The Essential Guide to Flex 2 with ActionScript 3.0

Charles E. Brown

friendsof

DESIGNER TO DESIGNER™

an Apress® company

The Essential Guide to Flex 2 with ActionScript 3.0

ISBN-13 (pbk): 978-1-59059-733-0

ISBN-10 (pbk): 1-59059-733-8

Printed and bound in the United States of America 9 8 7 6 5 4 3 2

Trademarked names may appear in this book. Rather than use a trademark symbol with every occurrence of a trademarked name, we use the names only in an editorial fashion and to the benefit of the trademark owner, with no intention of infringement of the trademark.

Distributed to the book trade worldwide by Springer-Verlag New York, Inc., 233 Spring Street, 6th Floor, New York, NY 10013. Phone 1-800-SPRINGER, fax 201-348-4505, e-mail orders-ny@springer-sbm.com, or visit www.springeronline.com.

For information on translations, please contact Apress directly at 2855 Telegraph Avenue, Suite 600, Berkeley, CA 94705. Phone 510-549-5930, fax 510-549-5939, e-mail info@apress.com, or visit www.apress.com.

The information in this book is distributed on an "as is" basis, without warranty. Although every precaution has been taken in the preparation of this work, neither the author(s) nor Apress shall have any liability to any person or entity with respect to any loss or damage caused or alleged to be caused directly or indirectly by the information contained in this work.

The source code for this book is freely available to readers at www.friendsofed.com in the Downloads section.

Credits

CONTENTS AT A GLANCE

CONTENTS

ABOUT THE AUTHOR

 **Charles E. Brown** is one of the most noted authors and teachers in the computer industry today. His first two books, *Beginning Dreamweaver MX* and *Fireworks MX Zero to Hero*, have received critical acclaim and are consistent bestsellers. In early 2004, Charles coauthored a book on VBA for Microsoft Access—*VBA Access Programming*.

In addition to his busy writing schedule, he conducts frequent seminars as an Adobe Certified Trainer. His topics include Flex, Flash, Dreamweaver, and ActionScript programming.

He is also frequently called in as a consultant for major websites involving Adobe technologies.

Charles is also a noted classical organist, pianist, and guitarist, and studied with such notables as Vladimir Horowitz, Virgil Fox, and Igor Stravinsky. It was because of his association with Stravinsky that he got to meet, and develop a friendship with, famed artist Pablo Picasso. Charles can be contacted through his website at www.charlesebrown.net.

ABOUT THE TECHNICAL REVIEWER

Sas Jacobs is a web developer who set up her own business, Anything Is Possible, in 1994, working in the areas of web development, IT training, and technical writing. The business works with large and small clients building web applications with .NET, Flash, XML, and databases.

Sas has spoken at such conferences as Flashforward, webDU (previously known as MXDU), and FlashKit on topics related to XML and dynamic content in Flash. In her spare time, Sas is passionate about traveling, photography, running, and enjoying life.

ACKNOWLEDGMENTS

This has been a long journey.

I heard the first murmurings of Flex 2 early in 2005. I never felt that Flex 1, due to the limitations and quirkiness of ActionScript 2.0, was a very viable product. Based on sales, many felt as I did.

I was not surprised that Flex 2 would mean a completely restructured ActionScript. It was also apparent to me why the Adobe/Macromedia merger had to happen.

In the fall of 2005, the full beta for Flex 2 was unveiled at the MAX convention in Anaheim, California. This also marked the beginning of the Adobe policy of public betas.

About that time, Chris Mills, my editor at friends of ED, approached me about doing a book on the subject. What I thought would be the easiest job in the world turned out to be the most difficult I have ever encountered. Between the beta's first release and the final product release in the summer of 2006, there were several major overhauls. This required that we throw out huge sections of the book and start over. I can honestly say we wrote this book three times before we arrived at what you hold in your hands right now.

It also meant taking nearly everything I knew about ActionScript and throwing it out. In other words, I had to relearn this knowledge myself.

Along the way, I wanted a book that could adapt with the inevitable changes that will come. As a result, the site www.charlesebrown.net came into being to continue this book long past publication.

I couldn't have done it alone, and some thanks are in order:

First of all, I want to thank my editor, Chris Mills, for his wisdom and guidance, as well as many mornings on Messenger listening to me gripe about what a tough book this was to write.

Every time I thought I wrote the perfect chapter, Sas Jacobs, my technical editor, brought me back to reality. This book would not have been possible without her guidance and wisdom.

ACKNOWLEDGMENTS

I have to thank my project manager, Beth Christmas, twice: First for persistently nudging me back on schedule every time I slacked off. Second, for a wonderful dinner in Philadelphia (with some friends) on a lonely night when I was conducting a training seminar there. Beth, I still owe you dinner at the City Tavern.

Finally, I want to thank all of my many friends and supporters of this project (including some students at my training classes) for their invaluable suggestions and insights.

I hope this book brings you, the reader, the knowledge you need to be a successful Flex programmar.

INTRODUCTION

Welcome to the future!

No, I am not making some metaphysical statement here. Instead, it is a statement about how many of us will build websites in the future. There is no doubt that Flash is playing an increasing role in web design, and Flex is the next evolutionary step for Flash.

In many ways, I struggled with this book. Was it to be a book about rich Internet websites? Was it to be a book about the MXML language that Flex uses? Was it to be a book on the next generation of ActionScript, ActionScript 3.0? Instead, I tried to make it a book that takes a very broad view of all three disciplines and how they fit together.

Let me start off by saying that many of the explanations are uniquely mine. After years of doing technical training, where I have only a few days to cover large topics, I have learned to substitute shorter explanations that clarify a concept in place of larger more technical (and often confusing) explanations. In other words, I often like to get right to the point without taking circuitous routes.

Please keep a few things in mind when reading this book. First, you will find that the techniques I show you are techniques that reflect my style of programming and design. Certainly there are many alternative ways of arriving at the same point. It is impossible for any one book to cover all possible variations, especially with topics as large as I cover here. If you find a different way of doing something, by all means use it if it works for you.

Second, I very purposely kept my examples simple in order to illustrate a point. I do not want you, the reader, to get caught up in just following recipe-like instructions that do little more than test your ability to follow instructions. While I have a case study in this book, it is far from complete. I have given details of a website at the end of this book where I am going to invite you, the reader, to submit various solutions and to join in various discussions. I hope you will take advantage of this.

Third, I am assuming that you already have at least a cursory knowledge of object-oriented programming concepts. While I do review these concepts in earlier chapters, it is only a very basic introduction. OOP is a very large subject in which large volumes have been written.

OK, enough of the warnings and disclaimers.

What I hope this book does is give you enough of a taste of Flex and the ActionScript 3.0 environment that you will be able to solve the unique problems your own situations will require. I spend a great deal of time discussing how to find help by using the ActionScript 3.0 Language Reference, for example.

If you have ever used ColdFusion, you probably know that it uses a simple language (CFML) to write a more complex language in the background (Java). Essentially, Flex does exactly the same thing: it uses MXML, the Flex equivalent of CFML, to write more complex ActionScript 3.0 in the background. In this book, I try to show you how to accomplish the same tasks in MXML and ActionScript 3.0.

I hope you walk away from this book with the same sense of excitement that I have about Flex 2. I really encourage you to experiment and study further. Look upon this book as the beginning, not the end.

On to the future.

Layout conventions

To keep this book as clear and easy to follow as possible, the following text conventions are used throughout:

Important words or concepts are normally highlighted on the first appearance in **bold type**.

Code is presented in fixed-width font.

New or changed code is normally presented in **bold fixed-width font**.

Menu commands are written in the form Menu ➤ Submenu ➤ Submenu.

Where I want to draw your attention to something, I've highlighted it like this:

> *Ahem, don't say I didn't warn you.*

Sometimes code won't fit on a single line in a book. Where this happens, I use an arrow like this: ➥.

```
This is a very, very long section of code that should be written all on the same ➥
line without a break.
```

1 INTRODUCING RIAS AND INSTALLING FLEX BUILDER 2

I am going to begin by giving you good news and bad news: The good news is that if you are presently an ActionScript programmer, you will be in some familiar territory, as you already know some of the syntax you will find in this book. The bad news is that if you are presently an ActionScript programmer, you will also be in entirely new territory with the new syntax, and you will need to rethink your understanding of ActionScript. This apparent contradiction will become clear as you move through this chapter.

This chapter, as well as subsequent chapters, is going to need to do double-duty. As you will see, it is nearly impossible to talk about ActionScript without talking about Flex. As a matter of fact, ActionScript is becoming more closely associated with Flex (even though it is a separate product) than it ever was with Flash.

In this chapter, you will look at how RIAs (Rich Internet Applications) are different from traditional websites, and take a broad tour of the ActionScript 3.0/Flex 2 environment, with the details saved for subsequent chapters.

In this chapter, you will

- Explore the new ActionScript 3.0/Flex 2 environment.
- Learn what RIA is.
- Install the ActionScript 3.0/Flex 2 environment.

Understanding the ActionScript 3.0/ Flex 2 environment

Let's begin with a little test.

1. Go to a traditional HTML website like the Apress site (www.apress.com) and look for different books and authors (as shown in Figure 1-1).

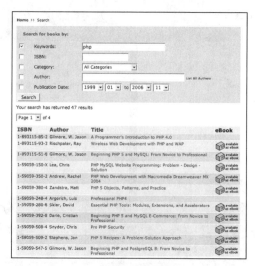

Figure 1-1. Search results on the Apress site

2. Now go to the Watergate Hotel reservation site at https://reservations. ihotelier.com/onescreen.cfm?hotelid=2560&languageid=1 (see Figure 1-2). Try out the reservation system by selecting check-in/check-out dates.

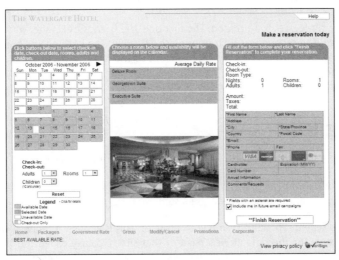

Figure 1-2. The Watergate Hotel reservation system

3. Finally, go to http://flexapps.macromedia.com/flex15/flexstore/flexstore. mxml?versionChecked=true and you should end up at the Flex Store, shown in Figure 1-3. Try to drag and drop items into the shopping cart and then go through the process of completing the purchase (don't worry, you're not really buying anything—this is only a demo site).

Figure 1-3. The Flex Store

Did the Friends of ED site have the look and feel of a desktop application? Or did it feel like a typical Internet site experience? Did the Watergate Hotel's reservation system start to feel a lot more like a desktop application? Finally, did the Flex Store *really* feel like a desktop application?

I chose these three sites for a reason. The first one, the friends of ED site, was a traditional HTML website. The second was built using Flash MX 2004. The last one was built using Flex, the newest of the technologies. It is the concept of the last site we will be concentrating on in this book.

Thinking RIA

In order for us to get started, you will need to change your thinking a bit.

When you build a web page, you traditionally think of going from page to page. Now, let's think about what goes on here. I will use a somewhat simplified example.

Typically, you type a URL address into your browser. This is actually a request, whether you realize it or not, for the default web page of that site (typically called the **home page**). After your request is bounced all over the world by routers in microseconds, it ends up on the web server of whoever's page you are requesting. That web server then sends the requested HTML page back, once again through routers all over the world, to your web browser, where that browser reads the HTML code on the page and displays the results. If that request is for information stored in a database, the receiving web server has to pass the information on to an application server (ColdFusion, JSP, ASP, ASP.NET, or PHP), which in turn passes the information to a database server. The database server then passes the information back to the application server, which writes the HTML code with the data. The application server then passes it back to the web server which, as before, sends it back to your browser for display.

While experience has shown us that all of this technology works most of the time, and fairly quickly, there is one small problem: every time we request another page, the whole process must begin again from scratch. I think most would agree that, while it does work well, it is not terribly efficient.

What's more, I think most people can easily distinguish between an Internet application, like the friends of ED site, and a desktop application such as Microsoft Word. The whole look and feel is different (among many other differences).

Wouldn't it be nice if the whole process ran much more efficiently? And wouldn't it be even nicer if desktop and web applications had more or less the same look and feel?

To address that challenge, Macromedia (now Adobe), with the introduction of Flash MX, introduced a new term: **rich Internet application (RIA)**. This technology, which is Flash based, overcomes many of the limitations of traditional HTML in that it is nearly indistinguishable from a desktop application.

As you may have seen in the two RIA examples earlier, the pages do not need to be rebuilt completely. Only the requested data is returned and plugged in where needed. This results in smoother and quicker responses, decreased demands on the servers, and much smaller file sizes (which lends itself nicely to mobile technology).

Also, in a traditional HTML environment, user interactivity is limited to forms and just a few buttons, and normal desktop items, such as menus, often perform poorly. The addition of these desktop tools often causes file sizes to increase dramatically, which makes for slower loading times.

As mentioned previously, with the release of Flash MX, Macromedia addressed these user concerns with a new set of programming tools, allowing developers to create RIAs to provide for greater interactivity with the user. This new set of tools overcame many of the limitations of HTML/JavaScript Internet applications. Suddenly, in an RIA environment, users could have the same interactive experience in an Internet environment that they enjoy in a desktop environment. As a bonus, this additional interactivity could be added without dramatically increasing the file size.

The release of Flash MX also saw the arrival of the first Flash server: **Flash Remoting MX**. This new server gave RIA environments a greater ability to interact quickly and smoothly with database servers as well as integrate with the Java and .NET server environments. This meant that Flash could now work as a presentation tool over a variety of programming environments. As a matter of fact, some writings have referred to Flex as a **presentation server**.

> *As a Flash programmer, I found this to be a welcome alternative to the less-than-ideal Java Swing classes.*

Many developers, however, complained that to develop an RIA, they needed knowledge of many of the complexities of the Flash environment (timelines, scenes, and so on). To address this issue, Macromedia introduced Flex in 2004. Flex presented a more traditional programming environment without many of the complexities of Flash. As you will see throughout the book, Flex combines the ease of ColdFusion, by using a proprietary markup language called MXML, with the Java-like programming capabilities of ActionScript 3.0.

There was one further issue that needed to be addressed: state.

In traditional HTML environments, there had to be a way to remember who you are going from page to page. For instance, as you shopped for books on, say, Amazon.com, how would the site's servers remember what books you added to the shopping cart? Typically, a variety of techniques, such as cookies, session variables, etc., are used. The ability of the server to remember who you are while going from page to page is called **state**. RIA applications do not have these problems because they run on the client's machine and only access the server when needed. In other words, if Amazon.com were an RIA, the shopping cart would be located inside of the application running on your machine. At the end, when you made the purchase, all of the purchase information would be sent to Amazon.com's servers. Once again, this drastically reduces the number of times you access Amazon.com's servers and makes the whole process run a lot more efficiently.

In case you think RIA is not important, let me show you some statistics about the Watergate Hotel reservation system you tried out earlier. Since implementing the RIA system, the hotel has seen

- 89% increase in reservations
- 50% increase in revenue
- 70% decrease in call-center usage
- 50% increase in sales leads

Take numbers like that and apply them to a site like Amazon.com or eBay. The results could be staggering.

While Flash MX and MX 2004 went a long way to develop RIA, Flex takes it to a whole new level. You will be seeing why that is as you progress through this book. Here, however, let's tackle one question you may be asking yourself: "How do I build an RIA application in Flex?" The short answer: you begin with a whole new programming environment called **Flex Builder 2**. In addition, with that new programming environment, you need to stop thinking about page-to-page websites and start thinking in terms of smooth-flowing desktop-like applications.

Flex Builder 2 and Eclipse

If you surf around on the web and look at various programming sites, you'll realize that a significant proportion of programmers use two programming environments—Java and .NET.

Java is a programming language introduced by Sun Microsystems in the mid-1980s and is an evolutionary step to the popular C++ environment. It is platform independent and utilized by many Internet and non-Internet applications today. (I have a toaster that uses Java. On the other end of the spectrum, the US Space Shuttle utilizes Java programming.)

The **.NET environment** was introduced by Microsoft in 2000 and is a multilanguage programming environment being utilized by many web applications today. It can employ a variety of different programming languages and compile them to a unified code on a variety of platforms.

.NET programmers mostly use Microsoft's **Visual Studio** to develop their programs. This **integrated development environment**, or IDE, employs tools to help build an application visually while it automatically writes bug-free code in the background.

A variety of IDE tools are available for Java. However, one of the most utilized ones is **Eclipse**. Eclipse is a multilanguage environment that can assist the programmer in a number of routine tasks common to all programming, such as properly formatting the code, renaming variables, and so on. You can learn more about Eclipse at www.eclipse.org.

Remember, Eclipse is not language specific. Instead, a number of members in the programming community have developed extensions or **plug-ins** to assist Eclipse with understanding programming languages like Java, C++, ColdFusion, and a variety of others. The nice part is that Eclipse, as well as most of the plug-ins available for it, is free of charge.

Because of the immense popularity of Eclipse, as well as its power as a traditional programming environment, Macromedia (now Adobe) made the decision to develop the Flex IDE, Flex Builder 2, around it. This will help many programmers to develop RIAs while working in a familiar environment. Although Flex Builder is an Eclipse plug-in, sadly it is not free.

Before you can use it, you need to install it. Let me turn your attention to installing the Flex development environment.

Installing Flex Builder 2

As of this writing, Flex Builder comes in two varieties: with and without the ability to create charts. Once you have decided on which one you want, you have two ways of purchasing it: either you can download it and, within the 30-day trial period, purchase an activation key online; or you can order a boxed copy.

Flex Builder 2 comes bundled with Eclipse, Flash Player 9 (which is needed for Flex applications to run), and a single licensed version of the Flex server for testing purposes.

Once you have received your copy of Flex Builder, you need to install it. I'll walk you through the steps now.

1. Start the installation process by either downloading Flex 2 from the Adobe site or inserting the disk that was shipped to you with your purchase. You'll be asked in what directory you want to save the installation files for Flex 2 (see Figure 1-4). Remember, this is not where Flex Builder 2 will be installed, but just a temporary holding place for the install files. Where you want these files is entirely up to you, but I typically like to put them in C:\Program Files\Flex 2.

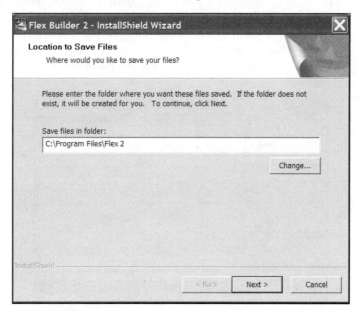

Figure 1-4. Initial install screen

2. Clicking the Next button will start some file extractions. There is nothing for you to do here.

3. The next screen is the opening screen for installing Flex Builder 2 and is shown in Figure 1-5. If you do not already have Eclipse installed on your computer, select the first option, Flex Builder and Flex SDK. If you are an experienced Eclipse user, you may want to select the second option. This will just extract the necessary Flex Builder files. You would then need to manually install them, using Help ➤ Software Update. Once you have made your choice, click Next.

Figure 1-5. Choosing the installation option

4. The next couple of screens are just typical license agreement and introduction screens. Click Next twice.

5. You will be brought to the screen shown in Figure 1-6. This will let you decide where you want Flex Builder 2 installed. I typically let it install in the default location of the Adobe folder. Specify your install location and click Next to continue.

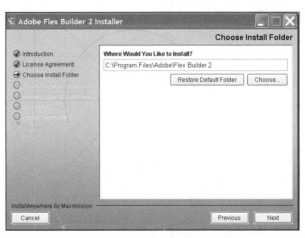

Figure 1-6. Choosing the installation location

6. The next screen, shown in Figure 1-7, prompts you to install the Flash 9 player for each browser on your computer. Flex 2 will not work without Flash Player 9 or higher. It is important that each browser is selected.

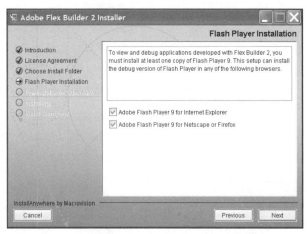

Figure 1-7. Installing the Flash Player for each browser

7. Click the Next button, and you are presented with the summary screen for installation (see Figure 1-8).

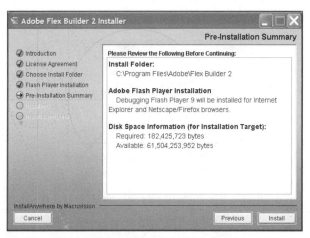

Figure 1-8. The confirmation screen before installation

8. Click the Install button, and Flex Builder will be installed along with everything else you need to develop RIA applications in Flex.

If all went well, you should see a final screen telling you that everything was installed successfully, and you are now ready to start building RIAs, as shown in Figure 1-9.

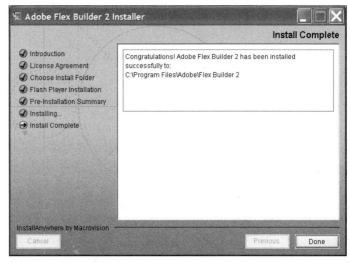

Figure 1-9. Final install screen

9. Go ahead and click Done. You should be presented with a very strange-looking message, as shown in Figure 1-10.

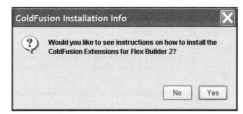

Figure 1-10. Accessing instructions for linking ColdFusion to Flex Builder 2

Although you've now successfully installed Flex Builder 2, as this dialog box hints, you're not quite done. You'll want to install the Flex-ColdFusion extensions, and we'll get into that in the next section.

Installing the ColdFusion Extensions for Flex Builder 2

The primary job of Flex is to build Flash-based graphic user interfaces to present data from a variety of platforms. However, Flex has no capability of linking directly to a database. Instead, as Chapter 2 discusses in detail, you will need to use **middleware**. This is software that sets the rules for connecting with databases and handling data. Middleware could be ColdFusion, Java, .NET, or PHP. By far the easiest to use is ColdFusion (not to mention that it is also an Adobe product).

If you are going to use ColdFusion (and I highly recommend you do, since the examples in much of the later part of the book rely on it), you need to make sure that you have the latest edition (version 7.02 as of this writing) installed in order to successfully link it to Flex. Instructions for installing ColdFusion version 7.02 can be found in Appendix A in the back of this book.

> *As of this writing, you can download ColdFusion at* www.adobe.com/
> products/coldfusion/. *You can go ahead and install the Flex-ColdFusion
> extensions if you do not have ColdFusion installed yet. You just cannot use them
> without version 7.02 at a minimum.*

In addition to ColdFusion itself, you need the Flex-Coldfusion extensions to link Flex Builder 2 to ColdFusion. Let's assume you have version 7.02 of ColdFusion installed and want to install the extensions. When the ColdFusion Installation Info dialog box back in Figure 1-10 appears, click Yes. You will be presented with two files, as shown in Figure 1-11. One is the HTML instructions.

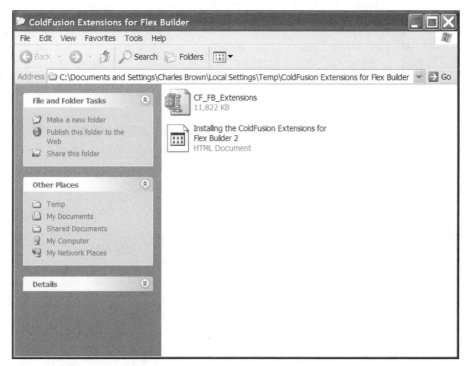

Figure 1-11. Files for installing the ColdFusion extensions

If you open the HTML instructions, it will give you step-by-step directions for installing these extensions on your own. I will also walk you through these instructions here if you want to install them as you work through the rest of this chapter.

> *Now your first instinct is to want to unzip the* CF_FB_Extensions.zip *file shown in Figure 1-11. It is not necessary.*

1. Since you've already installed it, go in and fire up Flex Builder 2. You'll first see the screen shown in Figure 1-12. You will be prompted for the serial number provided with your purchase. If you don't have a number yet, just click the Try button for a 30-day trial.

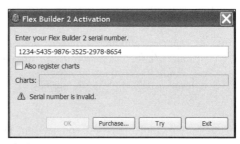

Figure 1-12. The opening screen for Flex Builder 2

> *For obvious reasons, the serial number shown in Figure 1-12 is not a valid one.*

2. If you purchased the charts option with Flex 2, you will also need to click the Also register charts check box and enter a valid serial number for that. When the correct serial numbers are entered, the boxes will gray out, and a message will confirm that the serial numbers are valid. Click OK. You should be taken to the opening screen of Flex Builder 2 (see Figure 1-13).

Figure 1-13. The opening screen for Flex Builder 2

3. To install the extensions, just select Help ➤ Software Update ➤ Find and Install to bring up the dialog box you see in Figure 1-14 —this will allow you to install any software updates that are available. It's always a good idea to make sure that your installation is as up to date as possible.

Figure 1-14. The Install/Update screen allows you to search for new features.

4. Select the Search for new features to install **option** and click Next to move on to the next screen (see Figure 1-15).

Figure 1-15. Here you specify the sites on which you want to install new features.

5. From here you want to click the New Archived Site button on the right side and maneuver to the directory containing the ZIP file (see Figure 1-16). The file is in a folder located in the directory you decided to extract files into back in step 1 of the section "Installing Flex Builder 2." (I had suggested `C:\Program Files\Flex 2`.) Once you are in that directory, you should see a folder called `Cold Fusion Extensions for Flex Builder`. Go into that folder.

Figure 1-16. Selecting the CF_FB_Extensions ZIP file

6. Select the ZIP file and click Open. You are presented with the dialog box shown in Figure 1-17 to do some renaming if necessary.

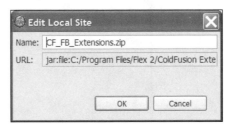

Figure 1-17. The Edit Local Site dialog box

7. Do not change any names. Just click OK. This brings you back to the original screen with the `CF_FB_Extensions.zip` file selected (see Figure 1-18).

Figure 1-18. The Install dialog box with the ZIP file selected

8. Click the Finish button. This brings you to the Updates dialog box (see Figure 1-19). Select the check box beside the ZIP file.

> *In Figure 1-19, I show the dialog box with the tree extended. When you select the topmost selection, the subselections get selected.*

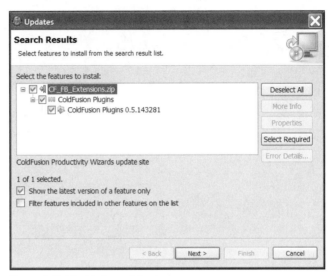

Figure 1-19. The Updates dialog box

9. Make sure the features are all selected, then click Next to move to the next screen, which is for accepting the license (see Figure 1-20).

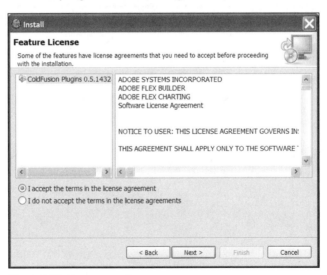

Figure 1-20. License acceptance

10. Click Next. This brings up the confirmation screen you see in Figure 1-21.

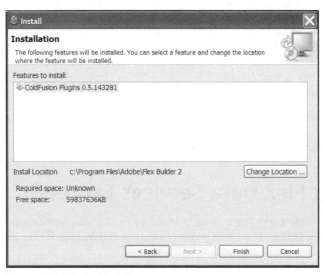

Figure 1-21. The final install screen

11. Just click the Finish button.

Just when you thought you were finished, you are presented with yet one more screen to verify version numbers and locations (see Figure 1-22).

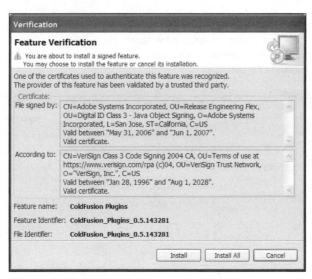

Figure 1-22. Final verification screen

12. Click Install All.

13. You will see the install process run. However, once the extensions are installed, you will be prompted to restart Flex Builder 2 (actually Eclipse), as you see in Figure 1-23. Click Yes.

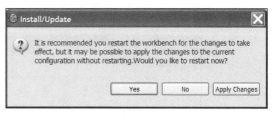

Figure 1-23. Restarting Flex Builder 2

Well, if you didn't get any nasty error messages, chances are things installed just fine. Looks like you are up and ready to rock-and-roll. However, we have one more small installation job ahead of us.

Installing Flex Data Services Express

Flex Data Services 2 (FDS2) is a server technology to help integrate data throughout your application. In addition, it can help end users work with data even if they are offline.

I will be speaking extensively about FDS2 later in this book. The main focus here is to install it.

Like all Adobe server technologies, you can install a free, single-user licensed version of it (this version is called **Flex Data Services Express**) to test your application locally. This version does not require a serial number to activate and will only work locally on your computer. It comes bundled when you purchase the Flex Builder 2 disk, or you can download it from the Adobe website.

1. Starting the install from either the download (You can download Flex Data Service Express at http://www.adobe.com/products/flex/dataservices/. Look for the relevant link at the bottom of the page.) or the disk, you should see the opening screen shown in Figure 1-24.

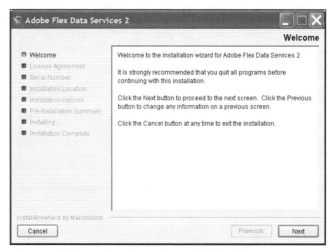

Figure 1-24. The opening screen of the FDS2 installation

2. Click Next, accept the license agreement, and click Next again.

3. You should be on the screen shown in Figure 1-25. This is where you would enter the serial number if you were working with a production version of the program. However, without the serial number, as I said previously, it is just a single-user version that can be run locally. It has all of the same functionality as the full version, but cannot run in a full server environment. For testing purposes, it is perfect. Just click Next.

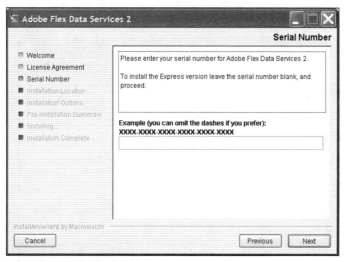

Figure 1-25. The serial number screen for the installation

4. The next screen, shown in Figure 1-26, allows you to decide the location of the server installation. The default, C:\fds2, should be fine and is the one we will reference later in this book. Click Next.

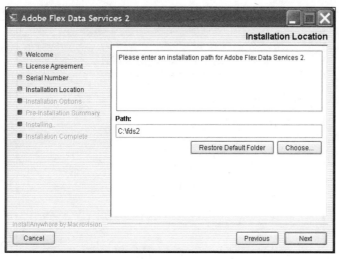

Figure 1-26. The server location

5. FDS2, like all Adobe server technology, is built over the Java programming environment. As a matter of fact, if you have ever worked with Adobe's popular ColdFusion environment, you know Java code is being written in the background while you are writing simple HTML-like tags.

Figure 1-27 shows the screen for selecting the Java server option. If you are not working with one of the several Java (J2EE) servers available, select the first option. This will install a runtime version of the Adobe Java server called JRun. If you are working with an existing server, select the second option. This will integrate FDS2 with the server.

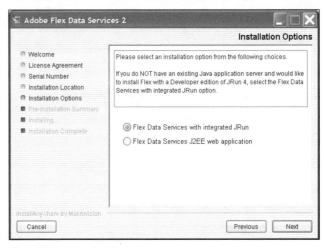

Figure 1-27. Selecting the Java option

6. The final screen before installation, shown in Figure 1-28, displays the preinstallation summary of your selections. If everything is as it should be, go ahead and click the Install button.

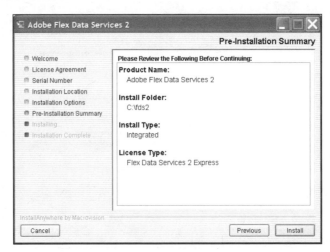

Figure 1-28. The preinstallation summary

7. If everything was successful, you should have gotten the Installation Complete screen shown in Figure 1-29. We will give it a test in a moment. However, for now, just click Done.

Figure 1-29. The Installation Complete screen

At this point, a read-me screen may pop up. It is worth spending some time browsing through it. However, you may want to give your server a quick test. Go ahead and try it:

1. Click Start ➤ All Programs ➤ Adobe ➤ Flex Data Services 2 ➤ Start Integrated Flex Server. The first time you try this, it may take a few moments to start up. But you will end up with a command window that looks something like Figure 1-30. You must leave that opened, and minimized, in order for the server to work.

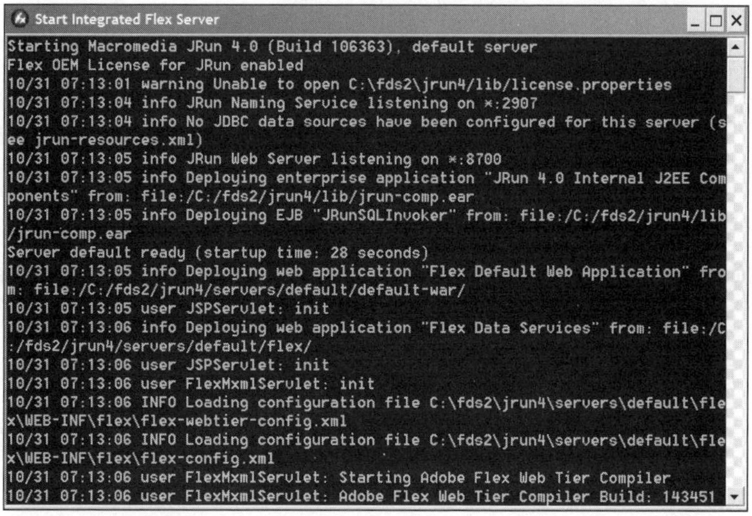

Figure 1-30. The FDS2 command window

FDS2 can be accessed by using `localhost:8700`. If you have ever used a server locally, it traditionally uses the word *localhost* followed by a colon and a port number. For instance, ColdFusion uses `localhost:8500`. Each server uses its own port. That way, they don't bump into each other.

2. Open the browser of your choice and enter http://localhost:8700/samples. You should get something like Figure 1-31. If you do, everything is working perfectly.

Figure 1-31. The FDS2 sample page

Don't worry too much about going through this information for now. You just want to be sure everything is working properly.

3. To shut down the FDS2 server, simply close the command window like you would any other window. You will see a few brief messages about data in the computer's memory being destroyed, and then the window will close.

Everything should now be installed and ready to work.

Summary

Now that you know what Flex is all about, and hopefully you have successfully installed it, you are probably anxious to start building your own RIA applications. For that, you will need to turn to the next chapter.

In the next chapter, you will learn the parts of Flex, explore some object-oriented programming concepts, and start to build some simple applications.

Ready? Let's move forward!

2 INTRODUCING FLEX AND FLEX BUILDER 2

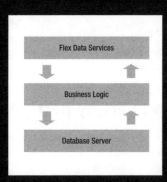

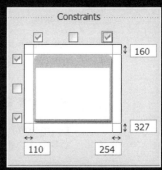

In Chapter 1, you learned what Flex is, why it is important, and how to install it. This chapter is going to focus in on the mechanics of how to build a Flex application. Admittedly, it will be a broad overview, with greater detail provided in subsequent chapters.

In this chapter, you will

- Examine the anatomy of a website.
- Explore the Flex application framework.
- Use Flex Builder in Code view.
- Understand some simple XMXL concepts.
- Use Flex Builder in Design view.
- Create a constrained layout.

Web design and Flex

Most enterprise-level web designs require three layers, or tiers, of structure:

- **Presentation Tier**: This is the level in which you build what the user sees. You'll see this sometimes referred to as the **graphical user interface (GUI)**.
- **Business Logic Tier**: The behind-the-scenes work happens at this level. It is here that programming code to determine what is or is not permissible resides, as well as the connections to other servers and databases. This is where the real work is done.
- **Backbone Tier**: At this level you'll find the database server that is collecting and distributing the data according to the rules stated in the Business Logic Tier.

A design such as this is sometimes called an *n*-**tier** design; beyond the basic three-tier design just outlined, some designs feature additional server and data levels.

As I stated in Chapter 1, Flex is primarily concerned with the Presentation Tier. As a matter of fact, Flex is frequently referred to as a **presentation server**. Its primary function is to create user interaction employing tools designed to create RIAs (which were introduced in Chapter 1).

You may not have realized it, but when you installed Flex as you worked through Chapter 1, what you installed was the **Flex application framework**.

The Flex application framework, part by part

Let me refine what I just said. What you installed was the **Flex software development kit (SDK)**, of which the Flex application framework is a part.

The Flex application framework has its very own tier structure that looks roughly like Figure 2-1.

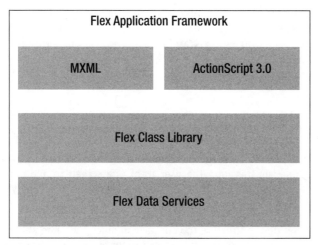

Figure 2-1. The Flex application framework architecture

At the very top is MXML and ActionScript 3.0. This is quite significant because it means Flex is using the two most popular tools in web design: **XHTML** and **object-oriented programming** (**OOP**). MXML is similar to XHTML, and ActionScript 3.0 adheres to the strictest principles of OOP.

Now, if that weren't enough, both MXML and ActionScript 3.0 harness the power of the Adobe Flash Player 9. This means you are actually getting the best of three worlds: an XHTML-like language (MXML), OOP (ActionScript 3.0), and the power of Flash. You have it all in one package.

Flex also comes with a rich collection of class files (prebuilt programs) that contain most of the tools needed for building successful RIAs (including Flex Data Services, discussed a little later in this chapter, for connecting to data sources.) In other words, most of what you will need is already built, and all you have to do is call it up, where needed, and add whatever customization you may want. The Flash Player knows how to handle these pre-built class files and uses them to build an RIA presentation to interact with the user.

Let's take a *very brief* tour of each of these parts.

MXML

Have you ever worked with XHTML? Or, if your skills are a little more advanced, have you ever worked with XML? If you can answer "Yes" to either of these questions, you will have no problems learning MXML.

MXML is an XML-based language that provides an easy way to call up and manage the visual elements of your application. Again, most of those visual elements are prebuilt and waiting to be called.

In case you don't understand what an XML-based language is, it is a descriptive language, or more specifically a **markup language**, that describes the various structures in a document. For instance, if you were working in XHTML, it would describe where the title, body, headers, etc., of your document are. A markup language does not have any of the structures normally associated with a programming language such as Java or JavaScript. It cannot make decisions for loop code.

Like XHTML and XML, MXML provides the structure for your application. However, in Flex, it goes one step further: you can use MXML to call up prebuilt components or, if you need to, create new ones from scratch. As you saw with the Flex Store website in Chapter 1, you can easily create such things as draggable data items or events to define specialized behaviors. You can seamlessly transition the user from one screen to another. And you can change the look of your application through means such as Cascading Style Sheets (CSS) and skins.

With MXML, you set up the structure to your page in much the same way you would XML. However, unlike XML, MXML allows you to lay out sophisticated interfaces with visual effects and behaviors. In other words, don't let the simplicity of MXML fool you. The simplicity does not limit what you can do—it speeds up your development productivity dramatically.

ActionScript 3.0

As great as MXML is, it has (as does any markup language) some limitations. As I mentioned earlier in the chapter, you can't use it to make a decision or to loop through a block of code for a certain number of times.

In the early days of web design, these limitations were addressed with the development of JavaScript, which augmented the ability of HTML. In the Flex environment, ActionScript is analogous to JavaScript: you use ActionScript 3.0 to augment the power of MXML.

With ActionScript 3.0, you can add dynamic interaction between your components. For example, you might want a label to dynamically show a certain piece of information based on a check box the user might have selected.

As you progress through this book, you will see that MXML has some capabilities to include interaction among components. However, for really sophisticated interactions, you need ActionScript 3.0.

Let me fill you in on a little secret I have been hinting at: all the components I talked about earlier are created using ActionScript 3.0. As a matter of fact, if you want to build your own components, you will need to know some ActionScript. What's more, when you compile your application into a SWF file, it transforms the MXML code, discussed earlier, into ActionScript 3.0 code.

Flex Data Services

Remember, Flex is a very sophisticated RIA presentation system. But what good is it if it cannot integrate with your current systems and database? In order for Flex to have any content to present, it must integrate with your current database and middleware (business logic). Flex Data Services is what connects Flex to dynamic server-side code such as Java, .NET, ColdFusion, PHP, ASP, or web services.

Please keep in mind that Flex does not connect directly with a database server. You must have code, using one of the technologies just mentioned, make the connection with the database, as Figure 2-2 illustrates. The Data Services components of Flex then connect with the code. The code determines what is, or is not, permissible (business logic).

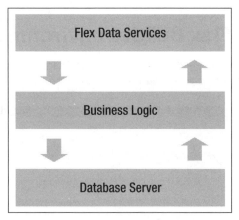

Figure 2-2. How Flex Data Services interact with the outside world

The Flex application framework goal: rapid development

The main goal of the Flex application framework is rapid development. I know I am being redundant, but you are going to be working with components that are built up as much as possible while still providing you control over how they should look and work. You have available dozens of prebuilt controls, containers, and managers that provide a complete set of UI components you can either use right out of the box or customize in any way you need to. You use MXML to tell Flex how to assemble these prebuilt containers and components on the screen, ActionScript to connect the components together, and Flex Data Services to connect them to the outside world.

In theory, the Flex SDK works on the command line. As an example, in Flash you would publish the FLA file (or press Ctrl+Enter) in order to generate the necessary SWF file to run the application. Like Java, the Flex SDK is platform independent in that it really does not install into the operating system. In Flex, as in Java, this would normally mean you would need to issue the commands to generate a SWF file from the command prompt.

> *The command prompt, in the old days of Windows 98 and before, was called the DOS prompt.*

Now, before you go running for the hills, don't worry! Notice I used words like "in theory" and "would normally mean." Eclipse, the development environment that runs Flex Builder 2, handles all of that automatically for you. So, unless you are developing Flex applications without using Flex Builder, you should never need to go to the command prompt.

Well, you are probably getting sick of hearing me babble. It is now time to put your initial knowledge to work, familiarize yourself with Flex Builder, and build some simple examples.

Let's begin by having a first look at Flex Builder.

Flex and the Flex Builder environment

Assuming you installed Flex Builder 2 as instructed in Chapter 1, go ahead and fire it up. When it loads, you should be presented with the screen shown in Figure 2-3.

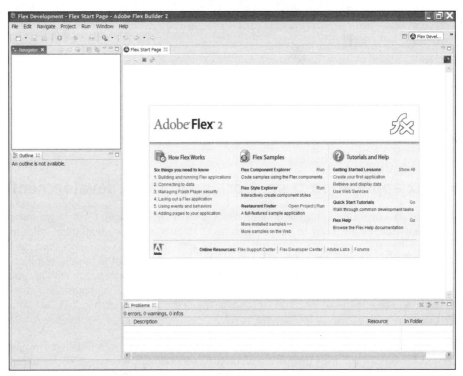

Figure 2-3. The opening screen for Flex Builder 2

Here you see some tutorials and sample applications to help you get started using Flex. It is worth taking some time and going through the Getting Started Lessons, especially the "Create your first application" tutorial. This tutorial is laid out in a step-by-step manner and serves as a good introduction to Flex.

As you progress through the book, you may also want to study the code in the sample applications. This will help you see how the concepts discussed are applied in a variety of situations.

> *If you have used Flex Builder before going through this book, you may not see the same opening screen as in Figure 2-3. If you don't, just go to* Help ➤ Flex Start Page.

Once you've had a chance to explore a bit, it is time for you to build your first simple Flex project.

Creating your first Flex project

In order to create a Flex application, you must start by creating a Flex project. This means that Flex Builder will create all of the necessary directories as well as create and manage the files necessary to run your project. Start creating your Flex project by following these steps:

1. Select File ➤ New ➤ Flex Project. You should be presented with the dialog box shown in Figure 2-4.

Figure 2-4. The New Flex Project dialog box

2. Here you can specify what server technology you want to hook Flex into. For the time being, keep it simple: choose Basic and click Next.

3. In the next screen, you name your project. Use the name Chapter2Welcome for this example (see Figure 2-5).

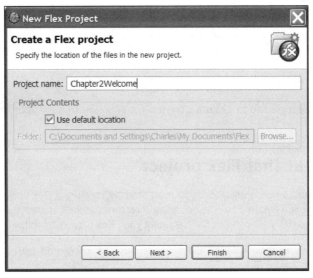

Figure 2-5. Giving the project a name

Of course you could use any name you want. However, it is important not to use any name previously used or put a space at the end of the name. If you do, the dialog box will give you a warning as shown in Figure 2-6.

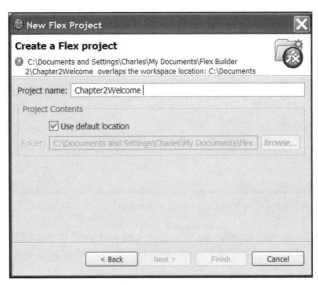

Figure 2-6. A naming error message

Staying away from spaces will give you the most trouble-free results.

4. This screen is also where you specify a location for your project. For the time being, stay with the Use default location option. This will set up your project as a subfolder under the My Documents directory.

5. You could click Next to specify some additional options. But for the time being, keep it simple and click Finish. You will now be presented with the screen shown in Figure 2-7.

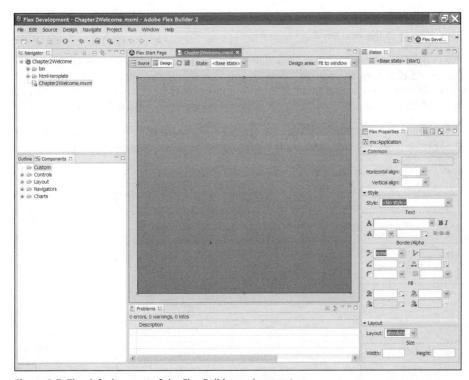

Figure 2-7. The default screen of the Flex Builder environment

This is the Flex Builder environment. Actually, more correctly, it is the Eclipse IDE running the Flex Builder environment.

> If you were to explore the documentation for the Eclipse environment (found at www.eclipse.org), you would learn this environment is called the workbench. Some of the Flex 2 literature also uses this term.

Eclipse divides the window into various panes. Again, for the sake of clarifying some inconsistent terminology, some of the Flex Builder literature refers to these panes as **views**. This is to conform with some of the terminology traditionally used with Eclipse.

Along the left side is the **Navigator pane** where you can see and manage your various project files.

Along the bottom are the **Output panes**. I used the plural "panes" on purpose because Eclipse uses this area to relay various messages and outputs to you. As you progress, you will see various message panes open in this area.

The large gray area in the center is the **Editor pane**, which will be the place where you will write and edit your code or do your design work.

Notice that Flex Builder already created some code for you. You'll learn more about these lines of code in the next section.

If you used the default location, Flex Builder set up the project directories under the My Documents directory on your hard drive. If you look there, you will see a directory called Flex Builder 2. Underneath that directory are three other directories (usually .settings, bin, and html-template). Most of your work will be stored in the bin directory.

If you look at the Navigation pane in Eclipse (see Figure 2-8), you will also see the Chapter2Welcome directory with the other project directories underneath of it.

Figure 2-8. The Navigator pane

You can get to the contents of the directories by clicking the small + icon to the left of each directory. Also, the Navigator pane shows you that Chapter2Welcome.mxml is the active file opened in the Editor pane.

Flex application files have the file extension .mxml (unlike ActionScript files, which have the extension .as).

Notice the two buttons in the upper-left corner of the Editor pane, Source and Design:

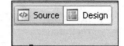

The Source button allows you to build your application, or modify it, by using code. The Design button allows you to do your design work visually by using drag-and-drop techniques.

> *If you have ever worked with Adobe's Dreamweaver, you will see many similar features here. Source view is the equivalent of Code view. And Design view gives you a graphic environment while writing code in the background.*

You will see how to work in Design view later in this chapter. For now, however, you'll stay with Source view.

Working in Source view

As you have probably figured out already, MXML code is placed inside of an MXML file. Most Flex applications have, or need, only one MXML file. When it becomes time to run the application, that file, similar to an FLA file in Flash, will compile into a SWF file.

Let's take a look at the code that Flex Builder places into an MXML file by default:

```
<?xml version="1.0" encoding="utf-8"?>
<mx:Application xmlns:mx="http://www.adobe.com/2006/mxml"➥
  layout="absolute">

</mx:Application>
```

MXML files begin with an **XML declaration**. This is because they must follow the rules of XML, which are quickly summarized here:

- For every opening tag, there must be a corresponding closing tag.
- The tags are case sensitive.
- Each tag can contain attributes.
- There must be a strict hierarchy of tags.

The **root tag** is the tag named Application. All the other tags must be within the opening and closing Application tags. Notice that MXML tags begin with the identifier mx:. This has to do with a feature of Flex called a **namespace**. We will talk about that in a bit.

As I said in Chapter 1 and earlier in this chapter, when you build Flex applications, you are actually building a configuration of containers that could hold other containers or visual elements such as buttons, text fields, check boxes, etc. The Application tag, in addition to being considered the root XML tag, is also the main container.

> *If you have ever done Java programming, an analogy can be drawn to the* main *method.*

Without the Application container, nothing else can effectively happen.

Let's build a simple label to display the text "Welcome to Flex and ActionScript 3.0" as follows:

1. Position your cursor between the Application tags.

2. Type an opening bracket, <.

As soon as you type the opening bracket, just like an HTML or ColdFusion tag, Flex Builder gives you a list of tags available, as shown in Figure 2-9.

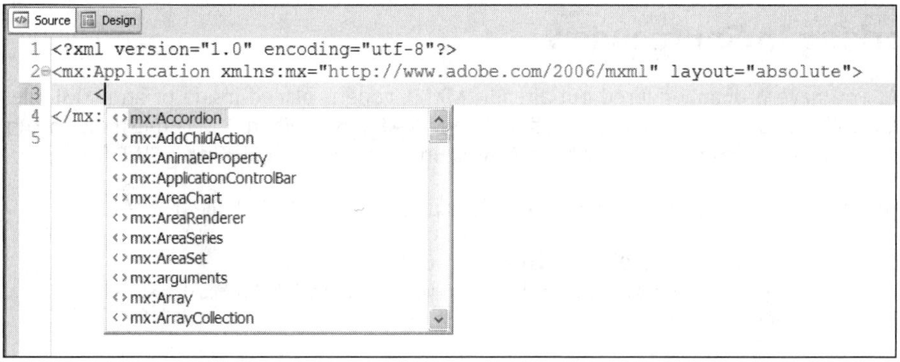

```
1  <?xml version="1.0" encoding="utf-8"?>
2  <mx:Application xmlns:mx="http://www.adobe.com/2006/mxml" layout="absolute">
3      <
4  </mx:   <> mx:Accordion
5          <> mx:AddChildAction
            <> mx:AnimateProperty
            <> mx:ApplicationControlBar
            <> mx:AreaChart
            <> mx:AreaRenderer
            <> mx:AreaSeries
            <> mx:AreaSet
            <> mx:arguments
            <> mx:Array
            <> mx:ArrayCollection
```

Figure 2-9. List of tags available

> *I like to indent the code between* Application *tags. I find it makes for easier reading. However, this is not a requirement.*

3. Either scroll down to mx:Label or type mx:Label.

> *Notice that the names of the components begin with a capital letter. You have probably already figured out that they are based on corresponding class files.*

4. Press the spacebar and type T, and you will be given a list of attributes starting with *t* for the tag (see Figure 2-10).

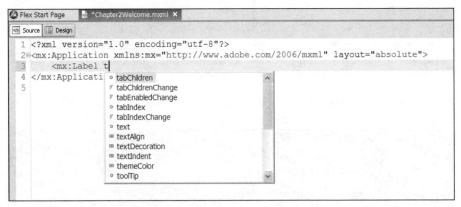

Figure 2-10. The list of attributes available for the Label component

5. Select the text attribute.

This attribute controls the text content of the label. Notice that Flex Builder automatically places the double quotation marks for your text.

Type in the text you want to appear in the label—in this case, Welcome to Flex and ActionScript 3.0. This is the only attribute you are going to use for the time being.

At the outset of this discussion, I mentioned a rule of XML is that all tags must have a corresponding closing tag. Let me refine that just a bit here. If the tag is going to have another tag contained within it, you can close the tag with just a closing bracket, >. However, if your tag is not going to have another tag within it, you can close your tag using />. In XML, this is sometimes referred to as an **empty tag**. The same is true for Flex.

6. Since you won't be putting another tag within the one you just created, type />.

Your finished code should look as follows:

```
<?xml version="1.0" encoding="utf-8"?>
<mx:Application xmlns:mx="http://www.adobe.com/2006/mxml" xmlns="*"➥
  layout="absolute">
  <mx:Label text="Welcome to Flex and ActionScript 3.0" />
</mx:Application>
```

All that remains is for you to test your little masterpiece of web design.

7. Save your file and click the Run button:

If you do not save your file first, Flex Builder will prompt you to save it.

The end result is that you see your label in the browser output (as shown in Figure 2-11).

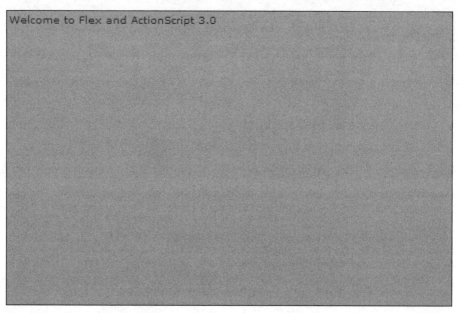

Figure 2-11. The Flex SWF output

OK, not very imaginative or exciting for now. But it helps illustrate the underlying concepts. You may be wondering why your label was located all the way in the upper-left corner. Hold tight on that. An explanation is coming soon.

As soon as you ran the application, Flex created a SWF from the MXML file as well as the appropriate HTML code for the browser to be able to call the Flash Player plug-in, which in turn calls and runs the SWF file. As I mentioned earlier, all the MXML code was converted to ActionScript 3.0 code.

If you look in the Navigator pane, you should see the files, including the SWF file, that were created (as shown in Figure 2-12). They were put into the bin directory, which is located under the Chapter2Welcome root directory.

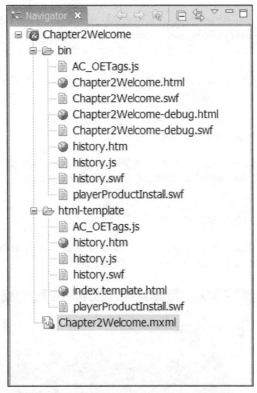

Figure 2-12. The files created for your first project

Recall that the various components you put into Flex are self-contained. The actions associated with a component, called **behaviors**, are simply another attribute of the tag. Let's take a look at a very simple example:

1. Click right after the closing double quote in the Label tag and press the spacebar.

2. Either scroll to mouseDownEffect or type mouseDownEffect.

In the double quotes, you are going to call the class file that controls the action you want. In this case, it is going to be WipeRight.

3. Type WipeRight.

Your code should now look as follows:

```
<?xml version="1.0" encoding="utf-8"?>
<mx:Application xmlns:mx="http://www.adobe.com/2006/mxml" xmlns="*"➥
  layout="absolute">
  <mx:Label text="Welcome to ActionScript 3.0 and Flex"
    mouseDownEffect="WipeRight" />
</mx:Application>
```

> *Flex is case sensitive. If you type* wiperight, *the effect will not work. By OOP tradition, class files always begin with a capital letter.*

4. Once again, give your code a test. But this time, while in the browser, click the label.

You should see the text refresh itself to the right. You will learn about effects in greater detail as you progress through this book.

5. Delete your Label tag, because now you're going to try a different approach to implementing the same label: visually using the Design view.

Working in Design view

If you now click the Design button, you are presented with an environment reminiscent of Microsoft's famed Visual Studio, as you see in Figure 2-13.

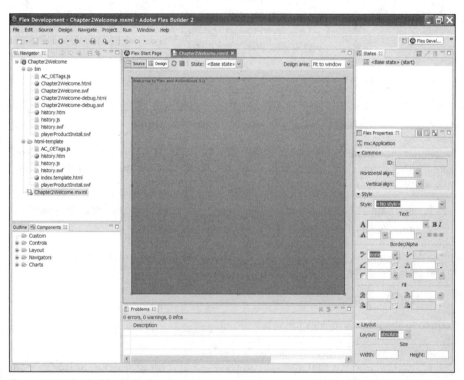

Figure 2-13. Flex Builder in Design view

Here you have an environment to design your layout visually. The lower-left pane—the Components panel—displays a listing of all the components available to you. Along the right side are all the various controls needed to set the component's attributes. You are going to create your label again, this time visually.

2

1. If you scroll down the lower-left pane to Controls, and expand them if necessary, you will see the Label control. Click and drag it to about the middle of the stage (the exact position is not important at this time). The control should appear similar to what you see in Figure 2-14.

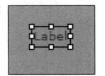

Notice on the right side of Flex Builder you have the Flex Properties panel. It is here that you can set the attributes of your Label control. One of them is the text attribute.

Figure 2-14. The Label control on the stage

2. Type the text Welcome to Flex and ActionScript 3.0 into the Text field, as shown in Figure 2-15.

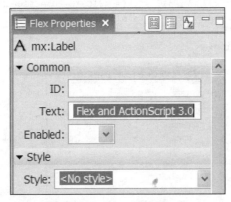

Figure 2-15. The Flex Properties panel

Once you press Enter, your Label control should reflect the changes on the stage. If necessary, you can drag the control so that is it recentered on the stage. Notice that you can use the Flex Properties panel to change the width, height, x-position, and y-position of the label (for the purposes of this example, the position is not too important at this time).

3. Go ahead and run the application like you did before. You should see your label nicely centered in the browser.

But what about the WipeRight behavior you had before when you clicked the mouse button on your text? You can add that visually also.

Notice the buttons just to the right on the top of the Flex Properties panel. The second button is called Category View, as you see here:

4. Click this button, and your Flex Properties panel now shows you more options grouped by the category of the options (see Figure 2-16).

5. Notice that one of the categories is Effects. If you click in the Value column to the right of mouseDownEffect, you can specify the class file you want that contains the effect you want. Like before, use WipeRight.

6. If you go ahead and run your application now, it should run exactly as it did before.

The only difference is that this time you did not need to do any coding. As a matter of fact, if you look at the code using Source view, it should be similar to what you did before with the exception of the x and y position attributes.

```
<?xml version="1.0" encoding="utf-8"?>
<mx:Application xmlns:mx="http://www.adobe.com/2006/mxml" xmlns="*"➥
layout="absolute">
  <mx:Label x="497" y="317" text="Welcome to ActionsScript 3.0➥
    and Flex" mouseDownEffect="WipeRight"/>

</mx:Application>
```

Figure 2-16. Category view

Whether you work directly in a visual environment or use code depends entirely on which you prefer. As you progress through the book, you might find that you can do a few more things in code than you can in the visual environment, especially when you start to combine Flex with ActionScript 3.0. However, for many developers, it is customary to start in Design mode to build the overall look and general behaviors. Then, from there, you move into code to fine-tune things a bit.

Why Flex?

What advantages does Flex offer over traditional HTML web design?

I'll tackle this question over the course of this book. Here, however, I'll show you one major advantage Flex has over HTML.

As more users move to mobile devices, as well as other means of accessing the Internet, the size of the browser is not always going to be the size that they see when accessing sites using a PC. For that reason, your applications will need to adjust easily to a variety of sizes and situations.

If you have worked with XHTML, you know that the flexibility needed to adjust to a variety of situations is not always easy to achieve. Let me demonstrate how easy it is to accomplish in Flex.

In order for Flex to easily adjust to a variety of sizes, the layout must be set to absolute. You can check this one of two ways:

From Design mode, make sure the Label control is not selected and look in the lower-left corner of the Flex Properties panel. It should say absolute as shown in Figure 2-17.

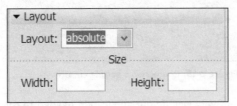

Figure 2-17. The absolute property in the Flex Properties panel

The other way you can check it is by going into Source view and looking at the layout attribute of the Application tag:

```
<mx:Application xmlns:mx="http://www.adobe.com/2006/mxml" ➥
layout="absolute">
```

As you will learn in Chapter 4, an absolute layout means that you must set the x and y properties of the various components you put into your application. If you don't, all the components will be stacked up in the upper-left corner. This is why the earlier Label control ended up there. We will be discussing this in greater detail in Chapter 4.

1. Delete the label you created in the previous section.

2. On the stage, use two Label controls, a TextInput control, and a TextArea control to create an application that looks something like Figure 2-18 (again, it does not have to be exact at this point nor do the labels have to be the same).

The text attribute you give to the Label controls is not important.

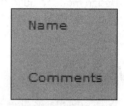

Figure 2-18. The layout needed for this demonstration

3. If you now run your application in the browser and then make your browser smaller, you will get something that looks like Figure 2-19.

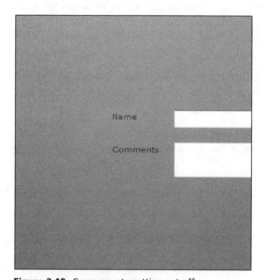

Figure 2-19. Components getting cut off

This would not work out very well if your application needed to run in a smaller environment, such as a mobile device.

Now return to Flex Builder and make some changes to your little form. For starters, you'll position and size things a bit more precisely. I'm going to have you deliberately oversize things a bit here just to demonstrate a point.

1. Select the top label and, using the Flex Properties panel, give it an x-position of 40 and a y-position of 80.

2. Select the TextInput field and give that an x-position of 90, a y-position of 80, and a width of 250.

3. Select the bottom label and give that an x-position of 40 and a y-position of 160.

4. Select the TextArea field and give that an x-position of 110, a y-position of 160, a width of 250, and a height of 110.

5. Select the TextInput field again. You will notice that right below where you set the x- and y-positions, there is a section called Constraints, as shown in Figure 2-20.

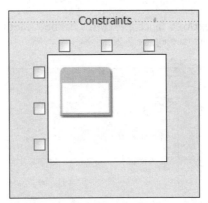

Figure 2-20. The Constraints panel

Each of the check boxes is called an **anchor**. An anchor locks the position of the component relative to the browser size. For instance, you can have the component always stay a certain distance from the left, right, top, and bottom of the edge of the browser. If the browser resizes, the component will resize to keep that distance.

6. As an example, with the TextInput still selected, click the left and right check boxes, as shown in Figure 2-21.

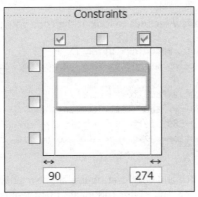

Figure 2-21. Constraints put on the TextInput control

43

Notice that the width and x attributes have now disappeared because they are now relative to the size of the browser. The x-position will be the one you originally set, 90. However, in this example, the right side of the TextInput will always be 274 pixels from the right edge of the browser.

If your number for the right side is a little different, don't worry about it. If you want, you can experiment with different widths.

7. Now select the TextArea. Since a TextArea has both width and height, you need to set the four corners (see Figure 2-22).

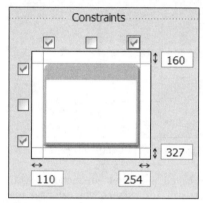

Figure 2-22. The constraints on the TextArea control

Here all four corners are set for the TextArea component. Notice that now all the original attributes are relegated to the anchor positions. Again, if your numbers are slightly different, do not be concerned.

It might be worth taking a few seconds to look at the code you just generated.

```
<?xml version="1.0" encoding="utf-8"?>
<mx:Application xmlns:mx="http://www.adobe.com/2006/mxml" ➥
layout="absolute">
  <mx:Label x="40" y="80" text="Name"/>
  <mx:Label x="40" y="160" text="Comments"/>
  <mx:TextInput y="80" left="90" right="274"/>
  <mx:TextArea bottom="327" top="160" left="110" right="254"/>
</mx:Application>
```

Notice that the original width and height attributes are now gone. In their place are attributes such as left, bottom, top, and right. This means that these components should always stay that number of pixels from the position indicated (for example, 274 pixels from the right or 160 pixels from the top). These attributes indicate anchoring taking place.

If you now run the application, you should see something like Figure 2-23.

Figure 2-23. The constrained components in a full-sized browser

But if you now resize the browser, the components adjust accordingly, as Figure 2-24 shows.

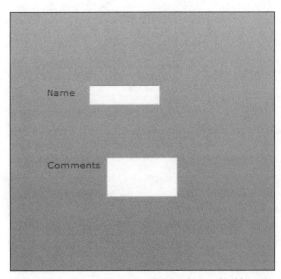

Figure 2-24. The components adjusting in a resized browser

As you can see, your application can now easily adjust to a number of different Internet clients (for example, your cell phone).

Try playing with some different settings and experiment a bit with the constraints. This is fairly significant when viewing applications in regular browsers, but imagine the power of this feature when users are viewing your application using alternative browsing devices such as handhelds.

OK, this is just one major advantage. You will see many others in the coming chapters.

Summary

You've seen a lot of the Flex basics in this chapter. In Chapter 3, you are going to explore the fundamentals of ActionScript 3.0 (as well as some OOP concepts). Then, beginning with Chapter 4, you will begin to examine the various types of containers and how to use them.

Let's get to work!

3 INTRODUCING ACTIONSCRIPT 3.0

Contents

- 📖 **Adobe Flex Builder**
- 📘 **Adobe Flex 2 Help**
- ⊞ 📖 How Flex Works
- ⊞ 📖 Getting Started with
- ⊞ 📖 Using Flex Builder 2
- ⊞ 📖 Flex 2 Developer's
- ⊞ 📖 Building and Deploy

⚙ New ActionScript File

New ActionScript file

Create a new ActionScript file

Enter or select the parent fold

Chapter3_Practice

In Chapter 1, you got to install Flex and the Flex Builder environment. And in Chapter 2, you learned some of the fundamentals of MXML. However, as powerful as MXML is, it is limited. MXML by itself cannot make decisions or loop code as needed. For that reason, a second component is needed: ActionScript 3.0.

In this chapter, you will

- Explore the fundamentals of object-oriented programming.
- Learn the ActionScript 3.0 syntax.
- See how to combine ActionScript 3.0 and MXML.
- Examine reusability, including putting the ActionScript code into a separate file.

Roll up your sleeves, you have a lot of work to do here.

Creating an ActionScript 3.0 project

As I stated in Chapter 2, when using the Flex Builder/Eclipse environment, you must set up a **project** before you can develop ActionScript 3.0 or Flex application programs. This helps Flex Builder organize and track the various files (assets) associated with your project.

Go ahead and open up Flex Builder.

If you completed the exercise in Chapter 2, the project files are probably still there. They won't interfere with what you are doing here. However, since you won't be using them again in the remainder of this book, it may be a good idea to delete them (or at least disconnect Flex Builder 2 from them).

To delete the project files, follow these steps:

1. Right-click the Chapter2Welcome root folder in the Navigator pane, and then click Delete (as shown in Figure 3-1).

When deleting a project, you have a choice (see Figure 3-2) as to whether you just want to delete the project from Flex Builder or physically delete the file from your local drive.

Figure 3-1. Deleting a project

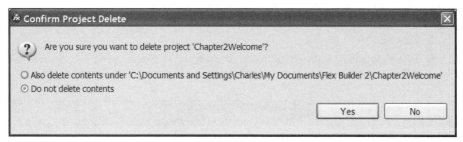

Figure 3-2. Confirm Project Delete dialog box

3

2. Select the option that starts Also delete contents under . . .

3. Click Yes.

As you will be learning, there are a number of ways to use ActionScript 3.0. However, for now, let's look at ActionScript 3.0 by itself and create a new ActionScript project.

4. Select File ➤ New ➤ ActionScript Project and enter a name for your new ActionScript project, as shown in Figure 3-3.

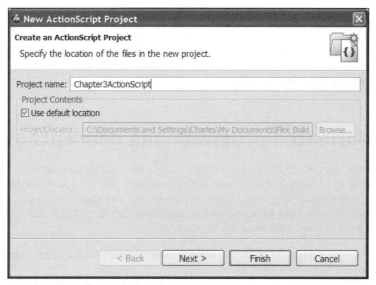

Figure 3-3. Starting a new ActionScript project

> *Chapter 2 discussed naming conventions. I am going to use the name* Chapter3ActionScript, *but feel free to use any name that you want.*

Once again, as in Chapter 2, you going to go ahead and use the default location.

5. Click Finish.

6. Take a close look at the default code onscreen (as shown in Figure 3-4). Notice how different the default code is from that you saw for the Flex project in Chapter 2.

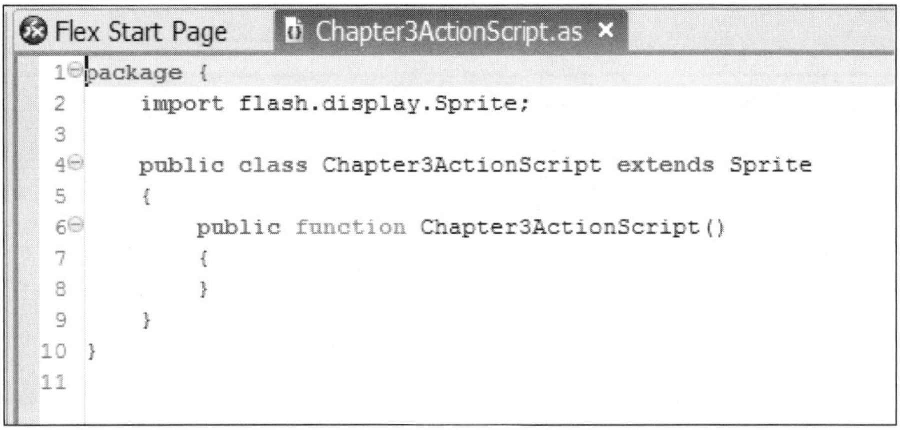

```
1  package {
2      import flash.display.Sprite;
3
4      public class Chapter3ActionScript extends Sprite
5      {
6          public function Chapter3ActionScript()
7          {
8          }
9      }
10 }
11
```

Figure 3-4. The default code for an ActionScript project

Don't worry if the code looks strange to you—I will explain it all very soon. However, at this point it is important for you to learn some object-oriented programming (OOP) concepts to aid you in understanding the code.

Object-oriented programming concepts

Over several years, ActionScript has evolved from a fairly minor programming language that handled some Flash animation routines to its present form as a sophisticated object-oriented programming language. However, before you can start analyzing and writing ActionScript 3.0, you need to learn some fundamental concepts about OOP and what it is—this is what you will achieve in this section.

As you progress through this book, you will see these concepts built and expanded on. For this reason, the following explanations are just brief overviews.

Understanding what a class file is

In the early days of programming, developers relied on a technique called **procedural programming**. This meant that nearly all of the code needed for a project was contained in relatively few files, each containing thousands, or sometimes hundreds of thousands, of lines of code that ran in pretty much a sequential fashion. This made coding, and the subsequent debugging, a nightmare sometimes. Among the early programming languages that relied on procedural programming were FORTRAN (FORmula TRANslator), Pascal, COBOL (COmmon Business-Oriented Language), and Ada.

In the early 1970s, Dennis Ritchie of Bell Laboratories developed a fast-running procedural language called C. Approximately 10 years later, Bjarne Stroustrup, also of Bell Labs, developed the next generation of the C programming language called C++. With this, a new breed of programming was introduced called **object-oriented programming**. This served as the basis for several additional programming languages including Java, C# .NET, Visual Basic .NET, and now ActionScript.

What distinguishes an OOP program from a procedural program is how the work is divided up. As I just mentioned, a procedural program uses long sequences of code. However, an OOP program breaks the work up into smaller, more specialized files called **class files**.

A class file is a self-contained program containing all the variables (called **properties**) and methods needed to perform either one specialized task or a group of related tasks. They also serve as the basis, or template, for something I will be discussing a lot throughout this book: **objects**. An object is a copy of the class file in memory. In all projects, class files and the objects they create can call on each other as needed.

Since class files are self-contained and specialized, you can use them in any of your projects at any time. Essentially, ActionScript 3.0, like other OOP programming environments, is nothing more than a large collection of class files. As you work with ActionScript 3.0, your library of class files will probably grow. You will write your own, as you will be doing shortly in this chapter, or download them from a variety of sources. The end result is that, over time, you will be doing less coding and more research on what class files are available and how to use them. Less coding means faster project completion with fewer bugs. As you progress through this book, you will get to use a variety of class files. Bottom line: don't try to reinvent the wheel. If it is already available, use it!

All classes have two potential programming constructs attached to them: **properties** and **methods**. I say "potential" because a class file is not required to have either or both. Properties and methods are OOP terms. A property is nothing more than a variable attached to a class file, and a method is a function attached to a class file.

> *Some books will identify a third construct attached to a class file: an* **event listener**, *or simply* **event**. *It is my opinion that an event listener is just a specialized method.*

Let me clarify a fine point in the terminology:

In the previous paragraphs, I used the word *method*. However, in ActionScript programming, the term *function* is used. In most OOP programming environments, a method is a function that is located inside a class file (along those same lines, a *property* is a variable located inside a class file). Interestingly, however, ActionScript does not make that distinction and uses the word *function* and *method* interchangeably.

To keep to OOP standards, I tend to use the word *method* when talking about class files.

Inheritance

By now it should be clear that a class file is a powerful way to modularize your applications into small, reusable building blocks. However, **inheritance** gives you even more of a reusability factor. This can sometimes be a difficult concept to grasp. For that reason, I like to use the following analogy when I teach about OOP languages.

Imagine you have a class called Animals. In it are the properties and methods associated with *all* animals regardless of the type of animal it is. Now let's say you need to write a class called Cats. Is a cat an animal? While my two cats, Max and Shadow, may disagree, obviously they are. Do you, as a programmer, want to recode all of the properties and methods associated with animals and then add the particular properties and methods associated with cats? Most likely not! That would be time consuming. Instead, all you have to do is write one line of code:

```
public class Cats extends Animals
```

This line of code allows your new class, Cats, to access the properties and methods associated with Animals.

Let's now assume you want to write two more classes, LongHair and ShortHair. Each of these classes could **extend** the class Cats, which in turn extends the class Animals.

As you move down the hierarchy, the class files become more specialized in their focus.

Inheritance is identified with the word *extends*.

Interestingly, as you move up all hierarchies, you will come to an all-encompassing starting point. That starting point is a class called Object. As you will soon see, virtually all other class files automatically inherit from this one class file.

Packages

With the potential of hundreds, or even thousands, of class files in your library, you will want to organize them into related groups. In OOP programs, you organize them by creating directory structures, much like you would arrange other things on your hard drive. However, class files need to call each other when needed. To make that process flow a bit easier, rather than enter directory paths, we call these directory structures **packages**. Each class file will have code in it that identifies what package it is a part of. All you need to do is create references to the packages when needed.

ActionScript 3.0 takes the concept of packages one step further. Most OOP environments, such as Java, only allow you to package entire class files. ActionScript 3.0 allows you to package individual methods and properties. This means that you can build libraries of properties and methods without them necessarily being associated with a particular class file. What's more, you can then have your class files access these properties and methods when needed. This powerful feature can save you a lot of potential programming time and headaches.

Packages can also control what information can be seen by who with the keywords public and private, as discussed in more detail in the "Understanding the code" section later in this chapter.

ActionScript 3.0 Language Reference

As I stated earlier, as an ActionScript 3.0 programmer (like any OOP programmer), you will be spending a lot of your time researching the properties and methods of the many class files available to you, rather than coding. But where do you go to learn about the class files that come with ActionScript 3.0? The best place to start is the online language reference.

To get to the language reference, select Help ➤ Find in Language Reference. The library should appear as shown in Figure 3-5.

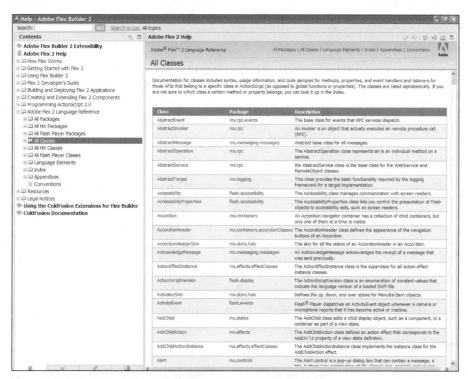

Figure 3-5. ActionScript Language Reference

During your career as an ActionScript 3.0 programmer, you will be spending a fair amount of your time on this site. It is here you can look up the properties and methods associated with each of the many class files that come with ActionScript 3.0.

In the left pane is the listing of all of the packages associated with ActionScript 3.0. As you click a package, the right pane will show the class files associated with that package.

The large pane will then give you all of the details of the class you selected.

For example, assume you want to find out how to create and use a text input field. The class names are pretty descriptive. For that reason, you are going to assume that there is a class called TextInput (as you will see when you familiarize yourself with the class library, nearly anything you do will have a class file associated with it), but you don't know what package is associated with it.

For starters, click the All Classes link along the top, which gives you the screen shown in Figure 3-6.

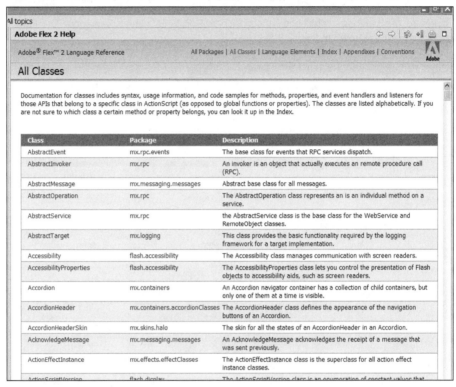

Figure 3-6. The All Classes list

This brings up the complete listing of class files in alphabetical order. Now scroll down to the Text classes You will see that there is a class called TextInput and that it is part of the package mx.controls. What's more, you get a brief description of what it does.

Go ahead and click the TextInput class link—this will bring up the wealth of information shown in Figure 3-7.

Don't worry if you don't understand everything that is here yet. All of the details will be explained as you work through the book. However, let's look at a few general areas here.

Notice under the package and class the line of inheritance, discussed earlier. As you can see, the TextInput class is inherited from the UIComponent class, which is inherited from the FlexSprite class, and so on. Eight levels of hierarchy exist above TextInput, and at the very top, as you expect, is the Object class.

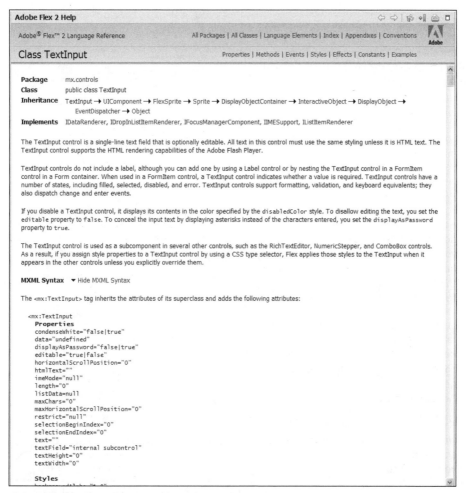

Figure 3-7. The ActionScript Language Reference for the TextInput class

After a description of what this class does, you next see a general listing of the properties available for this class.

As you scroll down, you will see a discussion of the public and protected properties specific to the TextInput class.

Scrolling further down, you will then see similar information for styles, events, and methods.

The left side of the Language Reference allows you to navigate quickly through the classes. For instance, you can expand All Classes, as shown in Figure 3-8, and scroll down to TextInput. If you expand TextInput, you will see listings for the various parts of the class.

You can use the list on the left to get quick information about a class as well as click the links to navigate to detailed information that will appear in the right side of the window.

Again, do not be too concerned if you do not understand all of the details, as you will be spending a great deal of time at this site. You will quickly find that this site is going to be your lifeline for understanding ActionScript 3.0.

I cannot emphasize enough the importance of getting to know this Language Reference. Without a working knowledge of it, you will utilize only a small percentage of the functionality of ActionScript 3.0.

As you progress through this book, you will learn several other techniques to access the ActionScript 3.0 information you may need.

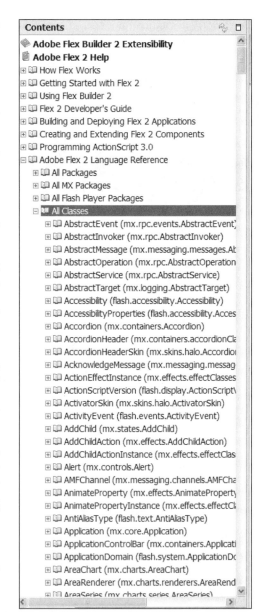

Figure 3-8. The left side of the Language Reference

Notice the class reference has links that will allow you to view the inherited properties from other classes in the hierarchy.

Object-oriented system design

Anything beyond a light discussion about designing and architecting OOP systems is well beyond the scope of this book. Voluminous volumes have been written on just that very subject, with numerous books focusing on just particular aspects of it. As a matter of fact, OOP design even has its own **architectural language**: **UML**, which stands for **Unified Modeling Language**. This is not a programming language. UML is used to design how the vast number of objects, necessary in some high-level applications, interact with each other. It also addresses the design and architecture of the class files themselves. However, a few simple rules of thumb will allow you to do some simple OOP designs quickly.

Assume you just completed all of the planning documents needed for your project and have also completed the write-up of your case study. Start going through the write-up sentence by sentence. Odds are the nouns in each sentence will represent the class files needed. For each class file, the adjectives will be the properties associated with that class file, and the verbs will be the methods also associated with that class file.

If you think that sounds like an oversimplification, it is not. As a matter of fact, several of the high-end (and expensive) UML design programs take your write-up document and analyze it for the nouns, adjectives, and verbs. From there, they automatically design class files with properties and methods. While the end results are admittedly far from complete and at times a bit bizarre, such an approach creates a time-saving foundation upon which to edit and build.

I will be referring to this simple noun, adjective, and verb paradigm throughout this book.

Your first class files

In nearly any book or class on programming, it is traditional to start with a simple program that outputs "Hello, World." You will be doing something similar to that here so that you'll get an overview of the general concepts that subsequent chapters will analyze in greater detail.

Understanding the code

Begin by returning to the Chapter3ActionScript class file you created earlier. As you can see, Flex Builder 2 did a lot of the routine setup for you. Let's begin by analyzing what this code means. Much of it will tie into the earlier discussion about OOP concepts.

As mentioned earlier, a package is a way of grouping class files that are related. It groups them within directory structures.

Unlike any other OOP programming environment today, ActionScript 3.0 requires that all class files be part of a package. This is not optional. Thus, the code for all package files must begin with the keyword package followed by an opening and closing curly brace.

> *A keyword is a reserved word that can be used only by ActionScript 3.0 and not to name a variable, method, or class file.*

Let's return to the default code written for you by Flex Builder 2:

```
package {
    import flash.display.Sprite;

    public class Chapter3ActionScript extends Sprite
    {
        public function Chapter3ActionScript()
        {
        }
    }
}
```

As you look at the curly braces associated with the package designation, notice that they encompass all the code for the class file (you can easily see that due to indenting). Also notice that there is no name after the keyword package. This means that the present directory, Chapter3ActionScript/bin, is the package. Why not just move class files around as necessary? This is not a good practice. In many instances, those class files may need to access other class files, which may need to access yet other class files, and so forth. If you start moving things around, no class or code file will know where to find anything, and you will end up with mass confusion.

> *When using curly braces, after typing an opening brace, it is good programming practice to immediately type the corresponding closing brace and then indent the code between them. This will allow you to easily see what code goes with what brace and make debugging much easier later on.*

So now that you have the package defined, how does the code it contains work?

The first line of code within the package is, if needed, an import statement. In this case, it is

```
import flash.display.Sprite;
```

An import statement allows the class file to talk to a class file in another package. It doesn't physically move the other class file or make a copy of it. It simply creates a path or reference, effectively importing the functionality of that class into your package so you can make use of it.

If you have never done ActionScript 2.0 programming in Flash, you are probably asking what the heck a **sprite** is. In its simplest terms, the Sprite class is the same as the MovieClip class, but without the timeline functionality. However, like the MovieClip class, Sprite serves as the basic class for building displays, and it can also contain children displays. You'll find it worthwhile spending a few minutes in the Language Reference learning about the Sprite class.

> *I know I am being redundant all over again, but when I am talking about a class file in this book (or anytime you see a new class file), please spend time reading about it in the Language Reference.*

But what happens if you don't use any of the properties and methods associated with the Sprite class? Not to worry! All the import statement is doing is creating a reference. It does not add any additional size to your subsequent SWF file.

Notice that the Sprite class file is part of the flash.display package. Even though a package is a directory structure, most OOP environments use a dot (.) to designate another level of subdirectory. This means that there is a directory called flash with a directory called display underneath of it.

> *Do not go looking for the directory. You won't find it. The internal ActionScript 3.0 packages are archived in compressed files called JAR files (JAR stands for Java Archived).*

> *Here is a little exercise. What other class files are available in the flash.display package? You will see an additional 33 classes available. I will be addressing a few more of them as you progress through this book.*

Let me take a few moments to address the term *statement*. In programming parlance, a **statement** is simply an instruction to do something (in the example I showed, display a sprite). In ActionScript 3.0 (as well as most OOP environments today), a statement ends with a semicolon (;). If you had programmed in ActionScript 2.0, you know the semicolon rule was not enforced very strongly. In ActionScript 3.0 it is.

The next line, repeated here:

```
public class Chapter3ActionScript extends Sprite
```

is referred to as the **class definition**.

> *The class definition is not a statement, so no semicolon is needed at the end of the line.*

The keyword public indicates that any other class file, from any other package, can access it at anytime. In some cases, you can make a class **private**. This means that only classes within the same package can access it. Thus, packages can not only designate where something is, but also control who has access.

By tradition, class file names always begin with a capital letter. However, and this is important, the name used here must match the name of the file, Chapter3ActionScript.as, containing the class. If the two names do not match, the class file will not run. You cannot name the ActionScript file Welcome and then define the class as having a different name like Chapter3ActionScript.

Notice that Flex Builder automatically makes your new class file, Chapter3ActionScript, an extension of the Sprite class. You learned about inheritance earlier (remember, the keyword extends means inheritance). It may seem like a redundancy to have Sprite in both the import statement and the class definition. However, if you think about it, it makes perfect sense. How can this class file extend another class file if it can't first see what it is extending? The import statement allows Chapter3ActionScript to see the class file Sprite so it can extend it.

Notice that the class definition is the next level of curly braces. This is easy to see because Flex Builder indents each level of braces.

Within the class definition is an automatically placed method called the **constructor**. You'll get much more experience of constructors later in the book. However, for now, it is important to know that a constructor is a special method that is required in all class files. As a matter of fact, most class files will not run properly without it. The constructor must have the same name as the class file (including case) and will run automatically as soon as the class file is called. It is a standard practice to place any code that must run automatically within the constructor. However, even if the constructor does nothing, it is still required in the class file.

Now that you have a basic understanding of the default code in your ActionScript project, let's get your class file to do something.

Giving the class file functionality

As it stands, the default code for your ActionScript project does not do anything. You will now add some custom code specific to what you want done. You will also add some comments so that should you decide to pack it in and move to Tahiti for good, the next person who picks up your code can easily see what you have done.

Comments

It is always a good idea to heavily comment your code. That way when either you or others look at your code, it is easy to see the purpose of various parts of your code.

Like most OOP environments, ActionScript 3.0 supports two types of comments:

- Single-line comments:

    //This is an example of a single-line comment

- Multiple-line comments:

    /* This is an example of a multiple-line comment,
    which encompasses several lines in one block*/

It's a good practice to include a header comment indicating when and why your file was created and to comment the closing curly braces. Following are the comments I would add to the Chapter3ActionScript class file:

```
/*This file was created on 4/10/2006
   by Charles E. Brown
   to demonstrate the parts of an ActionScript 3.0 class file*/

package {
   import flash.display.Sprite;
   public class Chapter3ActionScript extends Sprite {
      public function Chapter3ActionScript() {

      }//End of constructor
   }//End of class definition
}//End of package
```

When the file is converted to a SWF file, the comments are ignored and do not add to the size of the file.

If you are working along with this book, why don't you go ahead and add some comments to the code file now.

Using the trace() method

If you ever did programming in Flash, you probably used the trace() method. This was a handy little tool that, during code development, would send an output of some sort to the Output window. You could use it to test whether variables had the proper values, whether a method was being called properly, and so on.

Happily, the trace() method is still available in ActionScript 3.0. However, because you are not working in Flash, there is no output window. Instead, the output of the trace() statement is sent to the Output pane of Eclipse. In programming parlance, this is sometimes referred to as **console output**. In other words, this is the same as sending the output to the command prompt of the operating system. Eclipse is just doing the work for you by accessing the command prompt and handling all of the behind-the-scenes tasks for you.

Return to the ActionScript 3.0 Language Reference. Follow these steps to find info on the trace() method:

1. Click the Index link at the top of the library and then the letter T along the line marked Symbol.

> As an alternative method, you can expand the Index listing in the left pane and select T from there.

2. Scroll down to Trace and click the link to go the details about using the trace() function—you should now see the screen shown in Figure 3-9.

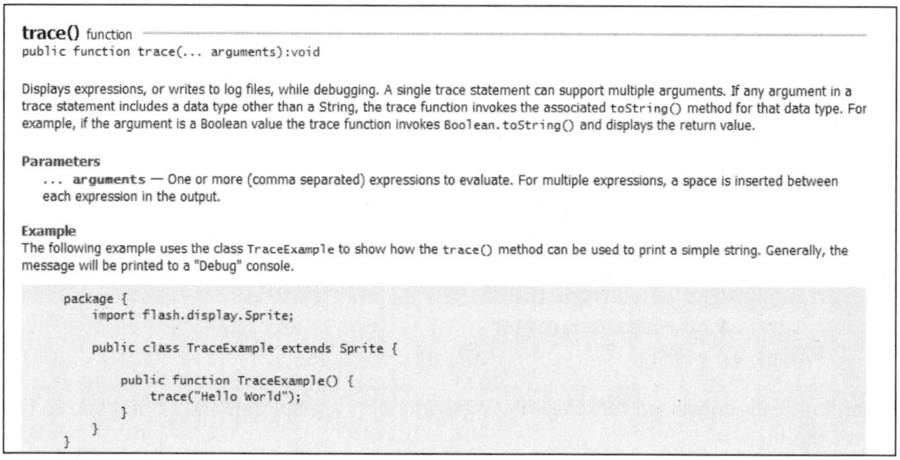

trace() function

```
public function trace(... arguments):void
```

Displays expressions, or writes to log files, while debugging. A single trace statement can support multiple arguments. If any argument in a trace statement includes a data type other than a String, the trace function invokes the associated toString() method for that data type. For example, if the argument is a Boolean value the trace function invokes Boolean.toString() and displays the return value.

Parameters

   ... arguments — One or more (comma separated) expressions to evaluate. For multiple expressions, a space is inserted between each expression in the output.

Example

The following example uses the class TraceExample to show how the trace() method can be used to print a simple string. Generally, the message will be printed to a "Debug" console.

```
package {
    import flash.display.Sprite;

    public class TraceExample extends Sprite {

        public function TraceExample() {
            trace("Hello World");
        }
    }
}
```

Figure 3-9. The details about using the trace() function

From the example, you can see that the trace() function is one of a group of functions called **top-level functions**. A top-level function is one that is available to all parts of your code automatically without the need to use an import statement. In other words, you can just call a top-level function whenever one is needed. They are sometimes referred to as **global functions**.

There are also **top-level constants**. These are values that never change and are **global**. For instance, you specify a value is not a number by using NaN. If you look in the upper-right corner of the Language Reference, you will see the Constants hyperlink. Click it, and you will see the screen in Figure 3-10.

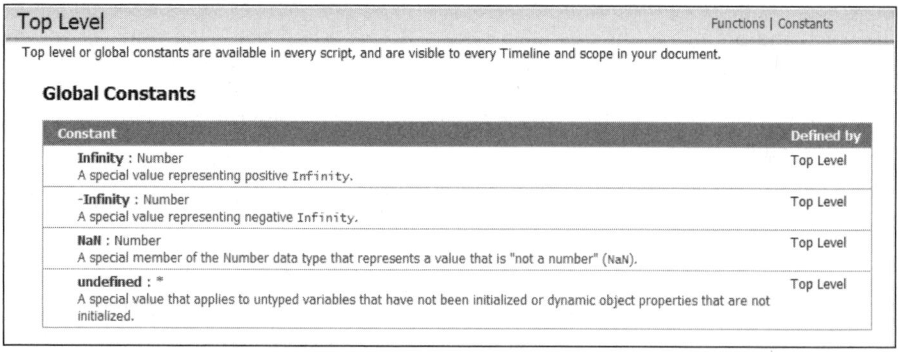

Top Level	Functions | Constants
Top level or global constants are available in every script, and are visible to every Timeline and scope in your document.	

Global Constants

Constant	Defined by
Infinity : Number A special value representing positive Infinity.	Top Level
-Infinity : Number A special value representing negative Infinity.	Top Level
NaN : Number A special member of the Number data type that represents a value that is "not a number" (NaN).	Top Level
undefined : * A special value that applies to untyped variables that have not been initialized or dynamic object properties that are not initialized.	Top Level

Figure 3-10. The global constants

Recall that everything inside the constructor will run automatically. Since you want this trace() statement to run automatically, put it within the curly braces of the constructor, as shown here:

```
package {
    import flash.display.Sprite;

    public class Chapter3ActionScript extends Sprite
    {
        public function Chapter3ActionScript()
        {
            trace("Welcome to Flex 2 and ActionScript 3.0");
        }
    }
}
```

Notice that the text you want to send to output needs to be enclosed in quotes. In most programs, you enclose strings of text in quotes.

You are now ready to see the results. In Flex Builder, look at the toolbar near the top of the window. You will see a button with a little bug icon on it, like the one shown here:

When you roll over it, you'll see a tooltip with the message "Debug Welcome."

> You must use the debug feature to see the results of a trace() statement.

3. Click the Debug button. You may be prompted to save the file first. Just click OK, and you will then see a window open up showing the build process.

After a few seconds you see . . . WHAT? . . . A gray, blank browser window?

Don't worry, you didn't make a mistake. Flex Builder automatically tries to test all ActionScript 3.0 code in Flex. However, you didn't direct any output to go to Flex. You will change this shortly in the upcoming section. But for now, close the blank window and go back to Flex Builder.

You should see the Console pane open at the bottom of Flex Builder (as shown in Figure 3-11).

```
Problems  🖵 Console ⊠
<terminated> Chapter3ActionScript [Flex Application] file:/C:/Documents and Se
Welcome to Flex 2 and ActionScript 3.0
[SWF] C:\Documents and Settings\Charles\My Documents\Flex Buil
```

Figure 3-11. The Console pane

Notice that Flex Builder created a file called Chapter3ActionScript-debug.swf and sent the results to the Console pane.

> The trace() *method is only used for testing purposes and is not meant to be carried through to final applications.*

Escape sequence

As I mentioned earlier, the text inside of the trace() method, "Welcome to Flex 2 and ActionScript 3.0", forms a string. As you may have guessed, there is a class file called String. You will be visiting it a bit more in the next chapter. However, for now know that you can do some basic manipulations with strings in the output. One of the most common involves using an **escape sequence**. An escape sequence has two parts: the backslash (\), which is called the **escape character**, and the instruction that tells the string what to do. Table 3-1 shows the available escape commands.

Table 3-1. Escape sequences

Escape sequence	Definition
\n	Positions the cursor at the beginning of a new line
\"	Allows you to put a double quote within a string
\\	Allows you to put a backslash within a string
\t	Moves the cursor to the next tab stop
\r	Positions the cursor at the beginning of the line, and subsequent text overwrites existing text

Let's see the newline sequence, \n, in action. Modify your trace() statement as follows and then run the debug feature.

```
trace("Welcome to Flex 2 \n and ActionScript 3.0");
```

The output will now look like Figure 3-12.

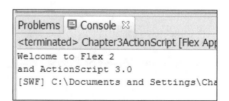

Figure 3-12. Inserting a line break (escape sequence) into the code

You inserted the newline sequence in the middle of the string, which forced the rest of the string to start on the next line.

> *You can use escape sequences only in strings.*

Go ahead and experiment a bit with the other escape sequences to see how they work.

You just got your first little taste of OOP and ActionScript 3.0. Of course, you have a lot more to learn along the way. However, now that you have had a taste of MXML in Chapter 2 and ActionScript 3.0 here, it is time to bring the two languages together.

Combining MXML and ActionScript 3.0

Before you see how to combine the power of MXML and ActionScript 3.0, a bit of house-keeping is in order. Start a new Flex project as discussed in Chapter 2. I call my example Chapter3_Practice. However, you can call yours whatever you want.

> *If you want to delete the ActionScript project created earlier, go ahead and do so; you will not be using it again in this book. Simply right-click the project name in the* Navigation *pane of Flex Builder and select* Delete. *You are then presented with the option to delete just the project from Flex Builder or delete the associated files also. Choose whichever option you want.*

Layout containers

Beginning in the next chapter, I will be discussing containers in greater detail. However, for the time being, let's take a quick look at the various types available in Flex and a little on how they interact with ActionScript 3.0.

Create a new Flex application using the techniques you have learned already. The name you choose is not important. Also, go ahead and use the default location for now.

Even though you did so for the exercises in Chapter 2, it is not a good idea to just put form controls on the stage.

> **Form controls** *are things such as labels, buttons, text input fields, and so on.*

If you have only a few controls, this will work. But if your applications start becoming more complex, you will have increased difficulty controlling their proper placement. Instead, it is far better to start with a **layout container**. These are boxes that allow you to group related controls together. In addition, they automatically handle placement of the controls you place within them.

In Design view, you can see the layout containers available in the Components panel located in the lower-left side of Flex Builder, as shown in Figure 3-13.

The two most commonly used containers are the VBox and the HBox. Quite simply, the former arranges your controls vertically, while the latter arranges them horizontally.

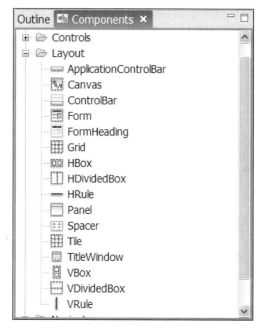

Figure 3-13. The Components panel

To add a layout container to your project, follow these steps:

1. Drag the VBox container onto the stage. As soon as you drop it on the stage, a small dialog box (see in Figure 3-14) pops up that allows you to do some initial sizing.

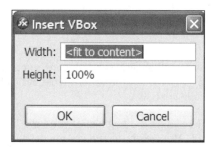

Figure 3-14. The Insert VBox dialog box

2. Go ahead and leave the defaults for now. (You learn more about these sizing options in Chapter 4.) Click OK, and your design view should now look like Figure 3-15.

You can go ahead and use the resizing handles to reshape the VBox container any way you want. For the purposes of this exercise, the size is not critical.

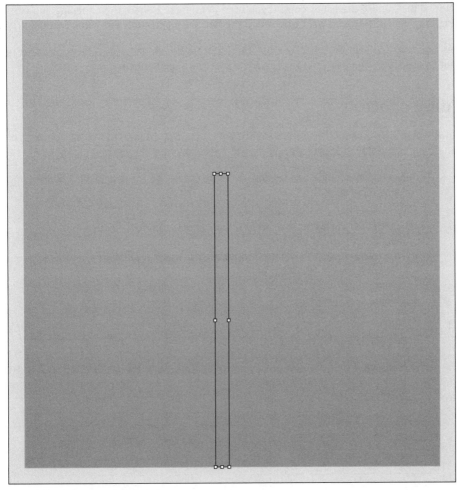

Figure 3-15. The VBox initial state onstage

3. It is worth taking a few moments and looking at the resulting code by clicking the Source button. It should look like the following:

```
<?xml version="1.0" encoding="utf-8"?>
<mx:Application xmlns:mx="http://www.adobe.com/2006/mxml" ➥
  layout="absolute">
  <mx:VBox x="213" y="110" height="290" width="218">
  </mx:VBox>
</mx:Application>
```

If your dimensions are a little different, don't worry about it for now.

Notice that, unlike the Label control you used in Chapter 2, there is an opening and clos-ing tag. Any controls you want to put into the box are placed between these two tags.

As discussed in Chapter 2, because the layout property of the Application container is set to absolute, you need to specifically position the VBox container.

Adding controls

In Chapter 2, you had your first experience with a control: Label. Let's revisit it a bit. For the time being, stay in Source view and code the following examples.

1. Between the opening and closing VBox tags, enter the following Label control and run the application:

```
<?xml version="1.0" encoding="utf-8"?>
<mx:Application xmlns:mx="http://www.adobe.com/2006/mxml"
  layout="absolute">
  <mx:VBox x="213" y="110" height="290" width="218">
    <mx:Label text="Charles" />
  </mx:VBox>
</mx:Application>
```

2. Go ahead and jump into Design view and see what happened—it should look something like what you see in Figure 3-16.

Notice that the VBox container is controlling the placement of the Label control. You did not need to specify the x and y attributes. As a matter of fact, if you click the Label con-trol, you won't even see the x and y properties in the Flex Properties panel.

> *Some of the containers will give you the ability to control placement. We will discuss them in Chapter 4.*

Let's take a look at a couple of new concepts.

Since you want to have these various controls interact with each other, and eventually with ActionScript, you need to give each control a unique identifier. For instance, let's say you want ActionScript to change the text of a label. What label?

To help you to this end, controls have an attribute called id, which you'll add to your proj-ect code here:

3. Modify your Label control as follows:

```
<mx:Label id="myLabel" text="Charles" />
```

> *The order of the attributes is not critical. They can be in any order.*

From here on in, whenever another control, or ActionScript, refers to myLabel, Flex will know that you are referring to that particular label, so now you can do things to it like update the text and its properties such as color and font. But how do you do that? You'll find out next.

Figure 3-16. Adding a label to the VBox container

Binding controls

OK, so you gave the label an `id` attribute. What does that buy you?

1. To see how you can make use of it, place your cursor right above your Label control, and add the code line shown in bold:

```
<?xml version="1.0" encoding="utf-8"?>
<mx:Application xmlns:mx="http://www.adobe.com/2006/mxml"➥
  layout="absolute">
```

```
<mx:VBox x="213" y="110" height="290" width="218">
    <mx:TextInput id="inputFirstName" />
    <mx:Label id="myLabel" text="Charles" />
</mx:VBox>
</mx:Application>
```

Remember that Flex and ActionScript 3.0 are case sensitive.

Anyway, your new code line has resulted in the addition of a TextInput control into your container, as you'll find out if you have a look in Design view (see Figure 3-17).

Figure 3-17. The VBox container, now with two controls in it

Notice that the VBox container stacked the TextInput control above the Label control entered earlier.

For purposes of this little exercise, you want the Label control to draw its content from the TextInput control, by referencing its id. A little bit of logic and a discussion of some new OOP concepts are in order here.

As you have already seen, the contents of both the Label and TextInput controls are handled by the text attribute. So what you need to be able to do is get the text attribute of the Label control to read the text attribute of the TextInput control.

2. In Flex, this is really quite easy and will require only a slight adjustment to the code of the Label control as follows—do this now:

```
<mx:Label id="myLabel" text="{inputFirstName.text}" />
```

In place of the actual text, the name Charles in the example, you put in a pair of curly braces containing the id of the TextInput control, followed by a period (.) and then the attribute text. Don't worry about the exact syntax of this code now; I'll explain it in more detail a little later in this section.

3. If you now run the application, you should see the text of the Label control copying the text of the TextInput control as you type different things into it—try it!

You just built your first interactive Flex application. Wasn't that easy?

> Remember from Chapter 2 that when you run the application, it gets compiled into a SWF file. In the process of compiling it, all the MXML code gets translated into ActionScript 3.0 code.

So much for the logic. Now for the new OOP concepts I mentioned.

You will recall from Chapter 2 that in ActionScript and Flex everything is built on a class file. I also stated that class files form the basis, or template, for objects. Basically, an object is a copy of the class file located somewhere in memory.

When you create an object from a class file, it's called **instantiating** (or creating an instance of) the class file.

In Flex, as well as in Flash, as soon as you use a control or layout container, you are creating an instance of the class file it is based upon. For example, in your small example project, you are now using three objects: an instance of the VBox class file, an instance of the TextInput class file, and an instance of the Label class file.

It is easy to see that you could have multiple instances of any class file anytime. So you have to be able to identify which object you are speaking about if you want to have controls speaking to each other or using ActionScript. You already accomplished that using the id attribute. However, in OOP parlance, the id attribute is referred to as the **object reference**. Flash uses the slightly more intuitive **instance name**. So the words *object reference*, *instance name*, and *ID* all mean the same thing. They are all referring to the unique name we give to each object for identification purposes.

However, referring to what I said earlier in this chapter, an object has two potential constructs in it: properties and methods.

A property is simply a variable (that you can modify, such as color) attached to an object, and a method is a function (such as a request to change that color) attached to an object. This creates a readjustment in your thinking and use of terminology.

If you have done any HTML or XML coding, you have already encountered the term *attribute*. An attribute is quite simply extra information the tag needs to do its job properly. Just in this chapter and the previous one of this book, you have used the id, text, x, and y attributes. However, more correctly, these attributes are actually properties associated with the class file the object is based upon. You would more correctly say that you have used the properties id, text, x, and y. This distinction is about to become an important one.

All OOP environments use a syntax called **dot notation** to allow objects to talk to each other. For example, when you typed inputFirstName.text into the Label control, you used dot notation.

On the left side of the dot is the object you want to address, and on the right side of the dot is the name of the property or method you are asking the object to use. In essence, the label object, myLabel, just asked the object inputFirstName to send over the contents of its text property.

ActionScript works exactly the same way.

Wait! Does that mean that when you work in Flex, ActionScript is being written somewhere in the background? That is *exactly* what it means.

> If you have ever worked with ColdFusion, it follows exactly the same concept. Even though you use tags in ColdFusion (much like you use tags here), ColdFusion is actually writing Java in the background.

By now, even in this simplified example, you are starting to see the pieces fit together quite nicely. All you need to do now is build on the foundation you already have.

Adding ActionScript code

In many of your projects, you will want to add your own ActionScript code in order to get your applications to carry out whatever specialized jobs you may need. In programming parlance, this is sometimes called adding **behaviors**.

Add a tag to your code:

1. Begin by doing some minor surgery on your file and remove the line of code for the TextInput control.

2. Right after the Application tag, but before the VBox tag, put the following tag in:

```
<mx:Script>
```

As soon as you complete the tag, some strange-looking lines of code will be added. Your code should now look as follows:

```
<?xml version="1.0" encoding="utf-8"?>
<mx:Application xmlns:mx="http://www.adobe.com/2006/mxml" ➥
  layout="absolute">
  <mx:Script>
    <![CDATA[

    ]]>
  </mx:Script>
  <mx:VBox x="213" y="110" height="290" width="218">
        <mx:Label id="myLabel" text="{inputFirstName.text}" />
  </mx:VBox>
</mx:Application>
```

The bold lines you see in the preceding code are known as the **CDATA section**, which is a common construct in XML documents. In essence, it isolates part of the document for special handling and prevents the code contained within it from being parsed along with the rest of the XML document; it usually is used to add non-XML code. However, in Flex, it is used primarily to add ActionScript code to your MXML document.

> CDATA tells Flex not to process the script contained within it as MXML.

In addition to parsing out the code in this section, it also helps to make your code more readable. Imagine how it would look if your MXML tags and ActionScript code were all jumbled together. As a matter of fact, later in this chapter, in the section "Reusability," you will be separating things out altogether by putting your ActionScript in separate files.

If you are using Flex Builder, the proper syntax for the CDATA section is automatically added after you enter the Script tag.

The next thing you want to do is add some variables and methods. But before you do, some background on both.

ActionScript constructs

As I stated in earlier in this chapter, there are two fundamental programming constructs in programming: variables and methods. Let's examine both, starting with variables, and see how you can integrate them with Flex.

Variables

A **variable** is a place somewhere in memory to temporarily hold data for later use. In order to find the data, you give the variable a name, which serves as a pointer to the place in memory where the data is being held.

The authors of the book *Foundation ActionScript for Flash 8* (Bhangal, Besley, Powers, Dolecki, friends of ED, 2006) liken variables to containers. If you look around, you will see that many containers are designed to hold specific things. For instance, your refrigerator is designed to hold food. Your wallet is designed to hold your money and credit cards. Would you put a package of frozen vegetables in your wallet? Or your money in the refrigerator? (All right, I had a grandmother who did that many years ago.)

Logic would dictate that if you liken a variable to a container, and that a container is designed to hold a specific type of item, then a variable should hold only a specific type of item. But how do you tell a variable to hold only certain types of items?

In programming terms, this is known as **strict typing**. It means that you assign the variable to, you guessed it, a class file. The properties and methods of that class file tell the variable what it can and cannot do.

The three most common class files used in relationship to variables are

- Strings: These are sequences of alphanumeric characters that are enclosed in double quotes (" "). For instance "Charles", "Today is 4/16/2005", or "This is working".
- Numbers: This is a broad category that could mean an integer such as 12 or 5, or it could mean a decimal number such as 12.5 or 5.768.
- Booleans: This means that something is either true or false.

This has important meaning. Let's assume that you defined two variables, num1 and num2, as Strings. Now, later on, assume that you try to use the following formula:

```
num1 * num2
```

ActionScript will not know what you are talking about because the class file, String, makes no provision for multiplication. The variable has no means of figuring it out on its own.

Older versions of programs like Visual Basic and the last version of ActionScript did not require strict typing. So if you wanted to multiply the two numbers, the program might use reasoning something like this:

"Well, let's see. num1 looks like a number, so maybe I can use the class number. Same goes for num2. So if I use Number for the class for both, that might tell me what to do with that asterisk."

Needless to say, you can imagine that using reasoning like that for every variable operation can drink up an enormous amount of processing power and make your programs run far less efficiently. Also, it could make for a lot of programming errors. A formula may end up with a String when it is expecting a Number.

So how do you name a variable and tell it what type it is?

Naming variables

Variables begin with the keyword (reserved word) var. This tells ActionScript that you are about to name a variable. Let's explore this construct.

1. In the CDATA section, enter var myName. Your CDATA section should now look as follows:

```
<mx:Script>
    <![CDATA[
        var myName
    ]]>
</mx:Script>
```

The next thing you need to do is assign your variable, myName, a type or class file. Enter the colon (:) and you should see the list of available class files come up. You can tell they are class files because they begin with capital letters.

2. For now, select the String class.

Assigning a value

Once you have the variable declared, you need to initialize it with a value as follows:

```
<![CDATA[
    var myName:String = "Charles Brown";
]]>
```

The single equal sign (=) is often known as an **assignment operator**. This means that whatever is on the right side of the equal sign is assigned to the left side of the equal sign.

You are now ready to give your little program a test. However, before you can, you must change one thing.

1. Your Label control still does not know where to look for its text. Change it so that it looks as follows:

```
<mx:Label id="myLabel" text= "{myName}" />
```

Logic dictates that the text property should read the variable myName and populate the Label control with the contents.

If you save your file before running it, you may get two warning messages along the bottom of Flex Builder 2 (more on this later, in the "Passing parameters" section of this chapter). You will learn about various warnings you might encounter as you progress through this book. In this case, since the warnings are exclamation points and not red x warnings, your small application won't be prevented from running. For the time being, just disregard the errors.

2. Run your program, and once again, you should see your name, or whatever you put into the variable myName, in the Label control. Believe it or not, you just combined ActionScript with Flex.

As you start to build your applications, it is a good idea to keep an eye on your Outline pane located in the lower-left side of Flex Builder. As you can see in Figure 3-18, this pane gives you a visual representation of the hierarchy of the structure of your page.

You have just finished your first combination of Flex and ActionScript. Now let's go a bit deeper.

Functions

Odds are pretty good that you want your ActionScript to do a bit more than fill in a label from a hardwired variable. The real workhorses of any program are the **functions**. A function is simply a block of code that does a specific job and can be called at anytime.

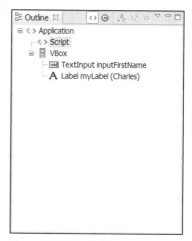

Figure 3-18. The Outline pane

Imagine for a moment that you need to add two numbers together, and that this job needs to be done several times in the code. It would be terribly inefficient to keep writing the same code over and over again. Instead, you build a function once and then call it every time that particular job needs to be performed.

There are two basic types of function: functions that just perform a job and functions that return a value.

> *The words functions and methods mean the same thing. A method is a function inside a class file, just as a property is a variable inside a class file.*

The first line of the function is called the **signature**. If the function does not return anything, its signature would look something like this:

```
function addNumbers():void
```

The void at the end indicates that the function does not need to return anything to whoever called it.

> *If you have used ActionScript 2.0, or most OOP programs, the keyword void is capitalized. However, in ActionScript 3.0, void is lowercase.*

If the function does need to return a value to the caller, you must specify the type of information being returned. For instance, if the function returns a String, you replace void with String.

```
function fullName():String
```

The code the function needs to do its job is enclosed in the open and closed curly braces ({ }).

Next, you'll do a little variation of the ActionScript code for your label.

1. Start by removing the variable, and in its place build the following function:

```
<mx:Script>
  <![CDATA[
    function myName():String
    {
      var myLabel:String = "Charles";
      var myLastName:String = "Brown";
      return myLabel + " " + myLastName;
    }
  ]]>
</mx:Script>
```

There is a bit to talk about here. This function returns information of type String. You indicate that in the signature. You then set two variables to hold the first and last names, respectively.

The next line is an important one. When a function has a return type other than void, you must specify what is to be returned with the keyword return. If the return type is void, you cannot use the keyword return. They are mutually exclusive.

The return line is an example of a **concatenation**. This is a fancy word for connecting multiple items together. In this case, you connect the first variable, then quotes with a space, then the second variable. In a concatenation, everything (whether it be numbers or strings) is converted into a string.

You need to do one last thing before this will work properly. In order to work, a function must be called by something. The calling code simply uses the name of the function, followed by the open and closed parenthesis (()).

2. Modify your Label control as follows:

```
<mx:Label id="myLabel" text="{myName()}" />
```

Notice you need to include the name of the function followed by parentheses.

> *You would put any parameters or arguments that the function needs to do its job in the parentheses. You will see an example of this in the next section.*

Your code should now look as follows:

```
<?xml version="1.0" encoding="utf-8"?>
<mx:Application xmlns:mx="http://www.adobe.com/2006/mxml" ➥
  layout="absolute">
```

```
<mx:Script>
  <![CDATA[
      function myName():String
      {
          var myFirstName:String = "Charles";
          var myLastName:String = "Brown";
          return myFirstName + " " + myLastName;
      }
  ]]>
</mx:Script>
<mx:VBox x="213" y="110" height="290" width="218">
    <mx:Label id="myLabel" text="{myName()}" />
</mx:VBox>
</mx:Application>
```

You may end up with the warning messages I discussed earlier. Again, you can just ignore them for now. If you go ahead and run it, your label should be populated with your name as before. Now you can simply call your function up wherever you need it, rather than writing the same code over and over again!

Passing parameters

Many times a function needs information before it can do its job properly. The caller needs to send it those parameters, and the function then needs to process them as necessary. Let's take a look at an example:

1. Change your function as follows:

```
<mx:Script>
  <![CDATA[
      function myName(myFirstName:String, myLastName:String):String
      {
          return myFirstName + " " + myLastName;
      }
  ]]>
</mx:Script>
```

Notice that in this case, you removed the two variables and replaced them with parameters inside of the parentheses. The parameters must specify not only the order in which they must be sent, but also the types. In this case, the function is expecting the first name and the last name, in that order, and both of them must be strings. This requires an adjustment to your function call in the Label control:

2. Make the following change to your Label control:

```
<mx:Label id="myLabel" text="{myName('Charles', 'Brown')}" />
```

Here the necessary parameters are in the function call in the order that they are expected. However, there is a small trap here. Normally, you would pass strings using double quotes ("). However, in this case, there would be a problem. MXML brings data into the form (data binding), as you have seen, using quotes. This is why you need single quotes here.

If you were to surround the first and last names with double quotes, it would confuse MXML as to where the binding ends, and you would get two error warnings. The first one would be a warning dialog box, as shown in Figure 3-19.

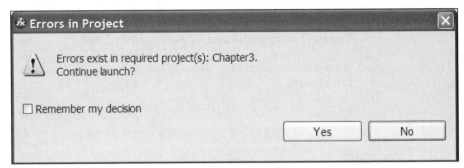

Figure 3-19. Errors in Project warning dialog box

If you continue on by clicking Yes, you may or may not get the result you want (in this case, it would probably work). However, it is usually a good idea to click No when you get this warning. But there is also a second troubleshooting area.

Flex Builder shows the problem in the Problems pane located along the bottom of the environment (see Figure 3-20).

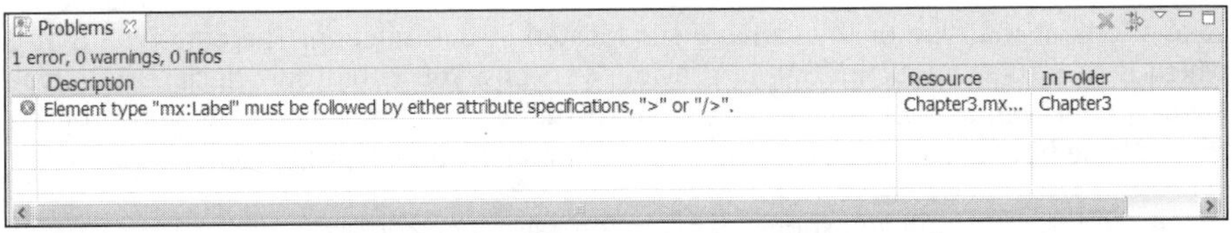

Figure 3-20. The Problems pane

> *If you do not see the* Problems *pane, go to* Window ➤ Show View ➤ Problems.

You should also see a red x to the left of the code line causing the problem. It is common to send strings within strings, as you are doing here, with single quotes ('). By using the single quotes, you have avoided the error just described.

> *In Chapter 4, you'll learn more about the various types of problems you might encounter and how to handle them.*

Let's do one more slight variation where you pass numbers instead of strings. The return will also be a number. However, if you have done ActionScript 2.0 coding, you will see an interesting new feature.

3. Change the code as follows. At this stage, you should be able to see the logic.

```
<?xml version="1.0" encoding="utf-8"?>
<mx:Application xmlns:mx="http://www.adobe.com/2006/mxml"➥
  layout="absolute">
  <mx:Script>
    <![CDATA[
        function mySum(number1:Number, number2:Number):Number
        {
            var sum:int = number1 + number2;
            return sum;
        }


    ]]>
  </mx:Script>
<mx:VBox x="213" y="110" height="290" width="218">
    <mx:TextInput id="inputFirstName" />
        <mx:Label id="myLabel" text="{mySum(2, 3)}" />
</mx:VBox>
</mx:Application>
```

There are a few points worth mentioning here. First of all, since you are passing numbers, the quotes, either single or double, are not needed in the function call. Also, the return type of the function is now Number.

Take a look at the type of the variable sum located in the function. The data type is int, which is new to ActionScript 3.0. In previous versions, you could only declare it as type Number. However, as type int, you can return the whole number only. As you progress through the book, you will be introduced to several new data types to ActionScript 3.0.

4. Run this file, and you should see 5 in the Label control.

If you wanted to perform a concatenation here, you might think you could do it by changing the return line to

```
return "The sum of the numbers is:" + " " + sum;
```

5. Go ahead and make this change and run the example again.

Whoops! NaN? **NaN** means not a number. But what went wrong here? Take a few moments and see if you can discover what the problem is.

Give up?

You will recall earlier that I said a concatenation turns the returned value into a string, even if there are nonstrings in it. So the function is now returning a string. However, if you look at the return type of the function, it is still declared as type Number. You need to change the return type to String if you are going to do a concatenation. It should work fine after you do.

As you can see, ActionScript 3.0 enforces the rules pretty strictly. The end result, however, is code that runs more efficiently and more bug free.

Handling events

Up to this point, all of your code has run as soon as you started the application. But many times you may not want some of the code to run until an **event** has happened.

An event could be a click of the mouse button, a press of a key, a roll of the mouse over a component, something just loaded, and so on. All events have to have two parts: an **event listener** and an **event handler**.

An event listener is something that is doing just as it says, listening for a certain event to happen. Once the event happens, the event listener needs to let a function know to do its job. That function is the event handler.

Every component has a set of events appropriate to that particular component. Let's return to the ActionScript Language Reference and locate the Button class.

Scroll down to the Events section, shown in Figure 3-21.

Events
▶ Show Inherited Events

Event	Summary	Defined by
buttonDown	Dispatched when the user presses the Button control.	Button
change	Dispatched when the selected property changes for a toggle Button control.	Button
dataChange	Dispatched when the data property changes.	Button

Figure 3-21. The events for the Button class

At first, it appears that the Button class has only three events associated with it: buttonDown, change, and dataChange. But here is where you need to do some detective work.

Remember earlier you learned about inheritance. The Button class inherits properties, methods, and events from the classes above it.

Notice that right above the list of events there is a link to Show Inherited Events. If you click it, you will see all the events available for the Button class (see Figure 3-22).

Events

▼ Hide Inherited Events

Event	Summary	Defined by
⬆ activate	Dispatched when Flash Player gains operating system focus and becomes active.	DisplayObject
⬆ add	Dispatched when the component is added to a container as a content child by using the addChild() or addChildAt() method.	UIComponent
⬆ added	Dispatched when a display object is added to the display list.	DisplayObject
buttonDown	Dispatched when the user presses the Button control.	Button
change	Dispatched when the selected property changes for a toggle Button control.	Button
⬆ click	Dispatched when a user presses and releases the main button of the user's pointing device over the same InteractiveObject.	InteractiveObject
⬆ creationComplete	Dispatched when the component has finished its construction, property processing, measuring, layout, and drawing.	UIComponent
⬆ currentStateChange	Dispatched after the view state has changed.	UIComponent
⬆ currentStateChanging	Dispatched after the currentState property changes, but before the view state changes.	UIComponent
dataChange	Dispatched when the data property changes.	Button
⬆ deactivate	Dispatched when Flash Player loses operating system focus and is becoming inactive.	DisplayObject
⬆ doubleClick	Dispatched when a user presses and releases the main button of a pointing device twice in rapid succession over the same InteractiveObject when that object's doubleClickEnabled flag is set to true.	InteractiveObject

Figure 3-22. The complete list of events associated with the Button class

The most common event associated with a button is click, which means the mouse button was clicked.

Here, you'll make some changes to your code to demonstrate using events:

1. After the Label control, add a Button control.

```
<?xml version="1.0" encoding="utf-8"?>
<mx:Application xmlns:mx="http://www.adobe.com/2006/mxml"➥
  layout="absolute">
  <mx:Script>
    <![CDATA[
        function mySum(number1:Number, number2:Number):String
        {
          var sum:int = number1 + number2;
          return "The sum of the numbers is:" + " " + sum;
        }


      ]]>
  </mx:Script>
  <mx:VBox x="213" y="110" height="290" width="218">
      <mx:Label id="myLabel" text="{mySum(2, 3)}" />
    <mx:Button label="Add the numbers" />
  </mx:VBox>
</mx:Application>
```

This will result in a button being added to your container, as shown in Figure 3-23.

Figure 3-23. The Button control added

For a moment, you will not use the mySum() function, although you will return to it shortly.

2. Modify the Label control so it looks as follows:

```
<mx:Label id="myLabel" />
```

You just got rid of the text property. This will make sense in a moment.

3. Return to the Button control and add the following event:

```
<mx:Button label="Add the numbers"➡
    click="myLabel.text = 'Button has been clicked'" />
```

The keyword click is an event listener. The event handler, within double quotes, tells the Label control (myLabel) to set its text property to 'Button has been clicked'.

Your code should now look as follows:

```
<mx:Label id="myLabel" />
<mx:Button label="Add the numbers"➡
    click="myLabel.text = 'Button has been clicked'" />
```

4. Run the application and give the button a click. You should see that the Label control now displays the text "Button has been clicked".

> *Once again, since the handler is within quotes, you need to put the text the Label control will display as a substring inside single quotes.*

The combination event listener/handler found inside of controls is good for simple tasks as you just saw. However, if you want to accomplish more complex tasks, you will need to write your own handler.

An event handler is really nothing more than a function that responds to an event. There are several different ways you can write a handler, and the next chapter will be discussing this in a bit more detail. For the time being, let's look at a simple example:

5. Modify the function so that it looks as follows:

```
<?xml version="1.0" encoding="utf-8"?>
<mx:Application xmlns:mx="http://www.adobe.com/2006/mxml"➥
  layout="absolute">
  <mx:Script>
    <![CDATA[
      function mySum(number1:Number, number2:Number):void
      {
          var sum:int = number1 + number2;
          myLabel.text = "The sum of the numbers is:" + " " + sum;
      }
      ]]>
  </mx:Script>
  <mx:VBox x="213" y="110" height="290" width="218">
    <mx:TextInput id="inputFirstName" />
    <mx:Label id="myLabel" />
    <mx:Button label="Add the numbers"➥
      click="myLabel.text = 'Button has been clicked'" />
  </mx:VBox>
</mx:Application>
```

In the many classes I teach, students often ask whether the function isn't, in fact, returning something to the Label control. The answer is a resounding *no*! Let's work through the logic:

6. First, change the Button control as follows:

```
<mx:Button label="Add the numbers" click="mySum(2, 3)" />
```

In order to say that a function has a return type, it has to return its results to the original caller, which in this case is the Button control. That is not the case here. All the function is doing is instructing the text property of the Label control to populate with the text indicated.

7. Run this code, and you should see the results in your Label control.

These examples work fine if you always want to add the same two numbers. But you will probably want to make things a bit more interactive. With just a few minor alterations, you can easily accomplish that.

8. Above the Label control, add two new TextInput controls with the ids of inputNumber1 and inputNumber2. Give both controls a width of 5.

```
<?xml version="1.0" encoding="utf-8"?>
<mx:Application xmlns:mx="http://www.adobe.com/2006/mxml"➥
  layout="absolute">
  <mx:Script>
    <![CDATA[
      function mySum(number1:Number, number2:Number):void
      {
```

```
                var sum:int = number1 + number2;
                myLabel.text = "The sum of the numbers is:" + " " + sum;
            }
        ]]>
    </mx:Script>
    <mx:VBox x="213" y="110" height="290" width="218">
        <mx:TextInput id="inputNumber1" width="50" />
        <mx:TextInput id="inputNumber2" width="50" />
        <mx:Label id="myLabel" />
        <mx:Button label="Add the numbers" click="mySum(2, 3)" />
    </mx:VBox>
</mx:Application>
```

The finished form should look like Figure 3-24.

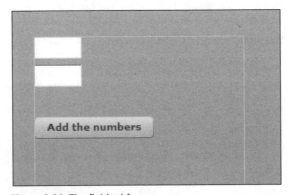

Figure 3-24. The finished form

9. Change the button's code as follows:

```
<mx:Button label="Add the numbers"➥
    click="mySum(inputNumber1.text, inputNumber2.text)" />
```

Here you pass the text properties of the two new TextInput fields into the click listener, which in turn passes it on to the handler function. Just another step beyond what you have done already.

10. Go ahead and run it.

Whoops again! The Error Warning box you saw earlier just popped up. The code seemed pretty logical. What went wrong?

Think about what you just did. You passed text into the button event and you then passed text into the function. But the two parameters of the function are defined as type Number. So somehow you need to convert the contents of the two text properties (which by definition are strings) into type Number. This is easily accomplished with a simple modification.

11. Make the following modification to the button click listener:

```
<mx:Button label="Add the numbers"➥
    click="mySum(Number(inputNumber1.text),➥
    Number(inputNumber2.text))" />
```

The Number and String classes are sometimes referred to as **wrapper classes**. By *wrapping* a string in the Number class, the class converts the string to a number. You could also use the String class to convert a number to a string.

12. If you run your code now, it should work fine. Change the numbers and click the button again. You do not need to restart the application each time. Save your project and close it.

> *Flex has some remarkable ways of handling unexpected events called* **exceptions**. *Try putting text (strings) into the two TextInput fields. Rather than crashing, as many programs do, it simply returns 0, as shown in Figure 3-25.*

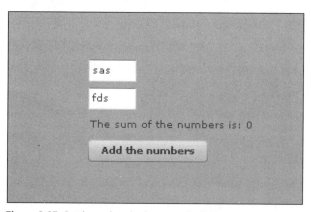

Figure 3-25. Putting strings in the numeric fields

> *As an exercise, try building an application in which the user inputs two numbers and, when the button is clicked, the application returns the sum, difference, product, and quotient of the two numbers. Then try building an application that has separate buttons to get the sum, difference, product, and quotient. Here is a hint for the second exercise: you will need to build separate functions for each calculation.*

As you can see, even with this limited experience, you can start building some effective applications. Let's talk about code placement next.

Reusability

The key to object-oriented programming is **reusability**. You don't want to reinvent the wheel each time a wheel is needed. You want to build the wheel once and then just attach it whenever it is needed.

As you progress through this book, you will learn several ways to facilitate reusability. For now, let's take a quick look at one method: using the source property. (Chapter 4 will discuss components in detail.)

In simpler situations, placing all of your code on one page, as you have done here, is perfectly fine. But when things start getting more complex, you might want to separate out the ActionScript code from the MXML code. You will find that this practice will facilitate easier debugging because each file will contain the code necessary to do one particular job. But, even more importantly, it will add to reusability.

If you ever did programming in Flash using ActionScript 2.0, chances are you separated out your ActionScript code and referenced it using the #include statement. Flex does not use #include. Instead, you use the source property of the Script tag. Here you'll give it a try:

1. Begin by starting a new ActionScript file by selecting File ➤ New ➤ ActionScript File, and entering a name for your file, as shown in Figure 3-26.

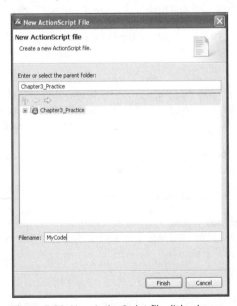

Figure 3-26. New ActionScript file dialog box

2. Click Finish.

As you can see, I call the file MyCode.as (remember, ActionScript files end in .as). Feel free to use this file name or any name you desire.

3. Cut the multiple functions you created in the previous section and paste them into the newly created ActionScript file. Your finished ActionScript file should look something like Figure 3-27.

```
1  // ActionScript file
2  function mySum(number1:Number, number2:Number):void
3         {
4              var sum:int = number1 + number2;
5              myLabel.text = "The sum of the numbers is:" + " " + sum;
6         }
```

Figure 3-27. Code now located in the ActionScript file

4. Return to the MXML file and delete the entire <mx:Script> section. In its place, just put a one-line Script tag as follows:

<mx:Script source="MyCode.as" />

From here on, everything works exactly as before. If you want to attach multiple ActionScript files, just use multiple Script tags as shown.

As you can see, by putting your code in separate files, you can call and reuse it whenever it is needed. After a while, you will build up entire libraries of code.

Before finishing up, let's take a look at one other way of getting help using MXML or ActionScript.

> As you may have figured out already, MXML and ActionScript 3.0 are fundamentally the same thing; they're just being used a little differently.

Return to the MXML document and, in Source view, click within the tags of any of the components, for instance, the Button control.

Now go to Help ➤ Find in the Language Reference.

Notice that Flex Builder took you right to the documentation for the Button class. You didn't need to select All Classes or scroll down. This is a handy way to get to information quickly.

Summary

You have just put a lot pieces together. Not only did you learn the basics of ActionScript 3.0, but you also used it to control MXML. You even broke the code out into a separate file.

From here on in, the text will build on the concepts you learned in this chapter as well as in Chapter 2. You will now turn your attention to containers and what they mean to developers. You will also explore the power of components as well as some powerful debugging techniques.

So turn the page and let us start putting everything together.

4 CONTAINERS AND COMPONENTS

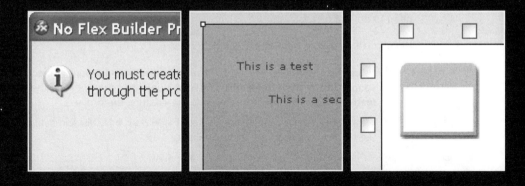

Chapters 2 and 3 painted a very broad overview of the Flex and ActionScript environment. I have presented the most general of concepts in order for you to understand what Flex is all about. Now it is time to start digging into a greater level of specifics.

This chapter will revisit many of the concepts discussed in Chapters 2 and 3, but discussing them in far greater detail than before so you understand the "why" of what you are doing.

In this chapter, you will

- Create a project.
- Examine the structure of an MXML file.
- Learn the concept of a container.
- Build a form entirely in Design view.
- Use the debugging features of Flex Builder 2.
- Pass data from components.
- Create custom components.
- Pass parameters to and from a component.
- Clean up the project files.

In many ways, this chapter is going to bring a lot of pieces together. You are going to build a simple form using layout containers and then turn it into a component.

I will be frequently referencing Chapters 2 and 3. So, if you need to, you may want to review those chapters again before continuing on.

Creating a project

In this section, you are going to try a small variation on creating a project to give you some tips on how to better set up your projects. If you were following along with the examples in Chapters 2 and 3, you started and subsequently deleted projects. But did you really need to do that?

Here, you'll try a little experiment.

1. Using the techniques shown in Chapters 2 and 3, delete any projects that are in your Navigator pane (remember, you don't need to actually delete the files and can reattach them at some future point by re-creating the project).

2. With the Navigator pane cleared, select File ➤ New ➤ MXML Application. You should see the warning message shown in Figure 4-1.

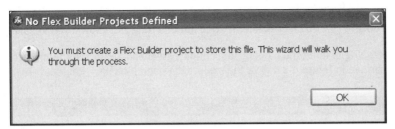

Figure 4-1. Warning message to create a project

The Flex Builder project or ActionScript project serves as a container to hold all of the project's assets. By assets, I mean the various files (MXML, AS, graphic, XML, etc.) your project needs to run. Flex Builder keeps track of these various assets for you. As a result, Flex Builder 2 requires that you create or import these assets only within a project.

4

3. Click OK, and you are brought to the New Flex Project dialog box shown in Figure 4-2.

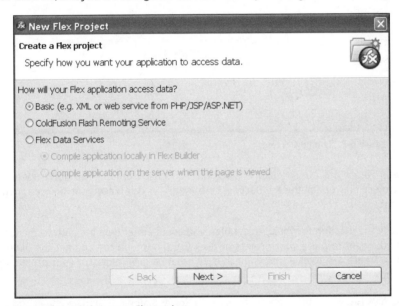

Figure 4-2. Creating a new Flex project

4. You are not going to be concerned about data-driven sites until a bit later on in the book, so keep the Basic radio button selected and click Next.

5. In Chapters 2 and 3, you learned what is and isn't permissible in a project name. You also saw that Flex Builder is good about letting you know if you violated a rule.

Keeping in mind the naming conventions, go ahead and name the project. As you can see in Figure 4-3, I gave the project the name Chapter4_Project.

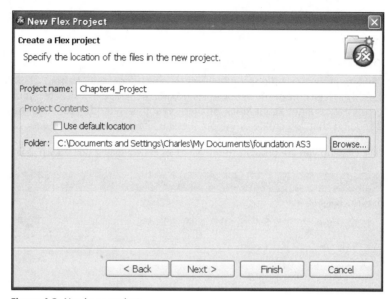

Figure 4-3. Naming a project

Notice in Figure 4-3 I unchecked the Use default location option. You don't need to put your project files under the My Documents folder; you can place your project anywhere you want.

To specify the location for your project files, you could either type the path to the location where you want to place your project or click the Browse button and get the dialog box shown in Figure 4-4. Notice that you can even create a new folder for your project in this dialog box if you want.

6. Click Browse to bring up the Browse For Folder dialog box, and go ahead and set up any directory you want for your project. When you have set it up, click OK—you are now returned to the New Flex Project dialog box.

7. In Chapters 2 and 3, you were instructed to just click Finish, and the MXML or AS file was set up. Here, however, rather than click Finish, click Next to bring up the screen shown in Figure 4-5.

Figure 4-4. Browsing for a folder

Figure 4-5. Changing the main application name

As stated in Chapters 2 and 3, you usually have only one MXML file, and this file serves as the "gateway" for everything else. As this is the file that comes up when the user goes to the site, it's a bit analogous to index.htm in standard web design.

Up to this point, when you've clicked Finish after accepting the default project location, Flex Builder has been naming the MXML file with the same name as the project. However, in many situations, you may not want this to be the case. For instance, assume you called your project myProject. Would you want your main file to be myProject.mxml? Most likely not.

It is common to want to give your main application file a name different from your project's name, and this is the place to do so.

8. In the Main application file field, change the file name to Container_Demo.mxml (see Figure 4-6).

Main source folder:		Browse...
Main application file:	Container_Demo.mxml	Browse...
Output folder:	bin	Browse...
Output folder URL:		

| < Back | Next > | Finish | Cancel |

Figure 4-6. Renaming the main MXML file

Notice that you can also change the output folder from bin to some other folder. However, I *strongly* suggest not changing this unless you really know what you are doing. Moving your main file outside of the bin folder will cause you to lose a lot of the testing ability of Flex Builder. You would change this destination if you need to test on a server with a different directory structure.

9. Leave the other fields blank, and click Finish.

Once all the housekeeping is done by Flex Builder, take a look in the Navigator pane (see Figure 4-7).

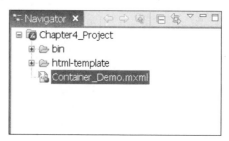

Figure 4-7. The Navigator pane with your newly created project

Flex Builder did exactly what you told it to do: it gave the project one name and the main application file a different name. But what makes it the *main* application file? Let's take a look at that now.

Main application file

Let's begin by looking at the initially generated code:

```
<?xml version="1.0" encoding="utf-8"?>
<mx:Application xmlns:mx="http://www.adobe.com/2006/mxml"➥
  layout="absolute">

</mx:Application>
```

A Flex application starts, and subsequently exits, through the opening and closing Application tags. Everything else that goes on *must* happen either directly or indirectly between these tags.

Every Flex project should have only one file containing the Application tags, and this file is referred to as the **main application file**.

If your project were a symphony orchestra, the Application tag would be the conductor. Nothing happens without it issuing the order.

> *If you have ever programmed in Java, C++, or C# .NET, the* **main method** *is comparable to the* Application *tags. What's more, in Flash, the main timeline is analogous to the* Application *tags.*

Now, let's take the concept of the Application tag one step further.

As I have repeatedly said in Chapters 2 and 3, the purpose of Flex is to present data. In fact, it is often called a presentation server. As you have had a taste of, and as you will be learning throughout the rest of this book, Flex applications are built by creating containers within containers within containers.

It is quite correct to think about the Application tags as the outermost, or main, container. It is within that container that all the other containers are placed.

> *In many ways, this concept is similar to the way Java builds its user interfaces.*

Now, how do you work within that main container? Let's take a look, and in the process take what appears to be a slight diversion that will help you in creating your projects. You'll look at how to add features to your application by adding code to your main application file, and you'll also see how easy it is to debug Flex applications.

Building within the main container

Start by adding a line of code (shown in bold) to the main container called Application.

```
<?xml version="1.0" encoding="utf-8"?>
<mx:Application xmlns:mx="http://www.adobe.com/2006/mxml" ➥
  layout="absolute">
  <mx:Label text="This is a test" />
</mx:Application>
```

This is nothing you haven't seen in Chapters 2 and 3, however, before we take you on to bigger and better things, let's take a little side trip for a moment.

True or false: You never make a mistake typing code.

You may have answered "True! I am perfect," but while you may think you are always perfect, there will be times when you will be less perfect than others. During those less-perfect moments, you will want to take advantage of the very powerful error and debugging tools in Flex Builder 2.

Debugging in Flex Builder 2

This section may seem a bit out of place when talking about working with the main application file (or so my editor complains). However, the debugging techniques you are about to learn are essential to help you work through all your projects, not just those for this book.

Start by making a slight modification to your label so that it's wrong:

1. Select the Project menu item. If Build Automatically is not checked, go ahead and select it so that it is.
2. Next, make the following change to the Label tag:

   ```
   <mx:Label text="This is a test />
   ```

   Notice that the closing quote is "accidentally" left out.
3. Save the project by pressing Ctrl+S (or selecting File ➤ Save).

Look in the Problems pane along the bottom of Flex Builder. You should see an error as displayed in Figure 4-8.

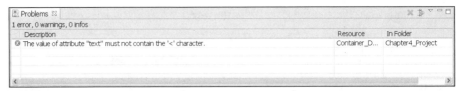

Figure 4-8. The Problems pane showing an error

All Flex errors come under one of two categories: **compile errors** and **runtime errors**.

In most programs, **compiling** means turning the code you wrote into a binary file (zeros and ones) that the processor of the computer can easily read. However, in Flex, like Flash, it means turning the code into a SWF (small web format) file.

When you selected Build Automatically a moment ago, you told Flex Builder to go ahead and create the SWF file before you ran the file. Take a look in the bin directory in your Navigator pane. You should see the Container_Demo.swf file there, as shown in Figure 4-9.

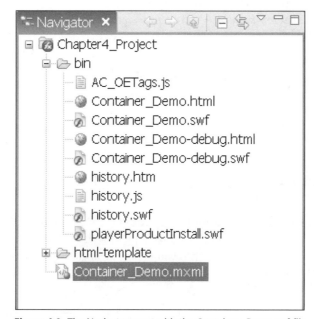

Figure 4-9. The Navigator pane with the Container_Demo.swf file

By creating the SWF file before you save, Flex has a chance to check through the code and flag most of the errors it may contain before they become problems during runtime (when the application is actually running).

If that isn't enough, switch to Design view. Here you have a bigger-than-life warning, as you see in Figure 4-10.

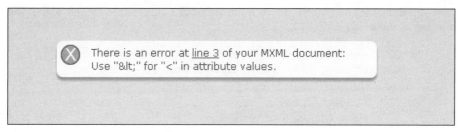

Figure 4-10. The error shown in Design view

Go back into Source view and fix the missing quote. When you save again, the SWF file is re-created and rechecked. The error message subsequently goes away.

The Flex debugging capability certainly does not end there. To further demonstrate, follow these steps:

1. Add a Script tag (which you know how to do from working through Chapter 3), set a variable, and make some changes to your Label tag (which you also saw in Chapter 3).

```
<?xml version="1.0" encoding="utf-8"?>
<mx:Application xmlns:mx="http://www.adobe.com/2006/mxml"➥
  layout="absolute">
<mx:Script>
  <![CDATA[
    private function showAge():Number
    {
      var myAge:Number = 30;
      return myAge;
    }
  ]]>
</mx:Script>
  <mx:Label x="30" y="30" text="{showAge()}" />
</mx:Application>
```

This simple application has the Label tag call the showAge function, which in turn returns the value of the variable, myAge, to the label.

2. Now you'll do something to help you debug. Right-click the line number, located along the left margin, that contains the variable myAge and select Toggle Breakpoint (see Figure 4-11).

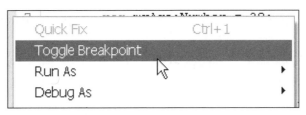

Figure 4-11. Toggling a breakpoint

Now you should see a small dot, which is the breakpoint indicator, to the left of that line number, as shown in Figure 4-12.

```
7       var myAge:Number = 30;
8       return myAge;
```

Figure 4-12. The breakpoint indicator

The purpose of the breakpoint is to stop the program at that point in order for you to examine what may or may not be happening in the code. For instance, you may want to test to see whether a variable received or passed the value that it should have.

If you click the Run button, the application will run normally. However, you're going to do something else here:

3. Click the Debug button. You should now see the message shown in Figure 4-13.

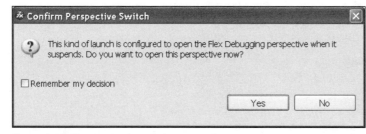

Figure 4-13. The perspective switch

4. Go ahead and click Yes to bring up the Debugging perspective, as shown in Figure 4-14. Recall from Chapter 3 that when you debug, the browser still opens up. You can close it since you won't need it for debugging.

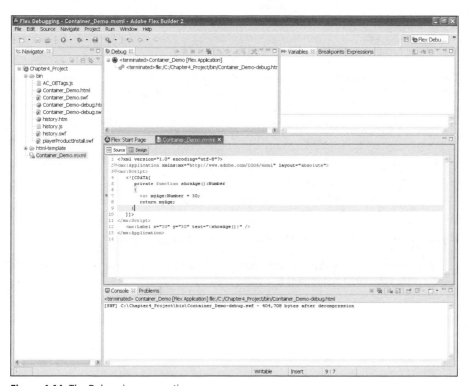

Figure 4-14. The Debugging perspective

Flex Builder offers two perspectives: the **Development perspective** and the **Debugging perspective**. Choosing a perspective allows you to open and arrange tools and panes relevant to the job you are doing.

Take a look at the Variables pane located in the upper-right corner (see Figure 4-15).

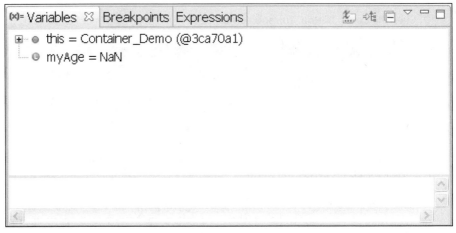

Figure 4-15. Seeing the values in the variables

If you look at the myAge variable, it seems to have a value of NaN (not a number).

Wait! How can that be if you set the value to 30?

Code is a very sequential process that moves step by step. When you set your breakpoint on Line 7, the code stops at the *beginning* of that line. This means it has not gotten to the point where the value, 30, is set. Located right above the Debug pane are a series of buttons that will tell Flex Builder how to continue with the code, including the Step Into button:

If you click the Step Into button, the code will advance only one line.

1. Click the Step Into button and look at the variable now (which should resemble what you see in Figure 4-16).

Figure 4-16. The variable is now set.

The pane shows not only the value in the variable, but also its memory position.

2. Now click the Terminate button, which is a couple of buttons to the left of the Step Into button. This stops all code from running.

There is one other powerful way to test your code also. Just to the right of the Variables pane you should see the Expressions pane, which allows you to write custom expressions that may be needed to test your code. Let's see how it works:

1. Click the Expressions tab.

2. Right-click the pane and select Add Watch Expression.

3. The Add Watch Expression dialog box appears. Here you can set a custom expression. Enter the small expression shown in Figure 4-17.

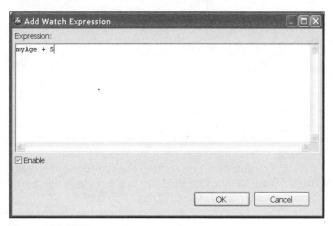

Figure 4-17. Writing a custom expression

4. Click OK, and then run the debug feature again.

5. When you first hit the breakpoint, you will see myAge + 5=35. Just step into the variable like you did before. The variable should now contain the correct value (see Figure 4-18).

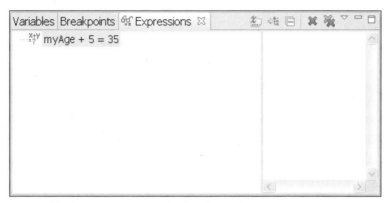

Figure 4-18. The watch expression showing the results

I hope you are seeing how powerful the debugging features of Flex Builder are. As you progress through this book, you will be looking at more of Flex Builder's debugging features.

Once you are through with debugging, you will want to return to the Development perspective (although this is not necessary). To do so, look in the upper-right corner of Flex Builder and click the button just to the left of the Flex Debugging label and select Flex Development, as shown in Figure 4-19.

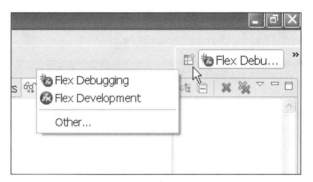

Figure 4-19. Returning to Flex Development perspective

Once you are back in Development perspective, you can toggle the breakpoint off the same way you toggled it on. So much for this little, but important, side trip. I hope you use this feature a lot to test your code as you progress.

Using containers

Now that you know how to debug, let's get back to the job at hand: building a way to present your data using Flex. As you are about to see here, as well as in the next chapter, the key to doing this job is understanding containers. The focus here is on layout containers; you'll learn about navigation containers (or navigators, which is the official Flex term) in the next chapter.

Let's get started:

Go back into Design view and return to your original code:

```
<?xml version="1.0" encoding="utf-8"?>
<mx:Application xmlns:mx="http://www.adobe.com/2006/mxml"
layout="absolute">
    <mx:Label text="This is a test" />
</mx:Application>
```

Notice the position of the label, as shown in Figure 4-20. Notice also that the layout property in the Application tag is set to absolute. Because you did not specify an x- or a y-position in the code, the label automatically appears in position 0, 0. Recall from Chapter 2 that when you set the layout to absolute, you must set the x and y properties.

Figure 4-20. Position of the label in Design view

2. Now define a second Label tag:

```
<?xml version="1.0" encoding="utf-8"?>
<mx:Application xmlns:mx="http://www.adobe.com/2006/mxml"➥
  layout="absolute">
  <mx:Label text="This is a test" />
  <mx:Label text="This is a second test" />
</mx:Application>
```

3. Save and run the code, and you'll see the following result:

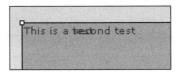

As you can see, Flex does not automatically position the labels properly due to the absolute layout.

In Flex, position 0, 0 is the upper-left corner of the work area. As you increase the x-position, the label moves to the right. As you increase the y-position, the label moves down.

4. Now make a slight modification to the Label tags and add x and y attributes.

```
<mx:Label x="30" y="30" text="This is a test" />
<mx:Label x="60" y="60" text="This is a second test" />
```

Measurement is in pixels.

5. Save and return to Design view. Your label should have moved to the right and down, as shown in Figure 4-21.

You could have adjusted the position a second way without going into the code by staying in Design view, clicking on a label, and going to the Layout panel, shown in Figure 4-22.

If for some reason you cannot see the Layout *panel in Design view, go to* Window ➤ Flex Properties.

Finally, there is a more visual way of changing position. Just put your mouse pointer in the middle of the label, click, and drag it to the position you want. You can also resize the label by using the resizing handles around the label box. Whichever technique you are the most comfortable with, Flex Builder will make sure the proper code is generated.

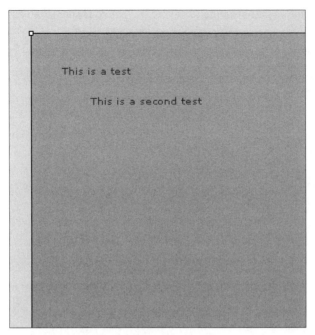

Figure 4-21. The moved label

Width:		Height:	
X:	60	Y:	60

Constraints

Figure 4-22. The Layout panel

A little bit of terminology is in order here. Since the Label tag is within the Application tags, the label is said to be a **child** of the application container. Understanding the hierarchy of your page will be quite important. Also, MXML shares a bit of terminology with XML/XHTML. Properties within the tags, such as text, x, y, width, etc., are called **attributes**.

Let's try a little experiment now:

1. Return to your Label tags and remove the x and y attributes.

Notice the Application tag has an attribute called layout—this defines where a component is placed. The default value is absolute.

2. Change the layout attribute to vertical. Your code should look as follows:

```
<?xml version="1.0" encoding="utf-8"?>
<mx:Application xmlns:mx="http://www.adobe.com/2006/mxml"➥
  layout="vertical">
  <mx:Label text="This is a test" />
  <mx:Label text="This is a second test" />
</mx:Application>
```

3. Now go into Design view or run the application. Your labels should be vertically stacked and centered, as shown in Figure 4-23.

> If you look in the Flex Properties panel and click one of the labels, you will notice that the x and y properties aren't even available anymore.

Figure 4-23. The labels vertically stacked

4. Try changing the layout to horizontal, so that the result resembles Figure 4-24.

> You can change the layout in Design view by clicking in the Editor pane and changing the layout in the Flex Properties panel.

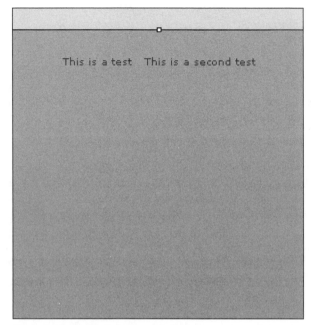

Figure 4-24. The labels horizontally laid out

If you're familiar with CSS, I'm sure you will liken this to CSS positioning . . . you'll notice more similarities later on, especially when you start looking at using CSS with Flex in Chapter 8!

Anyway, if this were all you could do, it wouldn't be very powerful. As you are about to see, it is not a great idea to put form controls right into the application container.

If you look in the Components panel, you'll see two broad categories of container: Layout and Navigators (see Figure 4-25).

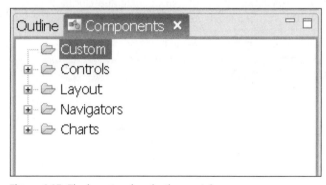

Figure 4-25. The layout and navigation containers

> *You have to be in Design view to see the* Components *panel.*

As you can see, there are 16 layout containers. Throughout this book, we will cover nearly all of them. However, for now, you'll just be concerned with the seven most commonly used ones, described in the following list. Any components located within the container, including other containers, are called **children**.

- HBox: Children are laid out horizontally from left to right.
- VBox: Children are laid out from top to bottom and centered.
- Canvas: This container uses an absolute layout. As you have previously seen, this means that you must specify the x and y properties, or the children will stack up in the upper-left corner.
- Panel: The Panel container can act as an HBox, VBox, or Canvas depending on the layout you choose within it. In addition, this container has a title bar area that can have text added to it.
- Tile: This arranges the children in either vertical columns or horizontal rows with each cell being the same size. Also, like the Panel container, the Tile container has a title bar area.
- ApplicationControlBar: This container can act either like a VBox or HBox. You would put components into this container that will affect the whole application. It is usually declared right after the Application tag, and by using the dock property, the container docks to the top of the application for the full width of the application.
- ControlBar: This container can act as either a VBox or HBox. It is used to dock a toolbar at the bottom of the Panel container.

As I mentioned earlier in the chapter, you'll explore the layout containers here, with navigation containers discussed in the next chapter. You'll start by making some modifications to your code.

1. Change the layout, if necessary, to horizontal, and add two more Label tags containing whatever text you want.

2. Surround the first two labels with an opening and closing VBox tag. Then do the same with the next two labels. Your finished code should look as follows:

```
<?xml version="1.0" encoding="utf-8"?>
<mx:Application xmlns:mx="http://www.adobe.com/2006/mxml"➥
  layout="horizontal">
  <mx:VBox>
     <mx:Label text="This is a test" />
     <mx:Label text="This is a second test" />
  </mx:VBox>
```

```
   <mx:VBox>
      <mx:Label text="This is the third test" />
      <mx:Label text="This is the fourth test" />
   </mx:VBox>
</mx:Application>
```

> *I like to indent code within the containers a bit for greater readability.*

3. Go into either Design view or run your code in the browser. Your labels should be arranged similarly to what you see in Figure 4-26.

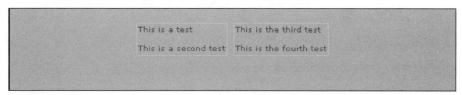

Figure 4-26. Labels contained in VBoxes

The application layout arranges the two VBox tags horizontally. Each of the VBox containers in turn arranges its contents vertically. Each container has a built-in **layout manager** that handles the placement of the components within it.

Let's go one step further now:

4. Surround each of the VBox tags with a Panel tag. Give the first Panel tag a title attribute of "1st Labels" and give the second Panel tag a title attribute of "2nd Labels".

```
<?xml version="1.0" encoding="utf-8"?>
<mx:Application xmlns:mx="http://www.adobe.com/2006/mxml"↪
  layout="horizontal">
   <mx:Panel title="1st Labels">
      <mx:VBox>
         <mx:Label text="This is a test" />
         <mx:Label text="This is a second test" />
      </mx:VBox>
   </mx:Panel>
   <mx:Panel title="2nd Labels">
      <mx:VBox>
         <mx:Label text="This is the third test" />
         <mx:Label text="This is the fourth test" />
      </mx:VBox>
   </mx:Panel>
</mx:Application>
```

5. Run the code. Your results should resemble Figure 4-27.

Figure 4-27. The panel container added

I am sure you are starting to get the idea of what is going on. You are setting up your presentation by using containers within containers, and then letting each container do its respective layout.

You can now control how much browser real estate each panel occupies.

6. In your code, give each of the two panel containers a height and width attribute of 50%:

```
<mx:Panel title="1st Labels" height = "50%"  width = "50%">
```

7. Run your code, and you should see results like those in Figure 4-28.

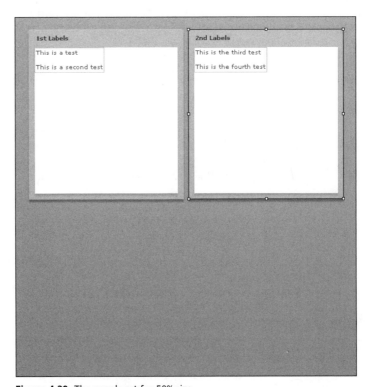

Figure 4-28. The panels set for 50% size

When you test, it is usually a good idea to test in the browser window. As handy as Design view is, depending on your settings, it may not always give you an accurate representation of what things really look like.

I was very particular to have you set the size to a percent. What this did was tell the SWF file to allow that panel, and any of its contents, to occupy 50% of the width and height of the browser. But 50% of *what* width and height?

Here is a variation of something you looked at in Chapter 2:

8. With the application running in your browser, resize your browser to any size you want. The panels and all of their contents automatically adjust to occupy 50% of the width and the height.

You can run the application in nearly any environment, and it will adjust accordingly. What makes this different from what you looked at in Chapter 2 is that in the earlier chapter you used constraints. Here, you are just setting the panel size as a percent of the browser size. You may find this technique a bit easier to work with.

This technique will not automatically adjust font sizes. However, even at small sizes, SWF files make fonts very clear and readable. I will be discussing fonts a bit more throughout this book.

Flex Builder comes with a great way of seeing ways containers can be used. Follow these steps:

1. Select Help ➤ Flex Start Page to bring up the page shown in Figure 4-29.

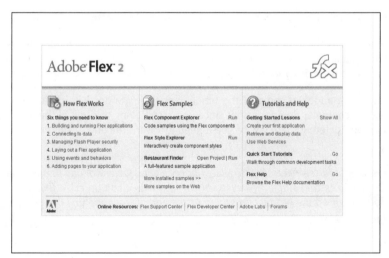

Figure 4-29. Flex Start Page

2. Click the Run link just to the right of Flex Component Explorer. This opens a new browser window that should look similar to Figure 4-30.

Figure 4-30. The Flex 2 Component Explorer

3. On the left, expand the Visual Components folder, then expand the Containers folder.

4. For each container, there is an example of the container and the corresponding code. To see an example, select VBox to bring up the screen you see in Figure 4-31.

When working with Flex containers, I use this reference quite often.

OK, you now know the basics of building a simple interface. The next chapter discusses the navigation containers. However, sooner or later, you will want these various components to either talk to each other or talk to a database.

Next, you'll take a look at some of the fundamentals of working with data. So go ahead and close the container demo for now, since you aren't going to use it in the next section. However, don't delete it quite yet, as you'll need it toward the end of this chapter.

> *It is not absolutely necessary to delete unneeded files while working in the development or testing stage. However, you will want to clean up extra files before mounting it on the production server. At the end of this chapter, I am going to show you a really cool way to clean up your files.*

Figure 4-31. Example of how to build the VBox container

Data binding

This section will do a bit of double duty. Not only will you become familiar with data binding, but you are also going to do most of the work in Design view and not "mess up your hands" with code.

The term **data binding** means connecting data to a "data consumer." For instance, let's say a label needs to get a name from a database. The connection that permits the label to do that is called the **binding**. Data could come from any source including another part of the form. In Chapter 3, you saw an example where you typed something into a text input field and, as you typed, you saw the data appear in a label.

In this section, you'll first see how to perform data binding in Flex; later, you'll get an overview of data binding in ActionScript.

Binding with Flex

Flex makes data binding really quite easy. Let's do a quick review here with a couple of new concepts.

Inside the Chapter4_Project (or whatever you named the new Flex project you created near the beginning of this chapter), start a new MXML file:

1. Select File ➤ New ➤ MXML Application. As you can see in Figure 4-32, I named the application Binding_Demo. However, you can call it whatever you want.

Figure 4-32. New MXML Application dialog box

2. Notice that at the bottom of the dialog box you can select an initial setting for the application layout. This is the setting you looked at early in the chapter. Since it is so easily changed, as you have seen, it doesn't make a difference if you set it here. Click the Finish button.

Let's build a simple form within a VBox container. You will use the VBox because, as stated earlier, building directly in the application container poses some limitations.

Since you have mostly been working with code so far in this chapter, you'll try building the container in Design view.

One of the most interesting aspects of Design view, and a carryover from Dreamweaver, is the ability to design with a particular browser size in mind. A common browser size to plan for is 1024×768, and you'll use that here.

3. Go to the top-right corner of the Design pane, and in the Design area field, specify 1024×768 as shown here:

When you set the design area, you will notice that scroll bars turn on to give you a larger area to work in.

4. Drag a Panel component from the Components pane (Layout category) to the design area. Use either the Flex Properties panel or drag in the design area to set the following properties:

- X = 450
- Y = 175
- Width = 400
- Height = 300

5. In the Flex Properties panel, give the panel a title such as My Form (see Figure 4-33).

Figure 4-33. The Panel container in the design area with scroll bars

6. Within the Panel container, drag a VBox component. A small dialog box opens that asks you what dimensions you want for the VBox container (see Figure 4-34).

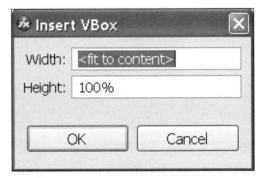

Figure 4-34. Insert VBox dialog box

This dialog box gives you the option of letting the width adjust itself depending on content. However, the Height option is 100%. This is an important point. Is it 100% of the Panel container? Or is it 100% of the browser size like you saw before?

The answer is the latter. Since you are placing the VBox within the Panel container, it is constrained by the size of the container.

7. Go ahead and click OK. Your VBox container now appears within the Panel container, as shown in Figure 4-35.

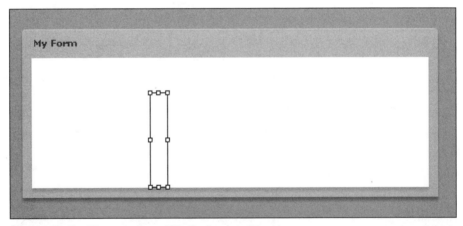

Figure 4-35. The VBox container within the Panel container

8. Add an HBox container inside of the VBox container. Be careful to watch the indicator mark to make sure it is in the container. Click OK when the Insert dialog box opens again. Your screen should resemble Figure 4-36.

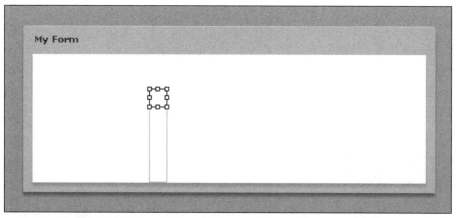

Figure 4-36. The HBox container within the VBox container

> **9.** Inside of the HBox container, put a Label control and set the text attribute to Enter Your Name: as you see here:

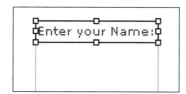

You want to put a TextInput control to the right of the Label control in the HBox container. The first time you do, it may be a little tricky. There are a couple of ways to do this:

> **10.** Click the HBox containing the Label control. Right at the top of the stage, just to the left, is the Show Surrounding Containers button. Click it, and your form should look like what you see in Figure 4-37.

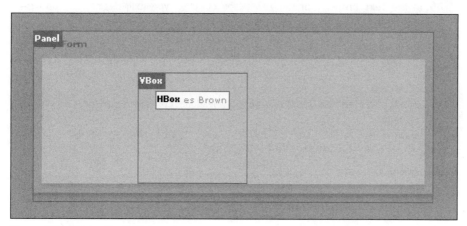

Figure 4-37. Turning the Container view on

117

This is a great way to help navigate through complex container designs.

11. Drag the TextInput control over and toward the right of the Label control with the text in it (if you are new to this, it may take a couple of tries). If you put the left border of the TextInput control over the *N* of *Name*, it should work fine.

12. You may find that your TextInput control, and subsequently your HBox container, now overflows the Panel container. If that happens, select the VBox container and reposition it within the Panel window so your form looks like the one in Figure 4-38.

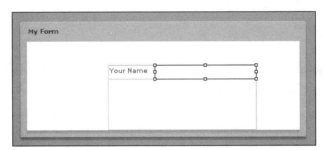

Figure 4-38. The form with the completed HBox container

> *Note that the surrounding* VBox *container adjusts automatically. This is because we used the* Fit to Size *setting earlier.*

13. You will be using the TextInput control in a programming environment shortly, so give it a unique id attribute (refer back to Chapter 3 if you need a refresher).

14. Select the TextInput control and, in the Flex Properties panel, give it the ID of txtMyName. In the VBox container, right below the HBox container, drag another Label control. Give it an ID of lblMyName. You will recall from Chapter 3 that to bind the data of one field with another, you need to use the curly braces to reference the control.

15. In the Text property of the lblMyName control, type {txtMyName.text}, and then press Enter to accept the changes.

Believe it or not, you just built an entire form, complete with data binding, without doing a drop of programming. The code generated looks something like this:

```
<?xml version="1.0" encoding="utf-8"?>
<mx:Application xmlns:mx="http://www.adobe.com/2006/mxml"➥
  layout="absolute">
  <mx:Panel x="450" y="175" width="400" height="300"➥
    layout="absolute" title="My Form">
    <mx:VBox x="35" y="10" height="100%">
      <mx:HBox width="100%">
        <mx:Label text="Enter your Name:"/>
        <mx:TextInput id="txtMyName"/>
      </mx:HBox>
```

```
    <mx:Label text="{txtMyName.text}" width="240" id="lblMyName"/>
  </mx:VBox>
 </mx:Panel>
</mx:Application>
```

16. Go ahead and run the form. Type your name in the TextInput control, and it should appear underneath in the form (see Figure 4-39).

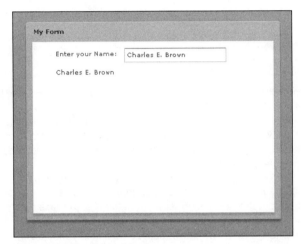

Figure 4-39. The finished form

Binding with ActionScript

What you just did is great for simpler bindings, but to really do more complex operations, you will need to use ActionScript. Recall from Chapter 3 that you add ActionScript using the Script tags.

1. Modify your code by adding the following Script tag and variable within it:

```
<?xml version="1.0" encoding="utf-8"?>
<mx:Application xmlns:mx="http://www.adobe.com/2006/mxml"➥
  layout="absolute">
<mx:Script>
  <![CDATA[
    var strMyName:String = "Charles";
  ]]>
</mx:Script>
<mx:Panel x="450" y="175" width="400" height="300" layout="absolute"➥
  title="My Form">
  <mx:VBox x="35" y="10" height="100%">
    <mx:HBox width="100%">
      <mx:Label text="Enter your Name:"/>
      <mx:TextInput id="txtMyName"/>
    </mx:HBox>
```

```
            <mx:Label text="{txtMyName.text}" width="240" id="lblMyName"/>
          </mx:VBox>
        </mx:Panel>
      </mx:Application>
```

2. When you save your file, you should see a warning, not an error, in the Problems panel (see Figure 4-40).

Figure 4-40. Variable warning message

Your application will work. What this message is politely saying is that if you run this, only data consumers within this MXML file (which I named Binding_Demo.mxml, as you see in the figure) will be able to see the ActionScript variable strMyName.

It is always advisable to give your variables a **scope**, which indicates who can or cannot use the variable. You should use one of two scope designations. **private** means only data consumers within this MXML file can see it. As you just figured out, that is the default scope, and Flex Builder is just letting you know. **public** means anyone can use the data in the variable. As you progress through the book, you will learn more about scope. It is good programming practice to make variables private and use functions within the MXML file to access them. That way, you can control who has access to them and what changes can be made.

3. For purposes of this exercise, change the variable to private:

```
private var strMyName:String = "Charles";
```

4. Save your file. When you do, the warning should go away.

5. Now change the data binding lblMyName label as follows:

```
<mx:Label text="{strMyName}" width="240" id="lblMyName"/>
```

Instead of the label being bound to txtMyName, like before, it is now bound to the variable strMyName in the ActionScript section.

6. Save your file. As soon as you save, another warning pops up (see Figure 4-41).

![Problems panel showing a data binding warning: "Data binding will not be able to detect assignments to 'strMyName'." Resource: Binding_Dem... In Folder: Chapter4_Project]

Figure 4-41. Data binding warning

This is a greatly misunderstood facet of Flex 2.

Flex 2 has greatly increased the power of ActionScript variables to interact with MXML tags. For instance, a variable tied to a TextInput control can both read and write from that control. However, before the variable can interact fully with the tag, you must instruct the variable to use those powers. You do that with a Flex metatag called [Bindable]. The [Bindable] tag gets placed on the line before each variable you want to have this power.

7. For this example, modify the ActionScript as follows:

```
<mx:Script>
  <![CDATA[
      [Bindable]
      public var strMyName:String = "Charles";
  ]]>
</mx:Script>
```

8. Save the file, and the new warning should disappear.

9. Go ahead and run the file. The Label control now reads the variable, and not the TextInput control as before (see Figure 4-42).

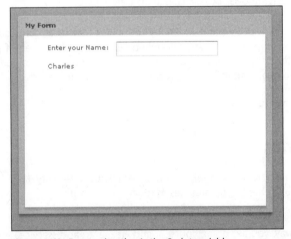

Figure 4-42. Form using the ActionScript variable

10. As one final variation, change the variable as follows so you can see a useful way to make use of this dynamic variable input.

```
[Bindable]
public var strMyName:String = "Welcome to Flex 2 " ;
```

11. Now change the Label control, lblMyName, as follows:

```
<mx:Label text="{strMyName} {txtMyName.text}" width="240"
id="lblMyName"/>
```

Here you have two bindings in the same Label control.

4

12. Now go ahead and run the application. When it is in the browser, type your name in the TextInput control, and you should get results similar to what you see in Figure 4-43.

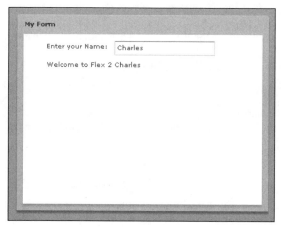

Figure 4-43. Two bindings in the Label control

Now that you have a working knowledge of containers as well as some additional knowledge about ActionScript 3.0, let's ask a couple questions: What happens if you want to use this form in multiple applications? And if you do, what if you want to modify the form a bit without having to change it in all the locations you may be using it?

There is one answer . . . components!

Components

In Chapter 3, I gave you a brief look at components and reusability. Here, I want to revisit the subject and examine the possibilities in much more depth.

If you put all of your code in one file, as you have been doing until now, it will work. But in doing it that way, you are doing yourself, and Flex, a great disservice.

By creating components, you can call something like the form you created in the last section on demand anytime you need it. What's more, if you modify the form, that modification will be reflected wherever the component is used, meaning that you don't have to update multiple pages when you are updating the same item.

As a rule of thumb, you will get greater flexibility and performance if you use many components in your application, each performing only one specialized job, than trying to put all of your functionality into one huge MXML file. As an example, suppose you had a login form you use in several places. Do you want to rewrite the code each time you need it? Or would you prefer to have it all in one place and just drag and drop it into wherever it is needed, ready to go?

As you are about to see, components are very easy to create in Flex Builder 2.

Component placement

As you progress through your Flex development career, odds are good that you will build entire libraries of reusable Flex components. Also, as will soon be obvious, many of these components may need to interact with yet other components. For that reason, you do not want to physically move component files around. Instead, you create links, which you will be doing in a moment, from your project to the required components.

You will want to eventually set up a directory structure to hold, and even classify, your components. For instance, a directory folder may hold a group of related components.

Most programming environments call these directory libraries **packages**. I spoke a bit about packages in Chapter 3.

For learning purposes, you are going to create a directory in your project to hold the component you are about to create. However, you will easily see how to build libraries of components that can be accessed by all your projects.

1. In the Navigator pane, select the root folder (if you followed the naming in this chapter, it is probably called Chapter4_Project). Next, select File ➤ New ➤ Folder to bring up the New Folder dialog box shown in Figure 4-44.

> *You could have also right-clicked the root folder in the* Navigator *pane and selected* New ➤ Folder.

Figure 4-44. The New Folder dialog box

2. Name the folder Components (or whatever name you want), and click Finish. You should now see the folder in the Navigation pane.

Creating the component

To create the component, follow these steps:

1. Select File ➤ New ➤ MXML Component. This brings up the New MXML Component dialog box shown in Figure 4-45.

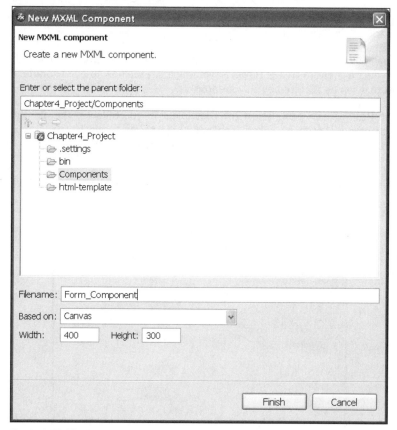

Figure 4-45. The New Component dialog box

2. Select the Components folder (or whatever you called it) as the save location. Give the component a name. In Figure 4-45, you can see I called it Form_Component.

Up to this point, all of our MXML files have used the Application tag as the main container. However, as discussed earlier in this chapter, only the MXML file that is serving as the main file can have the application container. If any other file with an application container is referenced, an error will occur. Since all MXML files must be within a container, you must base a component on one of the layout or navigation containers.

If you look at the Based on drop-down menu, you'll see all of the containers, as well as the other built-in components for Flex, are listed.

3. For purposes of this exercise, specify the most generic of all the containers: Box.

The Box container will arrange its children in either a single horizontal row or a single vertical column. To determine which one, you would use the direction attribute.

You choose this option because you are going to turn the form you created in the previous exercise into the component, and that form is contained within a Panel container already. Using a secondary Panel container could cause a conflict.

If you put a panel within another panel, the title attribute of Panel 2 seems out of position, nor do you have access to the content area of Panel 1. Putting a panel within a panel serves no real purpose (if you still don't believe me, give it a try).

4. At this point, you don't need to be concerned about the size. Just click Finish.

A new tab should open in Flex Builder with your component. Also, you should see your component saved under the Components folder in the Navigator pane as shown in Figure 4-46.

Figure 4-46. Flex Builder with the new component saved in the Components folder

Believe it or not, you have already built most of your component.

5. Click back on the Binding_Demo.mxml tab (the name may differ if you chose a different application name), and select all of the code *except* for the Application tags. Cut and paste the code between the Box tags in the Form_Component.mxml file—your component is now created. Go ahead and close the component file.

Calling components

Before you can call up a component, you need to tell Flex where the component is located. In the previous section, I talked briefly about creating folder libraries containing your various component files. You could easily enter the path each time you want to reference the component. However, this can be tedious after a while.

In Chapter 3, you saw the way ActionScript, Java, and C# .NET uses an import statement to predefine the path to get to a class file. However, MXML uses a technique employed by C++ and XML called a **namespace**.

A namespace is a way of giving a path a simple name so that every time you use that name, the program will know that you are referring to that path. We define a namespace inside of the Application tag using the xmlns attribute, followed by a colon (:), followed by the name you want to give it.

> There is already an xmlns *namespace inside of the* Application *tag that is used to verify the validity of the MXML code. You can have more than one namespace defined in the tag.*

If you want to call your namespace comp, you would use the following syntax:

    xmlns:comp

You follow that with an equal sign and the path in quotes.

In most programming syntax, a dot (.) indicates another level down of a folder. There are a few ways you can notate this, but the most reliable syntax is as follows:

    xmlns:comp="Components.Form_Component"

But what happens if there are five components you need to access in that folder? Do you need to create a separate namespace for each of them? By making a minor modification to the preceding namespace, you can access any component located in that folder.

    xmlns:comp="Components.*"

The asterisk is a wildcard that means access all of the components in that folder.

To call up the component you created in the previous section, do the following:

1. Return to the Binding_Demo.mxml file. If you cut and pasted the code properly in the previous section, you should have nothing left but the Application container tags.

2. Modify your Application tag as follows:

```
<mx:Application xmlns:mx="http://www.adobe.com/2006/mxml" ➥
    xmlns:comp="Components.*">
```

3. Now that you have the namespace defined, calling the component is easy. Between the Application tags, define a new tag as follows:

```
<comp:
```

When Flex sees comp instead of mx, Flex knows you are talking about the path you just defined. However, Flex Builder helps you out in one additional way (see Figure 4-47).

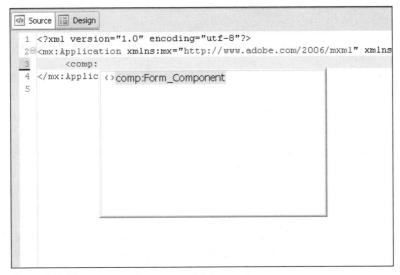

Figure 4-47. The namespace's component listing

As soon as you type the colon in, Flex Builder will automatically list all of the components located in that namespace. All you need to do is either press Enter or double-click with the mouse to select the one you want.

4. Select your component and close the tag. It should look as follows:

```
<?xml version="1.0" encoding="utf-8"?>
<mx:Application xmlns:mx="http://www.adobe.com/2006/mxml"➥
    xmlns:comp="Components.*">
    <comp:Form_Component />
</mx:Application>
```

5. Go ahead and run the MXML file, and your form should operate as before.

6. Save and close the Binding_Demo.mxml file.

Can it be any easier? The answer is *yes*!

1. Start a new MXML application file. Call it whatever you want (for this example, I called mine Component_Test.mxml).

2. If necessary, switch to Design view. Look in the Components panel, and you'll see that something curious has happened. A new folder called Custom was created and your new component is located in it, as shown in Figure 4-48.

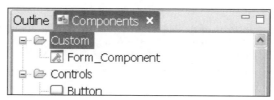

Figure 4-48. The custom component added to the Components panel

3. Drag the Form_Component from the Components panel to the stage and place it wherever you want.

4. Take a look at your code. It should look like this:

```
<?xml version="1.0" encoding="utf-8"?>
<mx:Application xmlns:mx="http://www.adobe.com/2006/mxml"➥
  layout="absolute" xmlns:ns1="Components.*">
    <ns1:Form_Component x="319" y="245">
    </ns1:Form_Component>
</mx:Application>
```

Flex Builder automatically built the namespace and called the component without a drop of programming on your part. By the way, notice that you just used that component in two separate files: your original Binding_Demo.mxml file and this one. See how easy and flexible it is? I have kept it simple for now, to easily illustrate the point—later on in the book I will show you some more real-world examples.

But, as you are about to see, you have even more power available.

Passing parameters

As you know, the component has a property in ActionScript called strMyName. And this property has a value of the string "Welcome to Flex 2". But let's say you want to change this string when you call it—let's make some slight modifications:

1. Go into the Form_Component file and change the scope of strMyName from private to public. Recall that the private scope will only allow the variable to be seen within the file. But if we want the calling file to be able to see it, as we do here, it needs to be public.

2. Return to the Component_Test file and start to type the name of the property strMyName. As you do so, Flex Builder helps you out by listing the properties that begin with those letters (see Figure 4-49). This will catch most of the spelling or case errors that could happen.

Figure 4-49. The properties listing

> The other properties listed in Figure 4-49 are ones that Flex automatically builds into an MXML file.

3. Finish the tag as follows:

```
<ns1:Form_Component x="319" y="245" strMyName="Hello">
```

4. Go ahead and run the application now. You should see the word "Hello" in place of the original "Welcome to Flex 2" text (see Figure 4-50).

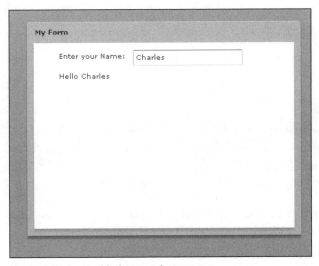

Figure 4-50. Form with the passed parameter

As you can see, you were easily able to pass the parameter and change the value of the string.

Receiving parameters from a component

The passing of parameters is a two-way street. You could also receive parameters from a component. However, since there is the potential to work with multiple components, you must give each component a unique ID, as discussed in Chapter 3 and again earlier in this chapter. This is similar to the Instance Name in Flash 8.

To see for yourself how to receive a parameter from a component, follow these steps:

1. Modify the call tag as follows:

```
<ns1:Form_Component id="myForm" x="319" y="245" strMyName="Hello ">
```

From here on in, every time you use the name myForm, Flex will know what you are talking about.

2. Add another Label control to the current MXML file. You can put it right below the component call in either Design or Source view (see Figure 4-51). The exact position is not critical.

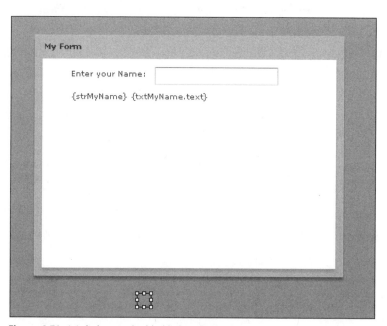

Figure 4-51. A Label control added below the component

You have done data binding with the curly braces several times already. But when you set the text attribute, it will be with an interesting feature.

3. Set your text attribute as follows:

```
<mx:Label text="{myForm.lblMyName.text}"  x="452.5" y="566"/>
```

Until this point, you have just used dot notation to call the control and the attribute associated with that control. Now, however, you begin the binding with the name of the component itself. The preceding code is saying to go to the component with the ID of myForm, and then go to the control lblMyName and read the text attribute (its contents).

4. Give it a try. As you type in the TextInput control, you should see the Label control set in both the form's label and the label in the main MXML file (see Figure 4-52).

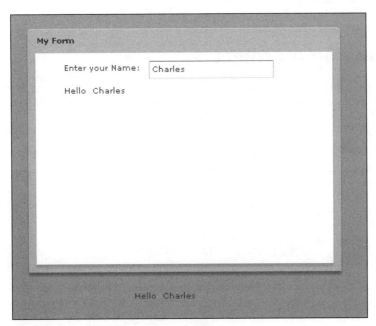

Figure 4-52. Label controls being set in both places

As you now see, it is very easy to both pass and receive parameters with components.

Let's take the idea of modularization one step further as an interesting little exercise:

1. Open the component file you created.

2. Select File ➤ New ➤ ActionScript File. Save the file in the Components folder and give it the name testScript.as.

3. Cut and paste the following two lines of ActionScript code in the component into the new ActionScript file:

```
[Bindable]
public var strMyName:String = "Welcome to Flex 2 " ;
```

4. Save and close the new ActionScript file.

5. In the components file, replace the entire mx:Script structure with the following:

```
<mx:Script source="testScript.as" />
```

6. Run the application; it should work exactly the same as before.

While you probably wouldn't want to create a new ActionScript file for just two lines of code, you can easily see how, in more complex situations, breaking everything out into separate files could give you greater reusability and maintainability while at the same time not harming performance.

Always look to break out code into separate files whenever possible.

You'll now look at how to clean up your project a bit.

Cleaning up a project

I purposely didn't have you delete any files you created in this chapter just so you could see how messy a project can get. A quick look at your Navigator pane, and you'll understand what I mean (see Figure 4-53).

Figure 4-53. The Navigator pane after working on a project

As Figure 4-53 demonstrates, for each MXML application file created, an array of support files is generated.

If you've been following along to this point, your project should have three MXML application files located at the bottom of the pane (Binding_Demo.mxml, Component_Test.mxml, and Container_Demo.mxml in the figure).

Assume that the only one you want to keep is Component_Test.mxml.

1. Go ahead and delete the other two MXML files. Now select Project ➤ Clean to bring up the Clean dialog box shown in Figure 4-54.

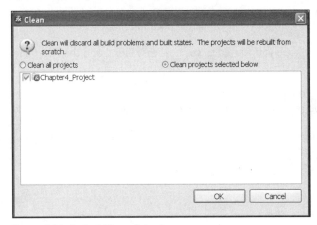

Figure 4-54. Project Clean dialog box

2. Select the Clean projects selected below option, click to check the Chapter4_Project check box, and then click OK. Any files associated with the two MXML application files you deleted are now cleaned up (see Figure 4-55).

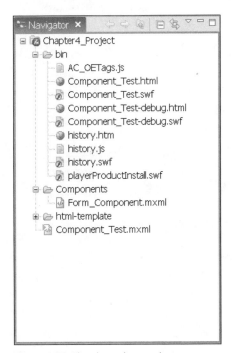

Figure 4-55. The cleaned-up project

Summary

You just covered a lot of ground in this chapter. Yet, in a lot of ways, this chapter has brought many pieces together. You used containers to build forms both programmatically and in Design view. You converted a form into a component. Finally, you passed parameters between the component and main application file.

Along the way, I hope you started to see how easy Flex 2 and the Flex Builder environment are to use.

You may want to take some time and review the concepts of this chapter several times. I am going to be referencing it quite often throughout the rest of the book.

The next chapter turns the focus on making things happen when they should, as it explores the concept of events.

5 NAVIGATION CONTAINERS

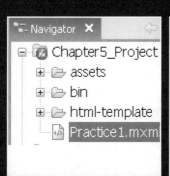

By now you are starting to see the philosophy behind Flex 2. It wants to give the web developer the ability to develop sophisticated, Flash-based user interfaces, over a variety of platforms, while minimizing the programming and complexity involved.

In Chapter 4, you saw how to use layout containers to build a GUI. Then you went on to turn them into components that can be used nearly anytime you need them by simply dragging and dropping them into an existing application. You even used some ActionScript to pass data to and from a component.

This chapter moves forward and talks about navigation containers. In this chapter, you will

- Learn how navigation containers work.
- Explore some of the different navigation containers: ViewStack, Accordion, and TabNavigator.
- Look at how to add LinkBar and TabBar controls to a ViewStack container.
- See how to add a navigation container to a project along with a Tile layout container.

This will really bring the concept of containers together. In this chapter, you will be mixing and matching almost all of the container structures. You will also see a slightly more complex layout than you have seen in the previous chapters.

Let's go to work . . .

Working with navigation containers

What good is any application without a good navigation system?

You want to either guide your users through the application or allow the users to choose where they want to go. In either case, a good navigation system is important.

This is the purpose of navigation containers. In essence, user movement is facilitated by controlling which containers (such as the VBox, HBox, and Panel containers you used in the last chapter) are visible and which are not.

If necessary, go into Design view and look at the Components panel. You should see an area for navigation containers (as shown in Figure 5-1).

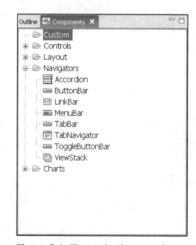

Figure 5-1. The navigation containers

While you see eight different navigation containers, you will soon see that the heart of all of them is the ViewStack class.

Before you begin, if you want to follow along with the rest of the exercises in this chapter, you will need to download a ZIP file containing the exercise files at www.friendsofed.com. Feel free to unzip it to wherever you want on your drive.

Up to this point, you have created projects from scratch. Here, you are going to need to create your project around the files you just downloaded. All that involves is a slight variation on what you have been doing.

As before, you can delete the project from the previous chapter if you want. Then follow these steps:

1. Select File ➤ New ➤ Flex Project.

2. Select Basic and then click Next to bring up the screen shown in Figure 5-2.

Figure 5-2. The New Flex Project dialog box

3. Give your project a name (you can use whatever name you want) and then uncheck the Use default location check box.

4. Browse to the folder where you unzipped the files you downloaded.

5. Click Finish.

Notice in the Navigator pane there is a file named Practice1.mxml (see Figure 5-3). In order for you to try the different navigation containers, it is not a bad idea to make a couple of backup copies of this file. That way you can experiment a bit.

Figure 5-3. The Navigator pane

1. Right-click Practice1.mxml and select Copy.

2. Right-click in an empty area of the Navigator pane and select Paste. The Name Conflict dialog box in Figure 5-4 appears.

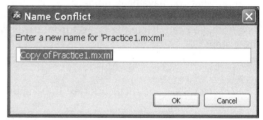

3. You get a warning of a potential name conflict. Change the name to Practice2.mxml.

Figure 5-4. The Name Conflict dialog box

4. Click OK. The renamed file should appear in your Navigator pane.

5. Go ahead and create a Practice3.mxml file.

Now that you've made your backup copies, open up Practice1.mxml, and you will see, as shown in Figure 5-5, that it is the badly designed website from hell (not that the books it sells are any better).

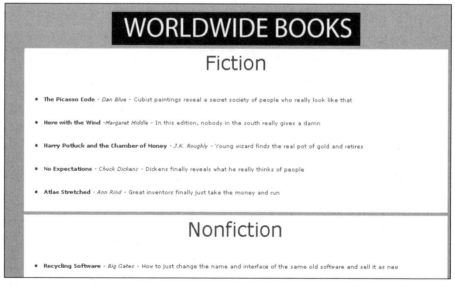

Figure 5-5. The Worldside Books website

Let's go over to Source view and see what is going on.

```xml
<?xml version="1.0" encoding="utf-8"?>
<mx:Application xmlns:mx="http://www.adobe.com/2006/mxml"➥
  layout="vertical">
    <mx:Image  alpha="100" source="assets/Banner.jpg"/>
<mx:VBox backgroundColor="white" id="Fiction" label = "Fiction">
    <mx:Text width="800" textAlign="center" fontSize="36"➥
      text="Fiction" />
    <mx:Text textAlign="left" width="100%">
        <mx:htmlText>
            <![CDATA[
                <li><b>The Picasso Code</b> - <i>Dan Blue</i> - Cubist
                paintings reveal a secret society of people who really look
                like that</li>
                <li><b>Here with the Wind</b> -<i>Margaret Middle</i>➥
                - In this edition, nobody in the south really➥
                  gives a damn</li>
                <li><b>Harry Potluck and the Chamber of Money</b> -➥
                <i>J.K. Roughly</i> - Young wizard finds the real pot➥
                of gold and retires</li>
                <li><b>No Expectations</b> - <i>Chuck Dickens</i>
                - Dickens finally reveals what he really thinks of people➥
                </li>
                <li><b>Atlas Stretched</b> - <i>Ann Rind</i> - Great➥
                inventors finally just take the money and run</li>
            ]]>
        </mx:htmlText>
    </mx:Text>
</mx:VBox>
<mx:VBox backgroundColor="white" id="Nonfiction" label = "Nonfiction">
    <mx:Text width="800" textAlign="center" fontSize="36"➥
    text="Nonfiction" />
    <mx:Text textAlign="left" width="100%">
        <mx:htmlText>
            <![CDATA[
                <li><b>Recycling Software</b> - <i>Big Gates</i> - How to➥
                just change the name and interface of the same old➥
                software and sell it as new</li>
                <li><b>Make Tons of Money</b> -<i>Donald Rump</i> - Rump➥
                explains how he became a billionaire while constantly➥
                declaring bankruptcy</li>
                <li><b>How to Win Enemies and Lose Friends</b> - <i>Dale➥
                Crochety</i> - The ultimate how-to book for people who➥
                want to stay loners</li>
                <li><b>My Lies</b> - <i>Swill Clinton</i> - This former➥
                American president tries to define what a lie is</li>
                <li><b>The Complete History of the World</b> - <i>David➥
                    McClutz</i> - McClutz gives you the entire history of➥
                    all civilization in less than 300 pages</li>
            ]]>
```

```
                </mx:htmlText>
            </mx:Text>
        </mx:VBox>
        <mx:VBox backgroundColor="white" id="Idiots" label =➡
          "For Idiot Series">
          <mx:Text width="800" textAlign="center" fontSize="36"➡
            text="For Idiots Series" />
          <mx:Text textAlign="left" width="100%">
            <mx:htmlText>
              <![CDATA[
                <li><b>Boiling Water for Idiots</b> - This book studies➡
                the intricacies of putting a kettle of water on the➡
                stove</li>
                <li><b>Solitaire for Idiots</b> - You will learn the➡
                highly competitive world of professional solitaire</li>
                <li><b>Concert Piano for Idiots</b> - In just 300 pages ➡
                you will learn to play like Horowitz and Rubinstein</li>
                <li><b>Writing Computer Books for Idiots</b> - Does➡
                wanting to write a computer book automatically make you➡
                an idiot?</li>
                <li><b>Turning on a Light Switch for Idiots</b> - Learn➡
                the technical intricacies of the various types of light ➡
                switches available</li>
              ]]>
            </mx:htmlText>
          </mx:Text>
        </mx:VBox>
        <mx:VBox backgroundColor="white" id="Technical"➡
          label = "Technical Books">
          <mx:Text width="800" textAlign="center" fontSize="36"➡
            text="Technical" />
          <mx:Text textAlign="left" width="100%">
            <mx:htmlText>
              <![CDATA[
                <li><b>Yet Another Flash Video Book</b> - ➡
                <i>Tom Greeny</i> - Tom shares more of his video➡
                secrets with us</li>
                <li><b>Flashing with XML</b> -<i>Sassy Jacobs</i>➡
                   - Sassy shows us how to spice up your life with XML</li>
                <li><b>How to Make Interesting Authors Boring</b> - <i>➡
                Chris Milled</i> - Chris reveals his secrets for making➡
                interesting manuscripts dreadfully boring</li>
                <li><b>Dreamweaver Made Hard</b> - <i>C.E. Brown</i> -➡
                Brown will show you how to do something in 20 steps➡
                instead of 5</li>
                <li><b>AJAX for Dirty Programming</b> - <i>Ben Forty</i>➡
                - This book squeezes the last breath from a dying➡
                technology</li>
              ]]>
```

```
            </mx:htmlText>
          </mx:Text>
      </mx:VBox>
      <mx:VBox backgroundColor="white" id="Videos" label = "Videos">
          <mx:Text width="800" textAlign="center" fontSize="36"➥
             text="Videos" />
          <mx:Text textAlign="left" width="100%">
             <mx:htmlText>
                <![CDATA[
                   <li><b>Mission Very Possible</b>  - Secret agent poses ➥
                   as an actor not very convincingly</li>
                   <li><b>Stuporman</b> - Man of aluminum saves the world➥
                   while posing for red underwear commercials</li>
                   <li><b>Lost in Transition</b> - Washed-up, middle-aged➥
                   actor and young and dumb starlet try to convince each ➥
                   other that they are good</li>
                   <li><b>Fallback Mountain</b> - This is how the west was➥
                   won?</li>
                   <li><b>Snoring in Seattle</b> - The coffee capital of ➥
                   the world and they are still asleep?</li>
                ]]>
             </mx:htmlText>
          </mx:Text>
      </mx:VBox>
   </mx:Application>
```

As you can see, this page is just a series of VBox containers. Each container has a Text container and, within that, an htmlText control. This control allows you to use some familiar (but not all) HTML tags and must be within the Text container. The CDATA tag is then used to prevent the HTML from parsing with the MXML and allows the browser to handle it like any other HTML code.

> *Flex supports the* <a>, <b>, <br>, <font>, <img>, <p>, <li>, <i>, <span>, *and* <u> *tags.*

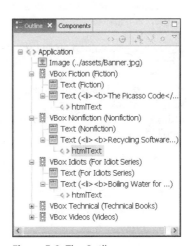

If you are going to set up navigation containers, you must give each of your layout containers id attributes and label attributes.

You can also see the structure of the application in the Outline pane, as shown in Figure 5-6.

Now that you understand the structure of the page, let's see how you can use various types of navigation containers to make it a bit more user friendly.

Figure 5-6. The Outline pane

ViewStack navigation container

The most generic of the navigation containers is the ViewStack container. This container is generic because it does not add navigation controls on its own. As you will see in a moment, you need to add some navigation controls. The other navigation containers bring their own controls with them.

Let's look at an example. You'll begin by enclosing all the VBox containers within a single ViewStack container that will act as a logical container for your data.

1. Put an opening ViewStack tag just before the first VBox.

```
<mx:ViewStack>
<mx:VBox backgroundColor="white" id="Fiction">
```

2. Now put the closing tag right after the last VBox.

```
</mx:VBox>
</mx:ViewStack>
```

3. Go ahead and run the application. You will get the somewhat strange result you see in Figure 5-7.

Figure 5-7. The results of adding the ViewStack container

What the ViewStack container does is stack the layout containers (in this case, the VBox containers) on top of each other. Each of the VBox containers is referred to as a **child container**. In other words, they are children of the governing ViewStack navigation container.

If you were to go behind the scenes, you'd see that the containers are set up as an array. The first container would be array position 0, the next array position 1, etc.

The reason the VBox labeled Fiction, the only one you can see now, looks collapsed is that the ViewStack container is not controlling the size of the VBox containers. You can fix this problem by adding height and width attributes to the opening ViewStack tag, which you'll do now.

4. Specify the following height and width attributes in the opening ViewStack tag:

```
<mx:ViewStack height="40%" width="25%">
```

As I stated in Chapter 4, using percents instead of absolute sizes gives it flexibility in browser sizes.

You now have the containers stacked and properly sized, as shown in Figure 5-8. The next step is to build some navigation.

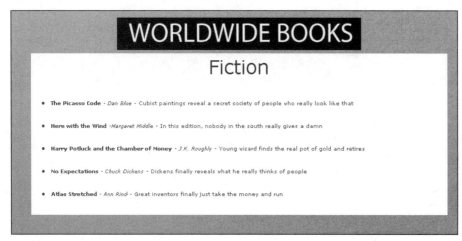

Figure 5-8. The container properly sized

The LinkBar and TabBar controls

If you go to Design view and look in the Components panel, under the Navigators category, you will see LinkBar and the TabBar (see Figure 5-9).

Figure 5-9. Controls in the Navigators category

These are controls that work nicely with the ViewStack container. However, before you can use them, you need to give the ViewStack container an id attribute so you can reference it later on from code or other components.

1. Define an id attribute in the opening ViewStack tag as shown here:

```
<mx:ViewStack height="40%" width="25%" id="bookCategories">
```

I find that setting up the LinkBar or the TabBar is little easier to do in Design view. There is a bit of programming involved, and Design view handles it automatically.

Let's begin with the LinkBar.

2. In Design view, drag LinkBar from the Components panel and put it underneath the VBox (see Figure 5-10).

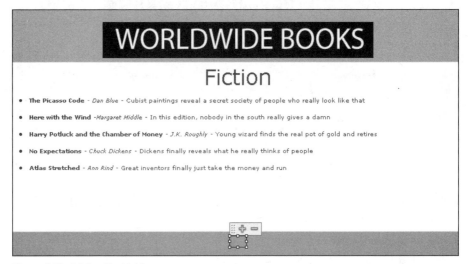

Figure 5-10. Adding the LinkBar

> *If you look in the code, it is really below the* ViewStack *container. But in Design view, all you are seeing is the* VBox.

Notice that there is a control with a + and – over the LinkBar. That is for adding and removing categories manually. Don't worry too much about that now.

The next step is to tie this LinkBar to the ViewStack container.

3. If you look in the Flex Properties panel, you will see a field for the data provider. Enter the value of the id you gave to the ViewStack container (see Figure 5-11).

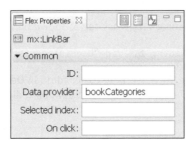

Figure 5-11. Adding a data provider to the LinkBar

4. Press Enter. Your LinkBar should appear as shown in Figure 5-12.

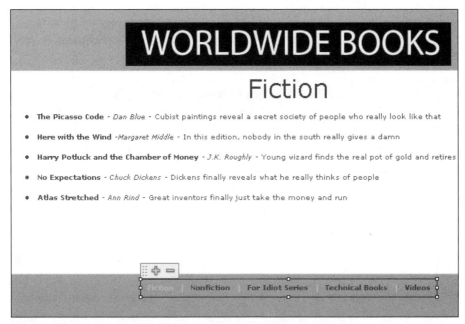

Figure 5-12. The LinkBar added

Notice that the LinkBar picks up the label attribute of each of the VBox containers within the ViewStack navigation container.

Run the application. As you click the links, the corresponding VBox containers come forward to display their contents.

The TabBar is similar in operation.

1. Drag a copy of the TabBar from the Components panel and put it between the banner and the VBox container (see Figure 5-13).

Figure 5-13. Adding the TabBar

Notice that it looks identical to the LinkBar. All you need to do, like the LinkBar, is tie the TabBar to the ViewStack container.

2. Specify the ViewStack id attribute (bookCategories) in the Data provider field of the Flex Properties panel and press Enter. When you run your application, your form should look like the one in Figure 5-14.

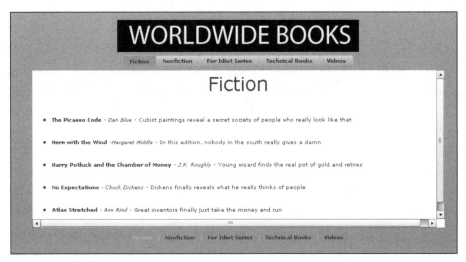

Figure 5-14. The TabBar added to the application

As you can see, you added some interesting navigation to your application.

You will notice that the Flex Properties panel, for both navigation bars, allows you to set font colors, size, background, rollover colors, etc. It is worth spending some time trying out these different attributes.

Now that you see how easy it is to build with layout and navigation containers, let's turn to a different navigation container.

Accordion navigation container

The Accordion navigation container is an interesting variation of the ViewStack container. Rather than stack the child containers one on top of the other, it collapses the children, leaving just a bar for selecting the container.

It is easy to adapt the previous example for an Accordion container.

1. Since they don't work well with the Accordion container, remove the two navigation bars (LinkBar and TabBar) you added by clicking them and pressing Delete.

2. Change the opening ViewStack tag as follows:

```
<mx:Accordion height="60%" width="25%" id="bookCategories">
```

Notice the slight adjustment to the height attribute. This is due to the nature of the Accordion container and the contents you are putting into it in this exercise—the area had to be expanded to accommodate the contents.

3. Change the closing ViewStack tag as follows:

```
</mx:Accordion>
```

4. Go ahead and run the application. Figure 5-15 shows the results.

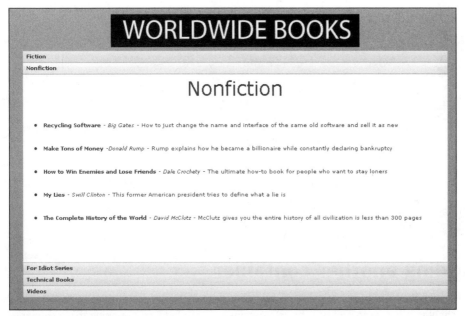

Figure 5-15. The Accordion container

Notice that each bar picks up the label attribute and, by clicking a bar, that container expands while collapsing the others.

TabNavigator navigation container

The **TabNavigator** navigation container attaches tab controls directly to the container. Let's see how it's done, using the same project as in the previous example:

1. Change the Accordion tag as follows:

```
<mx:TabNavigator height="50%" width="70%" id="bookCategories">
```

Notice the adjustments to the values for height and width.

2. Change the closing tag from an Accordion tag to a TabNavigator tag.

3. Go ahead and run the application. Your form should look like the one in Figure 5-16.

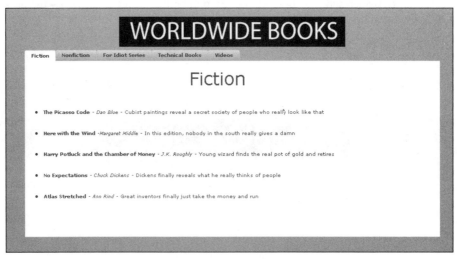

Figure 5-16. The TabNavigator

As you can see, the containers are easily navigable by clicking the tabs.

Now that you see how easy it is to work with all of these containers, let's take a look at a slight variation.

Adding another container

With your navigation structure set up using one of the techniques you learned in this chapter, it is easy to add or subtract containers as needed. You are going to do so manually now. (After you learn to work with dynamic data, later in the book, I will show you how to make the process a bit more automatic.)

1. Go into the code and move to the line just after the closing VBox tag for the container labeled Video, and build another VBox:

```
<mx:VBox backgroundColor="white" id="foED" label="friends of ED">

</mx:VBox>
```

2. Because you are building the VBox right within the navigation container, in this case the TabNavigator, it will be added automatically as a new tab, with the tab picking up the label attribute of the container. Go ahead and run the application; you should see the newly added tab shown in Figure 5-17.

Figure 5-17. New tab added

Unfortunately, the page is empty. For that reason, this would be a good place to show you another container.

3. Within the new VBox tags, put a Tile layout container tag and set the autoLayout attribute to True. The Tile container arranges objects, like graphics, in a grid-like manner.

```
</mx:VBox>
<mx:VBox backgroundColor="white" id="foED" label="friends of ED">
    <mx:Tile autoLayout="true">

    </mx:Tile>
</mx:VBox>
```

4. Now, within that, place four Image tags representing the four book covers located in the assets folder of your exercise files.

```
<mx:VBox backgroundColor="white" height="60%" id="foED"➥
  label="friends of ED">
    <mx:Tile autoLayout="true">
       <mx:Image source="assets/Green.jpg"/>
       <mx:Image source="assets/jacobs.jpg"/>
       <mx:Image source="assets/peters.jpg"/>
       <mx:Image source="assets/elst.jpg"/>
    </mx:Tile>
</mx:VBox>
```

5. Run the application, and go to your new container (the new tab in the application). Notice that the Tile container automatically arranged the graphics in a grid, as you see in Figure 5-18, but left a lot of empty space (hopefully to plug more books). You might be tempted to change the height of the container. However, if you did, it wouldn't help in that it is being controlled by the navigation container.

Figure 5-18. The Tile container

5

Notice that the Tile container also turns on the scroll bar should the content overflow the container.

So here you have a layout container, within another layout container, within a navigation container, within an Application container. As a matter of fact, if you look in the Outline pane, you will see the structure for the application (as shown in Figure 5-19).

Figure 5-19. The structure of the finished project

As you progress through this book, you will be revisiting navigation containers. More importantly, you will learn how to control these containers programmatically.

Summary

This chapter, as well as Chapter 4, covered containers pretty extensively. You mixed and matched most of the various layout and navigation containers.

It is now time for a change in direction. We are going to start to look at the purpose of Flex: to bring outside data into your GUI.

We have a bit of work ahead of us. I would attack the next chapter fresh.

Now that you have a good handle on building rich Internet application GUIs, you will now start to focus on putting content into them. After all, what good are all these tools if they are not tied into a data source?

In this chapter, you will

- Learn about the Event Object Model.
- Connect Flex to an XML file.
- Learn about E4X.
- See how the DataGrid component works.
- Explore security in the Flash Player

While you work through this chapter, I strongly suggest experimenting with the GUI building techniques you have learned up to this point when connecting with XML. As you will soon see, what applies to one control applies equally to many controls.

This chapter will start to bring a lot of little pieces together.

Data source

Let's begin with a simple question: What is a data source?

If you had asked this question 5 or 6 years ago, the answer would probably be a database. If you ever did programming in one of the earliest dynamic web technologies, ASP, you would have programmed direct references to a database, such as Microsoft Access or SQL Server, right into the dynamic page template. While many of today's dynamic technologies, such as ColdFusion, still have that capability, the trend is to move away from that toward a mixture of databases and XML. Let's see a simple example to demonstrate why this is happening.

Let's assume you want to build an online travel site where the user can compare flights and make a reservation. Let's say that a user wants a flight between Newark, NJ, and Orlando, FL, on a given day.

The user enters the dates, cities, flight times desired, and so on and the presses the Submit button. That site then "polls" all airlines such as Continental, American, JetBlue, and so on to see whether they have flights that match the specifications requested. If you followed the dynamic page model of ASP I mentioned previously, your site would have to have direct connection to the databases of dozens of airlines in order to work. Furthermore, it would have to take into account the individual database structures for each of those airlines. I am sure that you easily see this would not be very practical. You would need some sort of standardized way to allow your website to access the information from all the airlines easily.

XML is the standard to do just that: to exchange data easily over the Internet. Since it is a text-based format, it can be read without difficulty by both man and computer. Plus, it is flexible enough to adapt to a number of scenarios easily. Of course, many sites would still rely on databases to store their data, but this is not a problem for a site that uses XML—most databases can output data as XML for your site to use.

This new model is so prevalent that Macromedia (which made the decision before Adobe acquired the company) stripped the capability of Flex and Flash to access a database directly. In its place are a number of class files that allow for the easy access of XML files.

> In Chapter 12, I will be talking about the relationship of Flex and ColdFusion, which allows yet another way of accessing data.

As you will learn later on in this chapter, loading data from an XML file is an event. So before I talk about using XML data, you need a greater understanding of the concept of events.

6

Events

Let's begin with a bit of logic here from what you learned in Chapters 2 through 4:

Flex allows you to create graphic user interfaces over a variety of platforms. In order to make their construction easy, Flex employs the use of a variety of components, with some of those components acting as containers.

> Even though containers are used to hold other components, they are also themselves components.

A component further employs its own containers and ActionScript in order for it to do its job. However, let me give you a peek "under the hood" for just a moment.

Chapter 3 spoke briefly about ActionScript class files. I am not going to start making things complex here by introducing the intricacies of building class files. However, as you saw in Chapter 3, every class file has three potential programming constructs within it: properties (which are variables, located in the class file, that are not within a function), functions, and events.

Here is an interesting behind-the-scenes fact: the built-in components are actually derived from ActionScript class files. So if you place a Button control in your GUI, you are automatically calling the Button class file with all of its corresponding properties, functions, and events.

As you also saw in Chapter 3, these properties, functions, and events are all listed in the ActionScript Language Reference. For the sake of review, in Source view, go to Help ➤ Find in Language Reference. Once in the Language Reference, go to the Button class (or for that matter most any class) and scroll down to the Events section to see what events are available for that class—the list of events should look like what you see in Figure 6-1.

Events

▼ Hide Inherited Events

Event	Summary	Defined by
⬆ activate	Dispatched when Flash Player gains operating system focus and becomes active.	DisplayObject
⬆ add	Dispatched when the component is added to a container as a content child by using the addChild() or addChildAt() method.	UIComponent
⬆ added	Dispatched when a display object is added to the display list.	DisplayObject
buttonDown	Dispatched when the user presses the Button control.	Button
change	Dispatched when the selected property changes for a toggle Button control.	Button
⬆ click	Dispatched when a user presses and releases the main button of the user's pointing device over the same InteractiveObject.	InteractiveObject
⬆ creationComplete	Dispatched when the component has finished its construction, property processing, measuring, layout, and drawing.	UIComponent
⬆ currentStateChange	Dispatched after the view state has changed.	UIComponent
⬆ currentStateChanging	Dispatched after the currentState property changes, but before the view state changes.	UIComponent
dataChange	Dispatched when the data property changes.	Button
⬆ deactivate	Dispatched when Flash Player loses operating system focus and is becoming inactive.	DisplayObject
⬆ doubleClick	Dispatched when a user presses and releases the main button of a pointing device twice in rapid succession over the same InteractiveObject when that object's doubleClickEnabled flag is set to true.	InteractiveObject

Figure 6-1. Events for the Button class

Recall that many of the properties, functions, and events (including the all-important click event) are inherited from classes higher up in the hierarchy. For that reason, I always like to expand the Show Inherited Events link (or the Show Inherited Properties or Functions links if necessary).

Let's establish one metaphysical programming rule in object-oriented programming:

Nothing happens without an event.

The event could be the loading of the application, data loading completing, clicking a button, typing text, and so on. However, without the push of an event, nothing further happens. This is true in all OOP programming languages.

As you saw in Chapter 2, Flex makes event setup easy—we had some text, "Wipe Right," when we rolled the mouse over it. We'll review event setup here with some rather interesting variations.

1. Begin by starting a new project as you have in the previous chapters. Call it whatever you would like and, if you want, delete the previous projects.

2. Now set up a simple GUI—change the default code so it looks like the following:

```
<?xml version="1.0" encoding="utf-8"?>
<mx:Application xmlns:mx="http://www.adobe.com/2006/mxml"➥
  layout="absolute">
```

```
        <mx:Panel x="320" y="127" width="250" height="200"➥
            layout="absolute" title="Testing Events">
          <mx:VBox x="79" y="55" height="100%">
            <mx:Label id="myLabel"/>
            <mx:Button label="Test" id="myButton"/>
          </mx:VBox>
        </mx:Panel>
      </mx:Application>
```

The finished form should look something like Figure 6-2 in Design view.

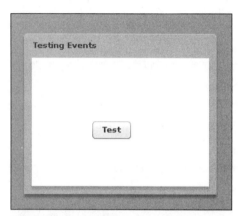

Figure 6-2. The test form

There is nothing here you have not seen before. You simply put a VBox container within a Panel container and add two controls: a Label component and a Button component. You delete the text attribute of the label and give it an ID of myLabel. You change the label attribute of the button to "test" and give it an ID of myButton.

Now, say you want the label to read "The Button is clicked" when you click the button. There are three ways you could approach this.

3. The first is certainly the easiest to do. Build the event right into the Button control tag.

```
<mx:Button label="Test" id="myButton"➥
   click="myLabel.text='The button is clicked'"/>
```

> *The text is enclosed in a single quote because the entire* click *event has to be enclosed in double quotes. This is how most programs define a string within a string.*

As a slight variation, you could skip programming altogether and in Design view, after selecting the Button component, click the Category view button in the Flex Properties panel, select the click category as shown in Figure 6-3, and in the values column type myLabel.text = 'The Button is clicked'.

Figure 6-3. The click category of the Flex Properties panel

4. Using either technique, your result should look like Figure 6-4 when you click the button.

Figure 6-4. The event triggering text

Getting the label to appear is pretty easy with little or no code involved; however, that ease comes at a bit of a price. The price is flexibility, so you should use this technique only in the simplest of circumstances.

5. To give your little form a bit more flexibility, add the following script to the top of the application:

```
<mx:Script>
  <![CDATA[
    private function fillLabel():void
    {
```

```
                myLabel.text = "The Button is clicked";
            }
        ]]>
    </mx:Script>
```

6. Next, change the click event in the Button component as follows:

```
<mx:Button label="Test" id="myButton" click="fillLabel()"/>
```

Here, rather than call the Label control directly, we pass it through the fillLabel() function in the Script tag.

> Recall that "private scope" means that only this file can see and use the fillLabel() *function it.*

7. Go ahead and run the application again—it should work exactly the same as before.

So how does this make things more flexible? Hold tight!

A bit of terminology is in order here.

The click event in the Button component is actually referred to in most programming environments as the **event listener**. This means its only job is to listen for its assigned event to happen. Once the event happens, it tells the assigned code (in this case, the fillLabel() function) to go ahead and do its job. That code is the **event handler**.

Coding by its very nature will give you the ability to respond to more complex situations easily. However, there is a third, and very powerful, way to handle events.

The event object

When an event happens in ActionScript, as is true of most programming languages today, an object is generated called the **event object**. This object contains two very important pieces of information: who generated the event, called the **target**, and what the event was, called the **type**.

These two properties have enormous consequences in programming. Can two separate buttons in a GUI generate click events? Does each component have potentially multiple events associated with it? The answer to both of these questions is a resounding *yes!*

Let's see how the event object works by modifying the code a bit.

1. First of all, modify the Button tag as follows:

```
<mx:Button label="Button 1" id="myButton" click="fillLabel(event)" />
```

Notice that when the click event now calls the event handler, in this case fillLabel(), it is passing a parameter. The name of that parameter, event, is not special. You could have called it anything you wanted to. Any name you pass with an event listener will be the name assigned to the event object. Programmers use the name event traditionally because it best describes what the object is doing.

Notice I changed the label attribute to Button 1. You will see why in a moment.

2. Now turn your attention to the fillLabel() handler. Modify your script as follows:

```
private function fillLabel(evt:Event):void
{
   myLabel.text = evt.target.id + " is pressed";
}
```

Again, programmers traditionally call the parameter receiving the event object evt. There is nothing significant in the name.

Recall from Chapter 3 that when a function receives a parameter, it must have a data type associated with it. With the event object, the data type is type Event.

> *Some ActionScript documentation shows the data type as being type* Object. *This is the most generic type there is, and many OOP programmers like to keep data types as generic as possible. This goes back to a discussion in Chapter 2 about hierarchies. I have tested it both ways, and both seem to work equally well.*

Once the event object is "caught" by the function, the function has access to the type and target properties I just discussed. But the target property has one more advantage: it can further access the properties of the component generating the event.

> *Of late, I have heard the term* **event dispatcher** *used to refer to the component generating the event.*

You can call the attributes in the myButton component. The line

```
myLabel.text = evt.target.id + " is pressed";
```

is calling the id attribute of the event dispatcher, in this case, myButton.

3. Go ahead and run the code, and you should get the result shown in Figure 6-5.

Figure 6-5. The id attribute showing in the label

The id attribute of the component generating the event, myButton, is shown.

4. Make the following minor alteration to the code:

```
myLabel.text = evt.target.label + " is pressed";
```

5. Now you are using the label attribute instead of id. Run your application again, and the result should be as shown in Figure 6-6.

Figure 6-6. The label attribute showing in the label

I am sure you are now starting to see the potential here.

6. Take this one step even further by adding a second Button control beneath the original one, like so:

```
<mx:Button label="Button 1" id="myButton" click="fillLabel(event)"/>
<mx:Button label="Button 2" id="myButton2" click="fillLabel(event)"/>
```

7. Test the code again, and click back and forth on the buttons. You'll see that the one event handler, fillLabel(evt:Event), can now handle the click event generated by either button. You no longer need to write a separate handler for each component.

8. Now take this even further with a slight variation—change the code in the event handler as follows:

```
private function fillLabel(evt:Event):void
    {
        if (evt.target.id == "myButton")
        {
        myLabel.text = "Button 1 is pressed";
         }
         if (evt.target.id == "myButton2")
         {
              myLabel.text = "Button 2 is pressed"
          }
    }
```

If necessary, you can build a series of decision statements to test which component is generating the event, and then respond accordingly.

> Note that a double equal sign is used here instead of a single one. The double equal sign means compare what is on the left side to what is on the right side. A single equal sign, known as an **assignment statement**, assigns what is on the right side to what is on the left side.

9. Go ahead and test the code. It should work exactly the same as before.

10. Finally, let's look at one more use of the event object by changing the handler as follows:

```
private function fillLabel(evt:Event):void
{
    myLabel.text = evt.type;
}
```

In this example, we are going to look at the type of event rather than who generated it or what it targets.

11. Try running the code and watch what happens when you click either button (see Figure 6-7).

Figure 6-7. The type of event being generated

The event object is reporting a click event when either button is pressed.

I am sure you can easily see the possibilities here. You could create code that will run only when a certain event happens, a particular component generated the event, or a combination of both factors. It will also allow the code to respond to a large range of events with a minimum amount of code.

As you progress through this book, you will be using all these event-handling techniques in a variety of situations.

Let's see how all of this now relates to data handling.

XML: A very brief introduction

You need to understand a few things first before we get into an overview of XML.

Flex, or for that matter Flash, cannot connect directly with a database; nor do you want it to. In Chapter 2, I talked a bit about business logic. **Business logic** simply means using a programming environment like Java, ColdFusion, .NET, or PHP to establish all the rules for connecting to a database, inserting data, deleting data, reading data, distributing data, and so on. The purpose of Flex, or Flash, is to present the data in a user-friendly manner. However, the business logic level establishes what is and is not permissible in accessing that data.

Also, an extensive discussion of the mechanics of XML is out of the scope of this book. If you are interested, I strongly suggest picking up copies of *Foundation XML for Flash* by Sas Jacobs (friends of ED, 2005) and *Beginning XML with DOM and Ajax: From Novice to Professional*, also by Sas Jacobs (Apress, 2006).

6

That said, time for your look at XML. The specifications for XML were first released by the W3C in 1998.

> In case you don't know, the W3C is the **World Wide Web Consortium**. Its purpose is to set standards for the various programming and markup languages used on the Web. If you want to learn more about these specifications, just go to www.w3.org.

Like XHTML, it is a markup language, meaning that it is text based and its purpose is to describe data. As a matter of fact, XML means Extensible Markup Language. But what does *Extensible* mean?

If you have done any design work with XHTML, you know you have a well-defined set of tags to work with—for example, <p>, <h1>, <head>, and so on. XML allows you to define your own set of tags depending on the particular needs of the data. As a matter of fact, there are libraries, or **vocabularies**, of XML tags for specific industries. One such example is Chemical Markup Language (CML) for the chemical engineering community.

Let's look at a small example. Say you wanted to represent your address book in XML. The structure might look something like this:

```xml
<?xml version="1.0" encoding="iso-8859-1"?>
<foed>
   <book ISBN="738493">
      <book_name>XML for Flash</book_name>
      <author>Sas Jacobs</author>
      <cover>assets/jacobs.jpg</cover>
   </book>
   <book ISBN="638212">
      <book_name>Foundation Flash 8 Video</book_name>
      <author>Tom Green</author>
      <cover>assets/green.jpg</cover>
   </book>
   <book ISBN="938201">
      <book_name>Object-Oriented Programming for Flash 8</book_name>
      <author>Peter Elst</author>
      <cover>assets/elst.jpg</cover>
   </book ISBN = "834732">
   <book>
     <book_name>Foundation ActionScript Animation: Making Things Move➡
      </book_name>
      <author>Keith Peters</author>
      <cover>assets/peters.jpg</cover>
   </book>
</foed>
```

You will notice several things about this XML structure.

First of all, the tag names are very descriptive of the data they contain. Second, notice that for every opening tag, there is a corresponding closing tag (signified by a / at the beginning). Third, the tags have a strict hierarchy. And fourth, they are case sensitive.

Notice that there are four book **elements**, which are known as **nodes**. Each one of these nodes has three child elements: <book_name>, <author>, and <cover>. In addition to the child elements, each node has an attribute called ISBN. Everything is contained within the root node called <foed>.

When Flex accesses the XML file, each node becomes a new object in memory.

> *While you will be working with hard-coded XML files, in actual working situations you would take the structure from the XML file and combine it with data in memory, so that each record becomes a new object.*

I know you are asking how programs like Java or ColdFusion create or use the XML files. Sorry, but that discussion is way outside the scope of this book. If you want to know more, consider picking up the books I mentioned at the beginning of this section.

6

Using XML in Flex

For starters, if you haven't done so yet, please download the exercise files for this chapter from the downloads section of www.friendsofed.com. Unzip them into a folder in a location of your choice. With that done, let's get down to business and run through an example of using XML in Flex. Again, by the end you'll be amazed at how easily you can do this stuff in Flex!

1. Like in the previous chapters, start a new Flex project, uncheck the Use default location option, and navigate to the folder containing the exercise files. Name the project using a name of your choice. If all went well, you should see a folder marked assets.

2. Navigate to the assets folder, and open the books.xml file. Let's examine it.

> *You will be using the file as soon as you get into* HTTPService, *a little later in this chapter.*

```
<?xml version="1.0" encoding="iso-8859-1"?>

<books>
    <stock>
        <name>The Picasso Code</name>
        <author>Dan Blue</author>
        <category>Fiction</category>
        <description>Cubist paintings reveal a secret society of➥
            people who really look like that</description>
```

```
    </stock>
    <stock>
      <name>Here with the Wind</name>
       <author>Margaret Middle</author>
        <category>Fiction</category>
         <description>In this edition, nobody in the south really➡
           gives a damn</description>
    </stock>
    <stock>
      <name>Harry Potluck and the Chamber of Money</name>
          <author>J.K. Roughly</author>
          <category>Fiction</category>
           <description>Young wizard finds the real pot of gold➡
             and retires</description>
    </stock>
    <stock>
      <name>No Expectations</name>
          <author>Chuck Dickens</author>
          <category>Fiction</category>
          <description>Dickens finally reveals what he really➡
            thinks of people</description>
    </stock>
    <stock>
      <name>Atlas Stretched</name>
          <author>Ann Rind</author>
          <category>Fiction</category>
          <description>Great inventors finally just take the➡
            money and run</description>
    </stock>
    <stock>
      <name>Recycling Software</name>
          <author>Big Gates</author>
          <category>Nonfiction</category>
          <description>How to just change the name and interface➡
            of the same old software and sell it as new</description>
    </stock>
    <stock>
      <name>Make Tons of Money</name>
          <author>Donald Rump</author>
          <category>Nonfiction</category>
          <description>Rump explains how he became a billionaire➡
            while constantly declaring bankruptcy
          </description>
    </stock>
    <stock>
      <name>How to Win Enemies and Lose Friends</name>
        <author>Dale Crochety</author>
          <category>Nonfiction</category>
```

```
         <description>The ultimate how-to book for people who➡
            want to stay loners</description>
      </stock>
      <stock>
         <name>My Lies</name>
            <author>Swill Clinton</author>
            <category>Nonfiction</category>
             <description>This former American president tries to ➡
               define what a lie is</description>
      </stock>
      <stock>
         <name>The Complete History of the World</name>
            <author>David McClutz</author>
            <category>Nonfiction</category>
             <description>McClutz gives you the entire history of all➡
               civilization in less than 300 pages</description>
      </stock>
   </books>
```

Normally, if you were working on a full system and getting data from a database, you would not see this data filled in. Instead, you would just see a basic XML structure. So how does data get used in it? I will give you a brief and generic insight.

When I teach XML, I usually tell my students to think of the outermost container, in this case <books></books>, as a giant container. Within that container, there are smaller boxes, in this case ten called <stock></stock>. Each one of those stock boxes holds the information about one book: the name, author, category, and description.

In truth, the technical explanation isn't much different. In this example, if a request were sent to a database that met all of the business logic rules, the database would return the data through the XML file. An object called books would be created. The books object in this case would refer to ten other objects called stock. Each stock object would have name, author, category, and description properties. All Flex needs to do is access these ten objects through the books object.

> *If you are an XML expert, remember that this is just a quick explanation and not meant to cover all of the technical issues of XML. So please don't send me nasty e-mails.*

Your next step is going to be to set up a Flex application that will read the objects created by the XML file.

3. Go ahead and start a new MXML application and give it any name you choose.

The Model tag

There are three possible scenarios for working with an XML file:

1. Embedding the XML data directly in the SWF file

2. Having an external XML file located on the same server

3. Having an external XML file located on a completely different server

The first scenario is rare and can be used only for limited and unchanging data. The second scenario is common, but not as common as the third scenario.

The Model class can handle the first two scenarios quite nicely, as you'll see in the following example.

> *As I am sure you are now seeing, the words* tag *and* class *are closely related. All MXML tags access ActionScript classes and, when compiled into a SWF file, MXML tags are converted to ActionScript.*

1. Begin by adding a Model tag below the opening Application tag. Give it an ID of bookStock.

```
<?xml version="1.0" encoding="utf-8"?>
<mx:Application xmlns:mx="http://www.adobe.com/2006/mxml"➥
  layout="absolute">
  <mx:Model id="bookStock">

  </mx:Model>
</mx:Application>
```

2. Within the Model structure, put in a simple XML structure with data that will not change.

```
<?xml version="1.0" encoding="utf-8"?>
<mx:Application xmlns:mx=http://www.adobe.com/2006/mxml➥
  layout="absolute">
  <mx:Model id="bookStock">
    <stock>
      <name>The Picasso Code</name>
      <author>Dan Blue</author>
      <category>Fiction</category>
      <description>Cubist paintings reveal a secret society of➥
        people who really look like that</description>
    </stock>
  </mx:Model>
</mx:Application>
```

3. Above the Model tag but after the Application tag, add a Script tag. You will put a function into it called bookHandler() as follows:

```
<?xml version="1.0" encoding="utf-8"?>
<mx:Application xmlns:mx="http://www.adobe.com/2006/mxml"➥
  layout="absolute">
<mx:Script>
  <![CDATA[
    private function bookHandler(theBook:Object):void
    {
       trace(theBook.name);
       trace(theBook.author);
    }
]]>
</mx:Script>
<mx:Model id="bookStock">
   <stock>
         <name>The Picasso Code</name>
         <author>Dan Blue</author>
         <category>Fiction</category>
          <description>Cubist paintings reveal a secret society of➥
             people who really look like that</description>
   </stock>
</mx:Model>
</mx:Application>
```

A bit of explanation is in order here. Understanding the concepts will be important for all three scenarios I listed earlier.

Using the Model tag, Flex does not differentiate between an embedded and an external XML file. (You will see an example of this in the "External files" section.) The Model tag runs automatically as soon as the application is called.

Upon a particular event, which you will define momentarily, you want to pass the entire XML file to the function you just defined in the script block. Since an XML file can hold a wide assortment of data, it is always passed with the most generic type you can use: Object.

Once the XML file is passed into the handling function, all Flex needs to do is use the reference name assigned by the function, in this case, theBook, and then a dot and the name of the XML node. In this example, you are going to put it in a trace() function.

> *If you have ever programmed XML access in Flash/ActionScript 2.0, you will appreciate how much this simplifies the process.*

As I just stated, none of this happens without an event of some sort. When dealing with XML files, the most commonly used event is creationComplete. This event is generated when the file is fully loaded and is usually placed inside of the Application tag. In this case, when the application is fully loaded, you want to pass the XML file (the ID of the Model tag) to the handling function (bookHandler).

THE COMPLETE GUIDE TO FLEX 2 WITH ACTIONSCRIPT 3.0

4. Modify the Application tag as follows:

```
<mx:Application xmlns:mx="http://www.adobe.com/2006/mxml"➥
    layout="absolute" creationComplete="bookHandler(bookStock)">
```

5. Since you are using the trace() functions, click the Debug button rather than run the code.

6. A blank browser screen will open up. You can close it.

7. When you return to Flex Builder, you will see the results of the trace() operation in the Console pane, as shown in Figure 6-8.

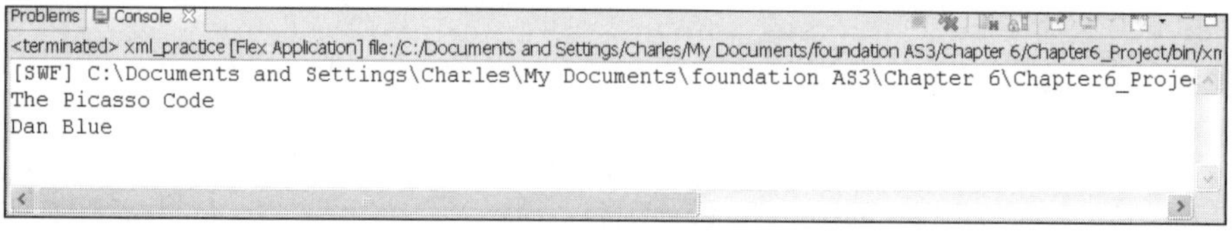

```
Problems  Console
<terminated> xml_practice [Flex Application] file:/C:/Documents and Settings/Charles/My Documents/foundation AS3/Chapter 6/Chapter6_Project/bin/xm
[SWF] C:\Documents and Settings\Charles\My Documents\foundation AS3\Chapter 6\Chapter6_Proje
The Picasso Code
Dan Blue
```

Figure 6-8. The results of the trace() operation

As you have done in the previous chapters, you could easily assign the results to whichever components you need to put them in.

Working with an external XML file

Let's look at scenario 2 now.

In the files you downloaded for this chapter, in the assets folder, you should find a file called testBooks.xml. It has exactly the same structure that you used inside the Model tag in the preceding section.

Remove the XML structure between the opening Model tag and the closing Model tag. In its place, modify the opening Model tag and use the source property as follows:

```
<mx:Model id="bookStock" source="assets/testBooks.xml"/>
```

If you debug the application again, you should get exactly the same result as before. ActionScript didn't care whether the source was embedded or external.

As tempting as it is to use the Model tag, this is not the best possible practice. The Model tag, in both cases, is compiling the XML file right into the SWF file. Not only does this increase the size of the SWF file, but it also makes it impossible to update the data in the XML file. You would only be able to use this technique if you were absolutely certain that the data was never going to change.

There is a better way. Let's take a look at that now.

Using the HTTPService tag

The HTTPService tag reads XML dynamically. By that, I mean that each time a given event occurs, a SWF file is requesting the latest data from an XML file. This is sometimes referred to as an **asynchronous request**. Also, using the HTTPService class, the XML file can be located on any server because you need to specify the URL of the XML file.

The HTTPService class makes the call for data using the send() method. When all of the data is received by the SWF file, an event is generated called a **result**. This tells whoever is listening for the event that the data is now available. HTTPService then stores the data in a property called lastResult and in the result property of the ResultEvent class. This will all become clearer as you work through the following steps:

1. Either create a new MXML file or delete everything but the Application tags from the last file you worked on.

2. Start the first tag by typing the following between the mx:Application tags. Note the id attribute with a value of bookData.

   <mx:HTTPService id="bookData"

The next attribute you want to add in is an important one: the URL of the XML file.

In this example, the URL target is located on the local drive. But it could just as easily be an http:// address in another location that uses a web service. The HTTPService class does not make a distinction.

3. Add the url attribute to the tag and close off the tag.

```
<?xml version="1.0" encoding="utf-8"?>
<mx:Application xmlns:mx="http://www.adobe.com/2006/mxml"➡
  layout="absolute">
  <mx:HTTPService id="bookData" url="assets/books.xml" />
</mx:Application>
```

As stated previously, in order for anything to happen in code, there must be an event of some kind. Just using the HTTPService class to connect with the XML file is not an event. An event would be the clicking of a button, the pressing of a key, and so on.

The creationComplete event is commonly included inside the <mx:Application> tag. What it does is report when the application is completely loaded, thus marking the completion of loading an event. However, now what do you want to happen after the event has occurred?

When you used the Model class, you called a handler to handle the data. HTTPService handles things a bit differently: it uses the send() function to make the call for data.

6

4. Go ahead and complete the `creationComplete` event as follows:

```
<?xml version="1.0" encoding="utf-8"?>
<mx:Application xmlns:mx="http://www.adobe.com/2006/mxml"➥
  layout="absolute" creationComplete="bookData.send()">
   <mx:HTTPService id="bookData" url="assets/books.xml" />
</mx:Application>
```

If you were to look at the documentation for the HTTPService class, you would see that the send() function tells the XML file to send its information. In actuality, it sends the information to the Flash Player and the objects discussed earlier are set up. Class HTTPService handles all of the mechanics in the background. All you need to do is set up the code as I am showing here.

It is not a bad idea to test the connection at this point. You are probably looking down at the Problems pane, not seeing any errors or warnings, and thinking you are in good shape. However, there is one problem: the Flash Player does not make the connection until the request is actually made. That request is not made until the application is running. This is called a **runtime process**.

5. Provided that there are no errors and warnings from other problems, go ahead and run the application. If you get no error messages in the blank browser, you are probably in good shape.

6. Just to show you what can happen, try going back into the code and changing the name of the XML file in the url attribute of the <HTTPService> tag. For instance, change it from books.xml to book.xml.

7. Run the application again, and you should see the error shown in Figure 6-9.

Figure 6-9. The error being returned from the Flash Player

The Flash Player returns a fault in the HTTPService request. Since there is nothing else going on in this application yet, it is a pretty safe bet that the XML connection is the fault.

8. You can click either Dismiss All or Continue and then close the browser.

9. Before you continue, don't forget to change the url attribute back to what it was and retest it to make sure everything is working fine.

Displaying data

Now that you have connected Flex to an XML data source, you will want to display the data. More accurately, you will want to have the ability to display the properties held inside of the ten stock objects. As with many of the other operations you needed to do, Flex has a tool to help you do exactly that: DataGrid.

With a minimum of effort and virtually no programming, the DataGrid component can read the properties of objects and display the data in a user-friendly format with some additional benefits, as you will see shortly.

1. Start by setting up a DataGrid control. Modify your code as follows:

```
<?xml version="1.0" encoding="utf-8"?>
<mx:Application xmlns:mx="http://www.adobe.com/2006/mxml"➡
  layout="absolute" creationComplete="bookData.send()">
   <mx:HTTPService id="bookData" url="assets/books.xml" />
   <mx:DataGrid x="56" y="250" width="950"/>
</mx:Application>
```

I purposely had you make the grid a bit wide to accommodate the data it will need to display.If you were to run the application now, you would get something that looks like Figure 6-10.

Figure 6-10. The empty DataGrid control

Unless you like the look of a big, blank box, it is not very useful as is. In order to fill it with data, you need to add an attribute to the DataGrid tag. I want to spend a few minutes talking about this attribute. It may be helpful if you refer to the contents of the XML file listed earlier.

Remember, the connection to the XML file, as well as the setting up of the objects, is all being handled by the <HTTPService> tag you set up earlier. That is going to be your dataProvider.

6

2. Return to the code and bind the DataGrid to the HTTPService as follows:

```
<mx:DataGrid x="56" y="250" width="950" dataProvider=➥
"{bookData.lastResult.books.stock}" />
```

We need to look at this a little more closely.

Notice, as you have done with other ActionScript bindings, that you enclose it in curly braces, { }. But what is going on after the first curly brace?

You know that bookData is the id attribute of HTTPService, and that HTTPService is the path to the XML objects. As mentioned previously, HTTPService stores the XML data in a property called lastResult, which updates itself every time fresh data comes in.

3. Now run your application. You should see output similar to that shown in Figure 6-11.

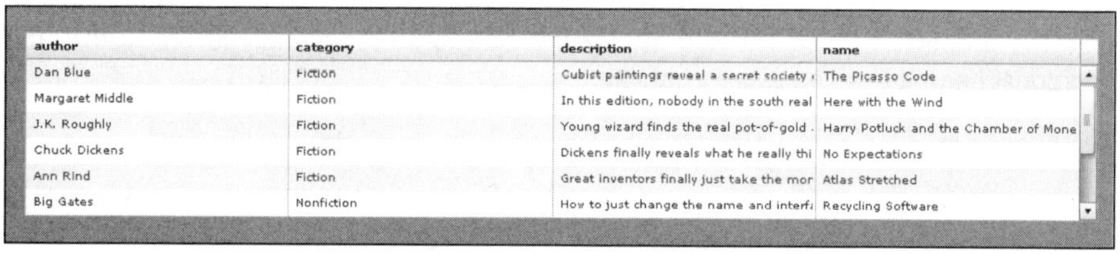

author	category	description	name
Dan Blue	Fiction	Cubist paintings reveal a secret society	The Picasso Code
Margaret Middle	Fiction	In this edition, nobody in the south real	Here with the Wind
J.K. Roughly	Fiction	Young wizard finds the real pot-of-gold	Harry Potluck and the Chamber of Mone
Chuck Dickens	Fiction	Dickens finally reveals what he really thi	No Expectations
Ann Rind	Fiction	Great inventors finally just take the mon	Atlas Stretched
Big Gates	Nonfiction	How to just change the name and interf	Recycling Software

Figure 6-11. The populated DataGrid control

Once the dataProvider is set up, the DataGrid class does most of the work. Notice that it uses the node names as headers. It brings them in alphabetically. You will see how to make some modifications to that in a bit.

4. Click one of the headings; notice the data is sorted on that criterion. For instance, if the user clicks the name header, the data will be sorted by the book names. Click the header again, and the data is sorted in descending order.

5. This control even gives the user the chance to rearrange columns and adjust their width using the same techniques you might use if you were in Excel. Give it a try.

6. Click the name column heading and drag it over to the first column. Then click between the category and description columns and make the description column wider.

This gives end users a tremendous amount of control over how they want the data displayed.

But as easy as all of this looks, let's examine things a bit more.

XML and ActionScript

As you have learned already in the course of this book, easy does not always equate to most flexible or efficient.

If you are working with simple data, as you are here, this doesn't present much of a problem, and the preceding techniques are fine. But if you are working in more complex situations, you will need to do these steps programmatically. For instance, depending on a response, you may want to select different data. Or you may need to write to complex data structures.

You will find that by learning a few basic programming concepts, you can cover a lot of potential situations. Let's start by examining the most important of these concepts: the ArrayCollection class.

What I am going to do here is have you reproduce programmatically what you just did automatically. While this may seem like a silly exercise, it helps you to understand the underlying ActionScript code, which in turn will aid you as you get into increasingly complex situations.

One of the first things any programming student learns is the definition of an array. You normally associate a variable with a single piece of data. For instance:

```
var fName:String = "John";
```

or

```
var myAge:Number = 35;
```

However, an array means multiple values associated with a single variable.

```
var myName:String = "John", "Mary", "Chris", "Tom";
```

Each value is assigned a number called the **index number**. In a typical array, the first index number is 0.

Like everything else, in ActionScript an array is handled by an ActionScript class. If you go to the Language Reference and scroll down, you'll find info on the Array class; it is worth taking a few minutes to study it over.

One thing a study of the class will show you is that there are a lot of methods and properties to manipulate the array but not the underlying data that makes up the array, except for a few basic functions. For instance, you can add data to or delete data from either the end or the beginning of an array. The bulk of the methods concern themselves with the array itself.

ActionScript offers you a second, and more powerful, class called ArrayCollection. This class literally wraps itself around the array and gives you tremendous ability to manipulate the actual data itself. If you look at the class ArrayCollection, you will see many more methods (native and inherited) that can manipulate data. In addition, it can handle a larger variety of events than the Array class can.

If you looked closely at what you did earlier, it shouldn't come as a great surprise that ActionScript created a multidimensional array with your XML data.

6

> *A **multidimensional array** is simply another array attached to an element of an existing array. For instance, a list of states could have a list of cities attached to each state. While most programs are capable of hundreds of levels of depth in an array, most programmers will not go beyond a couple of levels. Try to look for alternatives before using multidimensional arrays. They could slow performance of your applications.*

But what might come as a surprise is that HTTPService automatically wrapped that array inside of an ArrayCollection object. For that reason, if you want to programmatically control an array created with the HTTPService class, you will need to import and use the ArrayCollection class.

Let's make some modifications to the code to see how this works.

1. Begin by creating an <mx:Script> tag under the <mx:Application> tag.

```
<mx:Application xmlns:mx="http://www.adobe.com/2006/mxml"➥
  layout="absolute" creationComplete="bookData.send()">
<mx:Script>
  <![CDATA[

  ]]>
</mx:Script>
```

The first thing you have to do is import the ArrayCollection class, which is part of the mx.collections package. There are two syntaxes you could use:

```
import mx.collections.ArrayCollection;
```

or

```
import mx.collections.*;
```

I prefer the latter because it gives a bit more flexibility.

2. Add the following to your code:

```
<mx:Script>
  <![CDATA[
  import mx.collections.*;
  ]]>
</mx:Script>
```

ActionScript has a package of classes that deal with just web services and XML. This package is the rpc (remote procedure components) package. The rpc package has a class called ResultEvent whose primary function is to generate an object that reports when the XML data is successfully assembled into the objects discussed earlier.

> *The discussion here is necessarily elementary. I could literally devote an entire book to each of these classes. For that reason, I am focusing only on basic functionality.*

3. Next you need to import this package in order to gain access to the ResultEvent class. Add the following:

```
<mx:Script>
  <![CDATA[
  import mx.collections.*;
  import mx.rpc.events.*;
  ]]>
</mx:Script>
```

The next step would be to assign the ArrayCollection a variable name.

Recall in Chapter 4 I introduced the meta tag [Bindable]. Think of the variable it is attached to as the source; and think of the MXML using this source data as the destination. The [Bindable] tag tells ActionScript to update the destination if the source updates.

4. Modify your code as indicated here:

```
<?xml version="1.0" encoding="utf-8"?>
<mx:Application xmlns:mx="http://www.adobe.com/2006/mxml"➥
  layout="absolute" creationComplete="bookData.send()">
<mx:Script>
  <![CDATA[
  import mx.collections.*;
  import mx.rpc.events.*;
  [Bindable]
  private var bookStock:ArrayCollection;
  ]]>
</mx:Script>
  <mx:HTTPService id="bookData" url="assets/books.xml" />
  <mx:DataGrid x="56" y="250" width="950"➥
    dataProvider="{bookData.lastResult.books.stock}" />
</mx:Application>
```

Now that you have the necessary imports and variables, all that remains is for you to write a method. This method will accept only one argument, the event object. Earlier in this chapter, you specified the event object type as either Object or Event. However, since you are working with remote services, the event that is generated is of type EventResult (which is why you imported that package a few steps ago).

6

5. You are going to use this function to set the bookStock ArrayCollection, which in turn will send the data to the DataGrid control. Add the following highlighted lines to your code:

```
<?xml version="1.0" encoding="utf-8"?>
<mx:Application xmlns:mx="http://www.adobe.com/2006/mxml"➥
  layout="absolute" creationComplete="bookData.send()">
<mx:Script>
  <![CDATA[
      import mx.rpc.events.*;
      import mx.collections.*;
      import mx.rpc.events.*;
      [Bindable]
      private var bookStock:ArrayCollection;

      private function bookHandler(evt:ResultEvent):void
      {

      }
  ]]>
</mx:Script>
```

> If you forgot to import the necessary packages, Flex Builder helps you out. If it sees a call to a class that has not been imported properly, it automatically builds the requisite import statement.

Your last step is to fill in the functionality of the method. Recall that when an event object is passed, the target property contains the information about who sent the object, ostensibly creating a connection with the event broadcaster.

In this case, you are more interested in what the results are. As I mentioned earlier, the ResultEvent class has a property called result that returns just as you might guess, the results of the data connection. Recall also that the HTTPService class automatically saves the data to this property in addition to the lastResult property.

> The HTTPService class doesn't physically transfer the data but, like most OOP operations, just creates a reference to the objects that contain the data.

6. Fill in your function as follows:

```
private function bookHandler(evt:ResultEvent):void
{
    bookStock=evt.result.books.stock;
}
```

The ArrayCollection, bookStock, will now be the dataProvider and not the HTTPService class. However, the HTTPService class still needs to make the actual connection and then pass the results up to the function.

7. Make the following modification to the <HTTPService> tag (you will modify the DataGrid control in a moment):

```
<mx:HTTPService id="bookData" url="assets/books.xml"➥
    result="bookHandler(event)" />
```

This sends the result of the XML connection to the bookHandler() method by passing the event object of type ResultEvent.

8. You just have one more simple step to do:

```
<mx:DataGrid x="56" y="250" width="950" dataProvider="{bookStock}" />
```

9. If you go ahead and run your code now, it should work exactly the same as before.

As I said from the outset, the purpose of this exercise was to show you the basic skeletal structure of programmatically connecting to a web service or local XML file. From here, you have the powerful programming capabilities of ActionScript to use wherever you need it.

When good code goes bad

Earlier in the chapter, when you misnamed your XML file, you saw an error message returned by the Flash Player. Unfortunately, this is not a very graceful way of handling things.

In most programming environments, error handling is done with programming code. However, HTTPService can handle it simply through an attribute.

Let's take a look at how this works now.

You'll start by writing a function to handle the error. The event object you are going to use is FaultEvent, which is a class file and, conveniently, also part of the mx.rp.events package you imported earlier. So you won't need to do another import for this. Its sole purpose is to report an error connecting to a remote component (XML file or remote component).

1. Modify your script block as follows:

```
<mx:Script>
  <![CDATA[
    import mx.rpc.events.*;
    import mx.collections.*;

    [Bindable]
    private var bookStock:ArrayCollection;

    private function bookHandler(evt:ResultEvent):void
    {
```

```
            bookStock=evt.result.books.stock;
        }

            private function faultHandler(evt:FaultEvent):void
            {

            }
    ]]>
</mx:Script>
```

2. The next thing you will do is construct a variable to hold your message. Add the following to your code, in the position shown:

```
private function faultHandler(evt:FaultEvent):void
{
    var faultMessage:String = "Could not connect with XML file";
}
```

The next thing you are going to construct is something you saw way back in Chapter 3: an alert box.

3. Alerts are part of the mx.controls package, so add the following import statement along with the others:

```
import mx.controls.*;
```

4. Once that is done, all you need to do is set up the Alert class using its show() function as follows:

```
private function faultHandler(evt:FaultEvent):void
{
    var faultMessage:String = "Could not connect with XML file";
    Alert.show(faultMessage, "Error opening file");
}
```

The first argument in the show() function is the message to be displayed, and the second is the title of the pop-up box.

All that remains to be done is to have HTTPService call the method when a fault is encountered and the <HTTPService> tag has a fault attribute.

5. Make the following modification to your <HTTPService> tag:

```
<mx:HTTPService id="bookData" url="assets/books.xml"➥
    result="bookHandler(event)" fault="faultHandler(event)" />
```

Notice that if a fault occurs, the faultHandler function you just created will be called and the FaultEvent event object will be passed.

6. As you did earlier in the chapter, misspell the name of the XML file in the <HTTPService> tag and run the application. You should get the output shown in Figure 6-12.

Figure 6-12. Fault message

You can easily see where the message and title properties are placed. All you need to do is click OK and shut down the browser.

Let's take a look at a couple of other message possibilities.

Recall that an event object has a property called target that identifies what is generating the event. This is a good place to see this property in action.

7. Change your fault message string to the following:

```
var faultMessage:String = "The origin of this fault is: " + evt.target;
```

8. If you run your code now, you should see that HTTPService broadcasted the event, as shown in Figure 6-13.

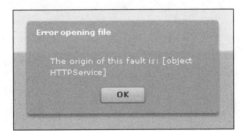

Figure 6-13. Dialog box showing the target property

While your previous dialog box would be friendly for the user, this last box would probably only be used in a debugging situation. Here you see that the source of the fault is an object of HTTPService.

9. If you want to see a way to look at all of the generated messages for debugging purposes, change your variable as follows:

```
var faultMessage:String = "The origin of this fault is:"➥
+ evt.message;
```

This will list all the messages as shown in Figure 6-14.

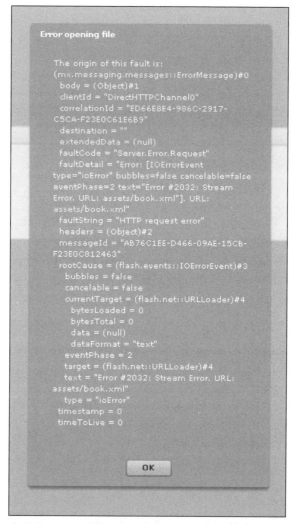

Figure 6-14. The message property generating all error messages

I am sure you wouldn't want your users to see this. As a suggestion, you may want to stick with the first dialog box.

If you are going to connect to outside services, you have to be very conscious of security. This is a good place to take a look at this issue.

Flash Player security

Flash Player security is pretty tight. Like most programs today, it has a **sandbox** around it. In other words, to spin a phrase from a commercial for Las Vegas:

What goes on in the Flash Player stays in the Flash Player

However, does that mean that it is 100% invincible to virus attacks? *No!* No program is.

Let's take a look at how the security features in Flash Player 9 work. For this part, you may want to just read through. However, if you want to try it out, you need to use the web server feature of ColdFusion, which you set up in Chapter 1.

> *The web server feature in ColdFusion is only available in the free Developer edition and is for testing purposes only.*

If you are familiar with web servers or have access to one, please feel free to follow along.

Here are the steps I followed for this demonstration:

1. Set up a folder, called test, under the wwwroot directory of ColdFusion (CFusionMX7). As I mentioned in Chapter 1, ColdFusion uses localhost:8500 if installed locally.

2. Place a copy of the books.xml file into the test directory.

3. Delete the fault attribute and function used in the last exercise.

4. Change the url attribute in the <HTTPService> tag as follows:

```
<mx:HTTPService id="bookData"➥
   url="http://localhost:8500/test/books.xml"➥
result="bookHandler(event)"  />
```

Again, notice that the fault attribute has been deleted. If you go ahead and run the application, it should run fine. When you test an application, you don't access all of the security features of the Flash Player.

> *The same is true for Flash when you press Ctrl-Enter to test.*

Internally, the SWF file generated knows to look for that XML file now at localhost:8500/test.

5. Copy the generated SWF file from the project folder to the web server folder (in this case test). In much the same way you would deploy it to a server, you can now use your web browser to enter the URL:

```
http://localhost:8500/test/chapter6.swf
```

6. This should work just like it would on a server. Now change the URL as follows:

```
http://127.0.0.1:8500/test/chapter6.swf
```

The output should be as shown in Figure 6-15.

Figure 6-15. Flash Player security error

The Flash Player returns a security error when you try to access the URL. One of the major security features of the Flash Player is that, by default, the SWF file cannot be at one URL while the XML is at another. Even though 127.0.0.1 means localhost, the Flash Player perceived the former as different from the latter and for safety reasons shut everything down.

But what happens if you need both URLs to be recognized as the same? You can override this security feature by creating an XML file in the directory of the web server. You must name this file crossdomain.xml and save it in the root folder of the web server, *not* the application folder—in this case, wwwroot.

7. Change the code as follows:

```
<?xml version="1.0"?>
<!DOCTYPE cross-domain-policy
  SYSTEM "http://www.adobe.com/xml/dtds/cross-domain-policy.dtd">
<cross-domain-policy>
   <allow-access-from domain="127.0.0.1"/>
</cross-domain-policy>
```

Notice that you just need to include the name of the accessing domain.

If everything was done correctly, `127.0.0.1` should have no trouble accessing the generated SWF file now.

You could also have substituted an asterisk for the domain name. However, this means that *all* domains will have access. I strongly recommend not doing this for obvious reasons.

Now that you know how to work with XML in Flex, let's change the rules a bit.

Introducing E4X

Until now, ActionScript had no way of directly working with XML data except to convert it into an `ArrayCollection`, as you just saw. The XML classes in ActionScript 2.0 were at best a patchwork that, although they worked, were not ideal.

The new and emerging standard is **E4X**, or **ECMAScript for XML**.

Before discussing this, I need to make a small disclaimer here. This is an emerging standard and subject to change. In addition, as of this writing, it doesn't have full browser support. For that reason, the discussion here will be very basic, and throughout the rest of the book you will be using what are now considered to be traditional practices.

That aside, let's see how E4X works:

1. Open E4X.mxml from the code download.

As you can see, this is the basic file—you are going to adapt it to E4X.

2. For starters, run a trace by modifying the bookHandler function as follows:

```
private function bookHandler(evt:ResultEvent):void
{
    trace(evt.result);
}
```

3. Remember, you can only use the `trace()` function with the Debug button. Go ahead and click Debug now. The browser will open. You can close it.

4. Take a look at the Console pane that should have opened (see Figure 6-16).

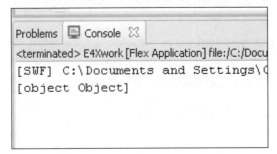

Figure 6-16. The results of the ArrayCollection

5. Now make a small adjustment to the <HTTPService> tag by specifying the attribute of resultFormat as e4x.

```
<mx:HTTPService id="bookData" url="assets/books.xml"➥
    result="bookHandler(event)" resultFormat="e4x" />
```

6. Now if you run the trace() statement in the debug feature, you get a very different result (see Figure 6-17).

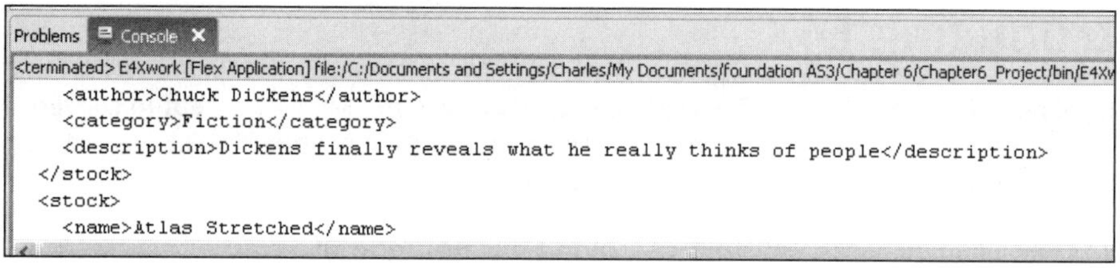

```
Problems  🖳 Console ✕
<terminated> E4Xwork [Flex Application] file:/C:/Documents and Settings/Charles/My Documents/foundation AS3/Chapter 6/Chapter6_Project/bin/E4Xw
      <author>Chuck Dickens</author>
      <category>Fiction</category>
      <description>Dickens finally reveals what he really thinks of people</description>
  </stock>
  <stock>
      <name>Atlas Stretched</name>
```

Figure 6-17. The trace() results of E4X

The actual XML file appears in the Console pane as opposed to just an object reference like before.

With E4X comes a different way of working with XML data. You will find the syntax to be more ActionScript-like. Let's begin by looking at one record in your XML file.

```
<books>
    <stock>
        <name>The Picasso Code</name>
        <author>Dan Blue</author>
        <category>Fiction</category>
        <description>Cubist paintings reveal a secret society of people➥
            who really look like that</description>
    </stock>
```

<books> is the root node. <stock> has a child node called <name>, and <name> has three child nodes: <author>, <category>, and <description>.

When you are using the E4X format, you use the dot operator like you do in other ActionScript statements. Also, you generally omit references to the root node (in this case, <books>).

For instance, say all you wanted to see was a list of book names. You could adjust the trace() function as follows:

```
private function bookHandler(evt:ResultEvent):void
    {
        trace(evt.result.stock.name);
    }
```

If you run the debug feature now, you should see results similar to Figure 6-18.

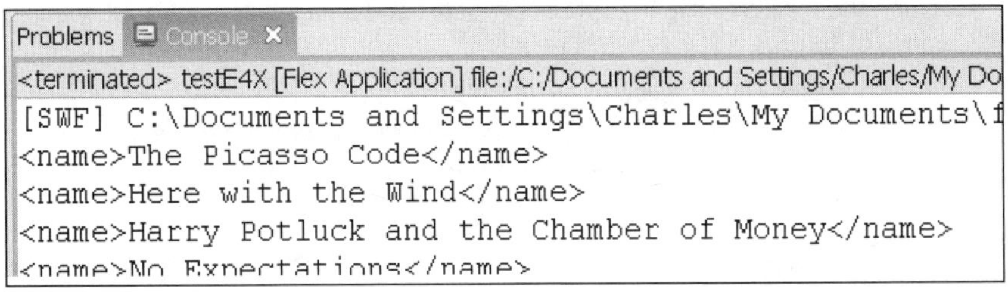

Figure 6-18. The results of the revised trace() function

You can also use two dots to jump to a child node. This is called the **descendant accessor**. For instance, if you want to see a list of authors, you could adjust your trace() statement as follows:

```
private function bookHandler(evt:ResultEvent):void
{
    trace(evt.result..author);
}
```

The result is shown in Figure 6-19.

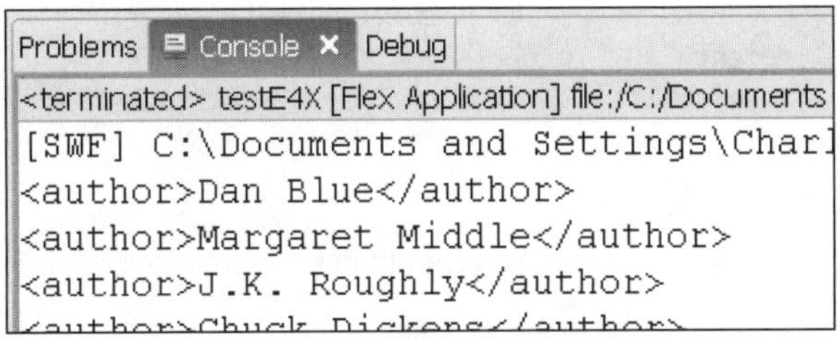

Figure 6-19. Using the descendant accessor

You can search the stock node for books whose category is fiction by using the parenthesis operator as follows:

```
private function bookHandler(evt:ResultEvent):void
{
    trace(evt.result.stock.(category=='Fiction'));
}
```

If you run this now, you should see data only on books that are fiction.

You have a few adjustments to make in order to use E4X:

1. Assign the results to the bookStock property, add a panel, and put a list within that panel, as follows:

```
<?xml version="1.0" encoding="utf-8"?>
<mx:Application xmlns:mx="http://www.adobe.com/2006/mxml"➥
  layout="absolute" creationComplete="bookData.send()">
<mx:Script>
  <![CDATA[
  import mx.rpc.events.*;
  import mx.collections.*;
  import mx.controls.*;
  [Bindable]
  private var bookStock:ArrayCollection;

  private function bookHandler(evt:ResultEvent):void
  {
      bookStock= evt.result.stock;
  }

  ]]>
</mx:Script>
<mx:HTTPService id="bookData" url="assets/books.xml"➥
  result="bookHandler(event)"  resultFormat="e4x"/>
<mx:Panel height="40%" title="Book Names">
    <mx:List height="100%" dataProvider="{bookStock}"/>
</mx:Panel>
</mx:Application>
```

2. Go ahead and run your code. You should get the error shown in Figure 6-20.

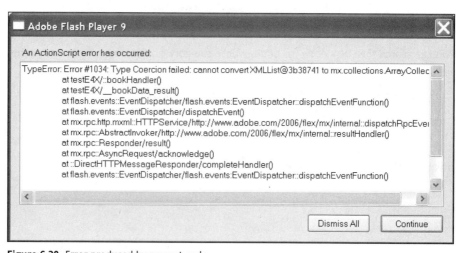

Figure 6-20. Error produced by present code

By converting the format of the result to E4X, you told Flex not to convert the XML objects to an ArrayCollection. This means that you can work with XML natively. However, it also means a change of syntax, as you will now see.

3. Change the type of your variable from ArrayCollection to XMLList.

```
private var bookStock:XMLList;
```

4. Run the application now. You should see the results shown in Figure 6-21.

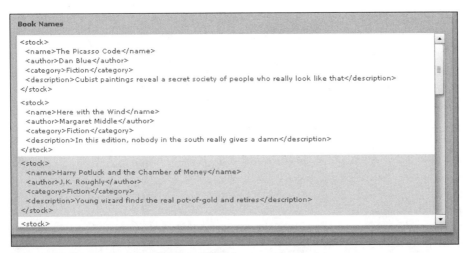

Book Names

```
<stock>
  <name>The Picasso Code</name>
  <author>Dan Blue</author>
  <category>Fiction</category>
  <description>Cubist paintings reveal a secret society of people who really look like that</description>
</stock>
<stock>
  <name>Here with the Wind</name>
  <author>Margaret Middle</author>
  <category>Fiction</category>
  <description>In this edition, nobody in the south really gives a damn</description>
</stock>
<stock>
  <name>Harry Potluck and the Chamber of Money</name>
  <author>J.K. Roughly</author>
  <category>Fiction</category>
  <description>Young wizard finds the real pot-of-gold and retires</description>
</stock>
<stock>
```

Figure 6-21. The results of changing to an XMLList

Changing the variable type gives you the result you want because E4X does not work with ArrayCollections. Instead, you have two classes associated with E4X: XML and XMLList.

The XML class deals mostly with the creation and deletion of XML objects. The XMLList deals with the manipulation of those objects. In other words, if you are opening an XML file that already exists, as you are here, you would use XMLList. But if you are creating XML objects from within the application, you would use the XML class.

> *ActionScript 2.0 had a class called* XML. *In ActionScript 3.0, that class has been renamed* XMLDocument. *The functionality of this class in ActionScript 3.0 is quite different.*

The List and ComboBox controls have a field called labelField. This controls what you want the List control to display. Without including this field, the control just assumes that you want to display the whole XML file. You want the labelField to display just the contents of the name nodes.

5. Change the List control as follows:

```
<mx:List height="100%" dataProvider="{bookStock}" labelField="name"/>
```

Notice that once E4X is set up, you can refer to the names of the nodes just as easily as you can refer to any other variable. This has the potential of reducing both the amount of code and the number of errors when handling an XML file.

6. Run the application. Your List control should look like Figure 6-22.

Figure 6-22. The List control with the name contents

You have now seen some of the power of E4X. However, please keep in mind that this is an emerging technology subject to many changes in the foreseeable future. Also, as of the time of this writing, some issues exist with using this technology with the Mozilla browser called Firefox. Use this technology carefully. You will be returning to it from time to time as you progress through this book.

Now that you know how to hook into and use an XML file, you'll next see how you can make the DataGrid control do more work for you, and in the process, learn more about some of the other controls such as the List control you just used.

Using the DataGrid control

When the DataGrid control was introduced with Flash MX 2004, I was astonished at its power and capabilities. Unfortunately, most Flash websites I have seen have not taken advantage of its power. Here, you will learn how, and hopefully incorporate that power into your own websites.

1. Start by opening the DataGrid.mxml file.

If you take a look at the code, you'll see there is nothing new or unusual here.

2. Go ahead and run the code. Notice all of the information is returned. But the columns may not be in the order that you want, nor will they necessarily have the text that you want. All the header controls did was pick up the node names.

In the next section, you'll see how you can fix this.

Modifying DataGrid columns

Here you will make some modifications to your DataGrid code. Since you need to put code between the opening and closing tags, you must modify how the tag closes.

1. Delete the `/>` and replace it with just the `>` character. Flex Builder should build a closing tag. If for some reason Flex does not automatically generate that closing tag, go ahead and type it yourself.

```
<mx:DataGrid x="56" y="250" width="950" dataProvider="{bookStock}">

</mx:DataGrid>
```

Within that, you need to tell your application that you are going to modify the columns.

2. Add `<mx:columns>` between the DataGrid tags.

```
<mx:DataGrid x="56" y="250" width="950" dataProvider="{bookStock}">
    <mx:columns>

    </mx:columns>
</mx:DataGrid>
```

3. Within the columns tags you define how you want the columns displayed with the `<mx:DataGridColumn>` tag. Let's start the tag with the following:

```
<mx:DataGridColumn
```

4. The first attribute you want to add is the `dataField` attribute. This allows you to specify which node you want to display. For instance, say you want to show the book's name first. Do so by specifying the following:

```
<mx:DataGridColumn dataField="name"
```

> You may want to have the XML file open to refer to the names as you go through these exercises.

5. Often the node names are not user friendly. You may want to specify what text you want users to actually see. You can do so with the `headerText` attribute. Make the following change:

```
<mx:DataGridColumn dataField="name" headerText="Book Name"
```

6

6. Now close the tag by adding `/>`. Your code so far should look like this:

```
<mx:DataGrid x="56" y="250" width="950" dataProvider="{bookStock}">
    <mx:columns>
        <mx:DataGridColumn dataField="name" headerText="Book Name" />
    </mx:columns>
</mx:DataGrid>
```

7. Go ahead and set up `DataGrid` columns for author and description. Add the bold lines shown here:

```
<mx:DataGrid x="56" y="250" width="950" dataProvider="{bookStock}">
    <mx:columns>
        <mx:DataGridColumn dataField="name" headerText="Book Name" />
        <mx:DataGridColumn dataField="author" headerText="Book Author" />
        <mx:DataGridColumn dataField="description"↬
          headerText="Book Description" />
    </mx:columns>
</mx:DataGrid>
```

8. Run the application. You should see the result shown in Figure 6-23.

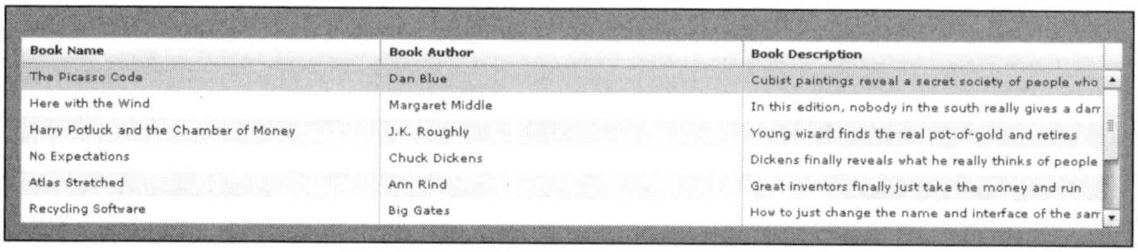

Book Name	Book Author	Book Description
The Picasso Code	Dan Blue	Cubist paintings reveal a secret society of people who
Here with the Wind	Margaret Middle	In this edition, nobody in the south really gives a dam
Harry Potluck and the Chamber of Money	J.K. Roughly	Young wizard finds the real pot-of-gold and retires
No Expectations	Chuck Dickens	Dickens finally reveals what he really thinks of people
Atlas Stretched	Ann Rind	Great inventors finally just take the money and run
Recycling Software	Big Gates	How to just change the name and interface of the sam

Figure 6-23. The modified DataGrid control

As you can see, the control is starting to look a lot nicer.

Frequently, you will be working with dates, time, and currency. The formats in many instances are not always the nicest to work with. For this reason, you are going to want to control the formatting of such items.

Changing date format

Here, you'll see how to change the formatting of dates in your `DataGrid` control by making a minor modification to your code.

1. In the `<HTTPService>` tag, redirect the `url` attribute from `"assets/books.xml"` to `"assets/books2.xml"`.

If you go ahead and open the `book2.xml` file, you will notice that it is nearly identical, but with some extra nodes. If you were to run the application at this point, it should work exactly the same as before.

2. You want to add a fourth `DataGridColumn` for the `publish_date` node and call the headerText `Publication Date`. Add this line below the others:

```
<mx:DataGridColumn dataField="publish_date"➥
headerText="Publication Date" />
```

3. Run your application again, and you should get the output shown in Figure 6-24.

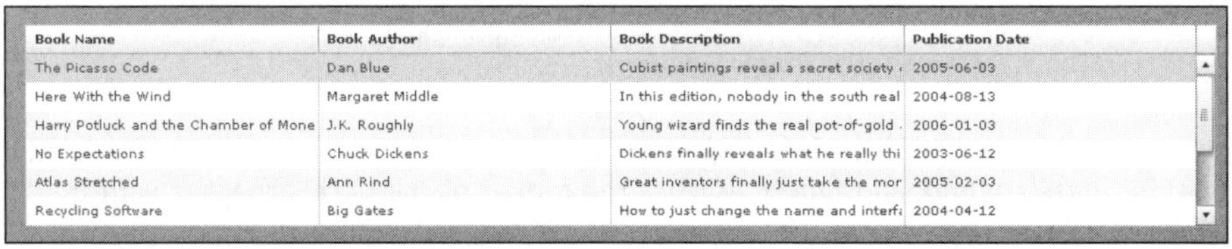

Book Name	Book Author	Book Description	Publication Date
The Picasso Code	Dan Blue	Cubist paintings reveal a secret society ↑	2005-06-03
Here With the Wind	Margaret Middle	In this edition, nobody in the south real	2004-08-13
Harry Potluck and the Chamber of Mone	J.K. Roughly	Young wizard finds the real pot-of-gold .	2006-01-03
No Expectations	Chuck Dickens	Dickens finally reveals what he really thi	2003-06-12
Atlas Stretched	Ann Rind	Great inventors finally just take the mor	2005-02-03
Recycling Software	Big Gates	How to just change the name and interfi	2004-04-12

Figure 6-24. DataGrid with publish_date added

It looks good, but you can do better.

4. Right above the `DataGrid` control, start an `<mx:DateFormatter>` tag.

This tag will allow you to predefine formats for the date by using the `formatString` attribute, which gives you the ability to use any format you might want. In this case, you'll use `MMMM DD, YYYY`.

5. Give this tag an id attribute:

```
<mx:DateFormatter id="publishDate" formatString="MMMM DD, YYYY" />
```

You now need to tell the `DataGrid` control to use this format for the `publish_date` field. Unfortunately, you cannot do this directly, only through a function.

Go up to your script block and add a new function called `dateFormat()`. This function will need to accept two arguments. The first argument you call is `dateItem`, which has to be of type `Object`. This represents each line of data. The second argument is the name of the column you want to format, in this case `publish_date`, and this must be of type `DataGridColumn`. The return type is `String`.

6. Add the following inside your script block, at the end of it, just before the closing `</mx:Script>` tag:

```
private function dateFormat(dateItem:Object, publish_date:➥
  DataGridColumn):String
{

}
```

Since there is a return type, as discussed in Chapter 3, there must be an instance of the keyword `return` in the function. But you have to decide what to return.

6

7. In this case, you want to return the contents of the DateFormatter, publishDate. In the process of returning the format, you want to format the publish_date column. For this reason, you must use the following syntax. Add the bold line shown here:

```
private function dateFormat(dateItem:Object, publish_date:➥
  DataGridColumn):String
{
    return publishDate.format(dateItem.publish_date);
}
```

What this does is it goes to each row of data in the DataGrid control, then goes to the publish_date column, and finally attaches the format of the DateFormatter with the id of publishDate.

8. Before you can run your application, you have to bind the DataGrid control to this function. The DataGrid control has an attribute to handle called labelFunction. Just add it to the DataGrid control as follows:

```
<mx:DataGrid x="56" y="250" width="950" dataProvider="{bookStock}">
    <mx:columns>
        <mx:DataGridColumn dataField="name" headerText="Book Name" />
        <mx:DataGridColumn dataField="author" headerText="Book Author" />
        <mx:DataGridColumn dataField="description"➥
          headerText="Book Description" />
        <mx:DataGridColumn dataField="publish_date"➥
          headerText="Publication Date" labelFunction="dateFormat"  />
    </mx:columns>
```

If you run the application, the dates should look as shown in Figure 6-25.

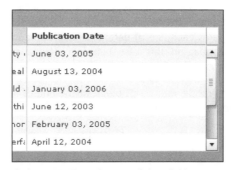

Figure 6-25. The reformatted date field

Editing and rendering data

The DataGrid control is not just for displaying data. It can also be used to edit existing data or enter new data. Let's take a look at this feature. Say you want to make the description field editable.

1. First, you must switch the editable feature of the entire DataGrid on by adding the editable attribute to the DataGrid control, like so:

```
<mx:DataGrid x="56" y="250" width="950" dataProvider="{bookStock}"➥
    editable="true">
```

This has one rather unfortunate side effect: it makes all of the fields editable.

2. Try running the application and click in each field. As you can see, you can change any data you want in the DataGrid control.

> *The changes you make to data will not be written back to the XML file at this point. We will be discussing that later on in the book.*

3. If you only want the description field to be editable, you have to make the following changes to the DataGrid structure:

```
<mx:DataGrid x="56" y="250" width="950" dataProvider="{bookStock}"➥
    editable="true">
  <mx:columns>
      <mx:DataGridColumn dataField="name" headerText="Book Name"➥
        editable="false" />
      <mx:DataGridColumn dataField="author" headerText="Book Author"➥
        editable="false"  />
      <mx:DataGridColumn dataField="description"➥
      headerText="Book Description" editable="true" />
      <mx:DataGridColumn dataField="publish_date"➥
        headerText="Publication Date" labelFunction="dateFormat"➥
        editable="false"  />
  </mx:columns>
</mx:DataGrid>
```

4. Run the application now. You should be able to change only the description field.

The next steps should change your thinking a bit so you can discover some powerful DataGrid features.

5. Change the structure of your DataGrid by adding a new column as follows:

```
<mx:DataGrid x="56" y="250" width="950" dataProvider="{bookStock}"➥
    editable="true">
  <mx:columns>
      <mx:DataGridColumn dataField="name" headerText="Book Name"➥
        editable="false" />
      <mx:DataGridColumn dataField="author" headerText="Book Author"➥
        editable="false"  />
      <mx:DataGridColumn dataField="description"➥
        headerText="Book Description" editable="true" />
      <mx:DataGridColumn dataField="publish_date"➥
        headerText="Publication Date" labelFunction="dateFormat"➥
```

6

```
        editable="false"  />
    <mx:DataGridColumn dataField="review"  headerText="New Reviews"➥
        editable="true" />
</mx:columns>
```

6. Try out the code. The changes should result in a new column in which users can write their own reviews, as shown in Figure 6-26.

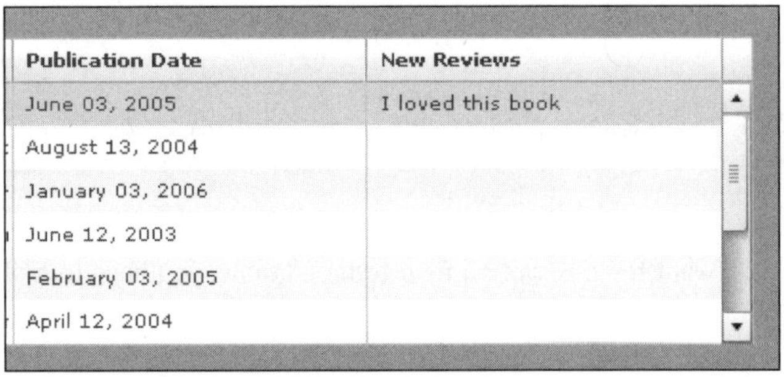

Figure 6-26. The DataGrid control with a new column

Now, let's assume you want to put a TextArea control into the cell in order to allow users to write reviews. You could go two possible routes: itemEditor or itemRenderer. Both attributes will allow you to enter controls into the cell. However, the attributes give you slightly different functionality. In both cases, the cell must be editable.

7. Add the following attribute to your new column:

```
<mx:DataGridColumn dataField="review"  headerText="New Reviews"➥
    editable="true" itemEditor="mx.controls.TextArea" />
```

Notice that you not only specified to put a TextArea into the field, but you also defined the package that contains it (mx.controls). You sort of combined the import and control into one simple MXML statement.

8. Run your application. Something will look wrong at first blush (see Figure 6-27).

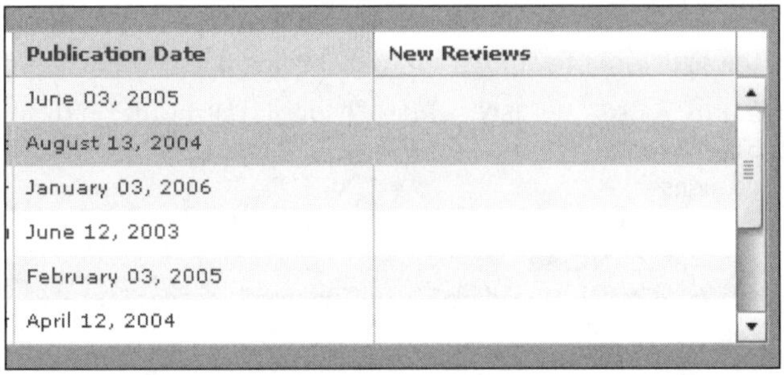

Figure 6-27. When the itemEditor first loads

9. It looks like nothing happened. However, click a cell and watch what happens—you should see a change, as shown in Figure 6-28.

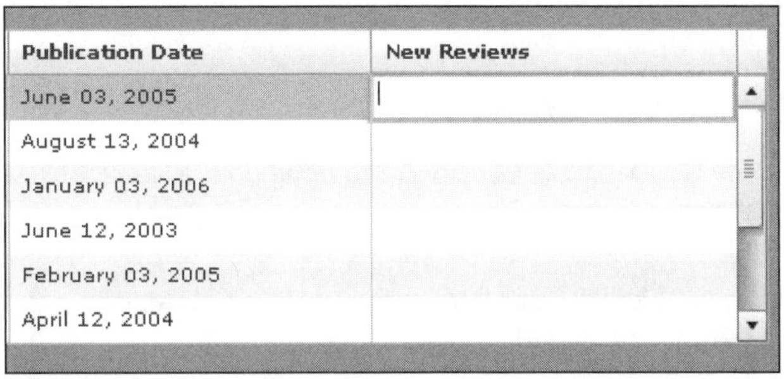

Figure 6-28. The clicked itemEditor

When you click a cell, the itemEditor clicks the TextArea control on and allows you type an entry.

10. Now change the itemEditor attribute to itemRenderer.

```
<mx:DataGridColumn dataField="review"  headerText="New Reviews"↵
    editable="true" itemRenderer="mx.controls.TextArea" />
```

11. Run your code now. You should see a significant difference in the results, as shown in Figure 6-29. The TextArea controls are automatically turned on for each row in the cell.

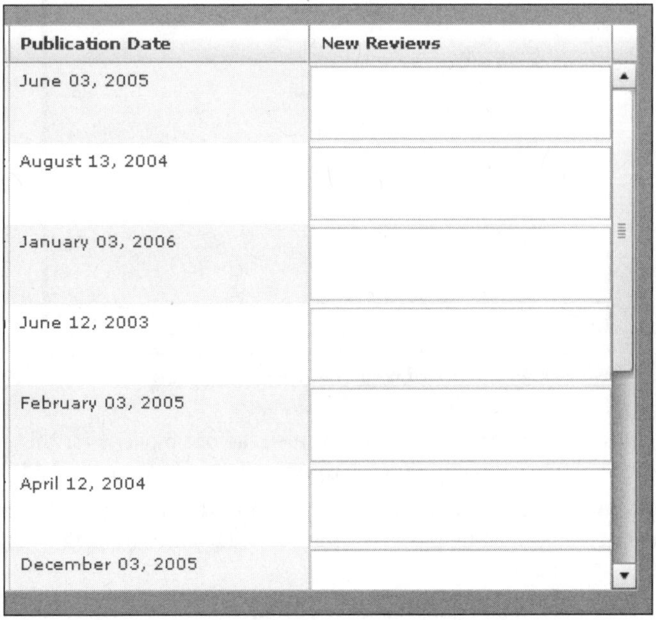

Figure 6-29. DataGrid with the itemRenderer control added

6

Deciding between itemEditor and itemRenderer is a matter of style and of appropriateness.

There is one drawback to the techniques you just saw. A cell can contain only one control at a time. What happens if you want the cell to contain several controls?

You can turn to a concept you learned in Chapter 4: components.

12. Select File ➤ New ➤ MXML Component to bring up the New MXML Component dialog box, shown in Figure 6-30.

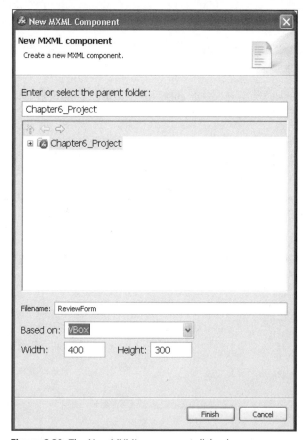

Figure 6-30. The New MXML component dialog box

13. Name this component ReviewForm. For the sake of simplicity for this exercise, save it in the Chapter 6 directory (or whatever you called your main folder).

14. Recall from Chapter 4 that a component cannot be based on the Application container. Instead, it must be based on one of the layout or navigation containers. For this exercise, choose VBox.

15. Leave the Width and Height properties as they are for now and click Finish.

16. Switch to Design view, if you are not already in it.

17. Drag a Label control into the VBox and give it the Text attribute of Please Enter Your Email Address (see Figure 6-31).

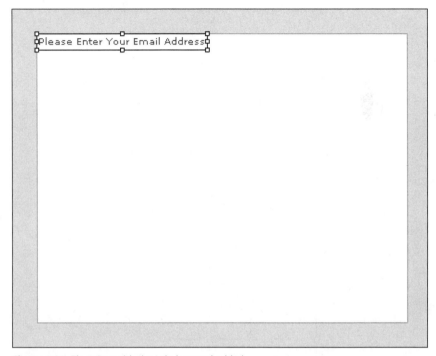

Figure 6-31. The VBox with the Label control added

18. Underneath this, add a TextInput control to enter the e-mail address, as shown in Figure 6-32.

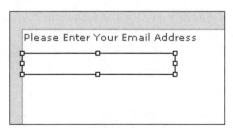

Figure 6-32. The TextInput control added

> *For purposes of this exercise, you are not going to add id attributes because you are not going to do any coding.*

19. Now add another Label control and give it the text Please Enter Your Review, as shown in Figure 6-33.

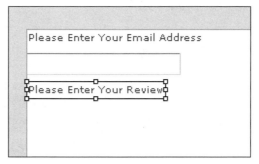

Figure 6-33. The Label control added

20. Next, add a TextArea control to write the review in, as in Figure 6-34.

Figure 6-34. The finished form

21. Next, click in the VBox container itself and, using the resizing handles, get rid of as much wasted space as possible, as shown in Figure 6-35.

Figure 6-35. The finished component

22. Save your component and, if you want, close it.

23. Return to your application file.

24. There is a way you can get the DataGrid control to automatically adjust the height of each row depending on its content. This can be done with the variableRowHeight attribute. Make the following change:

```
<mx:DataGrid x="56" y="250" width="950" dataProvider="{bookStock}"➥
    editable="true" variableRowHeight="true">
```

The only thing that is left for you to do is change the call in the itemRenderer attribute of the DataGridColumn you created earlier that now contains the TextArea control.

25. Replace mx.controls.TextArea with the name of your component, ReviewForm:

```
<mx:DataGridColumn dataField="review"  headerText="New Reviews"➥
editable="true" itemRenderer="ReviewForm" />
```

26. Go ahead and run the application. You should see the result shown in Figure 6-36.

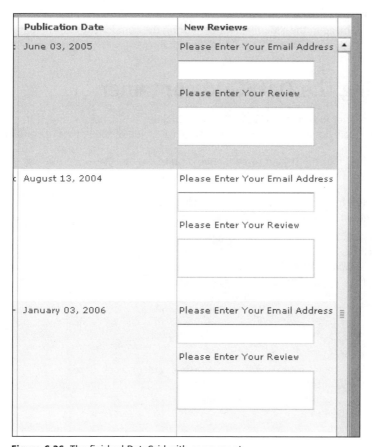

Figure 6-36. The finished DataGrid with component

As you can see, the component, with multiple controls, worked beautifully inside the cell of the DataGrid. You can set up all sorts of complex scenarios and programming situations by using this powerful feature. I have even seen applications where a component contained a secondary DataGrid.

> *Since you are not saving the user-input data yet, which you will be doing later on in the book (for example, using ColdFusion in Chapter 12), you will not see the entered reviews after you click off of them. Don't worry about this for now. Also, you will make your forms run more smoothly as you progress through the book.*

> *Chapter 4 discussed programming concepts using components. You may want to take the time to review them and try some of the concepts in this framework.*

A favorite trick of mine is to create a component with an Image control, tie that into the URL of the image in the XML file, and then bring the component into the DataGrid control. In that spirit, let's see what you can do with images.

Applying the DataGrid container

You had a brief look at the Tile and List containers in Chapters 4 and 5. In many ways, the functionality of both containers are combined inside of the DataGrid container.

You will find that the DataGrid container is quite easy to use while offering great functionality. Let's have a look at it.

1. Look in the assets folder of the Chapter6_Project files you downloaded; you should see a file called foed.xml, the contents of which are shown here:

```xml
<?xml version="1.0" encoding="iso-8859-1"?>
<foed>
    <book>
        <book_name>XML for Flash</book_name>
        <author>Sas Jacobs</author>
        <cover>assets/jacobs.jpg</cover>
    </book>
    <foed>
    <book>
        <book_name>Foundation Flash 8 Video</book_name>
        <author>Tom Green</author>
        <cover>assets/green.jpg</cover>
    </book>
    <foed>
    <book>
        <book_name>Object-Oriented Programming for Flash 8</book_name>
```

```
        <author>Peter Elst</author>
        <cover>assets/elst.jpg</cover>
    </book>
    <foed>
    <book>
        <book_name>Foundation ActionScript Animation: Making Things➥
          Move</book_name>
        <author>Keith Peters</author>
        <cover>assets/peters.jpg</cover>
    </book>
</foed>
```

You should also see a JPEG representing the cover of each book listed.

2. Open the file DataGrid2.mxml.

As you can see, it is fundamentally the same file you have been working with in that the HTTPService has been set up with the url attribute pointing to the foed.xml file. Also, the creationCompletion event has been set up in the Application tag.

3. Now, look at the bookHandler function to see how the results are handled.

Everything here has been discussed before. Let's move on to do some interesting design work.

4. Like before, you will adjust the column features of the DataGrid control. Only this time, the control will have just one column listing the book titles. You will also adjust the DataGrid's width. Make the following changes now:

```
<mx:DataGrid x="56" y="250" width="30%" dataProvider="{bookTitles}" >
    <mx:columns>
        <mx:DataGridColumn dataField="book_name"➥
          headerText="Book Name" />
    </mx:columns>
</mx:DataGrid>
```

5. Go ahead and run the application—you should see the result shown in Figure 6-37.

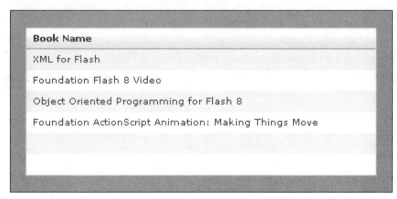

Figure 6-37. The DataGrid control with book titles

> *During the technical edit of this book, it was discovered that in some cases the browser cuts the text off. If this happens to you, feel free to change the width. This highlights the importance of testing applications in a variety of browser settings.*

Notice that some blank space appears under the last title. There are several ways of fixing this, which you will explore as you move through the rest of the book. But one of the easiest ways is with the rowCount attribute of the DataGrid, which you'll see now.

6. When you set the rowCount, you must count the header row as one of the rows. So, in this case, because there are four titles, you need to set the row count to 5, as follows:

```
<mx:DataGrid x="56" y="250" width="30%" dataProvider="{bookTitles}"➥
    rowCount="5" >
```

> *In a full application, you would want to do this programmatically, since you may not know how many rows will be needed. You will learn a bit more about this when you get to the case study later on in the book (it starts in Chapter 8).*

Your DataGrid should now look like Figure 6-38.

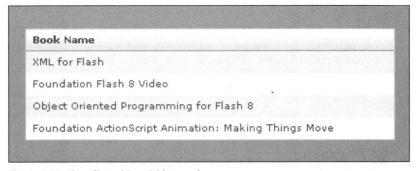

Figure 6-38. The adjusted DataGrid control

7. Now you'll do some design work—switch to Design view.

8. Move the DataGrid control by dragging it to the approximate position shown in Figure 6-39.

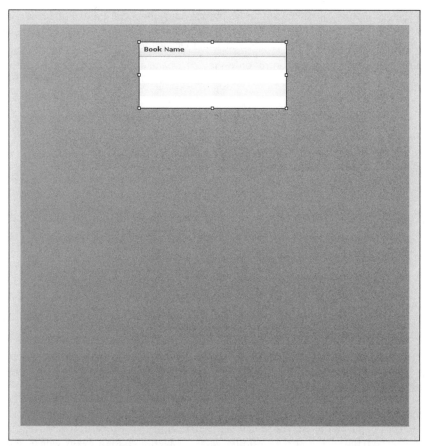

Figure 6-39. Positioning the DataGrid

9. Now drag a Label control onto the Editor pane. Use the Flex Properties panel to give it an id of book_name and place it under the left-edge of the DataGrid control.

10. Delete the default text of Label, as shown in Figure 6-40.

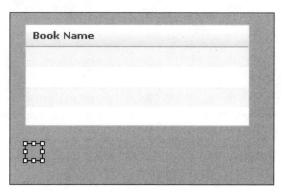

Figure 6-40. Placement of the Label control

11. Drag another Label control under the previous one. Give it an id of author_name and, again, delete the default text. Because you deleted the default text, the controls will seem to have disappeared. Don't worry, they are there.

12. Finally, drag an Image control onto the Editor pane and line up the right edge with the right edge of the DataGrid, as shown in Figure 6-41. Give it an id of cover_picture.

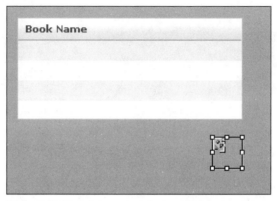

Figure 6-41. The placement of the Image control

13. Now that you have everything in place, return to Source view.

This is an excellent place to learn some very important programming concepts. In many respects, these concepts will tie a lot of pieces together.

Many of the controls that make lists of objects such as DataGrid, ComboBox, and List allow you to click items on the list. The item you select is called the selectedItem. Moving from one selectedItem to the next constitutes what is called a **change event** which, like all events, generates an event object of type Event. Because of this, you need to create a function, as you have done before, to handle the change event object. For the purposes of this exercise, you are going to call it changeHandler.

14. Create the following function structure in the script block:

```
private function changeHandler(evt:Event):void
{

}
```

As I have mentioned several times, the event object contains a property called target. The target property contains the name of the control broadcasting the event, as well as most of the information about the event. In this case, it also has the identification of the selectedItem selected in the DataGrid control.

15. Enter the following code to the function:

```
private function changeHandler(evt:Event):void
{
    book_name.text = evt.target.selectedItem.book_name;
    author_name.text = evt.target.selectedItem.author;
    cover_picture.source = evt.target.selectedItem.cover;
}
```

In addition to the information listed, the powerful event object contains a reference to the data contained by selectedItem. All you need to do is set the properties of the controls you included to the data referenced within selectedItem.

16. Tell the DataGrid control to call changeHandler(event) when a change occurs by modifying it as follows:

```
<mx:DataGrid x="200" y="55" width="30%" dataProvider="{bookTitles}"➥
    rowCount="5" change="changeHandler(event)">
```

17. Now test the application again, click a title, and you will be greeted with a display similar to the one shown in Figure 6-42.

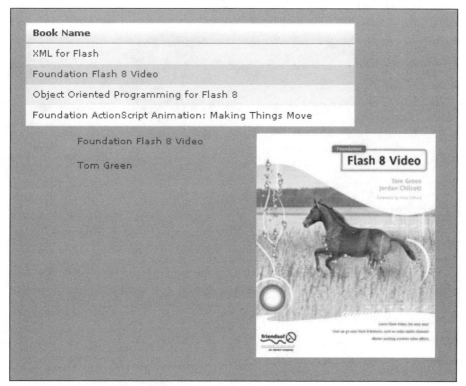

Figure 6-42. The finished exercise

As you can see, the event object is the glue that ties a lot together.

Try using the Flex Properties panel and change the font and size of the two Label controls. For instance, try making the following changes:

```
<mx:Label x="200" y="195" id="book_name" fontFamily="Arial"➥
  fontWeight="bold" fontSize="30"/>
<mx:Label x="200" y="221" id="author_name" fontFamily="Arial"➥
fontSize="24"/>
```

The result is shown in Figure 6-43.

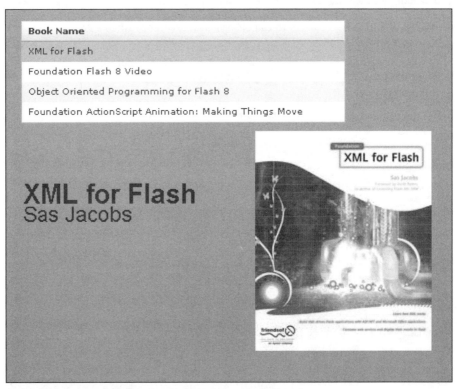

Figure 6-43. Results of further changing the Label control properties

Earlier in the chapter, you used the List control. As a little experiment, why don't you substitute that control for the DataGrid control you just worked on. You will find that the functionality is nearly identical.

Summary

By exploring event objects, XML (including E4X), and DataGrid controls, you just took a look at a pretty broad cross-section of Flex functionality. I hope you have become inspired enough to start to experiment on your own a bit. As a matter of fact, I have left tons of room in each of the exercises for you to do just that.

The next chapter takes a look at one of the most exciting features of Flex: states. States will give you timeline functionality without the timeline.

Turn the page and prepare to be wowed!

6

Flex creates SWF files and, in the past, such files were always associated with Flash. But Flex applications do not get built like Flash applications. The timeline and many of the Flash animation tools you have come to know and depend on are missing.

Or are they?

As you will see in this chapter, states capture many of the features you thought you may have lost from Flash. However, states handle those features in a very different way. With states, you can dynamically change forms based upon incoming data or a user's response.

In this chapter, you are going to explore some traditional Flash concepts; but in a very new light. You will

- Explore the concept of a state.
- Review a brief history of web design.
- Understand click properties.
- Create rollover effects.
- Use components with states.

Before you begin, let me make one point clear: Flex is not an animation program.

One of the questions I am most asked in my seminars is, "Will Flex be replacing Flash?" The answer is an unqualified *no*!

Flash started its life nearly 10 years ago as a powerful animation program. When versions MX and MX 2004 came along, we saw a move from an animation program to a web design program. As a result, many felt that Flash had become a hodge-podge of features that didn't always work together gracefully, and that Flash was losing its original purpose of providing powerful animation capabilities.

To address these issues, Macromedia (now Adobe) developed Flex to take up the web design duties of Flash with the hope of refocusing Flash on animation.

As you will see in this chapter, states give Flex many of the dynamic form capabilities seen in Flash MX and MX 2004.

Understanding states

States allow you to create dynamic forms that can respond to data or user events. For instance, based on a user response, form components may appear or disappear.

Before you dig into states, it will help for you to have a general understanding of web design in XHTML and Flash first, so I'll go over this briefly here.

Let's step away from the concepts of Flash for a moment.

Traditional non-Flash web design usually consists of many individual XHTML pages, arranged in some sort of hierarchy, tied together by some sort of common navigation system. The navigation system, at its most basic level, is a series of hyperlinks that moves users from page to page.

While this system works most of the time, it is very inefficient. Each time the user clicks a hyperlink, a request has to be sent to a web server, and the page has to be located by that server, sent over the Internet to the caller, and loaded into the browser. In some cases, a "Page Not Found" error occurs.

Flash addressed many of these issues by internalizing a complete website into one SWF file; in some very complex situations, two or three SWF files might be used and incorporated various ways into the main SWF file. In earlier versions of Flash, clicking a link in the navigation system moved the user from page to page by moving to a different point on the timeline or possibly a different scene. In Flash MX and Flash MX 2004, you could dynamically change the interface right in the same frame. In later versions, rather than using the timeline or scenes, pages were created using multiple SWF files that could be encased within the library of the main SWF file or loaded dynamically.

All of this improved the efficiency of web navigation in that each request did not need to go back to the server and be returned over the Internet. Once the main SWF file was loaded into the Flash Player, everything needed for that website to be fully operational would be loaded with it.

Flex suddenly changed things again, most notably by eliminating the now familiar timeline. But if the timeline is eliminated, how does one jump from page to page within an application?

One way is to use the navigation containers you saw in the previous chapters. Another way is by employing states. Moving between states is similar to jumping to different points on a timeline. You'll get a better understanding of this as you work through the examples in this chapter. In the process of building these examples, you will have a chance to review some previously discussed concepts.

Before you start, download the files, if you haven't done so already, for Chapter 7. These can be found on the code download page for this book at www.friendsofed.com.

The first example will be a simple one: you will make another panel, or panels, appear by clicking a hyperlink.

1. Delete previous projects and create a new Flex project using the downloads for Chapter 7 and start a new main MXML file. I am going to call this one Chapter7_States. However, use any name you might want. Just make the location wherever you unzipped the downloaded files.

2. Switch to Design view and drag a Panel container to the upper-left corner of the stage (see Figure 7-1).

Figure 7-1. Placement of the Panel container

3. Double-click in the header of the Panel container (the gray area). This is another way to enter a header, in addition to using either code or the Flex Properties panel.

4. Type in a header. (I will have a little fun and use Enemies of ED.)

5. Press Enter. Your screen should look similar to what you see in Figure 7-2.

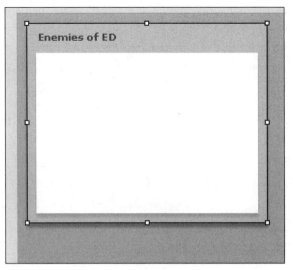

Figure 7-2. The Panel container with a header

6. Now you need to add some text to the body of the container. However, you can't type directly in the container, so drag a Text control into the body, as shown in Figure 7-3. The exact placement is not important.

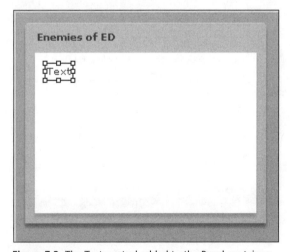

Figure 7-3. The Text control added to the Panel container

7. If necessary, highlight the word *Text* and type the following:

We would like to hear from you. Please click on the link below to find out how to contact us.

> *If you find it easier, you can also add the text using the* Text *field in the Flex Properties panel.*

7

213

8. Press Enter, and you should end up with a Text control that extends beyond the Panel container, as shown in Figure 7-4.

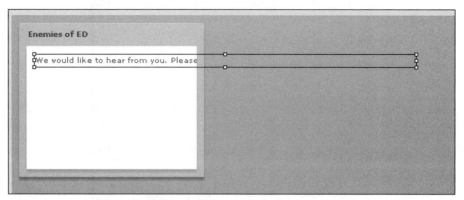

Figure 7-4. The initial state of the Text control

9. This is easily fixable—use the right-middle graphic handle to drag the right edge of the control back into the white area of the Panel container so that your screen resembles Figure 7-5.

Figure 7-5. The adjusted Text control

You want to make a new panel appear when an event happens. In order to accomplish this, what you want to do is create an event to trigger the new state. This is a good chance to look at a control you haven't seen before: LinkButton.

The LinkButton control is, in my opinion, a rather unfortunate name, as the result is not a button at all. Instead, it is closer to a hyperlink in XHTML.

10. Drag a copy of the LinkButton control and place it under the text you just created (see Figure 7-6).

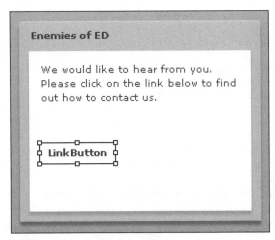

Figure 7-6. The LinkButton control added to the Panel container

11. Once again, you can either double-click the control or use the Text field in the Flex Properties panel to change the text. Type the text Click Here to Email Us.

12. Press Enter to lock in the changes.

13. Like all hyperlinks, you may want to change the color of the text to identify it as being a hyperlink. This can be easily done in the Flex Properties panel and the text color field, as shown in Figure 7-7.

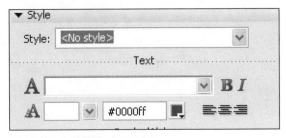

Figure 7-7. Setting the text color

14. Go ahead and test the application, and look at the LinkButton control (see Figure 7-8). The background color changes when you roll over the text, so you can easily see how this looks and feels more like a hyperlink than a button.

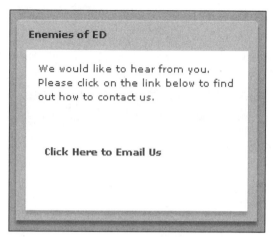

Figure 7-8. The finished Panel container

15. Go ahead and close the browser and return to Flex Builder.

Changing the state

Now the next trick is to use the LinkButton control to change the state of the application. Notice that in the upper-right corner, above the Flex Properties panel, there is a panel called States (see Figure 7-9).

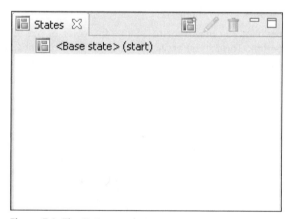

Figure 7-9. The States panel

> If your States panel is not visible, you can turn it on by selecting Windows ➤ States.

All Flex applications start in a base, or start, state. This is the default state. In other words, what you see in Flex Builder is what you get.

But now you are going to add an additional state.

1. Either right-click <Base state> in the States panel or click the New State button in the upper-right corner of the panel.

2. Select New State.

3. Name your state. You can see in Figure 7-10 that I called my new state Contact.

Figure 7-10. The New State dialog box

4. The Based on list is where you specify what state you want to build the new state over. Since you have no other states built, leave this set as <Base state>.

5. You can also make this new state the default or start state. For now, leave the Set as start state option unchecked.

6. Click OK. You should now see your new state appear in the States panel, as in Figure 7-11.

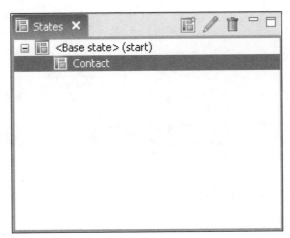

Figure 7-11. The new state added to the States panel

Everything looks exactly the same on the new state. But now you are going to change that.

7. Make sure that Contact is selected in the States panel.

8. Drag another panel onto the stage, place it to the right of the existing panel, and as shown in Figure 7-12, give it the heading of Send Us a Question.

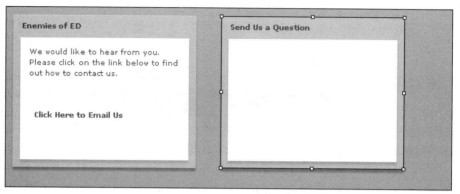

Figure 7-12. Adding a second panel in the Contact state

Let's build a simple e-mail form in this new Panel container as shown in Figure 7-13. Since you will not be actually e-mailing it now, the details of the form are not important.

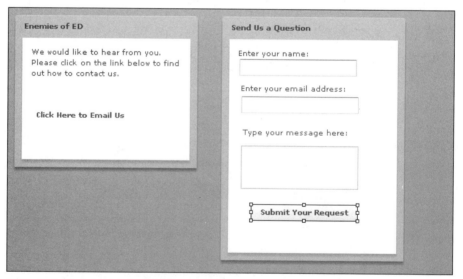

Figure 7-13. The completed contact form

9. Using Figure 7-13 as your guide, build a sample form using a combination of Label, TextInput, TextArea, and Button controls.

10. Resize the Panel container to accommodate the form you just created.

Let's see a little magic now.

11. In the States panel, click the `<Base state>` tag. The Panel container you just created disappears. If you click back on the Contact tag, your new Panel container returns.

Welcome to states!

As I said earlier in this chapter, this is similar to moving to a new point on the Flash timeline or using ActionScript to rebuild the interface.

You now have to add some code so that the LinkButton and Button controls can change state.

12. Return to the base state if you are not there already. Just the initial Panel container should be visible.

13. Click the LinkButton control.

14. In the Flex Properties panel, click the Category View button (see Figure 7-14).

Figure 7-14. The Category View button

15. Under the Events category, select the Value column to the right of the click event.

16. In the Value box, type the following code:

```
currentState='Contact'
```

Notice that Contact is enclosed in single quotes.

17. Press Enter.

As discussed in earlier chapters, this creates a string within a string, and ActionScript needs this inner string to work properly here. A quick analysis of the code will show the reason why.

```
<mx:LinkButton x="10" y="91" label="Click Here to Email Us"➥
    color="#0000ff" click="currentState='Contact'"/>
```

You can see that currentState is the main string for the buttonDown event. The state the event is selecting, Contact, is the inner string.

18. Give your code a test by saving and running the application. When you click the LinkButton control of the initial panel, the Contact panel should appear. This can create a pretty cool way of going from page to page.

19. You are not finished yet. Close the browser and return to your work.

20. Click the Contact tag in the States panel so you can see the Contact panel.

21. Click the Button control.

22. This time, in the buttonDown event, type the following code into the Value column:

currentState=' '

23. Press Enter.

24. Save and test the application. When you click the LinkButton control, the second panel should turn on. When you click the Button control on that panel, it should just return back to the original panel only (base state).

As you can see, you have not lost the gotoAndStop functionality of the Flash timeline. Instead, you are addressing it differently.

Let's take this concept yet one step further.

25. With the Contact state selected, right-click the States panel and select New State.

Notice that this time you are asked whether you want to base your new state on the Contact state. Flex will always ask whether you want to build on whatever state you have selected.

26. Name your new state Thankyou, as shown in Figure 7-15.

Figure 7-15. The New State dialog box for a state built over the Contact state

27. Click OK. Your States panel should now resemble Figure 7-16.

Figure 7-16. The States panel with a hierarchy of states

Notice that your new state, since it is built over the Contact state, is indented in the States panel. This makes it easy to see the hierarchy that is created by various states, as well as which states are built upon what others.

28. With the Thankyou state selected, bring a third Panel container onto the stage.

29. Give this Panel container a header of Thank You. Add some text to thank the user for submitting a question and add either a Button or LinkButton control (see Figure 7-17).

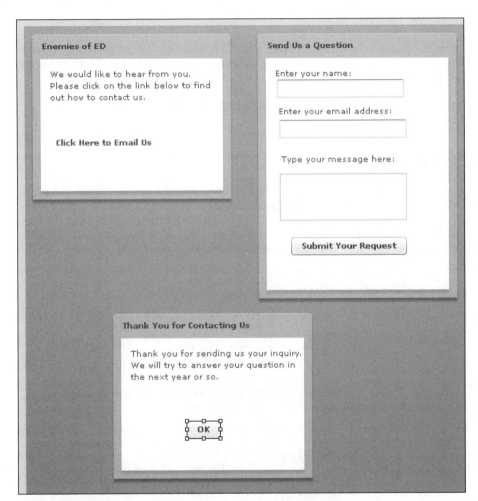

Figure 7-17. The finished states of the project

Now you need to make an adjustment to your application's functionality.

30. Click the Button control (or whatever control you used) in the new Panel container.

31. Set the buttonDown event to the following:

```
currentState = ' '
```

This will return the user to the default state.

32. Once you have completed that, click the Button control for the second state (Submit Your Request).

33. Change the currentState from ' ' to the following:

```
currentState='Thankyou'.
```

Needless to say, there are any number of variations you can try using these same ideas. For instance, you could have based the Thankyou state on the base state. By doing that, the e-mail form would become invisible when the Submit Your Request button is clicked.

It might be worth spending a bit of time looking at the code behind what you just did in Design view.

States and code

Throughout most of this book, I have been a strong advocate for using Source view over Design view. In my opinion, this gives you maximum control in creating your applications. However, when creating states, Design view may be the better choice, because the code can be daunting for a beginner. However, there are a couple of interesting concepts going on that you haven't seen yet. Take a look at the following code:

```
<?xml version="1.0" encoding="utf-8"?>
<mx:Application xmlns:mx="http://www.adobe.com/2006/mxml"➥
  layout="absolute">
  <mx:states>
    <mx:State name="Contact">
      <mx:AddChild position="lastChild">
        <mx:Panel x="294" y="10" width="250" height="321"➥
          layout="absolute" title="Send Us a Question">
          <mx:Label x="10" y="10" text="Enter your name:"/>
          <mx:TextInput x="14" y="26"/>
          <mx:Label x="14" y="56"➥
            text="Enter your email address:"/>
          <mx:TextInput x="17" y="75"/>
          <mx:Label x="17" y="114"➥
            text="Type your message here:"/>
          <mx:TextArea x="17" y="140" height="57"/>
          <mx:Button x="31" y="217" label="Submit Your Request"➥
            buttonDown="currentState='Thankyou'" id="button1"/>
        </mx:Panel>
      </mx:AddChild>
    </mx:State>
    <mx:State name="Thankyou" basedOn="Contact">
      <mx:AddChild position="lastChild">
```

```
                  <mx:Panel x="111" y="349" width="250" height="200"➥
                     layout="absolute" title="Thank You for Contacting Us">
                        <mx:Text x="10" y="10" text="Thank you for sending us➥
                           your inquiry. We will try to answer your question in➥
                           the next year or so." width="220"/>
                        <mx:Button x="82" y="100" label="OK"➥
                           buttonDown="currentState=''"/>
                  </mx:Panel>
               </mx:AddChild>
            </mx:State>
         </mx:states>
         <mx:Panel x="10" y="10" width="250" height="200" layout="absolute"➥
            title="Enemies of ED">
            <mx:Text x="10" y="10" text="We would like to hear from you.➥
               Please click on the link below to find out how to ➥
               contact us." width="210"/>
            <mx:LinkButton x="10" y="91" label="Click Here to Email Us"➥
               color="#0000ff" buttonDown="currentState='Contact'"/>
         </mx:Panel>
      </mx:Application>
```

The UIComponents class is part of the mx:core package. Recall from earlier discussions that anything in the mx:core package is automatically available to any Flex application without having to import the package.

One of the properties of the class UIComponents is states. The states property is of type Array. But what is it an array of?

In this case, it is an array of containers.

Notice that the two states beyond the base state, Contact and Thankyou, are wrapped within an <mx:states> tag. Then, each state is wrapped in an <mx:State> tag. This last tag automatically puts the state into a container called a **child container**. The outer <mx:states> tag then creates an array of the <mx:State> containers contained within it.

As soon as you click the component that calls the currentState handler, the AddChild class calls the <mx:states> tag to find the appropriate <mx:State> container in the array. The AddChild class has a property called position, which has a default value of lastChild. This just means to put the new container wherever you indicated during the design.

When the child container is no longer needed, <mx:states> calls a class called RemoveChild. This class has the appropriate methods for toggling off the child container.

As I said at the outset, this can be a bit daunting for a novice programmer. However, to help you get your toes a bit wet, let's try a small exercise involving rollover effects.

7

Rollovers and states

In traditional XHTML design, JavaScript can be used to create rollover effects. As soon as a mouse rolls over text or an image, an event handler in JavaScript catches the event, and the code instructs the browser to swap out one image for another (in the case of hyperlinks, the color of the text may change). This process, as easy and commonplace as it is by today's web standards, requires a lot of overhead in the resources used.

Flash handled the process much more efficiently by compiling, and compressing, all the necessary graphics and code into a single SWF file. Again, like the previous example, much of this was handled with the timeline. However, the timeline is no longer present in Flex.

Once again, states come to the rescue. Let's try a simple example. This time, rather than use Design view as before, you will create this example through code in the Source view.

1. Open the Chapter7_Rollover.mxml file found in the Chapter7_Project folder you should have downloaded from www.friendsofed.com. Figure 7-18 shows the contents of this file.

Figure 7-18. Initial state of the project file

As you can see, this is just an Image control referencing an image in the assets folder of the project. What you want to do is create a rollover effect so that the book's details will appear when the mouse rolls over the cover image.

2. If you are not there, go into Source view, where you should see the following code. You will be working in code for this exercise.

```
<?xml version="1.0" encoding="utf-8"?>
<mx:Application xmlns:mx="http://www.adobe.com/2006/mxml"➥
  layout="absolute">
    <mx:Image x="181" y="25" source="assets/jacobs.jpg"/>
</mx:Application>
```

Recall that the <mx:states> tag contains the additional states that will be built over the base state. Also, recall that it creates an array of containers to hold these states.

3. Add the following code in bold above the Image control:

```
<?xml version="1.0" encoding="utf-8"?>
<mx:Application xmlns:mx="http://www.adobe.com/2006/mxml"➥
  layout="absolute">
<mx:states>

</mx:states>
    <mx:Image x="181" y="25" source="assets/jacobs.jpg"/>

</mx:Application>
```

Each new state you want to add must be enclosed in an <mx:State> container.

4. You must give the state a name so that it can be properly identified by ActionScript.

```
<mx:states>
    <mx:State name="bookDetails">

    </mx:State>
</mx:states>
```

5. Just to prove a point, return to Design view and look at the States panel.

The state you just created with the <mx:State> tag should be listed in the panel (see Figure 7-19). Each subsequent state added will be listed.

Again, referring to the last example, the container is added with the <mx:AddChild> class. If you really dig into the mechanics, AddChild is yet another container in that it will take its contents, which you will build in a moment, and attach it as a container within the State container you just built (bookDetails). This class

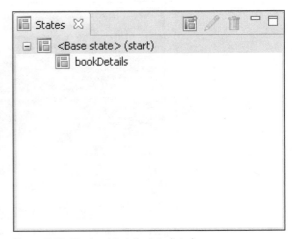

Figure 7-19. The bookDetails state listed

also decides the position of this subcontainer. The default position, as mentioned in the last section, is lastChild. This means the position of the bookDetails container, which, if you think about it, is a child of the base state (I warned you this was a bit confusing).

```
<mx:states>
  <mx:State name="bookDetails">
    <mx:AddChild position="lastChild">

    </mx:AddChild>
  </mx:State>
</mx:states>
```

You can now add your contents directly into the AddChild container.

In this case, you are going to keep it simple and add a Text control. You can add any text you want. However, if you want to use the text I show in this exercise, find the Rollover.txt file located with your exercise files.

6. Add the Text control as follows:

```
<mx:State name="bookDetails">
  <mx:AddChild position="lastChild">
    <mx:Text width="250" fontWeight="bold" text=""
  </mx:AddChild>
</mx:State>
```

In this code example, you have not added the text yet; all you did was give the control a width and an attribute to make the text bold.

7. In the quotes of the text attribute, either type some text or paste in the text from the Rollover.txt file. Don't forget to close the Text control with />.

8. Just to see what you have done so far, go over to Design view and click the bookDetails state in the States panel. Your screen should look similar to Figure 7-20.

Figure 7-20. Initial placement of the child container

9. As you may have noticed, the placement may be less than ideal. This is not a huge problem. As with any container, just click and drag this one to the position you want. You can also adjust the width if you want. Reposition the container so that your screen looks like Figure 7-21.

Figure 7-21. The repositioned child container

10. Now add another AddChild directly after the previous one.

```
<mx:State name="bookDetails">
    <mx:AddChild position="lastChild">
        <mx:Text width="387" fontWeight="bold" text="XML is a➡
            completely platform agnostic data medium. Flash is able to➡
            make use of XML data, which is very useful when you are➡
            creating Rich Internet Applications - it allows you to➡
            populate Flash web interfaces with data from pretty much any➡
            source that supports XML as a data medium, be it databases,➡
            raw XML files, or more excitingly, .Net applications, web ➡
            services, and even Microsoft Office applications such as ➡
            Excel and Word!" x="113" y="273"/>
    </mx:AddChild>
    <mx:AddChild position="lastChild">
        <mx:Text width="110" fontWeight="bold" text="ISBN:1590595432" />
    </mx:AddChild>
</mx:State>
```

11. As you did before, go back to Design view and position the container as you like (see Figure 7-22).

> *The* AddChild *class has the attribute of* relativeTo *so that you can position the container relative to another component in your application. If you use that, you can set your* position *attribute to before or after that component. You will get a chance to see this in action in a bit.*

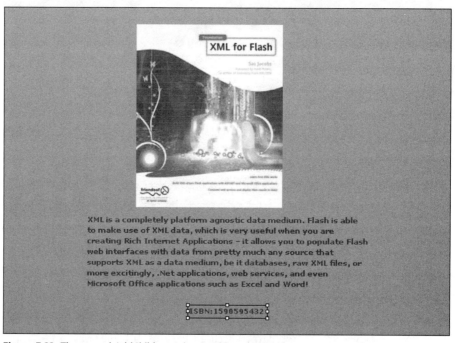

Figure 7-22. The second AddChild container positioned properly

Hopefully, you are now beginning to see how the AddChild class adds subcontainers within the State container.

You may be thinking that you could have added these Text controls directly into the State container. However, I strongly suggest that you don't do that. You will be sacrificing some interesting design possibilities that you will learn about later as you progress through the book.

It is now time to give your application some functionality.

12. Begin by giving your Image control an ID.

```
<mx:Image x="181" y="25" source="assets/jacobs.jpg" id="bookCover"/>
```

This is a good habit to get into whenever you work with ActionScript.

13. Recall that in your first exercise you assigned the currentState handler to the event buttonDown. You will do a slight variation here and assign this handler to a rollOver event for the image.

```
<mx:Image x="181" y="25" source="assets/jacobs.jpg" id="bookCover"➥
    rollOver="currentState='bookDetails'"/>
```

> *Please remember to enclose* bookDetails *in single quotes as discussed earlier.*

14. Save and test the application. As soon as you roll over the image, your AddChild containers and their contents should appear.

You now have one slight problem. When you roll off of the image, the containers remain.

15. Remedy this problem by adding a second event to the Image control as follows:

```
<mx:Image x="181" y="25" source="assets/jacobs.jpg" id="bookCover"➥
    rollOver="currentState='bookDetails'" rollOut="currentState=''"/>
```

Again, use single quotes after currentState.

16. Save and run your application now. You should see the text disappear after you roll the mouse away from the image.

Let's try a small variation in order to see an interesting programming tool in Flex Builder 2.

17. Delete the rollOut event in the Image control.

18. Right below the <mx:State> tag, start the tag shown here in bold:

```
<mx:State name="bookDetails" id="bookDetails">
    <mx:SetEventHandler
```

The SetHandler class allows you to define events outside of the component creating or dispatching the event. While this is a relatively simple example, you will be using this in increasingly complex situations—for instance, assigning multiple events and transitions to a state.

19. The first attribute you want to set is target. This is the component that will be dispatching the event. In this case, it will be the Image control with the id attribute of bookCover.

```
<mx:SetEventHandler target="{bookCover}"
```

20. The next attribute you need to set is name. This attribute should contain the event you want to trigger in the state. In this particular example, you want a rollOut event.

```
<mx:SetEventHandler target="{bookCover}" name="rollOut"
```

21. The final attribute you want to set is handler, which indicates what you want to happen when the event occurs. In this case, you specify currentState=' '. After this attribute, you can close out the tag.

```
<mx:SetEventHandler target="{bookCover}" name="rollOut"➡
    handler="currentState=''" />
```

22. Test your code now. It should work exactly the same way when you roll your mouse out.

When I give Flex seminars, I show the power of the SetEventHandler using an example similar to this. And, invariably, I am asked whether the rollOver event can be set up the same way. I have the attendees set it up and, when they go to test it, nothing happens.

The reason can be understood with a bit of logic. The SetEventHandler class is invoked within the State container. This means that it is not active until the State it is in is active. In this case, the State is not active until the rollOver event occurs. So you would be trying to call something that programmatically does not exist yet. It is a bit of cyclical thinking.

Along with SetEventHandler, there is the SetProperty event. The syntax for this event is very similar in that the target attribute will be the component whose properties you want to change. Likewise, name is the property you want to change.

In this example, you want to reduce the size of the image by 50% when the state is activated. This will require that you add two SetProperty instances: one for the scaleX property and one for the scaleY property. Where things change a bit is that you need to set a value attribute in place of the handler attribute used in SetEventHandler.

23. Make the following changes in bold to your code:

```
<mx:SetEventHandler target="{bookCover}" name="rollOut"➡
    handler="currentState=''" />
<mx:SetProperty target="{bookCover}" name="scaleX" value=".50" />
<mx:SetProperty target="{bookCover}" name="scaleY" value=".50" />
```

24. Run the application, and you should see results similar to those in Figure 7-23.

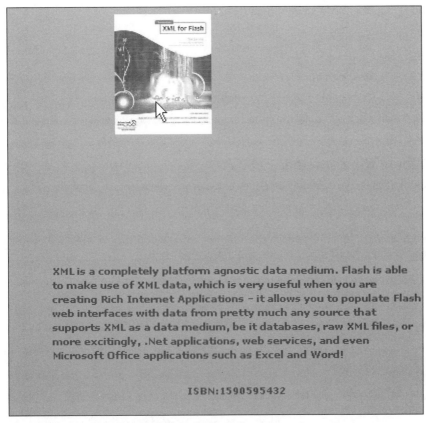

Figure 7-23. The effect with the mouse rolled over the picture

In all of these examples, the states seem to be making a rather ungraceful entrance and exit. Let's see how you could smooth things up a little bit.

Transitions

Once again, to address the loss of the Flash timeline in Flex, Flex has a corresponding feature associated with states: **transitions**.

A transition is a way to gracefully turn a state on or off. There is no way to set transitions up in Design view, and, as you are about to see, they require a bit of programming. The subject of transitions could take up an entire book; though a detailed discussion of transitions is outside the scope of this book, the following example will hopefully give you a good introduction.

Building transitions is actually a three-step process:

1. Build the container.

2. Create the states.

3. Program the transitions.

You have already done the first two steps in the previous exercises. So, in this exercise, you are going to work with a slightly more complex scenario. You will give the container some animation.

Building the container

You'll start this exercise by building the container you will eventually animate.

1. Start a new MXML file in your project and give it a name of your choice.

You are going to build a container to hold the information for the XML book you have been working with. This part will be pretty straightforward.

2. Change your MXML code to the following:

```
<?xml version="1.0" encoding="utf-8"?>
<mx:Application xmlns:mx="http://www.adobe.com/2006/mxml"➥
  layout="absolute">
  <mx:Panel title="Book" id="book" horizontalScrollPolicy="off"➥
    verticalScrollPolicy="off">
    <mx:Form id="bookForm">
      <mx:FormItem label="Foundation XML for Flash"➥
        fontWeight="bold" />
      <mx:FormItem label="Sas Jacobs" fontStyle="italic" />
    </mx:Form>
  </mx:Panel>
</mx:Application>
```

Your initial Panel container should appear as shown in Figure 7-24.

Figure 7-24. The initial Panel container

Next you need to add a LinkButton and Label control to the Panel container. As you saw in earlier chapters, the easiest way to do that is with a ControlBar. The purpose of the ControlBar is to provide a container for adding any controls that you might need.

You want to be certain that there is a space between the LinkButton and Label controls. In order to do this, you are going to call on a little-known class in Flex called Spacer.

In the past, HTML designers used to use spacers, which were usually a 1-pixel–by–1-pixel transparent GIF image, for a variety of needs, including preventing empty table cells from collapsing. In Flex, Spacer is an entire class whose main purpose is to allocate space in a parent container. In this case, the parent container is ControlBar.

In situations where the size of that parent container could be variable, the Spacer class has a number of properties for setting height, width, maximum height and width, minimum height and width, percent height and width, and so on. It would be well worth your time to study the documentation for this class. I am finding that it is coming in handy for a variety of situations.

3. Add the following code to the Panel container you just created:

```
<mx:Panel title="Book" id="book" horizontalScrollPolicy="off"➥
   verticalScrollPolicy="off">
      <mx:Form id="bookForm">
        <mx:FormItem label="Foundation XML for Flash"➥
          fontWeight="bold" />
        <mx:FormItem label="Sas Jacobs" fontStyle="italic" />
      </mx:Form>
      <mx:ControlBar>
        <mx:LinkButton label="Book Details" id="bookLink" />
        <mx:Spacer width="100%" id="spacer1"/>
        <mx:Label text="Book Title" id="title"/>
      </mx:ControlBar>
    </mx:Panel>
```

Your Panel container should now look like Figure 7-25.

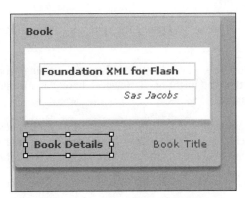

Figure 7-25. The completed Panel container

Now that the container is completed, your next step is to build the state for it.

Building the states

Recall from earlier in the chapter that states must be enclosed within the <mx:states> tags that create an array of containers. Each of those containers represent a different state and must be enclosed in <ms:State> tags.

Most of the following code example is similar to the previous states you built.

1. Place the following code before the Panel code you created earlier.

> *In this case, code placement is not critical. I am suggesting the placement so it will be easier to follow along with the book.*

```
<mx:states>
    <mx:State name="bookDetails" basedOn="">
        <mx:AddChild relativeTo="{bookForm}" position="lastChild"➥
            creationPolicy="all" >
            <mx:FormItem id="isbn" label="ISBN: 1590595432" />
        </mx:AddChild>
        <mx:SetProperty target="{book}" name="title"➥
            value="Book Details"/>
        <mx:SetProperty target="{title}" name="text"➥
            value="Book Details"/>
        <mx:RemoveChild target="{bookLink}"/>
        <mx:AddChild relativeTo="{spacer1}" position="before">
            <mx:LinkButton label="Collapse Book Details"➥
                click="currentState=''"/>
        </mx:AddChild>
    </mx:State>
</mx:states>
```

After the opening <mx:states> you create the state container, named bookDetails, using the <mx:State> tag.

As mentioned previously, the AddChild class adds a new container, and each container can contain any content that you might need. However, here you are using it a bit differently from the earlier examples.

In this example, you are adding the relativeTo attribute to the AddChild class to add the container to the <mx:Form id="bookForm"> container you created earlier. You are also telling it to position this container, containing form items, as the last child in the form.

The creationPolicy attribute decides when the child container is created.

> *Notice I said "created" and not "added." When it is created, it is just held in memory until called.*

The creationPolicy attribute has three possible values. The default is auto. An auto value means that the child is created when the state is activated. The all value, which you use here, means that the child is created when the application is started. When doing transitions, you might find that caching the child containers will facilitate smoother transitions since the pieces will be in place already. The none value means that the child will not be created until a method, createInstance(), is called to specifically create it. This can be handy in certain advanced programming scenarios.

You are using the all value here to help make a smoother transition.

Like any container, once the child container is created, you can put whatever content you want into it. For the sake of simplicity in this exercise, you just put a label into it showing the ISBN number of the book.

After the AddChild container is created, you use the SetProperty class discussed earlier in the chapter. Notice that, in this case, you are using two instances of the class to change the title value of the Panel container, book, and the text attribute of the Label control on the ControlBar, title. Remember, these actions will not occur until the state is activated.

The next few lines are where things start to become a bit different from before.

The <mx:RemoveChild> can literally remove any component or container from the user interface. In this case, you are telling it to remove the LinkButton control, bookLink, on the ControlBar.

Once the initial LinkButton is removed, you put a whole new one in its place. Notice that you position the new control before the Spacer, spacer1, using a combination of the relativeTo and position attributes. This raises an interesting programming issue: could you have used the SetProperty and SetEventHandler classes to do the same thing?

The answer to that is yes. In this case, either technique would have worked. The decision as to which technique to use is largely a matter of programming style and needs. As you progress through the book, and as you learn new techniques, you may want to go through previous exercises and try your newfound knowledge.

If you switch to Design view and activate the bookDetails state, your UI should look something like Figure 7-26.

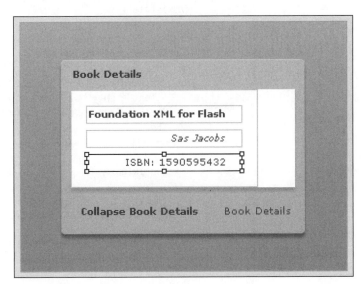

Figure 7-26. The design of the bookDetails state

Notice the change in the panel's title and the label's text. Also, there is an additional control in the form.

2. You have one more small thing to do. You need to tell the initial LinkButton control, located in the ControlBar, to switch to the bookDetails state when clicked.

```
<mx:LinkButton label="Book Details" id="bookLink"↝
click="currentState='bookDetails'" />
```

Again, do not forget to use single quotes around the name of the state.

At this point, your code should look as follows:

```
<mx:states>
    <mx:State name="bookDetails" basedOn="">
        <mx:AddChild relativeTo="{bookForm}" position="lastChild"↝
            creationPolicy="all" >
            <mx:FormItem id="isbn" label="ISBN: 1590595432" />
        </mx:AddChild>
        <mx:SetProperty target="{book}" name="title"↝
            value="Book Details"/>
        <mx:SetProperty target="{title}" name="text"↝
            value="Book Details"/>
        <mx:RemoveChild target="{bookLink}"/>
        <mx:AddChild relativeTo="{spacer1}" position="before">
            <mx:LinkButton label="Collapse Book Details"↝
                click="currentState=''"/>
        </mx:AddChild>
    </mx:State>
</mx:states>

<mx:Panel title="Book" id="book" horizontalScrollPolicy="off"↝
    verticalScrollPolicy="off">
<mx:Form id="bookForm">
    <mx:FormItem label="Foundation XML for Flash"↝
        fontWeight="bold" />
    <mx:FormItem label="Sas Jacobs" fontStyle="italic" />
</mx:Form>


<mx:ControlBar>

    <mx:LinkButton label="Book Details" id="bookLink"↝
        click="currentState='bookDetails'" />

    <mx:Spacer width="100%" id="spacer1"/>
    <mx:Label text="Book Title" id="title"/>

</mx:ControlBar>

</mx:Panel>
```

3. Go ahead and test the application. You should be able to change states as you did in earlier exercises.

Your next step is to start creating a transition so your state enters and exits gracefully.

Creating transitions

In many respects, the syntax for creating transitions is similar to the syntax for states. You are going to use a tag, `<mx:transitions>`, to create an array of transitions. You can have as many transitional effects as you want. In addition, you can make a decision whether you want them to play sequentially or parallel. You are going to add several to help make going from state to state a bit smoother.

I will give you all the code for the transition first and then discuss it line-by-line.

1. For this example, place the following code above the state code:

```
<mx:transitions>
        <mx:Transition fromState="*" toState="*">
            <mx:Parallel targets="{[book, bookLink, title, isbn]}">
                <mx:Resize duration="500" easingFunction=➡
                "Bounce.easeOut"/>
                <mx:Sequence target="{isbn}">
                    <mx:Blur duration="200" blurYFrom="0.0"➡
                        blurYTo="20.0" />
                    <mx:Blur duration="200" blurYFrom="20.0"➡
                        blurYTo="0.0" />
                </mx:Sequence>
            </mx:Parallel>
        </mx:Transition>
    </mx:transitions>
```

Just as the `<mx:states>` tag creates an array of states, the `<mx:transitions>` tag creates an array of transitions within it.

And, just as the `<mx:State>` creates a new state, `<mx:Transition>` creates a new transition. However, the fromState and toState attributes create an interesting programming possibility. Let's create a hypothetical situation here and say that your application has four states: stateA, stateB, stateC, and stateD. You could specify to use this particular transition only when going from stateB to stateC as follows:

```
<mx:Transition fromState="stateB" toState="stateC">
```

By using the asterisk, you are telling Flex to use this transition from any state to any state.

With transitions, you can choose whether they perform all together, in **parallel**, or one after the other, in **sequence**.

In this example, you choose to have parallel performance by selecting the Parallel class. But now you have to tell Flex what components you want to run in parallel. You do that with the targets attribute.

```
<mx:Parallel targets="{[book, bookLink, title, isbn]}">
```

The syntax is important here. The Parallel class is setting up its own array or components. Thus the [ ], which is array notation. So components book, bookLink, title, and isbn will all transition at the same time.

Within that Parallel container, you now need to specify the actions these components will perform. There are a large number of classes you could call here. But the one I decided to demonstrate is the Resize class.

```
<mx:Resize duration="500" easingFunction="Bounce.easeOut"/>
```

The first attribute you add is duration. This will decide how long the resizing transition will take measured in milliseconds. So 5000 milliseconds translates to 5 seconds.

The easingFunction attribute varies the speed of the animation and goes back to a feature of Flash. The best analogy is that of a ball. If you ever follow the calculus of throwing a ball in the air, gravity will cause it to slow as it rises and accelerate as it descends. This variation of velocity is called **easing**. For a great discussion on this topic, go to www.ericd.net/chapter7.pdf.

Rather than specify a value directly, you are going to let the value of the easingFunction be controlled by another class: Bounce.

The Bounce class does just as it says: it causes the easing to bounce like a ball. The easeOut property causes the bounce to begin quickly and then slow down. So, in this case, the resize transition will last 5 seconds and end with a bounce that will begin quickly and then start to slow down.

> If you were to look in the documentation for the Bounce class, you would not see the easeOut property at first. You need to expand the inherited properties to see it.

There is one quirk to using the Bounce class that you need to know. The Bounce class is part of the mx.effects.easing package. This package must be imported within a Script tag in order for you to use the Bounce class.

2. Right under the opening Application tag put the following Script tag:

```
<mx:Script>
        <![CDATA[
            import mx.effects.easing.Bounce;
        ]]>

    </mx:Script>
```

While all of this is going on, you run a second animation in the isbn label. You use the Sequence class instead of Parallel.

```
<mx:Sequence target="{isbn}">
```

An old trick of animators is to create a sense of motion by blurring an object and then bringing it back into focus. The Blur class does just that by creating a graphics effect called a Gaussian blur.

```
<mx:Sequence target="{isbn}">
    <mx:Blur duration="200" blurYFrom="0.0" blurYTo="20.0" />
    <mx:Blur duration="200" blurYFrom="20.0" blurYTo="0.0" />
</mx:Sequence>
```

The amount of blur you apply ranges from 0.0 to 255.0. In addition, you can apply blur either along the x- or the y-axis.

Looking at the preceding code, it should be fairly obvious why you did this sequentially. You first change the blur of the control from 0.0 to 20.0 over a time of 2 seconds. The second call to the Blur class reverses the process going from 20.0 to 0.0 over 2 seconds.

3. Now that you have the transitions all set, take a quick review of all of your code:

```
<?xml version="1.0" encoding="utf-8"?>
<mx:Application
    xmlns:mx="http://www.adobe.com/2006/mxml" verticalAlign="middle"
    width="340" height="250"
    viewSourceURL="src/DefiningStateTransitions/index.html">
    <mx:Script>
        <![CDATA[
            import mx.effects.easing.Bounce;
        ]]>

    </mx:Script>

    <mx:transitions>
        <mx:Transition fromState="*" toState="*">
            <mx:Parallel targets="{[book, bookLink, title, isbn]}">
                <mx:Resize duration="500"➡
                    easingFunction="Bounce.easeOut"/>
                <mx:Sequence target="{isbn}">
                    <mx:Blur duration="200"➡
                        blurYFrom="0.0" blurYTo="20.0" />
                    <mx:Blur duration="200"➡
                        BlurYFrom="20.0" blurYTo="0.0" />
                </mx:Sequence>
            </mx:Parallel>
        </mx:Transition>
    </mx:transitions>
    <mx:states>
        <mx:State name="bookDetails" basedOn="">
            <mx:AddChild relativeTo="{bookForm}"➡
                position="lastChild" creationPolicy="all" >
                <mx:FormItem id="isbn" label="ISBN: 1590595432" />
```

7

```
            </mx:AddChild>
            <mx:SetProperty target="{book}" name="title"↵
              value="Book Details"/>
            <mx:SetProperty target="{title}" name="text"↵
              value="Book Details"/>
            <mx:RemoveChild target="{bookLink}"/>
            <mx:AddChild relativeTo="{spacer1}" position="before">
                <mx:LinkButton label="Collapse Book Details"↵
                  click="currentState=''"/>
            </mx:AddChild>
        </mx:State>
    </mx:states>

    <mx:Panel title="Book" id="book" horizontalScrollPolicy="off"↵
      verticalScrollPolicy="off">
    <mx:Form id="bookForm">
        <mx:FormItem label="Foundation XML for Flash"↵
          fontWeight="bold" />
        <mx:FormItem label="Sas Jacobs" fontStyle="italic" />
    </mx:Form>


    <mx:ControlBar>

        <mx:LinkButton label="Book Details" id="bookLink"↵
          click="currentState='bookDetails'" />

        <mx:Spacer width="100%" id="spacer1"/>
        <mx:Label text="Book Title" id="title"/>

    </mx:ControlBar>

    </mx:Panel>
</mx:Application>
```

If all looks well, go ahead and give the code a test drive.

When you click the LinkButton control, you should see all the changes of the new state taking place. When you return to the initial state, the changes reverse.

While these transitions are fun and, once you get the idea, easy to program, I strongly recommend that you plan them out before you start to program. In very complex situations, they can get quite involved.

And you thought you lost the timeline?

Summary

I started off this chapter by saying that you could regard states as a replacement for the Flash timeline. I think after going through these pages you will agree with me. If you're interested in reading more about animation techniques achieved without a timeline, check out *Foundation ActionScript 3.0 Animation: Making Things Move!* by Keith Peters (friends of ED, 2007).

You are now ready to put all of the knowledge you've gained so far to work by creating a project from scratch in the next chapter.

7

8 CASE STUDY: PART 1

Up to this point, the text has been focusing on teaching you individual concepts, and most of the examples focused on those concepts in a somewhat isolated manner. It is now time to bring them together in a full-on case study.

In this chapter, you will

- Review many of the concepts already discussed, which will serve as a good reinforcement of what you've learned.
- Use these concepts differently from how you've used them in previous examples, thereby allowing you to see them in a different light.
- Learn some new concepts along the way. While these will not be major features, they will be new nonetheless.

Unlike the previous exercises in this book, in which you were given a lot of freedom to try things, please stick strictly to the steps outlined here. Everything is being done for a reason, and those reasons will become clear as you progress. Also, please take your time with these steps and make sure you understand why you took them.

Finally, as a developer, you may spot different ways to accomplish the same task. That is normal, and, in the writing of this book, I could only choose one of many possible choices.

Keeping all of this in mind, let's get to work . . .

The case study: a book publisher's website

For the case study, you are going to redesign the website for a well-known technical book publisher that needs a bit of a facelift (of course, the senior editor could do with a facelift also, but that is a different subject altogether, one that is well beyond the scope of this book).

In this part, you are going to create just the structure and components needed for your project. When you get to Chapter 10 (part 2 of the case study), you will start to tie it all together with data and coding. Along the way, you will also build some states and make some advanced preparations for part 2.

Just to give you an idea of what you are shooting for, Figure 8-1 is a screenshot of the finished part 1 of this project.

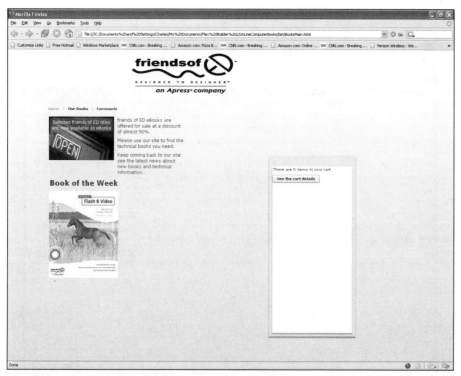

Figure 8-1. The finished part 1 for this project

Creating the project environment

I generally find that, although not 100% necessary, things become less confusing with only one project active at a time. That choice is up to you. However, for this project, let's work in a clean Navigator pane.

1. Delete any projects that you may have open in Flex Builder. Again, all you need to do is right-click the project name in the Navigator pane and select Delete.

   A dialog box will open that will ask whether you want to delete the actual files of the project or not. In most instances, I usually choose not to do that. By not doing that, you have the option of creating a project again, at some future point in time, using those same files.

2. Once all the projects are cleared, select File ➤ New ➤ Flex Project.

3. Select Basic.

4. Click Next.

5. Name the project onLineComputerBooks.

6. Select Use default location. Your dialog window should currently look like Figure 8-2.

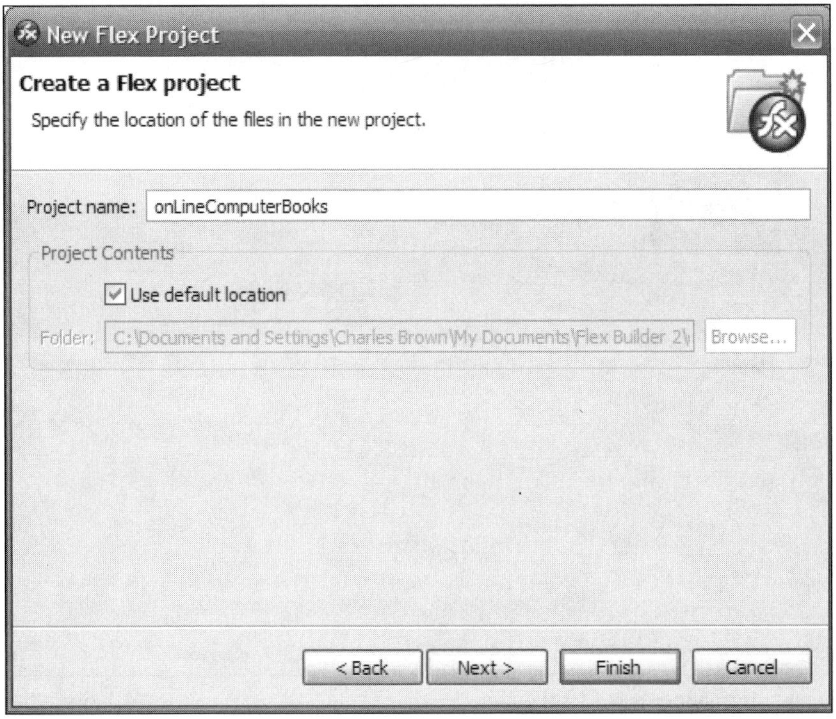

Figure 8-2. Specifying your project name in the Flex Builder New Project dialog box

7. Click Next.

8. Change the name of the main application file to BooksMain.mxml, as shown in Figure 8-3. You don't have to do this; if you keep the default name, which is the same as the project name, things will still work fine. But by putting the word *main* into the name, you make the main file a little easier to identify if you are going to have multiple files.

Remember, by OOP tradition, file names usually begin with a capital letter.

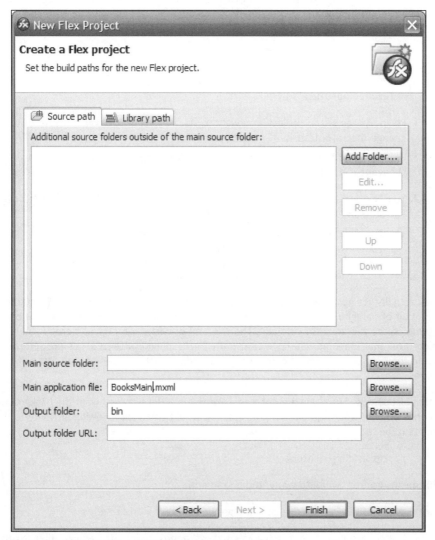

Figure 8-3. Changing the name of the main application file

9. Click Finish.

10. Switch to Source view.

As you already know from working through the previous chapters, the code needed for Flex must be put between opening and closing Application tags. Also, the Application tags have an attribute to decide how the various containers are going to be arranged automatically.

The default of this layout is absolute.

```
<mx:Application xmlns:mx="http://www.adobe.com/2006/mxml"
  layout="absolute">
```

11. For purposes of this project, you want to stack the container vertically. To do that, change the layout attribute to vertical.

```
<mx:Application xmlns:mx="http://www.adobe.com/2006/mxml"
  layout="vertical">
```

12. You also want to make the background color white. So add a backgroundColor attribute and change the value to #FFFFFF:

```
<mx:Application xmlns:mx="http://www.adobe.com/2006/mxml"
  layout="vertical" backgroundColor="#FFFFFF">
```

13. Switch over to Design view; the background should be white now.

Well, actually, it's not really white. You may notice that what you have is a bit of a gradient with a bit of darkening going on toward the bottom of the application. Flex handles background colors as gradients by default. There is a bit of backward thinking here: if you want to turn off that gradient, you have to use the backgroundGradientColors property. You would then set up an array of colors or, if you didn't want the gradient, an array of one color.

If that just confused you, you are not alone. For instance, let's say you want the background color to be pure white without the gradient. You would enter the following attribute to the Application tag:

```
backgroundGradientColors = "[#FFFFFF, #FFFFFF]"
```

This means go from white to white in the gradient.

For purposes of this case study, leave the gradient as is. It works fine.

14. If you have not done so already, go ahead and download the project files for this chapter from this book's page on www.friendsofed.com. Go ahead and unzip them to any directory that you would like.

In a normal workflow, you would probably have a graphic artist design the necessary graphics for the website using a program like Photoshop or Illustrator. You then import and use the graphics where needed. For purposes of this project, the graphic files have been completed already. However, before you can use them, you must import them into the project environment. Flex Builder cannot use files that are not within the environment.

15. To import the graphics files for the case study, select File ➤ Import. You will be greeted by the dialog box shown in Figure 8-4.

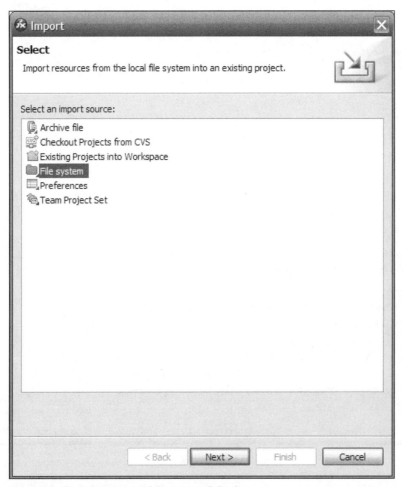

Figure 8-4. The Select screen of the Import dialog box

249

16. As you can see, you can select from a number of types of files. However, for the purposes of this case study, double-click File system to progress to the screen shown in Figure 8-5.

Figure 8-5. The File system screen of the Import dialog box

You are going to spend a few minutes in this box. As you are about to see, it has some pretty powerful features.

17. Using the Browse button, browse to the folder you downloaded containing the assets for this project, as shown in Figure 8-6.

Figure 8-6. The open assets folder

You can do one of several things here to select the files you want. You can click the check box next to the assets folder in the left window or click the Select All button to select all the files, or you could select the individual files you want to use.

18. Using one of the techniques I just stated, select all the files in the assets folder.

Notice that the Into folder field displays the project folder's name.

> If for some reason the name of your project folder is not appearing in the Into folder field, just use the Browse button to the right of the field to maneuver to that folder. When you click the Browse button, the folder should come right up first.

19. Make a minor modification to the entry in the Into folder field as shown in Figure 8-7.

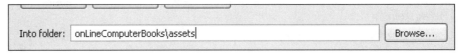

Figure 8-7. The modified Into folder field

20. Make sure the radio button option Create selected folders only is selected. This is located right above the Into folder field.

21. Click Finish.

22. Look in the Navigator pane. You should now see an assets folder created with all of the assets for this project in it (see Figure 8-8). They are now officially inside of this project and can be used.

Figure 8-8. The created assets folder

Starting to build the structure

Now that you have your environment set up, you'll start to build your structure.

1. You want to begin by adding a logo to the top of the page. In order to do this, go to Source view and, between Application tags, insert an Image tag to place the logo1.gif image.

Also, double-check the layout attribute of the Application tag to ensure it is set to vertical.

```
<?xml version="1.0" encoding="utf-8"?>
<mx:Application xmlns:mx="http://www.adobe.com/2006/mxml"
  layout="vertical" backgroundColor="#FFFFFF">
  <mx:Image source="assets/logo1.gif" />
</mx:Application>
```

2. This particular image is called a **transparent GIF**. This means that everything but the actual lettering is transparent and will reflect any color the background is. Just as a little experiment, change the backgroundColor attribute of the Application tag to any color you want, red for example.

> When setting colors in Flex, you can use either the name of the color or the hex code as you did previously. If you use the hex code, it must be preceded by a # symbol. Most designers feel you can get more precise colors using hex codes.

3. After you get through testing out the transparency of the GIF image, change the color back to white. Save and run the application. Your browser should look like Figure 8-9 now.

Figure 8-9. The page with the logo added

   4. Close the browser and return to Flex Builder.

The next step you are going to take is to create the components for your project.

Creating the components

Time to divide and conquer!

As I said in Chapter 4, you want to divide your project over several components. By doing this, you increase flexibility, reusability, and maintainability.

You will be building components for your home page, a gallery of book covers, a comments page, and a shopping cart. Later on, you will be using the components you are about to build to display different states.

Let's begin with the BookHome component, which will serve as your home page.

BookHome component

To build the BookHome component, follow these steps:

1. In the Navigator pane, right-click the root folder (onlineComputerBooks) and select New ➤ Folder.

2. Call the new folder components, as shown in Figure 8-10.

Figure 8-10. Naming the components folder in the New Folder dialog box

3. Click Finish.

4. Look in the Navigator pane, and you should now see the new folder, as shown in Figure 8-11.

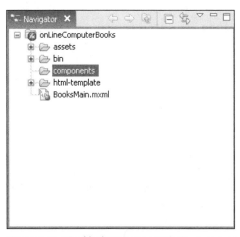

Figure 8-11. The Navigator pane with the components folder

5. Right-click the new components folder and select New ➤ MXML Component.

6. If you will recall, components have to be based on one of the container components and not on the Application tags. Call your new component BookHome and base it on a VBox component, as shown in Figure 8-12.

Figure 8-12. Defining the BookHome component in the New MXML Component dialog box

7. Click Finish.

The code for the new component should look as follows:

```
<?xml version="1.0" encoding="utf-8"?>
<mx:VBox xmlns:mx="http://www.adobe.com/2006/mxml"➥
    width="400" height="300">

</mx:VBox>
```

8. Within the VBox container, put an HBox container:

```
<?xml version="1.0" encoding="utf-8"?>
<mx:VBox xmlns:mx="http://www.adobe.com/2006/mxml"➥
    width="400" height="300">
    <mx:HBox>

    </mx:HBox>
</mx:VBox>
```

9. Now, within the HBox container, put an Image tag and make the source assets/ebooksHomeAd.jpg:

```
<?xml version="1.0" encoding="utf-8"?>
<mx:VBox xmlns:mx="http://www.adobe.com/2006/mxml"➥
    width="400" height="300">
    <mx:HBox>
        <mx:Image source="assets/ebooksHomeAd.jpg" />
    </mx:HBox>
</mx:VBox>
```

You will recall that a Flex application is built with containers within containers. The containers, in turn, handle the placement of whatever content is inside of them.

10. You now want to place some text below the image you just inserted. Put a VBox below the Image tag.

```
<?xml version="1.0" encoding="utf-8"?>
<mx:VBox xmlns:mx="http://www.adobe.com/2006/mxml"➥
    width="400" height="300">
    <mx:HBox>
        <mx:Image source="assets/ebooksHomeAd.jpg" />
        <mx:VBox>

        </mx:VBox>
    </mx:HBox>
</mx:VBox>
```

11. Recall that when I talked about UI components, I talked about Text. What you need to do is create a Text container to control the font, size, color, and so forth of the text. Place a Text container within the new VBox container. Give it a fontSize attribute of 12 and a color of blue, and make the container 200 pixels wide:

```
<?xml version="1.0" encoding="utf-8"?>
<mx:VBox xmlns:mx="http://www.adobe.com/2006/mxml"➥
    width="400" height="300">
    <mx:HBox>
        <mx:Image source="assets/ebooksHomeAd.jpg" />
        <mx:VBox>
            <mx:Text color="blue" fontSize="12" width="200">

            </mx:Text>
        </mx:VBox>
    </mx:HBox>
</mx:VBox>
```

As you may recall, within the Text container, you need to identify each block of code with an <mx:text> tag. Notice that this tag uses a lowercase *t*. The text you want to put into it is as follows: friends of ED eBooks are offered for sale at a discount of almost 50%.

12. Add the <mx:text> tag within the Text container as follows:

```
<mx:Text color="blue" fontSize="12" width="200">
    <mx:text> friends of ED eBooks are offered for sale➥
        at a discount of almost 50%.</mx:text>
</mx:Text>
```

13. Remember, you cannot run a component as an application because it has no Application tag of its own. However, you can see it in Design view. Compare your work so far against Figure 8-13.

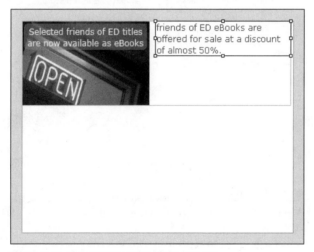

Figure 8-13. The component as of the last step

14. Return to Source view so you can add some additional text.

15. To save yourself some time, copy the entire <mx:Text> code and paste it below the present Text container. Inside of the <mx:text> tag of the new container, replace the text with the following:

Please use our site to find the technical books you need.

16. Follow the same procedure to add one more Text container with the following text:

Keep coming back to our site to see the latest news about new books and technical information.

Your code should look as follows:

```
<mx:VBox>
    <mx:Text color="blue" fontSize="12" width="200">
        <mx:text>friends of ED eBooks are offered for sale at a price➡
            almost 50% below that of their traditional, printed➡
            companions! Find out more.</mx:text>
    </mx:Text>
    <mx:Text color="blue" fontSize="12" width="200">
        <mx:text> Please use our site to find the technical books you➡
            need. </mx:text>
    </mx:Text>
    <mx:Text color="blue" fontSize="12" width="200">
        <mx:text> Keep coming back to our site to see the latest news➡
            about new books and technical information.</mx:text>
    </mx:Text>
</mx:VBox>
```

17. Switch to Design view; you screen should look like Figure 8-14.

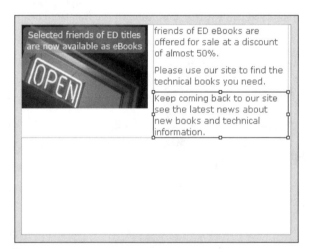

Figure 8-14. The component with text added

You still have a small gap in the lower-left part of the component, which you will use to show a featured book of the week. You are still not quite ready to handle that programmatically. However, since it is in a component and components are easy to edit, you can manually add it. You could add it now, but this might be a good time to demonstrate the updatability of components.

When you learned how to build and attach components, you used the drag-and-drop technique to bring them into the main page. In this case study, you could do that also. However, in this exercise you are going to do it manually just to reinforce the concepts you've learned and to make some changes.

18. Switch back to the BooksMain.mxml window.

Recall that in the Application tag you have to declare a namespace. For review, a namespace is simply a way of predefining a path to find objects that will be needed.

19. To define a namespace, use the xmlns attribute as follows.

```
<mx:Application xmlns:mx="http://www.adobe.com/2006/mxml"➥
    layout="vertical" backgroundColor="#FFFFFF"➥
    xmlns:comp="components.*">
  <mx:Image source="assets/logo1.gif" />
</mx:Application>
```

The asterisk signifies all components in the directory named components. As you may recall from Chapter 6, the name itself has absolutely no significance. However, it is a good idea to use a name that describes what is in the path. In this case, I used comp as a name to tell me that this path contains my components. Using precise terminology, the name (in this case, comp) is called a **prefix**.

20. Under the Image tag, place the component by starting the tag not with mx, as you have done with tags to this point, but with comp, which is the prefix of the namespace:

```
<comp
```

As soon as you type the colon after the namespace name, a list of components in the components directory (in this case there is only one so far) comes up, as shown in Figure 8-15.

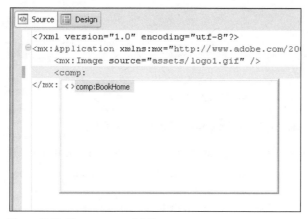

Figure 8-15. The component listing

21. Select the BookHome component.

22. For purposes of this exercise, you want the height and width of the component to be 50% of the size the application, as shown here:

```
<?xml version="1.0" encoding="utf-8"?>
<mx:Application xmlns:mx="http://www.adobe.com/2006/mxml"➥
   layout="vertical" backgroundColor="#FFFFFF"➥
   xmlns:comp="components.*">
   <mx:Image source="assets/logo1.gif" />
   <comp:BookHome height="50%" width="50%" />
</mx:Application>
```

23. Save the project and run it. Your output should be as shown in Figure 8-16.

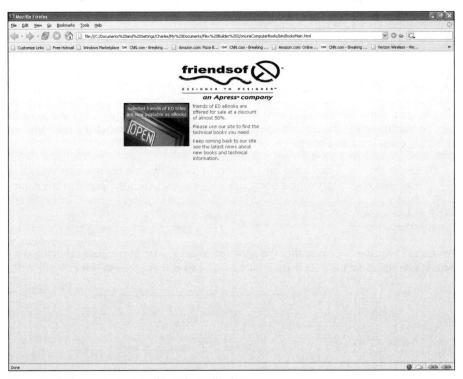

Figure 8-16. The component on the main application

This is a good place to show the power of components.

24. Close the browser and return to the BookHome component.

25. Under the closing HBox tag, insert a Text container with the following text:

```
</mx:HBox>
   <mx:Text fontSize="20" fontWeight="bold">
      <mx:text>Book of the Week</mx:text>
   </mx:Text>
```

26. Under the closing Text tag, place an Image tag calling the green.jpg file in the assets folder.

```
</mx:HBox>
 <mx:Text fontSize="20" fontWeight="bold">
   <mx:text>Book of the Week</mx:text>
</mx:Text>
<mx:Image source="assets/green.jpg" />
</mx:VBox>
```

27. Save the component.

28. If you switch back to BooksMain and run the application, you should see the page automatically updated due to the component being updated (see Figure 8-17). That is some of the real power of components.

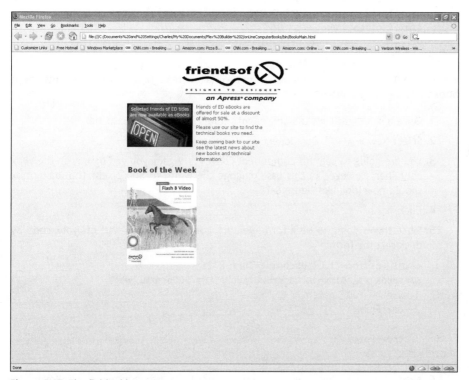

Figure 8-17. The finished home page

As you can see, once the component is updated, everything that uses that component is updated automatically as soon as the component is saved.

29. As you progress through this case study, you will be calling this component programmatically as well as building a navigation bar. For that reason, you need to give the call to the component the attributes of id and label. In this case, call both home. In the label attribute, you must enter the name exactly the way you want it to appear in the navigation bar. So you will use a capital *H* for home:

```
<comp:BookHome height="50%" width="50%" label="Home" id="home" />
```

Your finished code should look as follows:

```
<?xml version="1.0" encoding="utf-8"?>
<mx:Application xmlns:mx="http://www.adobe.com/2006/mxml"➥
    layout="vertical" backgroundColor="#FFFFFF"➥
    xmlns:comp="components.*">
    <mx:Image source="assets/logo1.gif" />
    <comp:BookHome height="50%" width="50%" label="Home" id="home" />
</mx:Application>
```

Comments component

You will now build another component that will allow readers to make comments about books sold by this publisher.

1. Once again, right-click the components folder in the Navigator pane.

2. Select New ➤ MXML Component.

3. You are going to call this component Comments. Again, you will base it on the VBox container. However, in this case, change the width to 500 pixels. The dialog box should now look like Figure 8-18.

4. Click Finish.

5. Since this is going to be a form, you are going to need to start off your code by declaring the form:

```
<?xml version="1.0" encoding="utf-8"?>
<mx:VBox xmlns:mx="http://www.adobe.com/2006/mxml"➥
    width="500" height="300">
    <mx:Form>

    </mx:Form>
</mx:VBox>
```

6. Next, declare a label telling the user to enter his or her comments, as follows:

```
<?xml version="1.0" encoding="utf-8"?>
<mx:VBox xmlns:mx="http://www.adobe.com/2006/mxml"➥
    width="500" height="300">
    <mx:Form>
        <mx:Label text="Please Enter Your Rating and➥
            Comments About Our Books" />
    </mx:Form>
</mx:VBox>
```

Recall from the discussion of forms that the FormItem container helps position, as well as format, the form's various components. In Flex, it is good practice to put each component in a separate FormItem container. The reason will be obvious in a moment.

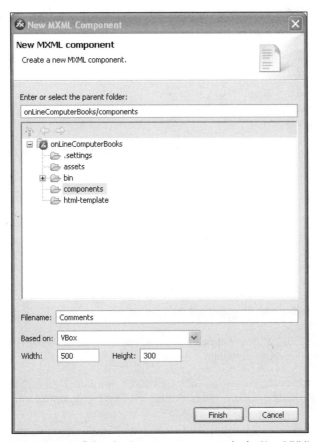

Figure 8-18. Defining the Comments component in the New MXML Component dialog box

7. Under the Label control, insert a FormItem container.

```
<?xml version="1.0" encoding="utf-8"?>
<mx:VBox xmlns:mx="http://www.adobe.com/2006/mxml" width="500"➥
  height="300">
  <mx:Form>
    <mx:Label text="Please Enter Your Rating and Comments➥
      About Our Books" />
    <mx:FormItem>

    </mx:FormItem>
  </mx:Form>
</mx:VBox>
```

As you've seen before, the label identifying the control does not get entered as text like you would in an XHTML design. Instead, in Flash and Flex forms, they are controlled by the container. For that reason, you need to give the FormItem container a label attribute.

8. For this first one, you will use Full Name.

```
<mx:FormItem label="Full Name">
```

9. Within the FormItem container, add a TextInput control and set the width to 250 characters.

```
<mx:FormItem label="Full Name">
   <mx:TextInput width="250" />
</mx:FormItem>
```

10. Just to see what is going on, switch over to Design view. Your screen should look similar to Figure 8-19.

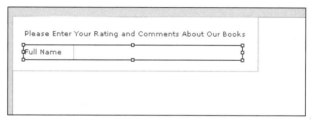

Figure 8-19. The Label and TextInput control

Notice how the label attribute appears to the left of the control. Again, it is all being controlled with the FormItem container.

11. Return to Source view—you will now build a new FormItem container. Give it the label attribute of Email, and put within it a TextInput control with a width of 250 pixels.

```
<mx:FormItem label="Email">
   <mx:TextInput width="250" />
</mx:FormItem>
```

12. Now you will build a similar structure that will allow users to enter the title of the book they are reviewing. Put the following underneath your Email FormItem:

```
<mx:FormItem label="Book Title">
   <mx:TextInput width="250" />
</mx:FormItem>
```

> *If you were actually designing a real website, you would probably use a ComboBox control or List control to give the user a list of books to select from. You have not seen that yet but will later on in the "BookCovers component" section.*

You now want users to enter their comments. For that, you will need to give them a larger area to work with. To accomplish that, the TextArea control works nicely.

13. Again, you need to use a FormItem container and give it the label of Please Enter Your Comments. Set the width of the TextArea control to 250:

```
<mx:FormItem label="Please Enter Your Comments">
   <mx:TextArea width="250" />
</mx:FormItem>
```

14. Switch over to Design view to preview the form, as shown in Figure 8-20.

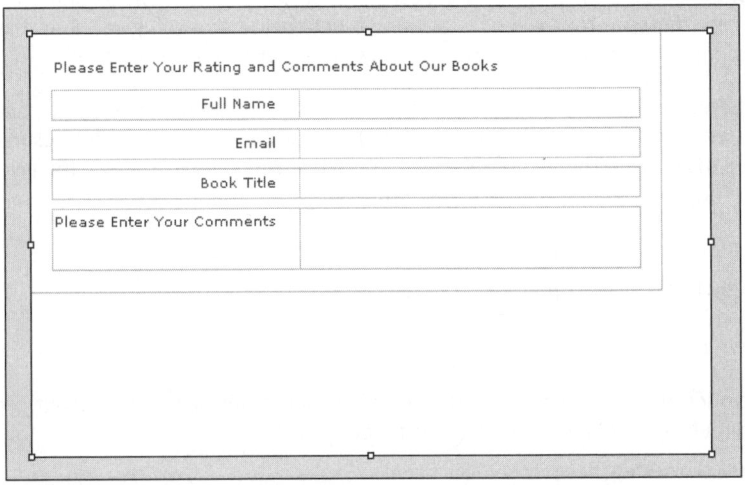

Figure 8-20. The partially completed form

Notice that the FormItem containers right-justify the labels and that each item on the form is in its own container. You don't need to be concerned about placement and alignment just yet.

You now want users to be able to rate books on a scale of 1 to 5. The NumericStepper control does this job nicely. You can give this control a minimum and maximum value. Users then just need to click the up or down arrow keys to set the value they want.

15. To achieve this, begin by switching back to Source view, setting up a new FormItem container, and giving it the label of Please Rate This Book.

16. Within the container, place a NumericStepper control with the attributes of minimum and maximum set to 1 and 5, respectively.

```
<mx:FormItem label="Please Rate This Book">
   <mx:NumericStepper minimum="1" maximum="5" />
</mx:FormItem>
```

17. Switch again to Design view. You will see the NumericStepper control, as shown in Figure 8-21. However, you cannot test it until you actually run the component from the main application, which you'll do in a bit.

Figure 8-21. The NumericStepper control

The final thing you want to do on this form is to create a Submit button and a Clear button. Initially, these buttons will not have any functionality. You will give them that a little further along in the process. However, initially, you have a small problem.

All of these controls are part of the larger VBox layout container. As you know, VBox arranges everything vertically. However, the FormItem container has an interesting attribute called direction. This attribute allows you to override the direction of the layout container for anything within that FormItem container.

18. Under the last FormItem, set up the following FormItem container:

```
<mx:FormItem direction="horizontal">

</mx:FormItem>
```

19. Notice that you didn't give it a label attribute. Instead, you will put the labels directly on the Button controls as follows:

```
<mx:FormItem direction="horizontal">
    <mx:Button label="Submit Your Comment" />
    <mx:Button label="Clear the Form" />
</mx:FormItem>
```

20. Test the form now—it should look like Figure 8-22.

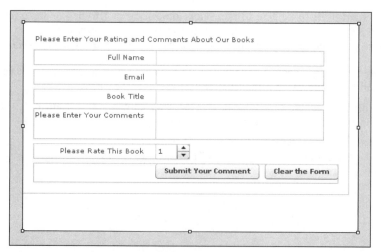

Figure 8-22. The finished comments form

Notice that the two new buttons are arranged horizontally and, by default, right-justified.

You are now finished with your form. The next step is to build a component to display your various book covers.

BookCovers component

To build the BookCovers component, which will display book covers, follow these steps:

1. As you have before, right-click the components folder in the Navigator pane and select New ➤ MXML Component.

2. Call this component BookCovers, and base it, as before, on the VBox container.

3. Set the width to 500 pixels. However, unlike before, delete the height setting. By doing this, the height of the component will adjust with content automatically. The completed dialog box should look like Figure 8-23.

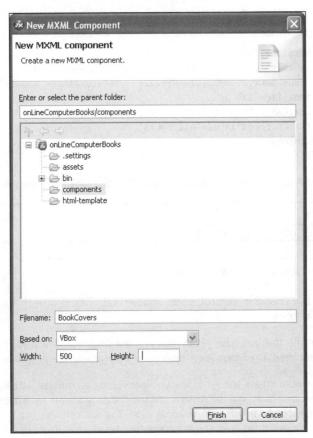

Figure 8-23. Defining the BookCovers component in the New MXML Component dialog box

4. Click Finish.

As you can see in Design view, the work area is nearly collapsed. You will fix that in a moment.

5. Switch to Source view and, within the VBox container, create an HBox container.

6. Give the new HBox container a backgroundColor attribute of #EE82EE. This is a light blue. Also, set the verticalAlignment attribute to middle. This will align graphics with a middle point. Finally, set fontSize to 12.

```
<?xml version="1.0" encoding="utf-8"?>
<mx:VBox xmlns:mx="http://www.adobe.com/2006/mxml" width="500">
    <mx:HBox backgroundColor="#EE82EE" verticalAlign="middle"➥
        fontSize="12" >

    </mx:HBox>
</mx:VBox>
```

7. Within the HBox container, place a Label control with the text Select the Books:.

8. Below that, place a CheckBox control with the label All Books.

```
<?xml version="1.0" encoding="utf-8"?>
<mx:VBox xmlns:mx="http://www.adobe.com/2006/mxml" width="500">
    <mx:HBox backgroundColor="#EE82EE" verticalAlign="middle"➥
        fontSize="12" >
        <mx:Label text="Select the Books:" />
        <mx:CheckBox label="All Books" />
    </mx:HBox>
</mx:VBox>
```

9. Test this functionality in the browser, and it should look like Figure 8-24.

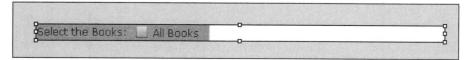

Figure 8-24. The Label and CheckBox controls

10. Under the CheckBox control, enter another Label control with the text Select Book Category.

One of the controls that you have yet to look at is the ComboBox, which you'll be adding to your component here. The ComboBox is essentially a menu within a drop box.

Normally, you would create the list in the ComboBox using an outside data source such as XML or web services, or even a database if you did it through some kind of server-side file such as those created by a PHP or Rails application. You will certainly see that in part 2 of this case study. However, for now, you are going to manually add items to this control. This will also give you a good chance to see some of the mechanics behind this control. You will be working through this part in a very step-by-step fashion. Please take your time.

11. Below the CheckBox control, create a ComboBox control.

```
<mx:HBox backgroundColor="#EE82EE" verticalAlign="middle"➥
    fontSize="12" >
    <mx:Label text="Select the Books:" />
    <mx:CheckBox label="All Books" />
    <mx:Label text="Select Book Category" />
    <mx:ComboBox>

    </mx:ComboBox>
</mx:HBox>
```

As you may recall from the discussion of XML in Chapter 6, many controls use an attribute called dataProvider. The dataProvider control links to the source of the data. You need this control when you are manually entering data, as you are doing here, or connecting to an outside data source. However, when manually entering data into a ComboBox control, you use the dataProvider not as an attribute, but as a container for data items.

12. The following code shows the syntax for doing this. Enter the code in bold.

```
<mx:HBox backgroundColor="#EE82EE" verticalAlign="middle"➥
    fontSize="12" >
    <mx:Label text="Select the Books:" />
    <mx:CheckBox label="All Books" />
     <mx:Label text="Select Book Category" />
    <mx:ComboBox>
        <mx:dataProvider>

        </mx:dataProvider>
    </mx:ComboBox>
</mx:HBox>
```

13. Again, referring to the previous discussion of XML, ActionScript holds the data in an ArrayCollection. However, because you are manually entering data into this control, you must explicitly tell ActionScript to use ArrayCollection by creating an ArrayCollection container, like so:

```
<mx:HBox backgroundColor="#EE82EE" verticalAlign="middle"➥
    fontSize="12" >
    <mx:Label text="Select the Books:" />
    <mx:CheckBox label="All Books" />
    <mx:Label text="Select Book Category" />
    <mx:ComboBox>
        <mx:dataProvider>
          <mx:ArrayCollection>

          </mx:ArrayCollection>
        </mx:dataProvider>
    </mx:ComboBox>
</mx:HBox>
```

8

Once you have all these mechanics set up, you must enter the items you want contained in the control as either Objects or Strings.

> As you will recall from earlier chapters, Strings are just a subclass of Objects. Since you are not using any of the real functionality of the String class, either type will work fine.

For purposes of this case study, you will use Strings.

14. You are going to create five items in the ComboBox control: Dreamweaver, Flash, Graphics, Web Design, and Other. You could add more, but for this example, you'll want to keep coding down to a minimum. Complete the ArrayCollection like so:

```
<mx:ComboBox>
    <mx:dataProvider>
        <mx:ArrayCollection>
            <mx:String>Dreamweaver</mx:String>
            <mx:String>Flash</mx:String>
            <mx:String>Graphics</mx:String>
            <mx:String>Web Design</mx:String>
            <mx:String>Other</mx:String>
        </mx:ArrayCollection>
    </mx:dataProvider>
</mx:ComboBox>
```

15. Look at your form now; it should look similar to Figure 8-25.

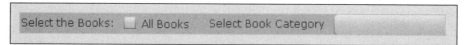

Figure 8-25. The completed search bar

Like the NumericStepper control you saw before, the ComboBox control will not work until you run it through the Application tags of the main application page (as a matter of fact, it doesn't even look like a combo box right now).

Now you'll add a Tile container to your component. You have had a brief look at using this type of container in Chapter 5; here you'll take a closer look at it.

The Tile container does just as it says: it creates a grid of square boxes to display a series of similar objects. In this case, it is perfect for displaying the 20 or so book covers you need to show.

16. If you are not there, return to the code in this component.

17. Under the closing HBox tag, create a Tile function.

```
</mx:HBox>
<mx:Tile>
```

```
        </mx:Tile>
      </mx:VBox>
```

I now have some good and bad news for you. The good news is that populating the Tile container is easy. The bad news is that you have a lot of code to enter because you are doing it manually. (But have no fear—I am coming to your rescue by providing a text file so you can copy and paste the code you want.)

All you need to do is to create a series of Image controls. In this exercise, you are going to use the images titled with -small. There are about 20 of them. However, you are going to go one step further here. You are going to give the images a click event that will call up another state, which you will be creating, called BookDetails. You will use this later on in the project.

You are doing this so that end users can click one of the tiled thumbnail book covers to bring up details about that book.

18. The code for each Image tag is as follows (with just the name of the image changing). Add this to your code:

```
<mx:Tile width="500">
    <mx:Image source="assets/andrew-small.jpg"↪
        click="currentState='BookDetails'" />
    <mx:Image source="assets/balkan-small.jpg"↪
        click="currentState='BookDetails'" />
    <mx:Image source="assets/besley-small.jpg"↪
        click="currentState='BookDetails'" />
    <mx:Image source="assets/briggs-small.jpg"↪
        click="currentState='BookDetails'" />
    <mx:Image source="assets/brown-small.jpg"↪
        click="currentState='BookDetails'" />
    <mx:Image source="assets/bryant-small.jpg"↪
        click="currentState='BookDetails'" />
    <mx:Image source="assets/budd-small.jpg"↪
        click="currentState='BookDetails'" />
    <mx:Image source="assets/burks-small.jpg"↪
        click="currentState='BookDetails'" />
    <mx:Image source="assets/donatis-small.jpg"↪
        click="currentState='BookDetails'" />
    <mx:Image source="assets/downs-small.jpg"↪
        click="currentState='BookDetails'" />
    <mx:Image source="assets/elbaga-small.jpg"↪
        click="currentState='BookDetails'" />
    <mx:Image source="assets/elst-small.jpg"↪
        click="currentState='BookDetails'" />
    <mx:Image source="assets/evans-small.jpg"↪
        click="currentState='BookDetails'" />
    <mx:Image source="assets/grannell-small.jpg"↪
        click="currentState='BookDetails'" />
    <mx:Image source="assets/green-small.jpg"↪
        click="currentState='BookDetails'" />
```

8

```
        <mx:Image source="assets/harkness-small.jpg"➥
           click="currentState='BookDetails'" />
        <mx:Image source="assets/jacobs-small.jpg"➥
           click="currentState='BookDetails'" />
        <mx:Image source="assets/keith-small.jpg"➥
           click="currentState='BookDetails'" />
        <mx:Image source="assets/kirkpatrick-small.jpg"➥
           click="currentState='BookDetails'" />
        <mx:Image source="assets/lifaros-small.jpg"➥
           click="currentState='BookDetails'" />
    </mx:Tile>
```

> As I mentioned, if you don't want to type all of the preceding lines of code, I have included a TXT file containing this code, `imageLinks.txt`, with the chapter's download files. You can copy and paste all of this code from there.

19. Take a quick look in Design view. Your screen should look something like Figure 8-26.

Figure 8-26. The finished BookCovers component

Now that you have the basic components built, you'll start to assemble them together.

Assembling the components

Let's return to the BooksMain application. You may recall that during the discussion of navigation containers in Chapter 5, I said that the ViewStack container was one of the easiest and most useful of containers to use. For that reason, you are going to use it here.

1. Right above the code for the home page, set up a ViewStack container. Because you are going to create a navigation bar from it, you will need to give it an id attribute. In this case, you will call it bookPages. You also want the container to automatically resize based on the content of the page called.

2. Cut the call to the BookHome component, already in the page, and paste it into the container. Your code should look as follows:

```
<?xml version="1.0" encoding="utf-8"?>
<mx:Application xmlns:mx="http://www.adobe.com/2006/mxml"➥
    layout="vertical" backgroundColor="#FFFFFF"➥
    xmlns:comp="components.*">
    <mx:Image source="assets/logo1.gif" />
    <mx:ViewStack id="bookPages" resizeToContent="true">
        <comp:BookHome height="50%" width="50%" label="Home" id="home" />
    </mx:ViewStack>
</mx:Application>
```

3. You also want to put the other components within the container—Comments and BookCovers. Because you want to build a navigator bar, you will need to do what you did for the BookHome component—give each call an id and a label attribute. You already know from earlier why you need to make the height and width 50%.

```
<?xml version="1.0" encoding="utf-8"?>
<mx:Application xmlns:mx="http://www.adobe.com/2006/mxml"➥
    layout="vertical" backgroundColor="#FFFFFF"➥
    xmlns:comp="components.*">
    <mx:Image source="assets/logo1.gif" />
    <mx:ViewStack id="bookPages" resizeToContent="true">
        <comp:BookHome height="50%" width="50%" label="Home" id="home" />
        <comp:Comments height="50%" width="50%"➥
            label="Comments" id="comments" />
        <comp:BookCovers height="50%" width="50%"➥
            label="Our Books" id="bookCovers" />
    </mx:ViewStack>
</mx:Application>
```

4. Your last step is to add a LinkBar control right under the Image tag. In this case, the dataProvider will be the id of the ViewStack.

```
<?xml version="1.0" encoding="utf-8"?>
<mx:Application xmlns:mx="http://www.adobe.com/2006/mxml"➥
    layout="vertical" backgroundColor="#FFFFFF"➥
    xmlns:comp="components.*">
```

8

```
<mx:Image source="assets/logo1.gif" />
<mx:LinkBar dataProvider="bookPages" />
<mx:ViewStack id="bookPages" resizeToContent="true">
    <comp:BookHome height="50%" width="50%" label="Home" id="home" />
    <comp:Comments height="50%" width="50%" label="Comments"➥
        id="comments" />
    <comp:BookCovers height="50%" width="50%" label="Our Books"➥
        id="bookCovers" />
</mx:ViewStack>
</mx:Application>
```

You are now ready to give your application an initial test.

5. Go ahead and save the main page, and then run it. The first thing that should come up is the home page, as shown in Figure 8-27.

Figure 8-27. Current view of the home page

6. Notice that the link bar picked up each of the `label` attributes of the component calls within the `ViewStack` navigation container.

7. Click the Comments link. Your display should now look like Figure 8-28.

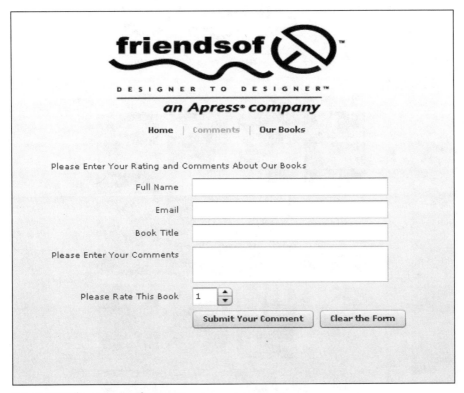

Figure 8-28. The comments form page

Notice that the `NumericStepper` control is now working, and you can set a number between 1 and 5 by either clicking the two arrow buttons or highlighting the field and typing in the number you want. If you try to put a number in that is larger than 5, the control will just default to 5.

The two buttons will not work yet. You will give them functionality in part 2 of this case study.

8. Click the Our Books link, and you will see your tiled book covers, as shown in Figure 8-29.

Figure 8-29. The Our Books page

Notice the ComboBox control now has the categories you created in it. While they do not have any functionality yet, you can click the control to see them, as shown in Figure 8-30.

Figure 8-30. The populated ComboBox control

9. Assume that you wanted the Our Books link to be the second selection in the navigation bar. All you need to do is go into the code and move the call to the component so that it is the second one.

```
<mx:ViewStack id="bookPages" resizeToContent="true">
    <comp:BookHome height="50%" width="50%" label="Home" id="home" />
    <comp:BookCovers height="50%" width="50%" label="Our Books"➥
        id="bookCovers" />
    <comp:Comments height="50%" width="50%" label="Comments"➥
        id="comments" />
</mx:ViewStack>
```

10. Close the existing browser session and rerun the application. You will see that the navigation has been rearranged, as shown in Figure 8-31.

Figure 8-31. The rearranged LinkBar component

By now your wow factor should be high. However, there is one little design wrinkle we need to discuss here.

If you look at your application carefully, you will notice that it is divided into three sections: the logo image, the LinkBar control, and the ViewStack container. Their positioning is being automatically handled by the layout attribute of the Application container. At present, it is vertical, and, as you can see, the three sections are arranged from top to bottom.

Using a layout such as vertical or horizontal has a few drawbacks. First of all, it limits your ability to arrange the application the way you may need to. In addition, because Flex needs to perform calculations to decide on the position of the parts each time the page is called, performance can be hurt. For that reason, there is a strong argument in favor of setting the `layout` attribute to `absolute` and using either Design view or ActionScript to position the various parts of your page.

11. Set the `layout` attribute to `absolute`.

```
<mx:Application xmlns:mx="http://www.adobe.com/2006/mxml"➥
    layout="absolute" backgroundColor="#FFFFFF"➥
    xmlns:comp="components.*">
```

12. Switch to Design view. Your screen should look something like Figure 8-32.

If your file looks a little different from Figure 8-32, after changing the layout *attribute to* absolute, *don't worry about it. You will be manually repositioning everything in a few moments.*

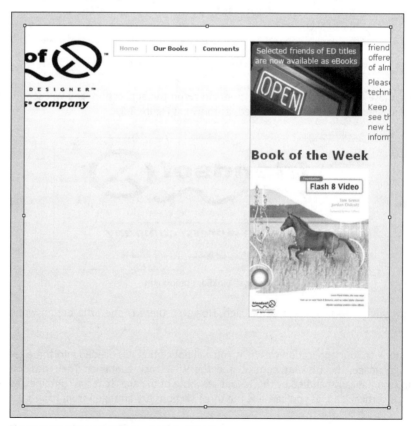

Figure 8-32. The page with an absolute layout

As you can see, it is not a pretty sight (or site).

There are two possible approaches you can take to fix this. You can either go into your code and give each of the three parts an x and y attribute, or you can simply drag in Design view to manually arrange the parts.

13. Use whichever approach you want to achieve approximately the results shown in Figure 8-33.

Figure 8-33. The repositioned components

Notice that the LinkBar and ViewStack sections appear a bit off to the left. You do this to make room for the shopping cart you will soon be building.

The positions I used to achieve the layout you see in Figure 8-33 are as follows:

- Logo image: x = "357", y = "10"
- LinkBar: x = "105", y="151"
- ViewStack container: x = "118", y="185"

14. Finally, in the Application tag, set both the width and height attributes to 100%. This will give you room to place your shopping cart shortly.

```
<?xml version="1.0" encoding="utf-8"?>
<mx:Application xmlns:mx="http://www.adobe.com/2006/mxml"➡
    height="100%" width="100%" layout="absolute"➡
    backgroundColor="#FFFFFF" xmlns:comp="components.*">
    <mx:Image source="assets/logo1.gif"  x="357" y="10"/>
    <mx:LinkBar dataProvider="bookPages"  x="105" y="151"/>
    <mx:ViewStack id="bookPages" resizeToContent="true" x="118" y="185">
        <comp:BookHome height="50%" width="50%" label="Home" id="home" />
        <comp:BookCovers height="50%" width="50%"➡
          label="Our Books" id="bookCovers" />
        <comp:Comments height="50%" width="50%"➡
          label="Comments" id="comments" />
    </mx:ViewStack>
</mx:Application>
```

Your next step will be to build a shopping cart in order for users to be able to purchase the books they see.

BookCart component

You are now going to build the BookCart component, which will be the shopping cart feature for your site. Again, you will not be giving it a lot of functionality till you get to part 2 of this case study later on in the book. However, you will be using states a bit here.

1. As you have done with building previous components, right-click the components folder in the Navigator pane and select New ➤ MXML Component.

2. Call the component BookCart, base it on the Canvas container, and specify no height or width, as shown in Figure 8-34.

3. Click Finish.

4. Within this Canvas container, add a Panel container. You will give it an id attribute of bookCart, a width of 250, and a layout of vertical.

```
<?xml version="1.0" encoding="utf-8"?>
<mx:Canvas xmlns:mx="http://www.adobe.com/2006/mxml">
    <mx:Panel id="bookCart" width="250" layout="vertical">

    </mx:Panel>
</mx:Canvas>
```

5. You need to set up a temporary holding place that you can use later on to give you a count of the number of items on your cart. In part 2 of the case study, you are going to replace information in the label with variables provided by ActionScript. For now, add the following inside your Panel container:

```
<mx:Label text="There are 0 items in your cart" />
```

6. You will also add a button that will allow users see the details of the books in their shopping carts later on.

```
<mx:Button x="5" y="30" label="See the cart details" />
```

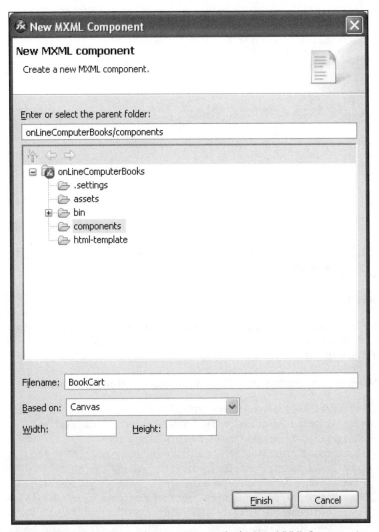

Figure 8-34. Defining the BookCart component in the New MXML Component dialog box

7. Switch to Design view; your screen should look something like Figure 8-35.

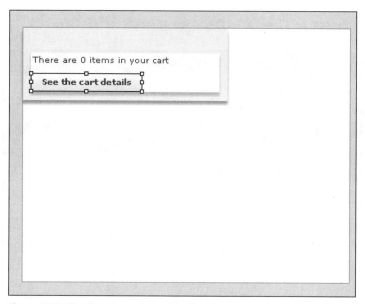

Figure 8-35. The shopping cart panel in the component

8. Save the component and return to the BooksMain window.

You need to put your BookCart component onto your BooksMain page. Placement in the code is not critical as long as it is not in the ViewStack container. The reason why is, as with the logo and link bar, you want to see the shopping cart at all times.

9. Make a call as you have with the other components on the page.

```
<?xml version="1.0" encoding="utf-8"?>
<mx:Application xmlns:mx="http://www.adobe.com/2006/mxml"➥
    height="100%" width="100%" layout="absolute"➥
    backgroundColor="#FFFFFF" xmlns:comp="components.*">
    <mx:Image source="assets/logo1.gif"   x="357" y="10"/>
    <mx:LinkBar dataProvider="bookPages"   x="105" y="151"/>
    <mx:ViewStack id="bookPages" resizeToContent="true" x="118" y="185">
        <comp:BookHome height="50%" width="50%" label="Home" id="home" />
        <comp:BookCovers height="50%" width="50%" label="Our Books"➥
            id="bookCovers" />
        <comp:Comments height="50%" width="50%" label="Comments"➥
            id="comments" />
    </mx:ViewStack>
    <comp:BookCart />
</mx:Application>
```

Again, like before, you may find it a little easier to position the component in Design view.

10. Switch to Design view and move your cart to the right of the ViewStack container. In this example, its x-position is 790 and its y-position is 290. If yours is slightly different, it is not critical, but your page should look something like Figure 8-36.

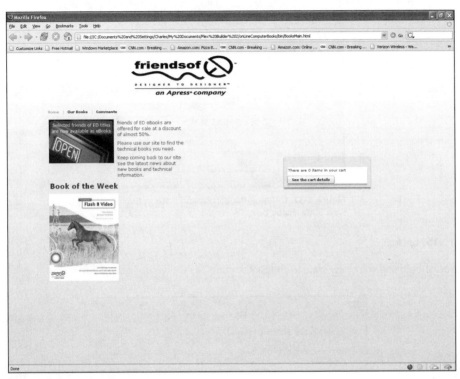

Figure 8-36. The shopping cart added

Now that you have the shopping cart in place, you want to develop a state for it so that it can expand to show details.

You have already seen that as soon as you update a component, everything that uses that component updates.

11. Return to BookCart.mxml.

12. Go into Source view and add a click event to the Button control. As you have done in the state exercises in Chapter 7, set the currentState to 'cartExpand'. (Don't forget to use single quotes around the name of the state.)

```
<?xml version="1.0" encoding="utf-8"?>
<mx:Canvas xmlns:mx="http://www.adobe.com/2006/mxml">
    <mx:Panel id="bookCart" width="250" layout="vertical">
        <mx:Label text="There are 0 items in your cart" />
        <mx:Button x="5" y="30" label="See the cart details"➥
            click="currentState='cartExpand'" />
    </mx:Panel>
</mx:Canvas>
```

13. Switch to Design view and create a new state by either clicking the New State button or right-clicking in the States window.

14. As you have probably figured out already, you are going to call the state cartExpand, so specify the settings in the New State dialog box as shown in Figure 8-37.

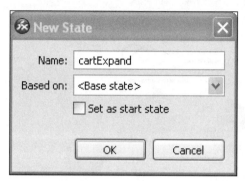

Figure 8-37. Defining the cartExpand state in the New State dialog box

15. Click OK.

You should see your new state in the States panel, as shown in Figure 8-38.

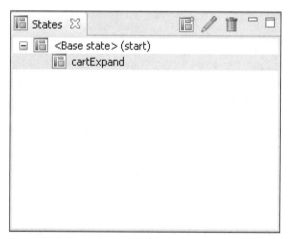

Figure 8-38. The States panel with the new state

Follow these steps carefully now:

16. Make sure that cartExpand is selected in the States panel.

17. Select the Panel container itself and, using the Flex Properties panel, change the height to 500, so that the Panel container appears as shown in Figure 8-39.

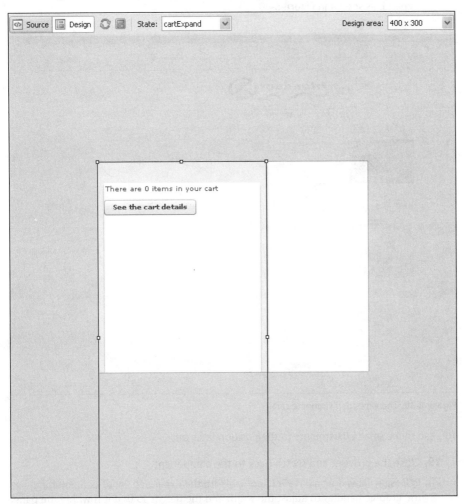

Figure 8-39. The expanded Panel container

> *The* Panel *container will look as though it is overflowing the* Canvas *container. But recall earlier that you didn't give the container a* height *attribute. As a result, it will expand when the* Panel *container expands.*

18. If you want to give this a quick test, save your work, switch back to BooksMain, and run the application. When you click the button in the cart, you should see it expand, as shown in Figure 8-40.

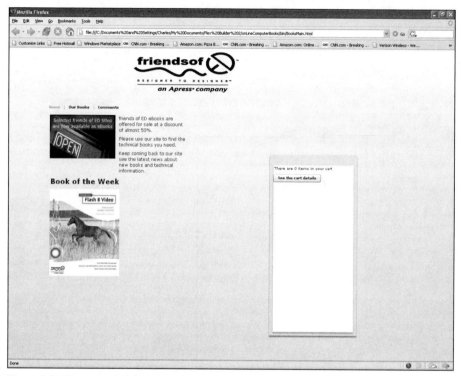

Figure 8-40. The expanded shopping cart

You can make small adjustments to the position later on.

19. Close the browser and switch back to the component.

20. In Design view, drag a DataGrid control into the expanded Panel container and use the graphic handles to adjust the width and the height so that it is within the panel and about three-quarters of the height or so. Leave enough room to add another button at the bottom of the panel. The component should look something like Figure 8-41.

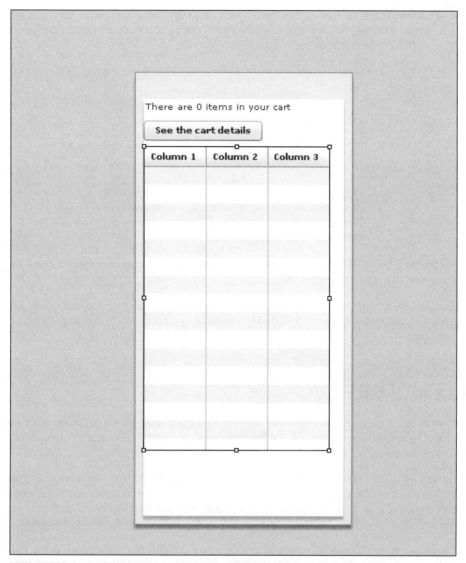

Figure 8-41. The expanded Panel container with the DataGrid control added

> *If you are having trouble seeing the expanded panel, try choosing* Fit to content *from the* Design area *drop-down menu.*

21. Now add a Button control to the bottom of the expanded Panel container, as shown in Figure 8-42. Give it a label attribute of Click to Checkout and an id attribute of checkOut.

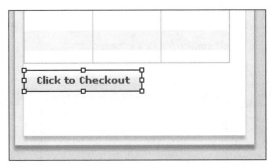

Figure 8-42. The checkOut Button control

For the time being, you are not going to add any events to the Button control. You will be doing that in part 2 of the case study when you hook everything up to a data source.

You are now through with the BookCart component, so you can save and close it. If you want, you can return to the BooksMain file and run your application to test your shopping cart feature.

Flex and CSS

Most modern web designers have worked with Cascading Style Sheets (CSS). As a matter of fact, good XHTML design calls for the separation of content, presentation, and structure, as follows:

In modern XHTML and CSS web design, XHTML handles the structure of a website. The content is either static, contained within the XHTML, or handled by a data source of some sort. Finally, the look of the site (the background color and images, colors, fonts, and so on) are handled by CSS. This dramatically increases the site's flexibility and maintainability.

I am about to give you good news without any corresponding bad news: you can use CSS in Flex. As a matter of fact, you can use CSS two ways: you can create an external style sheet like you would do for most site designs, or you can use the Style class to define the styles internally.

You will be using the latter technique here.

While knowledge and experience may teach me differently later on, it is my opinion that the use of CSS in Flex will be limited for reasons you shall see momentarily. For instance, CSS is frequently used to position the various objects within an XHTML page. As you have seen, you can position items within a Flex application very easily without using CSS. Please do not take this comment to mean that you won't want to use CSS at all. As you will soon see, it has some handy uses. For that reason, if you have never worked with CSS before, you will want to develop a working knowledge of the mechanics of it.

It is well beyond the scope of this book to enter into a lengthy discussion about the fundamentals of CSS design and structure. For the basics, pick up a copy of *Beginning CSS Web Development: From Novice to Professional* by Simon Collison (Apress, 2006). For more advanced techniques, check out *CSS Mastery: Advanced Web Standards Solutions* by Andy Budd et al. (friends of ED, 2006).

Keeping this in mind, let's review some basic terminology and mechanics of CSS.

CSS: The basics

If you have ever developed an XHTML page, you probably noticed that the page might look slightly different depending on the web browser it is being viewed in. For instance, a line in the page designated as Heading 1 (<h1>) may look a little smaller in Internet Explorer than in Firefox. The reason for this is that each browser has a set of built-in rules on how to present the various parts of the XHTML document.

Simply put, a Cascading Style Sheet overrides these browser rules by telling the browser that if you have an <h1> tag, for example, use the font, color, size, and so on of the designer's designation. That way, there is greater consistency of appearance within various browsers.

Keeping this in mind, a Cascading Style Sheet is simply a collection of rules telling the browser how the various elements of the XHTML document should look. These rules, however, must have a precise syntax. Let's take a look at that syntax here:

```
h1 {color:red}
```

The h1 part of this rule is called the **selector**—this is the element you are applying the rule to. The {color:red} portion is called the **declaration**.

Within the declaration, the word *color* is called the **property**, and the *red* designation is the **value** you are assigning to that property.

Within a declaration, you could set multiple properties as follows:

```
h1 {
  color:red;
  font:Arial;
  font-style:Italic
  text-align:center
}
```

I think what this rule does is pretty self-explanatory.

You could also assign the same rule to multiple elements as follows:

```
h1, h2, h3 {color:red}
```

289

Of course, this is saying that any time you have an <h1>, <h2>, or <h3> element, color the text red.

So far, you have only seen these rules applied to a specific tag. However, there is another type of rule called a **class rule**. A class rule begins with a dot and any name that you would want. For instance:

```
.myStyle {color:red}
```

The advantage of a class rule is that it can be applied anywhere at any time.

So, where do you put these rules?

You can put CSS rules in one of three places: in a text document that can be referenced by any page in the site, in the heading of a particular page where the rules would apply only to that page, or on a specific line where the rules would only apply to that line of markup. If you put a rule in an external file, this is called a **linked** or **external** stylesheet; if that rule is called within the heading of a particular document, this is called an **embedded** stylesheet. A rule on a particular line is called an **in-line** style.

Embedded styles get priority over the rules in external styles, and in-line styles get priority over everything else. So if you had an external CSS that had

```
h1{color:red}
```

and an embedded style that had

```
h1{color:blue}
```

the latter would override the former, so you would see blue headings, not red.

By now, it should be becoming obvious why I feel CSS will have limited use in Flex.

Flex does not use the browser except to call the Flash Player. So, because Flex applications display within the Flash Player (as SWF files), the issues regarding browser differences are simply not there.

Instead, you can use CSS to handle some general formatting issues that might apply to all of the components of your application. Let's take a look at how you would do this.

Working with CSS in Flex

Like everything else in Flex, you define a style (or call a style) with a class file. In this case, the class file would be created with the following:

```
<mx:Style>

</mx:Style>
```

The Style class has an attribute called source that can reference an external CSS file.

```
<mx:Style source="assets/myStyle.css">
```

You could embed a class rule much the same way you would as shown previously.

```
<mx:Style>
   .myStyle
   {
      font:Arial;
      font-style:italic;
   }
```

Later on, you could apply this to a component, say a Button, as follows:

```
<mx:Button styleName="myStyle">
```

The advantage of this is that if you apply the style to 10 different buttons, and you need to change the font from one type to another, you just change it in the one place and everything referencing it is automatically updated.

As you will see in your project shortly, you can replace the concept of a selector with a component name. As an example:

```
<mx:Style>
   ComboBox
   {
       selection-color:#32cd32
   }
</mx:Style>
```

Here, instead of using tag names for the selector, like h1, h2, body, and so on, you use the component name. That way, every time the component is used, in this case ComboBox, that style is applied.

The next logical question you might ask is what properties of a component can you set a style for.

The answer for that can be found, as you may have guessed, in the ActionScript Language Reference.

Let's open the documentation for the ComboBox class.

If you scroll down, you will find a section called Styles. These are the properties you can set in CSS. Figure 8-43 shows the selectionColor style.

rollOverColor	Type: uint Format: Color CSS Inheritance: yes The rollOverColor of the drop-down list.	ComboBox
selectionColor	Type: uint Format: Color CSS Inheritance: yes The selectionColor of the drop-down list.	ComboBox
selectionDuration	Type: uint Format: Time CSS Inheritance: no The selectionDuration of the drop-down list. The default value is 250.	ComboBox

Figure 8-43. The selectionColor style

You may have noticed that the preceding example uses selection-color. But the documentation calls for selectionColor.

ActionScript supports original CSS syntax, as well as its own proprietary syntax. That way, if you are already an experienced CSS user, you can use the syntax you know and love. But I strongly suggest that you get used to ActionScript syntax. History has shown, for most development environments, what is transitional today is mandatory tomorrow. By using the proper syntax now, you may save yourself a ton of work up the road.

It is now time to use all of this knowledge in your project.

1. Right under the Application tag in BooksMain.mxml, enter a Style tag, as follows:

```
<?xml version="1.0" encoding="utf-8"?>
<mx:Application xmlns:mx="http://www.adobe.com/2006/mxml"➥
    height="100%" width="100%" layout="absolute"➥
    backgroundColor="#FFFFFF" xmlns:comp="components.*">
    <mx:Style>

    </mx:Style>
    <mx:Image source="assets/logo1.gif"  x="357" y="10"/>
```

> The Style class has a property called source. You would use that if you were using an external CSS file.

2. Assume that you want the selections in the ComboBox control to be lime-green. You can use syntax very similar to what you may be used to working with in standard CSS. Add the following to your code:

```
<mx:Style>
    ComboBox
    {
        selectionColor:#32cd32
    }
</mx:Style>
```

3. Save and test the application. Switch to the Our Books page and click a selection in the ComboBox control. It should come up as the color you set.

4. What about if you want to change the color of all text to dark blue? You can define a global style to set the color as follows. Go ahead and add the following:

```
<mx:Style>
    ComboBox
    {
        selectionColor:#32cd32
    }
    global
    {
        color:#00008b
    }
</mx:Style>
```

This requires a short explanation. The global designation means just what it says: apply everything within the curly braces to all MXML files associated with this project.

> *"All files associated with a project"* means all files being called within the Application *tags of the main MXML file.*

The color property is the ActionScript syntax for the CSS designation of font-color.

> *Although I said earlier that some of the CSS syntax can be used, I have found that* font-color *does not always work correctly. Again, you would be well served to use the ActionScript syntax consistently throughout your applications.*

If you now run the application, all of your fonts should come up with the color specified.

I will be giving you an occasional look at more CSS as you move through the rest of this book

Summary

This completes part 1 of the case study. In this part, all you did was set up the basic structures. When you get to part 2, after you learn a few more concepts, you will make the site a bit more functional. You will begin with a short introduction to the Repeater control.

8

Place Book Title Here	Problems ⊠ Consc	1 XML for Flash
Add to Cart	1 error, 0 warnings, 0 inf	**Add to Cart**
Place Book Title Here	Description	2 ActionScript for Animation
Add to Cart	⊗ 1067: Implicit coercic	**Add to Cart**
Place Book Title Here		3 Foundation Flash 8 Video
Add to Cart		**Add to Cart**

In the last chapter, you did a tremendous amount of work setting up a little technical book site. However, as I stated at the end of the last chapter, that was only half of the project. The hard-wiring of the project is coming in the next chapter.

In this chapter, I am going to introduce you to what is, in my opinion, one of the most powerful components of Flex: Repeater. This component ties into a data source and will repeat whatever structures are inside of it for each instance of data.

As an example, let's say you want a button labeled "Add (name of book) to cart" in your e-commerce application. You could use the Repeater component for each book that comes up to add a button and add the name of that book to an array. You may think that this sounds like a lot of extra effort if you were selling only 5 books, say—but what if you had 300 books, and the books kept changing every week? The Repeater code could stay the same and generate all the buttons for you dynamically, no matter how many books were in the data source and how often they changed.

In this chapter, you will

- Learn about the Repeater component.
- Pass data with the Repeater component.
- Create an event using the Repeater component.

This chapter will be a relatively short one compared to the last chapter. But the information in it will be essential to complete the project you started in the last chapter.

Understanding the Repeater component

When you use the Repeater component, what you are doing is creating an MXML structure that will repeat for each record in the data source. If you are a little confused as to what I mean by that, it will become abundantly clear in just a few minutes. Before you get started, however, you need to do a little bit of housekeeping.

1. In order to have some data to work with, you will keep it simple. Create a new mxml file and create a short data structure using the Model tag under the Application tag:

```
<mx:Model id="bookData">
  <books>
    <bookName>XML for Flash</bookName>
    <bookName>ActionScript for Animation</bookName>
    <bookName>Foundation Flash 8 Video</bookName>
  </books>
</mx:Model>
```

Recall from the discussion of XML in Chapter 6 that Flex works best by converting XML data to an ArrayCollection. Even though you used the Model tag above, you created an XML structure within it to structure the data. So you need to convert the data to an ArrayCollection.

2. Do this by adding the following code underneath the Model tag you just defined.

```
<mx:ArrayCollection id="bookArray" source="{bookData.bookName}" />
```

In this case, the source is going to be the repeating node, bookName, of the Model tag bookData. You don't need mention the root, books, at all. Since you are referring to another MXML structure, you are enclosing the source, in addition to the quotes, in curly braces, {}.

Now that the data is structured and converted into an ArrayCollection, you are ready to start working with the Repeater component.

3. Create a Repeater structure using the ArrayCollection, bookArray, as the dataProvider. You will give the Repeater component an ID of bookRepeater. Place it right underneath the ArrayCollection you just defined.

```
<mx:ArrayCollection id="bookArray" source="{bookData.bookName}" />
<mx:Repeater id="bookRepeater" dataProvider="{bookArray}">

</mx:Repeater>
```

Once the Repeater component is set up, all you need to do is decide what you want to do within it. Let's start off with a very simple example.

4. Within the Repeater structure, add a Label control and give it the text attribute of "Place Book Title Here".

```
<mx:Repeater id="bookRepeater" dataProvider="{bookArray}">
    <mx:Label text="Place Book Title Here" />
</mx:Repeater>
```

If you run the code now, you may not see proper results. The reason for this is a concept you have already encountered several times: the layout attribute of the Application tag. If it is set to absolute, you would need to set the positions yourself. However, by changing it to vertical, all should work out fine.

Your finished code should look as follows:

```
<?xml version="1.0" encoding="utf-8"?>
<mx:Application xmlns:mx="http://www.adobe.com/2006/mxml"↩
    layout="vertical">
    <mx:Model id="bookData">
        <books>
            <bookName>XML for Flash</bookName>
            <bookName>ActionScript for Animation</bookName>
            <bookName>Foundation Flash 8 Video</bookName>
        </books>
    </mx:Model>

    <mx:ArrayCollection id="bookArray" source="{bookData.bookName}" />
    <mx:Repeater id="bookRepeater" dataProvider="{bookArray}">
```

9

```
    <mx:Label text="Place Book Title Here" />
</mx:Repeater>

</mx:Application>
```

5. Go ahead and save your code and run it. Your results should look like Figure 9-1.

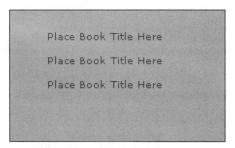

Figure 9-1. The Repeater component

You can see that the Label control, located inside of the Repeater component, repeats for each record (in this case, three times).

6. Take this out one step further and add a Button control with the label attribute set to Add to Cart. Add it right below the Label control.

```
<mx:ArrayCollection id="bookArray" source="{bookData.bookName}" />
<mx:Repeater id="bookRepeater" dataProvider="{bookArray}">
    <mx:Label text="Place Book Title Here" />
    <mx:Button label="Add to Cart" />
</mx:Repeater>
```

7. Run your code now, and you should see something similar to Figure 9-2.

Figure 9-2. The Repeater component with a Button control added

Quite obviously, you don't want your finished label to say Place Book Title Here. You need to do a bit of coding to fix that.

Passing data in a Repeater component

Each time the Repeater component creates a new repetition, the data that is causing the repetition is a property called the currentItem. So, in this case, the currentItem would be the bookName data.

1. Make a slight adjustment to the text attribute of the Label control as follows:

```
<mx:Label text="{bookRepeater.currentItem}" />
```

Here, the Label control is making a call back to the Repeater component. It is asking that Repeater what the currentItem is. The Repeater component is then returning the data in the currentItem back to the caller, which in this case is the text attribute of the Label control.

2. Save and run the code after making the change to the Label component. Your results should look similar to Figure 9-3.

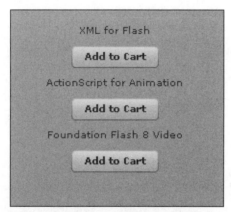

Figure 9-3. The data added to the Label control

There is also a useful property called currentIndex that returns the ArrayCollection position of the currentItem. This can be helpful when you want to number something.

3. Next you'll try creating a slight concatenation in the Label's text attribute. Make the following change:

```
<mx:Label►
    text="{bookRepeater.currentIndex}{bookRepeater.currentItem}" />
```

9

299

Notice that, unlike programming languages such as ActionScript, C++, Java, and so on, you don't need to set up a concatenation using the + character. In MXML, all you need to do is make the two calls and put a space between them.

4. Save and run the application. Your screen should look similar to Figure 9-4.

Figure 9-4. The Repeater component with numbering added

Whoops! Remember that arrays begin with the number 0. If you were running this application, I am sure you wouldn't want to see something numbered as 0.

5. This problem is easily remedied as follows:

```
<mx:Label➡
    text="{bookRepeater.currentIndex + 1} {bookRepeater.currentItem}" />
```

6. Try running the application again—Figure 9-5 shows the problem fixed.

Figure 9-5. The fixed numbering in the Repeater component

I am sure that, by now, you have figured out how this is all going to fit into the project you started in the last chapter. You are going to select a book, click a button to add it to the cart, and then pass the necessary data to the shopping cart component.

You are going to see the mechanics in a somewhat simplified form here.

The Button class, as well as many of the classes involving form items, has a method (not a property) called getRepeaterItem().

If you open the ActionScript Language Reference, go to the Button class documentation, and scroll down the methods, you will find getRepeaterItem() (see Figure 9-6).

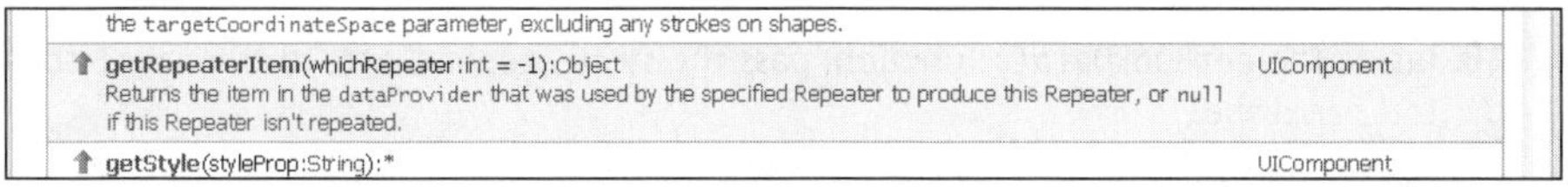

the targetCoordinateSpace parameter, excluding any strokes on shapes.

⬆ **getRepeaterItem**(whichRepeater:int = -1):Object   UIComponent
Returns the item in the dataProvider that was used by the specified Repeater to produce this Repeater, or null
if this Repeater isn't repeated.

⬆ **getStyle**(styleProp:String):*   UIComponent

Figure 9-6. The getRepeaterItem() method documentation

You have read about the Event Object Model already and have seen numerous examples.

As a quick review, the property event.target returns who generated the event. But you want to go one step further and not only return the name of who generated the event, but the currentItem of the Repeater component. Let's walk this through step by step.

7. Begin by creating a click event for the Button control. The event will call a method, which you have yet to create, called getBookData. You will pass the click event to the method along with the target and the results of the getRepeaterItem() method.

```
<mx:Button label="Add to Cart"➡
    click="getBookData(event.target.getRepeaterItem())" />
```

If you save your code, you will get a message in the Problems pane that getBookData() does not exist yet. You can ignore that for now because you are about to create this function.

8. Under the Application tag, as before, create a script block for ActionScript.

```
<?xml version="1.0" encoding="utf-8"?>
<mx:Application xmlns:mx="http://www.adobe.com/2006/mxml"➡
    layout="vertical">
<mx:Script>
    <![CDATA[

    ]]>
</mx:Script>
```

9. You have written event handlers before. In this case, the information sent by the getRepeaterItem() method is of type String. For this example, pass the information with the parameter repeatData as follows:

```
<mx:Script>
    <![CDATA[
        private function getBookData(repeatData:String):void
        {

        }
    ]]>
</mx:Script>
```

9

For purposes of this exercise, you are going to pass the data to a Label control outside of the Repeater component. You haven't created this Label control yet. But, when you do, it will be called nameLabel.

10. Inside the getBookData() function, pass the string, repeatData, to the Label control nameLabel.

```
<mx:Script>
  <![CDATA[
    private function getBookData(repeatData:String):void
    {
        nameLabel.text = repeatData;
    }
  ]]>
</mx:Script>
```

11. Under the Repeater structure, create a Label control called nameLabel as follows:

```
    </mx:Repeater>
    <mx:Label id="nameLabel" />
</mx:Application>
```

12. Save your code; there should be no errors now. The complete code is as follows:

```
<?xml version="1.0" encoding="utf-8"?>
<mx:Application xmlns:mx="http://www.adobe.com/2006/mxml"➥
    layout="vertical">
<mx:Script>
  <![CDATA[
    private function getBookData(repeatData:String):void
    {
        nameLabel.text = repeatData;
    }
  ]]>
</mx:Script>
    <mx:Model id="bookData">
        <books>
            <bookName>XML for Flash</bookName>
            <bookName>ActionScript for Animation</bookName>
            <bookName>Foundation Flash 8 Video</bookName>
        </books>
    </mx:Model>

    <mx:ArrayCollection id="bookArray" source="{bookData.bookName}" />
    <mx:Repeater id="bookRepeater" dataProvider="{bookArray}">
        <mx:Label➥
            text="{bookRepeater.currentIndex + 1}➥
            {bookRepeater.currentItem}" />
        <mx:Button label="Add to Cart"➥
            click="getBookData(event.target.getRepeaterItem())" />
```

```
        </mx:Repeater>
        <mx:Label id="nameLabel" />
    </mx:Application>
```

13. Save and run the application. You should see the `Label` control reflect the book title when you click any of the three buttons (see Figure 9-7).

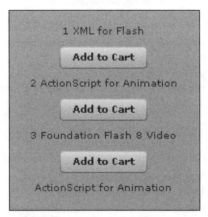

Figure 9-7. The new Label control populated

Based on this, I hope you are starting to see how data will be passed to the shopping cart component in your project. As you have seen in the past examples, there are several different ways you could configure the code to accomplish the same results and, in the second part of the case study, you will see some of those variations.

You are now going to turn your attention to bringing in your data from an XML file. As you will see, this will just be a variation on a theme.

Using XML data

In this section, you will pull your data from an XML file.

Inside the assets folder of your downloaded project files, you have an XML file called books.xml. You first saw this file in Chapter 6.

```xml
<?xml version="1.0" encoding="iso-8859-1"?>

<books>
    <stock>
        <name>The Picasso Code</name>
        <author>Dan Blue</author>
        <category>Fiction</category>
        <description>Cubist paintings reveal a secret➡
            society of people who really look like that</description>
```

```
      </stock>
      <stock>
        <name>Here With the Wind</name>
         <author>Margaret Middle</author>
         <category>Fiction</category>
         <description>In this edition, nobody in the south➡
            really gives a damn</description>
      </stock>
      <stock>
        <name>Harry Potluck and the Chamber of Money</name>
         <author>J.K. Roughly</author>
         <category>Fiction</category>
         <description>Young wizard finds the real pot➡
            of gold and retires</description>
      </stock>
      <stock>
        <name>No Expectations</name>
         <author>Chuck Dickens</author>
         <category>Fiction</category>
         <description>Dickens finally reveals what he really thinks➡
            of people</description>
      </stock>
      <stock>
        <name>Atlas Stretched</name>
         <author>Ann Rind</author>
         <category>Fiction</category>
         <description>Great inventors finally just take the money➡
            and run</description>
      </stock>
      <stock>
        <name>Recycling Software</name>
         <author>Big Gates</author>
         <category>Nonfiction</category>
         <description>How to just change the name and interface of the➡
            same old software and sell it as new</description>
      </stock>
      <stock>
        <name>Make Tons of Money</name>
         <author>Donald Rump</author>
         <category>Nonfiction</category>
         <description>Rump explains how he became a billionaire while➡
            constantly declaring bankruptcy</description>
      </stock>
      <stock>
        <name>How to Win Enemies and Lose Friends</name>
         <author>Dale Crochety</author>
         <category>Nonfiction</category>
```

```
            <description>The ultimate how-to book for people who want to➡
                stay loners</description>
        </stock>
        <stock>
            <name>My Lies</name>
            <author>Swill Clinton</author>
            <category>Nonfiction</category>
            <description>This former American president tries to define➡
                what a lie is</description>
        </stock>
        <stock>
            <name>The Complete History of the World</name>
            <author>David McClutz</author>
            <category>Nonfiction</category>
            <description>McClutz gives you the entire history of all➡
                civilization in less than 300 pages</description>
        </stock>
    </books>
```

1. Since you are bringing your data in from this XML file, you no longer need the Model tag and its contents. So go ahead and delete it. However, remember the name you gave it: bookData. That will save you some programming later on.

2. As you may remember from Chapter 6, you need to use the HTTPService class to call the XML file. In the place of the original Model tag, put an HTTPService tag, give it an id attribute of bookData, and make the URL assets/books.xml.

```
<mx:HTTPService id="bookData" url="assets/books.xml" />
```

3. You will need to adjust the dataProvider attribute of the Repeater component to reflect the new source. Recall from Chapter 6 that you need to use the lastResult property to build the data objects and keep them updated. In addition, you need to drill down the nodes of the XML file to get to the data you need.

```
<mx:Repeater id="bookRepeater"➡
    dataProvider="{bookData.lastResult.books.stock}">
```

4. Since HTTPService automatically creates the ArrayCollection, you no longer need ArrayCollection in your code. So go ahead and delete the ArrayCollection tag.

Finally, an HTTPService does not happen automatically as soon as the application is run. There must be an event that triggers it. While you can use any event, the common practice is to place a creationComplete event in the Application tag that instructs the HTTPService to send the request for data to the XML file.

5. Add the following to the Application tag:

```
<mx:Application xmlns:mx=http://www.adobe.com/2006/mxml➡
    layout="vertical" creationComplete="bookData.send()">
```

9

Since you made quite a few changes, please take a moment and review your completed code against the code shown here:

```
<?xml version="1.0" encoding="utf-8"?>
<mx:Application xmlns:mx="http://www.adobe.com/2006/mxml"➥
    layout="vertical" creationComplete="bookData.send()">
<mx:Script>
    <![CDATA[
        private function getBookData(repeatData:String):void
        {
            nameLabel.text = repeatData;
        }
    ]]>
</mx:Script>
    <mx:HTTPService id="bookData" url="assets/books.xml" />

    <mx:Repeater id="bookRepeater"➥
        dataProvider="{bookData.lastResult.books.stock}">
        <mx:Label➥
            text="{bookRepeater.currentIndex + 1}➥
            {bookRepeater.currentItem}" />
        <mx:Button label="Add to Cart"➥
            click="getBookData(event.target.getRepeaterItem())"  />
    </mx:Repeater>
    <mx:Label id="nameLabel" />
</mx:Application>
```

6. Save and run the code, and you will get a very odd result as shown in Figure 9-8.

Things did not quite work out as planned, as you can see.

When you used the Model tag, the Repeater component had an easy job. There was only one piece of data, bookName, that it needed to be concerned with. So the currentItem property was populated easily. However, if you look at the structure of the XML file, you will see that currentItem can be any one of three potential data items: name, author, or description.

The text object Object is ActionScript's way of telling you that it created the object for each data item, but it doesn't know which of the data items you want to put into it. You have to give ActionScript more specific instructions. Happily, this is not hard.

7. Make a small addition to the Label control in the Repeater structure.

```
<mx:Repeater id="bookRepeater"➥
    dataProvider="{bookData.lastResult.books.stock}">
    <mx:Label➥
        text="{bookRepeater.currentIndex + 1}➥
        {bookRepeater.currentItem.name}" />
    <mx:Button label="Add to Cart"➥
        click="getBookData(event.target.getRepeaterItem())"  />
</mx:Repeater>
```

8. You told the Label control which node to use to populate the text attribute. Save and run the application now, and your screen should look like Figure 9-9.

As you can see, the proper data is now being displayed. However, as shown in Figure 9-9, if you click any of the buttons, you are still getting the object Object indication in the nameLabel Label control.

9. Again, this is easily fixed by making a slight adjustment to the button's click event:

```
<mx:Button label="Add to Cart"➥
    click="getBookData(event.target.getRepeaterItem().name)" />
```

> *The use of* name *in the preceding code is not as a property. Instead, this refers to the* name *node of the XML file.*

By adding .name, you are telling the getRepeaterItem() method to get the name data of the current item.

Figure 9-8. The results of publishing the XML file in the Repeater component

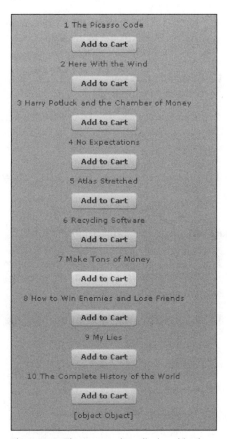

Figure 9-9. The proper data displayed in the Repeater structure

9

307

10. Run the application and click any of the buttons; the correct name should now appear in the Label control, as shown in Figure 9-10.

Figure 9-10. The corrected Label control information

While the code for the eventHandler, getBookData(), shows how all the pieces fit together nicely, it is not the most efficient way of doing things. For instance, it does not lend itself nicely to displaying multiple data items for each of the objects in the Repeater structure.

11. Make the following change to the click event in the Button control:

```
<mx:Button label="Add to Cart" click="getBookData(event)"  />
```

What this does is send all of the information, the entire object, to the getBookData() method rather than just the name data. Once this data is sent to the method, the method can then sort out what it needs.

12. Go ahead and save your application; you may notice a problem in the Problems pane (see Figure 9-11).

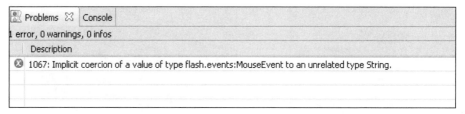

Figure 9-11. The problem in the Problems pane

A click event is generated by a mouse. This makes it of type MouseEvent. So what this is saying is the function, getBookData(), is expecting a String, but you are sending it a MouseEvent.

13. You need to make an adjustment to the signature of the function as follows:

```
<mx:Script>
  <![CDATA[
     private function getBookData(repeatData:MouseEvent):void
     {
        nameLabel.text = repeatData;
     }
  ]]>
</mx:Script>
```

This creates another problem that you will fix momentarily.

> *Since you are not using most of the functionality of the* MouseEvent *class, you could have also used the more generic type* Object, *and it would still have worked fine.*

14. Once the function has all the information, you can use getRepeaterItem() within it by adding the following line of code:

```
private function getBookData(repeatData:MouseEvent):void
    {
        var book:Object = repeatData.target.getRepeaterItem();
        nameLabel.text = repeatData;
    }
```

Notice that you given the new variable, book, the generic type Object. Why not set it as a String like you did earlier?

In this particular exercise, you are passing all strings to the function. However, that may not always be the case. You could be passing numbers, arrays, etc. By making the variable as generic as possible, it can handle a large variety of situations.

15. From here, all you need to do is tell the nameLabel what data, all of which is now available through the book variable you just created, you want to display in the text attribute. For instance, if you want to display the description, make the following change:

```
private function getBookData(repeatData:MouseEvent):void
{
    var book:Object = repeatData.target.getRepeaterItem();
    nameLabel.text = book.description;
}
```

16. Save and run the application; you should now be able to click a button and have the description appear in the Label control at the bottom of the Repeater component (see Figure 9-12).

Figure 9-12. The Label control showing the description

This will open up a variety of programming situations you will use for part 2 of the case study.

Changing component properties

There is one more aspect of the Repeater component I need to show you.

1. Give the Button control an id attribute. In this case, use cartAdd.

```
<mx:Button id="cartAdd" label="Add to Cart"➥
    click="getBookData(event)" />
```

Consider a question a friend asked me recently: Wouldn't this create a page with multiple instances of the button object with the same name? And, if that is the case, doesn't that violate every precept of programming known? After all, you cannot have two objects with the same name in the same application page.

On the face of it, that does appear to be happening. However, in reality, Flex is creating an array of Button controls (or whatever control is being replicated) with as many elements in that array as there are data items. If you could peek behind the scenes, you would see something like the following:

```
cartAdd[0]
cartAdd[1]
cartAdd[2]
etc.
```

Understanding this concept allows you to programmatically change the properties of the various components.

For the sake of simplicity, and to save you some code writing in this example, let's just look at the first instance of the Button control. Since it is the first element of the array, you would address it with cartAdd[0]. Let's assume that when the button is clicked, you want the button's label attribute to change from "Add to Cart" to "Added".

2. You can add one more line of code to the getBookData() function to accomplish this as follows:

```
private function getBookData(repeatData:MouseEvent):void
{
    var book:Object = repeatData.target.getRepeaterItem();
    nameLabel.text = book.description;
    cartAdd[0].label = "Added";
}
```

3. Save and run the application; everything will appear as before. But if you click the first Add to Cart button, the button's text should change, as shown in Figure 9-13.

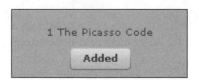

Figure 9-13. The changed button text

If you want, go ahead and add this functionality to the other buttons. But, for the purposes of this example, this is not necessary. I think you understand the point.

Of course, coding it like this assumes that there will always be exactly the same number of repetitions. This will not always be the case. Once you get into part 2 of the case study, you will make this code a bit more dynamic and flexible in order to handle a variety of scenarios.

Summary

You discovered a lot of potential power in this discussion of the Repeater component. You can create incredibly complex structures that will repeat for each new incidence of data.

You are now going to take this powerful knowledge and apply it to the case study you began in the last chapter.

Roll up your sleeves; you have a lot of work ahead.

9

In Chapter 8, you completed the first part of a case study involving the reconstruction of the site for the publisher of this book (if only I could reconstruct my editor that easily).

Part 1 is what I call the *designer stage*. Programming was minimal and all you did was design the layout, graphics, and components that are going to be needed. However, the components have only minimal functionality. For instance, you can't place things in the shopping cart, the book covers were manually inserted, and so forth.

In this part, you are going to enter into the *developer stage*. This is where you write the programming code necessary to make the application function like an enterprise commerce site.

Your focus here will be coding. Like I told you in the introduction of part 1, you will be seeing what you have already learned in a new light; and you will learn some new ActionScript concepts along the way.

One new concept you will be looking at in this chapter is how to write your own class files. It is surprisingly easier than you may think. However, there are certain rules that will need to be discussed when you get to that point.

Like part 1, I will not be giving you a lot of room to play around, as I have in the other chapters. In a case study such as this, we need to be on the same page. So please take your time and carefully test everything each step of the way.

Let's get to work . . .

Setup

If, for some reason, you do not have the files for part 1, I have included them with the download for this chapter. They are in the folder called Completed Part 1 Files.

1. If you need to, go ahead and set up a Flex project that uses the files created in Chapter 8. You can use any name for the project you want. However, for conventions in this book, I am going with the original name of onlineComputerBooks.

If Flex Builder set up an MXML file called onlineComputerBooks, close and delete it if you want. If you don't, it won't hurt anything.

Your Navigator pane should look something like Figure 10-1.

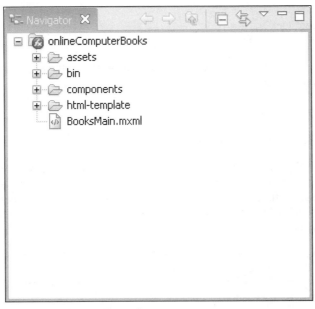

Figure 10-1. The opening Navigator pane

2. Open up the BooksMain.mxml file.

3. Take a few moments and review your code against the following:

```
<?xml version="1.0" encoding="utf-8"?>
<mx:Application xmlns:mx="http://www.adobe.com/2006/mxml"⮯
   height="100%" width="100%" layout="absolute"⮯
   backgroundColor="#FFFFFF" xmlns:comp="components.*">
  <mx:Style>
     ComboBox
     {
        selectionColor:#32cd32
     }
     global
     {
        color:#00008b
     }
  </mx:Style>
  <mx:Image source="assets/logo1.gif"  x="357" y="10"/>
  <mx:LinkBar dataProvider="bookPages"  x="105" y="151"/>
  <mx:ViewStack id="bookPages" resizeToContent="true" x="118" y="185">
     <comp:BookHome height="50%" width="50%" label="Home" id="home" />
     <comp:BookCovers height="50%" width="50%" label="Our Books"⮯
        id="bookCovers" />
     <comp:Comments height="50%" width="50%" label="Comments"⮯
        id="comments" />
```

10

```
    </mx:ViewStack>
       <comp:BookCart  x="750" y="291"/>
    </mx:Application>
```

4. If necessary, go ahead and run the application to review the application's functionality up to this point.

Coding the application

As I said at the beginning of this chapter, you are going to primarily place your efforts in coding this application in order to get everything to work together. I am going to begin this section with a little bit of a warning: a large amount of the coding will not always be easy to understand. While the syntax will be pretty straightforward, the concepts behind it may not always be clear.

While I will try and explain the flow and concepts along the way, it will be up to you to take a step back and make sure that you understand each step. Do not go on to the next step unless you understand the present step. If you try and speed the process, you might find yourself very lost after a while.

Keeping this in mind, let's begin by setting up the data source which, in this case, is an XML file.

Connecting the data source

Let's begin by importing the XML file containing the data for your application. In your Chapter 10 download files, you should have a file, located in the `resources` folder, called `books.xml`. You have already learned how to import files into your project. However, let's do a quick review:

1. Select File ➤ Import.

2. Select File System.

3. Browse to the `resources` folder, select it, and click OK.

4. Select the check box for `books.xml`.

5. For the Into folder field, browse to the assets folder for your project environment (see Figure 10-2).

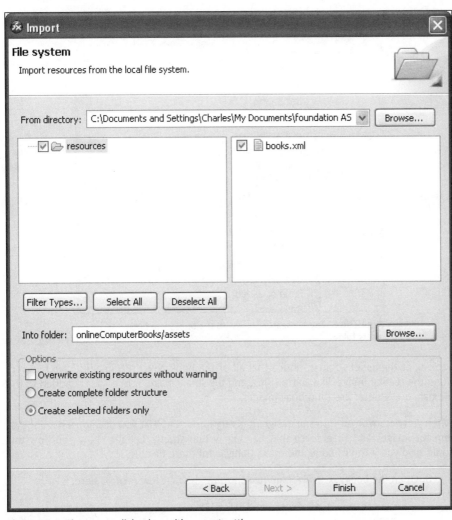

Figure 10-2. The Import dialog box with current settings

6. Click Finish.

7. Check your Navigator pane to make sure the file is in the assets folder, as shown in Figure 10-3.

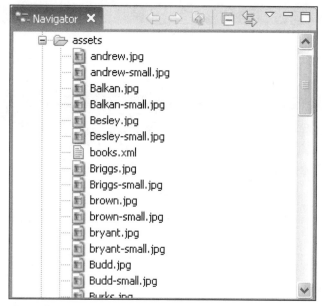

Figure 10-3. The Navigator pane with the books.xml file in the assets folder

Looking at the assets folder, notice that all of the book cover JPG images have two versions: the regular image, like Andrew.jpg, and the small image, with a -small added to the file name. The latter are thumbnail images.

When you get involved with site design, it is very important that you develop a naming system for images and to enforce that naming system strictly. Let me show you how this could save you a ton of code and make things a lot more flexible.

8. Open the books.xml file. I am just showing the first few records here:

```
<?xml version="1.0" encoding="UTF-8"?>
  <books>
    <stock filename="andrew" title="Dreamweaver MX 2004 Design➥
      Projects" author="Rachel Andrew" category="Dreamweaver">
      <desc>Dreamweaver MX 2004 Design Projects takes you➥
        through the process of creating four real-world case ➥
        studies, enabling you to take your Dreamweaver skills➥
        to a new level.</desc>
    </stock>
    <stock filename="balkan" title = "Flash 3d Cheats Most Wanted"➥
      author="Aral Balkan" category="Flash">
      <desc>Improve your depth of deception with an innovative ➥
        slice engine to create convincing 3D objects</desc>
```

```
        </stock>
                <stock filename="besley" title = "Learn Programming with Flash➥
                   MX" author="Kristian Besley" category="ActionScript">
                    <desc>This book employs a truly unique classroom-based➥
                       approach to learning, with the goal of establishing core,➥
                       practical programming skills.</desc>
                </stock>
                <stock filename="briggs" title = "Cascading Style Sheets"➥
                   author="Owen Briggs" category="CSS">
                    <desc>CSS is one of the trio of core client-side web➥
                       professional skills: HTML for markup, JavaScript for➥
                       dynamism, and CSS for style.</desc>
                </stock>
```

Notice that the root node is books. But below that is a node, for each book, called stock. The stock node contains an attribute called filename. This attribute contains the actual name of each image file for that book title. Let's take the andrew file name.

When you access these records, you will see that it is not that difficult to add fixed text around the name. For instance, you will add assets/**andrew**-small.jpg. What I have bolded is the original name.

Because of this, you now have a lot of potential programming flexibility. But, once again, in order for this to work, you must use a consistent naming convention.

Now that you understand the naming conventions, the next step is to connect to the XML file in the BooksMain.xml file. As you know, BooksMain.mxml is the main application file, and since everything passes through it, you only need to establish the connection there. Once the connection is made, the various components can access it easily.

9. Open BooksMain.mxml if it isn't opened already and, if necessary, go to Source view.

10. The placement of HTTPService to connect to the XML file is not critical. For the purposes of this exercise, put it right below the Application tag. You will give it an id of bookDataIn and set the url to the books.xml file located in the assets folder.

```
<?xml version="1.0" encoding="utf-8"?>
<mx:Application xmlns:mx="http://www.adobe.com/2006/mxml"➥
   height="100%" width="100%" layout="absolute"➥
   backgroundColor="#FFFFFF" xmlns:comp="components.*">
<mx:HTTPService id="bookDataIn" url="assets/books.xml" />
```

In previous chapters, you put an event called creationComplete into the Application tag which, when the application completed loading, would instruct HTTPService to call the XML file for the data. You could do that here just as easily. However, here you'll try something a little different.

10

11. In the Application tag, add the creationComplete event as you did before. But this time, rather than make the call back to HTTPService, have it call a function, which you will write shortly, called init().

```
<mx:Application xmlns:mx="http://www.adobe.com/2006/mxml"➥
   height="100%" width="100%" layout="absolute"➥
backgroundColor="#FFFFFF" xmlns:comp="components.*"➥
creationComplete="init()">
```

This may seem strange to you but, in reality, it is a standard programming practice and an excellent code organization tool. You always want to keep your code as organized as possible, for obvious reasons. Many programmers like to organize their setup code, such as database calls, variable initializations, calls to other files, and so forth, inside of a single method. Traditionally, that method is called init(). That way, with just one method call, all of the initial jobs the application needs to perform are run.

12. Keeping that in mind, you now need to set up your script block and create the init() function. This function will have a return type of void. The name "init" has no significance—it is just a programming convention for a function to organize code needed to set up the application. The return type of void means the function does not return anything. Again, placement is not critical but, for the purposes of this exercise, set it up under the Application tag and over the HTTPService call.

```
<mx:Script>
  <![CDATA[
     private function init():void
     {

     }
  ]]>
</mx:Script>
```

13. Of course, as you may have guessed, you will use the send() method of your HTTPService called bookDataIn. Add this in now.

```
<mx:Script>
  <![CDATA[
     private function init():void
     {
        bookDataIn.send();
     }
  ]]>
</mx:Script>
```

Many times events happen in ActionScript that you may not realize are happening. When the XML data gets fully loaded, that generates an event named results. This event contains just as it says, the results of the XML call. The results event can be used to trigger other things happening. As you work with this, you will see a lot of analogies to the target event you have worked with often.

Not surprisingly, ActionScript has a class for handling these results called ResultEvent, which is part of the mx.rpc.events package.

14. Right above the init() function you created, import the mx.rpc.events package. Rather than just call ResultEvent, I prefer to use the asterisk, as discussed in Chapter 4, to save having to write out a separate import statement for each class in the package.

```
<mx:Script>
    <![CDATA[
        import mx.rpc.events.*;
        private function init():void
        {
            bookDataIn.send();
        }
    ]]>
</mx:Script>
```

You are also going to want to save the results of the XML file data to a variable. Since HTTPService converts it to an ArrayCollection, the variable you save it to must be of type ArrayCollection.

15. In order to do this, you will need to import the package mx.collections, which also holds the ArrayCollection class.

```
<mx:Script>
    <![CDATA[
        import mx.rpc.events.*;
        import mx.collections.*;
        private function init():void
        {
            bookDataIn.send();
        }
    ]]>
</mx:Script>
```

16. Finally, you will need a variable to store the results of ArrayCollection to. You can easily set that up under the two import statements. Call it books and make it public.

```
<mx:Script>
    <![CDATA[
        import mx.rpc.events.*;
        import mx.collections.*;
        public var books:ArrayCollection;
        private function init():void
        {
            bookDataIn.send();
        }
    ]]>
</mx:Script>
```

10

If you are an experienced programmer, you may question why I am using public properties. Proper OOP calls for making most properties private and then writing a getter or setter method to control access to that property. This makes good programming sense. Would you want properties to be accessed without the ability to filter who is accessing them and what changes are being made? (I wouldn't mind having that ability with the balance property of my bank account.)

As an example, let's say you had a private property called myAge. A typical getter and setter method would have the following syntax:

```
public function getMyAge():Number
{
   return myAge;
}

Public function(age:Number):void
{
   myAge = age;
}
```

Of course, these are just skeletal structures. In actuality, you would probably have code in them controlling the rules that accesses or changes the property. Then the only access would be through the public properties.

With that all said, I am not enforcing this practice for this book's project, because I want to save you from having to type a lot of additional code.

As I stated earlier, when the XML data is finished loading, an event is generated that carries the results of that data. You haven't written the code yet to handle that, so let's do so now.

17. A\dd the following code to the HTTPService tag:

```
<mx:HTTPService id="bookDataIn" url="assets/books.xml"➥
   result="bookHandler(event)" />
```

Next, you'll write the bookHandler() function, which will not be called until all of the data is loaded from the XML file.

18. Add the bookHandler() function under the init() function you created earlier. It will accept one argument, and that argument will be of type ResultEvent. The return type will be void.

```
<mx:Script>
  <![CDATA[
     import mx.rpc.events.*;
     import mx.collections.*;
     public var books:ArrayCollection;
     private function init():void
     {
        bookDataIn.send();
```

```
        }
        private function bookHandler(event:ResultEvent):void
        {

        }
    ]]>
</mx:Script>
```

By now, you should be seeing the analogy to the target event you have used many times already.

Since the event contains all of the XML data, you now need to save it to the ArrayCollection variable, books, that you created earlier. But you need to tell it what node you will be using. If you refer to the XML file, you will see that books is the root node, but the data you need is contained within the stock node.

19. Set the books variable as follows:

```
private function bookHandler(event:ResultEvent):void
{
    books = event.result.books.stock;
}
```

Just to recap a bit, the HTTPService creates the connection to the books.xml file. When the creationComplete event happens, the init() function is called. The init() function has code that makes the HTTPService, bookDataIn, call to the XML file and get the data. Once the data is fully loaded, the result is sent to bookHandler() which, in turn, saves it to a variable, books, of type ArrayCollection.

Your code up to this point should look as follows:

```
<?xml version="1.0" encoding="utf-8"?>
<mx:Application xmlns:mx="http://www.adobe.com/2006/mxml"➥
    height="100%" width="100%" layout="absolute"➥
    backgroundColor="#FFFFFF" xmlns:comp="components.*"➥
    creationComplete="init()">
<mx:Script>
    <![CDATA[
        import mx.rpc.events.*;
        import mx.collections.*;
        public var books:ArrayCollection;
        private function init():void
        {
            bookDataIn.send();
        }
        private function bookHandler(event:ResultEvent):void
        {
            books = event.result.books.stock;
        }
    ]]>
```

```
        </mx:Script>
        <mx:HTTPService id="bookDataIn" url="assets/books.xml"➥
            result="bookHandler(event)" />
        <mx:Style>
            ComboBox
            {
                selectionColor:#32cd32
            }
            global
            {
                color:#00008b
            }
        </mx:Style>
        <mx:Image source="assets/logo1.gif"  x="357" y="10"/>
        <mx:LinkBar dataProvider="bookPages"  x="105" y="151"/>
        <mx:ViewStack id="bookPages" resizeToContent="true" x="118" y="185">
            <comp:BookHome height="50%" width="50%" label="Home" id="home" />
            <comp:BookCovers height="50%" width="50%"➥
                label="Our Books" id="bookCovers" />
            <comp:Comments height="50%" width="50%"➥
                label="Comments" id="comments" />
        </mx:ViewStack>
        <comp:BookCart  x="750" y="291"/>
    </mx:Application>
```

It is probably a good idea to test the connection now to make sure everything is talking properly.

Testing your code

If you go ahead and run the application, and don't get an error, there is a reasonable chance everything is working fine. However, that is far from a reliable test. Earlier in this book, you learned about the powerful debug feature of Flex Builder. This might be a good place to put it to work.

1. Click the line of code that assigns the result of the XML call to books:

```
books = event.result.books.stock;
```

2. Select Run ➤ Toggle Line Breakpoint. You should see a small dot just to the left of the line numbering, as shown in Figure 10-4.

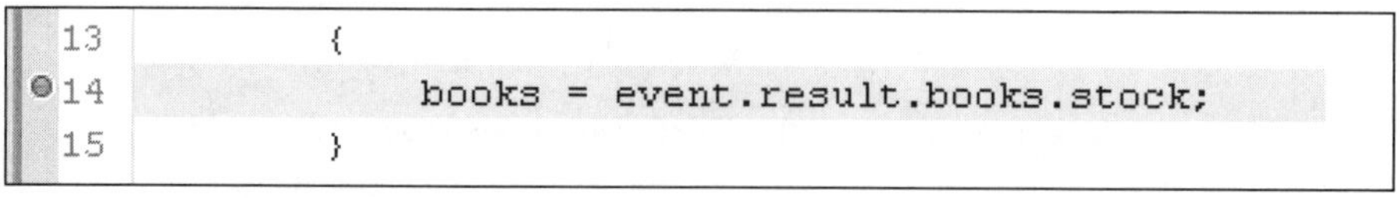

```
13              {
●14                 books = event.result.books.stock;
15              }
```

Figure 10-4. Setting the Toggle Line Breakpoint option

3. Click the Debug button rather than the Run button. You should get a message to start the Debugging perspective as shown in Figure 10-5.

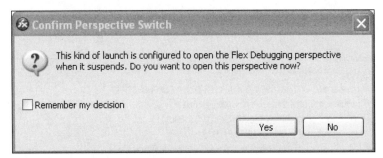

Figure 10-5. Confirming the perspective switch

4. Click Yes, and Flex Builder reconfigures itself to make the tools for debugging available, as shown in Figure 10-6.

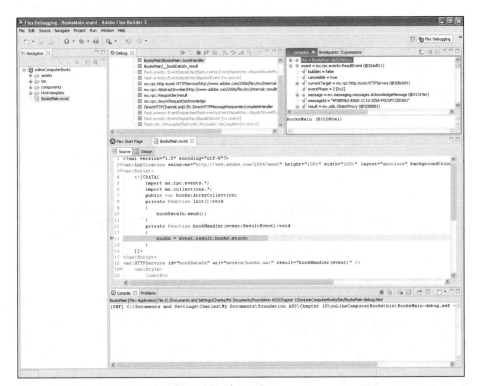

Figure 10-6. Flex Builder in Debugging perspective

If you look at the upper-right side, you should see a pane named Variables. If you scroll down, you should see result, which is the result from HTTPService.

5. Click the + to the left of result. As soon as you click down, you will start to see familiar objects from the XML file.

You will see the main node, books. Under that you will see stock and, under that, you will see author and a representation of the data, as illustrated in Figure 10-7.

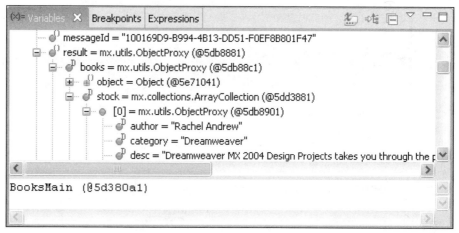

Figure 10-7. The Variables pane with the live data

As long as you see this data, you know the connection is working, and you are now ready to move forward.

6. Switch back to Development perspective by clicking the Perspective button, located on the upper-right side above the Variables pane, and selecting Flex Development.

> *In some cases, you may find your browser open and nonresponsive. At the time of this writing, this is a small bug. If this happens, just click the close button for the browser. Nothing will be affected.*

7. Select Run ➤ Remove All Breakpoints.

8. Click Yes.

Let's now proceed to the next step.

Handling the book cover images

If you did everything in part 1 (Chapter 8) of this project, you should have a component named BookCovers.mxml located under the components folder.

Your initial code should look as follows:

```
<?xml version="1.0" encoding="utf-8"?>
<mx:VBox xmlns:mx="http://www.adobe.com/2006/mxml" width="500">
    <mx:HBox backgroundColor="#EE82EE"➥
        verticalAlign="middle" fontSize="12" >
        <mx:Label text="Select the Books:" />
        <mx:CheckBox label="All Books" />
        <mx:Label text="Select Book Category" />
        <mx:ComboBox>
            <mx:dataProvider>
                <mx:ArrayCollection>
                    <mx:String>Dreamweaver</mx:String>
                    <mx:String>Flash</mx:String>
                    <mx:String>Graphics</mx:String>
                    <mx:String>Web Design</mx:String>
                    <mx:String>Other</mx:String>
                </mx:ArrayCollection>
            </mx:dataProvider>
        </mx:ComboBox>
    </mx:HBox>
    <mx:Tile width="500">
        <mx:Image source="assets/andrew-small.jpg"➥
            click="currentState='BookDetails'" />
        <mx:Image source="assets/balkan-small.jpg"➥
            click="currentState='BookDetails'" />
        <mx:Image source="assets/besley-small.jpg"➥
            click="currentState='BookDetails'" />
        <mx:Image source="assets/briggs-small.jpg"➥
            click="currentState='BookDetails'" />
        <mx:Image source="assets/brown-small.jpg"➥
            click="currentState='BookDetails'" />
        <mx:Image source="assets/bryant-small.jpg"➥
            click="currentState='BookDetails'" />
        <mx:Image source="assets/budd-small.jpg"➥
            click="currentState='BookDetails'" />
        <mx:Image source="assets/burks-small.jpg"➥
            click="currentState='BookDetails'" />
        <mx:Image source="assets/donatis-small.jpg"➥
            click="currentState='BookDetails'" />
        <mx:Image source="assets/downs-small.jpg"➥
            click="currentState='BookDetails'" />
        <mx:Image source="assets/elbaga-small.jpg"➥
            click="currentState='BookDetails'" />
        <mx:Image source="assets/elst-small.jpg"➥
            click="currentState='BookDetails'" />
        <mx:Image source="assets/evans-small.jpg"➥
            click="currentState='BookDetails'" />
        <mx:Image source="assets/grannell-small.jpg"➥
            click="currentState='BookDetails'" />
```

10

```
                <mx:Image source="assets/green-small.jpg"↪
                    click="currentState='BookDetails'" />
                <mx:Image source="assets/harkness-small.jpg"↪
                    click="currentState='BookDetails'" />
                <mx:Image source="assets/jacobs-small.jpg"↪
                    click="currentState='BookDetails'" />
                <mx:Image source="assets/keith-small.jpg"↪
                    click="currentState='BookDetails'" />
                <mx:Image source="assets/kirkpatrick-small.jpg"↪
                    click="currentState='BookDetails'" />
                <mx:Image source="assets/lifaros-small.jpg"↪
                    click="currentState='BookDetails'" />
            </mx:Tile>
        </mx:VBox>
```

If you run the BooksMain application and click the Our Books link, you will see the results of this component, as illustrated in Figure 10-8.

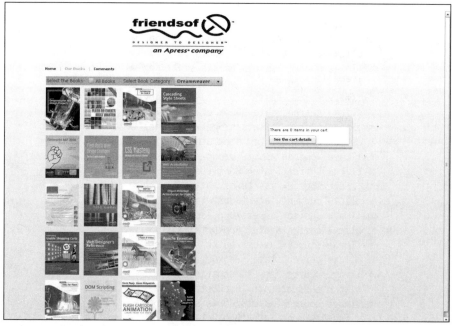

Figure 10-8. Clicking the Our Books link displays the BookCovers component.

As you can see, all of these book cover images are hard-wired into the component. While this certainly works, it does not allow for changes to be made easily.

> Note that the images are contained within a Tile container.

What you want to do here is populate the images programmatically so that if there are changes, you don't need to go into the code and make changes—instead, you can make the code handle the changes automatically.

1. The first thing you need to do is delete all of the Image tags between the opening and closing Tile tags.

```
<mx:Tile width="500" >

</mx:Tile>
</mx:VBox>
```

You are going to need to pass the ArrayCollection, books, into this component because that data contains the name of the image file (or at least part of the name as you saw earlier). There are a couple of ways you could do this. Let's look at the simpler method first.

2. At the top of the BookCovers component, right underneath the opening VBox tag, create a script block.

```
<?xml version="1.0" encoding="utf-8"?>
<mx:VBox xmlns:mx="http://www.adobe.com/2006/mxml" width="500">
<mx:Script>
  <![CDATA[

  ]]>
</mx:Script>
```

3. Within the block, declare a variable of type ArrayCollection, because that is the type of data you will be bringing over. In this case, call the variable coverData.

```
<mx:Script>
  <![CDATA[
      import mx.collections.ArrayCollection;
      public var coverData:ArrayCollection;
  ]]>
</mx:Script>
```

Notice that as soon as you do this, Flex Builder automatically sets up the import statement as discussed in Chapter 3.

You now need to get your data from the books variable in BooksMain.

4. Switch to BooksMain and scroll down to the three components in the ViewStack container. You should see the BookCovers component there.

```
<mx:ViewStack id="bookPages" resizeToContent="true" x="118" y="185">
    <comp:BookHome height="50%" width="50%" label="Home" id="home" />
    <comp:BookCovers height="50%" width="50%" label="Our Books"➥
        id="bookCovers" />
    <comp:Comments height="50%" width="50%" label="Comments"➥
        id="comments" />
</mx:ViewStack>
```

5. Go into the line that calls the BookCovers component and create a binding as follows:

```
<comp:BookCovers height="50%" width="50%" label="Our Books"➥
    id="bookCovers" coverData="{books}" />
```

What this simply says is make the coverData variable, which you just declared in the BookCovers component, equal to the books variable.

6. Save the application now; you may get a warning message. Don't worry about this for now. You can easily fix this with the [Bindable] meta tag discussed in earlier chapters.

7. Place the tag above the books declaration as follows:

```
<![CDATA[
    import mx.rpc.events.*;
    import mx.collections.*;
    [Bindable]
    public var books:ArrayCollection;
```

and place another instance above the declaration for coverData in the BookCovers component:

```
<![CDATA[
    import mx.collections.ArrayCollection;
    [Bindable]
    public var coverData:ArrayCollection;
]]>
```

8. Save your code; the warning should disappear.

What you are now going to do is create a component to hold the cover image and then have that component repeat in the BookCovers component using the Repeater component.

9. Right-click the components folder in the Navigator pane and select New ➤ MXML Component.

10. Call the component CoverDisplay and base it on the Image tag, as shown in Figure 10-9.

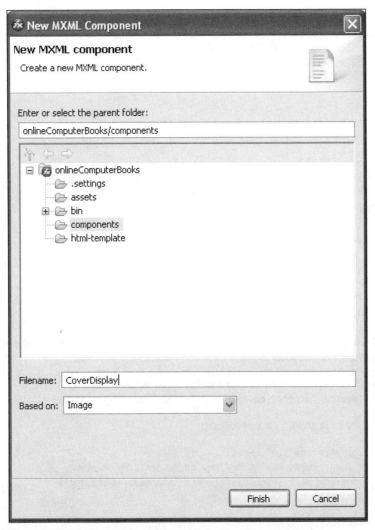

Figure 10-9. The New Component dialog box with your current settings

Notice that the size properties are not necessary when you base your component on the Image tag.

11. Click Finish. You should see the following code in Source view:

```
<?xml version="1.0" encoding="utf-8"?>
<mx:Image xmlns:mx="http://www.adobe.com/2006/mxml">

</mx:Image>
```

Here is where things are going to start to get a little confusing, so please follow carefully.

12. Create a script block under the Image tag.

```
<?xml version="1.0" encoding="utf-8"?>
<mx:Image xmlns:mx="http://www.adobe.com/2006/mxml">
  <mx:Script>
    <![CDATA[

    ]]>
  </mx:Script>
</mx:Image>
```

13. Create a bindable variable called coverImageData. In this case, you will not pass all the data from the XML file. Instead, you will just pass it the string filename, which contains the name of the image file. For that reason, you could make this either type String or type Object. To keep things as generic as possible, make it type Object.

```
<mx:Script>
  <![CDATA[
    [Bindable]
    public var coverImageData:Object;
  ]]>
</mx:Script>
```

14. Now set the source of the Image tag to call the assets folder, add the filename attribute of the XML file, and then add -small.jpg as follows:

```
<mx:Image xmlns:mx="http://www.adobe.com/2006/mxml"➥
  source="assets/{coverImageData.filename}-small.jpg">
```

Your finished code should look as follows:

```
<?xml version="1.0" encoding="utf-8"?>
<mx:Image xmlns:mx="http://www.adobe.com/2006/mxml"➥
  source="assets/{coverImageData.filename}-small.jpg">
  <mx:Script>
    <![CDATA[
      [Bindable]
      public var coverImageData:Object;
    ]]>
  </mx:Script>
</mx:Image>
```

15. Save this component and return to BookCovers.mxml.

16. Before you can use the CoverDisplay component, you will need to define the namespace in the VBox container as follows:

```
<mx:VBox xmlns:mx="http://www.adobe.com/2006/mxml" width="500"➥
  xmlns:comp="components.*">
```

17. Scroll down to the Tile container.

18. In between the Tile container tags, add a Repeater tag. You will give it an id of displayCovers and make the dataProvider control the coverData variable you defined in ActionScript.

```
<mx:Tile width="500" >
    <mx:Repeater id="displayCovers" dataProvider="{coverData}">

    </mx:Repeater>
</mx:Tile>
```

By doing this, you ensure that the Repeater component will repeat for as many items as there are in the XML file.

19. Within the Repeater component, call the CoverDisplay component and pass it the currentItem of the Repeater component to display the correct image.

```
<mx:Tile width="500" >
    <mx:Repeater id="displayCovers" dataProvider="{coverData}">
        <comp:CoverDisplay➡
            coverImageData="{displayCovers.currentItem}" />
    </mx:Repeater>
</mx:Tile>
```

The code for your finished BookCovers component should look as follows:

```
<?xml version="1.0" encoding="utf-8"?>
<mx:VBox xmlns:mx="http://www.adobe.com/2006/mxml"➡
    width="500" xmlns:comp="components.*">
<mx:Script>
    <![CDATA[
        import mx.collections.ArrayCollection;
        [Bindable]
        public var coverData:ArrayCollection;
    ]]>
</mx:Script>
    <mx:HBox backgroundColor="#EE82EE"➡
        verticalAlign="middle" fontSize="12" >
        <mx:Label text="Select the Books:" />
        <mx:CheckBox label="All Books" />
        <mx:Label text="Select Book Category" />
        <mx:ComboBox>
            <mx:dataProvider>
                <mx:ArrayCollection>
                    <mx:String>Dreamweaver</mx:String>
                    <mx:String>Flash</mx:String>
                    <mx:String>Graphics</mx:String>
                    <mx:String>Web Design</mx:String>
                    <mx:String>Other</mx:String>
                </mx:ArrayCollection>
            </mx:dataProvider>
```

10

333

```
            </mx:ComboBox>
        </mx:HBox>
        <mx:Tile width="500" >
            <mx:Repeater id="displayCovers" dataProvider="{coverData}">
                <comp:CoverDisplay➥
                    coverImageData="{displayCovers.currentItem}" />
            </mx:Repeater>
        </mx:Tile>
    </mx:VBox>
```

20. Save everything, return to BooksMain, and click the Our Books link. You should see book covers displayed exactly as before (see Figure 10-10).

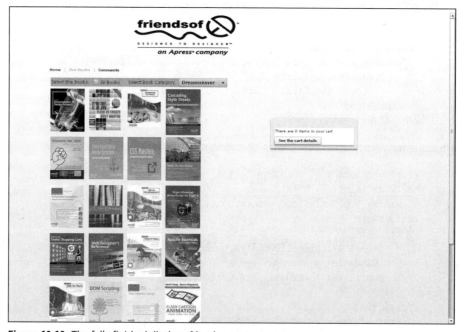

Figure 10-10. The fully finished display of book covers

You may have wondered why you went through the additional step of creating the CoverDisplay component. This will become obvious as you progress through the rest of the case study, but for now just understand the basic idea is to give you a little more flexibility, such as adding text or making selections.

Remember what I have been saying throughout much of this book: divide things into individual components as much as possible.

Hopefully, you also saw the importance of having proper naming conventions for images. If done properly, the system is almost self-running. All you need to do is place the properly named image into the assets folder and add the appropriate information to the data source.

You are now going to make it possible to click an image and see a larger version of it.

Changing states

As you already know, there are two versions of each of the cover images: the thumbnails, which you just worked with and which have the designation -small, and a larger version. What you want to do here is add the ability to click a thumbnail, close the gallery, and have the larger image appear in its place with an accompanying description. Then, once you are finished, you want to be able to return to the gallery.

Before you start, let's quickly review a couple of concepts about state that you have seen previously in Chapter 7.

As discussed in previous chapters, everything in Flex is held in a container. The entire application is held in a huge container called Application. Each of the containers under Application are child containers. So, based on that, the ViewStack container is a child container of Application. A child container can, in turn, have its own child containers.

When you change state, you are essentially removing one child container and putting another one in its place.

As long as you understand this relatively simple concept, the code you are about to enter will be easy to understand (well, relatively easy).

1. Begin by opening BookCovers.mxml if necessary.

2. Since you will need to remove the Tile container programmatically, you will need to give it an id. In this case, call it coverThumbnails.

   ```
   <mx:Tile width="500" id="coverThumbnails" >
   ```

3. Begin to build your states. Right underneath the script block, add an <mx:states> tag.

> Remember, the lowercase states *is the container for created states. The upper-case* State *creates each state.*

```
<?xml version="1.0" encoding="utf-8"?>
<mx:VBox xmlns:mx="http://www.adobe.com/2006/mxml"➥
   width="500" xmlns:comp="components.*">
<mx:Script>
   <![CDATA[
      import mx.collections.ArrayCollection;
      [Bindable]
      public var coverData:ArrayCollection;
   ]]>
</mx:Script>
<mx:states>

</mx:states>
```

10

335

4. Now you want to build a specific state called coverDetails.

```
<mx:states>
    <mx:State name="coverDetails">

    </mx:State>
</mx:states>
```

5. The first thing you want this state to do is to remove the Tile container, which you just named coverThumbnails. To do this, you use the RemoveChild tag and make the container you want to remove the target.

```
<mx:states>
    <mx:State name="coverDetails">
        <mx:RemoveChild target="{coverThumbnails}" />
    </mx:State>
</mx:states>
```

6. The next thing you want to do is add a new child in the same position where the Tile container was located.

```
<mx:states>
    <mx:State name="coverDetails">
        <mx:RemoveChild target="{coverThumbnails}" />
        <mx:AddChild position="lastChild">

        </mx:AddChild>
    </mx:State>
</mx:states>
```

You might need to make some adjustments later on once you have the state working and see where everything is positioned.

7. Next you need to build a container to hold the image. You can use the most generic of containers, Canvas.

```
<mx:states>
    <mx:State name="coverDetails">
        <mx:RemoveChild target="{coverThumbnails}" />
        <mx:AddChild position="lastChild">
            <mx:Canvas>

            </mx:Canvas>
        </mx:AddChild>
    </mx:State>
</mx:states>
```

You now need to start the coding process to make the image swapping described earlier happen. Again, follow the steps very closely. Please do not rush through this part.

8. Go down to the tag that calls the CoverDisplay component.

9. Add a click event there. The click event will call a function named displayBookDetails(), to which you will pass event.currentTarget. getRepeaterItem().

```
<comp:CoverDisplay coverImageData="{displayCovers.currentItem}"➥
  click="displayBookDetails(event.currentTarget.getRepeaterItem())" />
```

Your next step is, as you may have already guessed, to create the function displayBookDetails().

10. Return to the script block and create the displayBookDetails() function. Call the parameter event and make it of type Object. The return type is void.

```
<mx:Script>
  <![CDATA[
    import mx.collections.ArrayCollection;
    [Bindable]
    public var coverData:ArrayCollection;
    private function displayBookDetails(event:Object):void
    {

    }
  ]]>
</mx:Script>
```

11. You will need to pass the results to your state in a bit. In order to make this easier, create a bindable variable above the newly created function and call it selectedCover. Make it of type Object also.

```
<mx:Script>
  <![CDATA[
    import mx.collections.ArrayCollection;
    [Bindable]
    public var coverData:ArrayCollection;
    [Bindable]
    public var selectedCover:Object;
    private function displayBookDetails(event:Object):void
    {

    }
  ]]>
</mx:Script>
```

12. The first thing you are going to want to do with the function displayBookDetails() is to activate the new state, which you called coverDetails. Do not forget to use single quotes.

```
public var selectedCover:Object;
  private function displayBookDetails(event:Object):void
  {
    currentState = 'coverDetails';
  }
```

This would be a good place to do a quick test.

13. Return to BooksMain and run the application.

14. Click the Our Books link.

15. When you get to the gallery of book covers, click one of them. If they all disappear, as shown in Figure 10-11, you are actually in good shape.

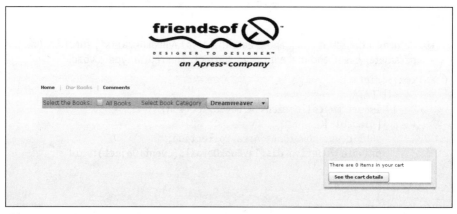

Figure 10-11. The empty current state

16. Close the browser and return to the function you were working on in the BookCovers component.

Since the getRepeaterItem() function is passing all of the requisite information to the event parameter, your job is going to be very easy, but you have to do a little object-oriented programming sleight of hand.

17. Create a new object using the selectedCover variable you created earlier.

```
private function displayBookDetails(event:Object):void
    {
        currentState = 'coverDetails';
        selectedCover = new Object();
    }
```

You now need to save all of the information passed to the event in the new object.

> *Why you created the object will become obvious in a few minutes. Here you could have used the technique you used earlier to bring up your small images. However, as I stated at the outset, I want to show you a variety of techniques. Thus, the slight difference.*

18. Return to your Canvas container and add an Image tag. Give the Image tag an id attribute of coverState.

```
<mx:AddChild position="lastChild">
    <mx:Canvas>
        <mx:Image id="coverState" />
    </mx:Canvas>
</mx:AddChild>
```

The Image class has a method called load(). The load() method calls an object for the URL of the image you want to display, including other SWF files. This is why you created the object: to be able to use the load() method.

19. In this case, you are going use the load() method in a fashion similar to the way you called the small images before. You are going to create a concatenation with the filename attribute of the XML file. The only difference is that you will not need to add -small. The file name itself is contained in the object you created, selectedCover.

```
private function displayBookDetails(event:Object):void
    {
        currentState = 'coverDetails';
        selectedCover = new Object();
        selectedCover = event;
        coverState.load('assets/' + selectedCover.filename + '.jpg');
    }
```

20. Save your code now; you should not see an error in the Problems pane.

21. Return to BooksMain.mxml and start the application. Click the Our Books link. When you get to the gallery of book covers, click one of the covers. The gallery should go away, and the larger book cover image should be displayed (see Figure 10-12).

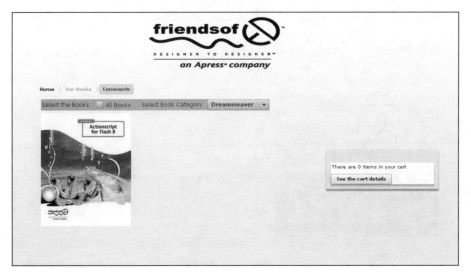

Figure 10-12. The new state displaying the book cover

Again, you will worry about the position a little later.

339

> *To minimize the complexity of this exercise, I decided not to have you use a transition effect. However, if you are feeling brave, you can apply the code discussed in Chapter 7.*

22. You need to create a button to return to the original state. This can be done easily by putting a Button control under the Image control in your state. Give it a label attribute of "Return to Book Covers" and a click event that returns the currentState attribute to ''.

```
<mx:states>
    <mx:State name="coverDetails">
        <mx:RemoveChild target="{coverThumbnails}" />
        <mx:AddChild position="lastChild">
            <mx:Canvas>
                <mx:Image id="coverState" />
                <mx:Button label="Return to Book Covers"➥
                    click="currentState=''" />
            </mx:Canvas>
        </mx:AddChild>
    </mx:State>
</mx:states>
```

23. When you run your application, the button may be bizarrely placed, as shown in Figure 10-13. Clicking the button should return you to the gallery.

Figure 10-13. The position of the Return to Book Covers button

24. Make an adjustment to the position by setting the x attribute of the image to 10 and the y attribute of the button to 300. You may need to make a further adjustment to this after the next couple of steps. But, for now, this will work fine (your results should be similar to Figure 10-14).

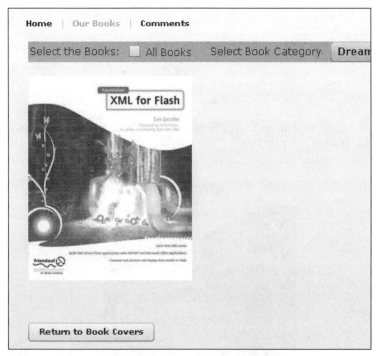

Figure 10-14. Proper placement of the button in the application

Now that the programming work is all set up, you can very easily add the additional information, such as the description. Remember, all of the information is held inside of the selectedCover object already.

25. Add yet another bindable variable and call it selectedAuthor.

```
public var coverData:ArrayCollection;
[Bindable]
public var selectedCover:Object;
[Bindable]
public var selectedAuthor:Object;
```

26. Inside the function displayBookDetails(), access the selectedCover object to access the author attribute.

```
private function displayBookDetails(event:Object):void
{
    currentState = 'coverDetails';
    selectedCover = new Object();
    selectedCover = event;
```

```
coverState.load('assets/' + selectedCover.filename + '.jpg');
selectedAuthor = selectedCover.author;
}
```

27. Between the Image and Button controls in the Canvas container, add a Text control and set the text attribute to selectedAuthor. Set the y attribute to 250.

```
<mx:Canvas>
    <mx:Image id="coverState" y="10" />
    <mx:Text y="250" text="{selectedAuthor}" />
    <mx:Button label="Return to Book Covers"➡
        click="currentState=''" y="300" />
</mx:Canvas>
```

28. Run the application and test the Text control. Your results should be similar to what you see in Figure 10-15.

Figure 10-15. The author's name added

29. Make the author name a little more pronounced by specifying a fontSize of 18 and fontWeight of bold. Figure 10-16 illustrates the results.

```
<mx:Text y="250" text="{selectedAuthor}" fontSize="18"↪
    fontWeight="bold" />
```

Figure 10-16. Changing the font size and weight

You are going to use an identical technique to create a description field now.

30. Start off by creating a bindable variable called selectedDescription and then access the desc node, which is what it is called in the XML file, in the displayBookDetails() function.

```
public var coverData:ArrayCollection;
[Bindable]
public var selectedCover:Object;
[Bindable]
public var selectedAuthor:Object;
[Bindable]
public var selectedDescription:Object;
private function displayBookDetails(event:Object):void
{
    currentState = 'coverDetails';
    selectedCover = new Object();
    selectedCover = event;
    coverState.load('assets/' + selectedCover.filename + '.jpg');
    selectedAuthor = selectedCover.author;
    selectedDescription = selectedCover.desc;
}
```

10

31. Add another Text control under the last one you created, and make the text attribute {selectedDescription}. For this example, set the fontSize attribute to 14 and set the y attribute to 300.

32. If you do not set a width attribute, the text will run off to the end of the browser. To prevent this, set this attribute to 400.

33. You will need to make an adjustment to the y attribute of the Button control below the Text control you just created. Set it to 400.

```
<mx:Canvas>
    <mx:Image id="coverState" y="10" />
    <mx:Text y="250" text="{selectedAuthor}" fontSize="18"➥
        fontWeight="bold" />
    <mx:Text y="300" text="{selectedDescription}"➥
        fontSize="14" width="400" />
    <mx:Button label="Return to Book Covers" click="currentState=''"➥
        y="400" />
</mx:Canvas>
```

34. Run the application, and your screen should look something like Figure 10-17.

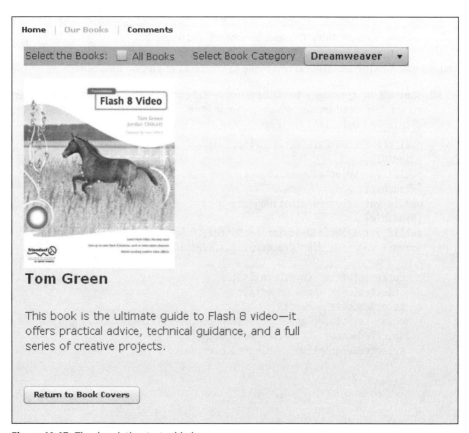

Figure 10-17. The description text added

The complete code in BookCovers.mxml should now look as follows:

```xml
<?xml version="1.0" encoding="utf-8"?>
<mx:VBox xmlns:mx="http://www.adobe.com/2006/mxml" width="500"➥
    xmlns:comp="components.*">
<mx:Script>
    <![CDATA[
        import mx.collections.ArrayCollection;
        [Bindable]
        public var coverData:ArrayCollection;
        [Bindable]
        public var selectedCover:Object;
        [Bindable]
        public var selectedAuthor:Object;
        [Bindable]
        public var selectedDescription:Object
        private function displayBookDetails(event:Object):void
        {
            currentState = 'coverDetails';
            selectedCover = new Object();
            selectedCover = event;
            coverState.load('assets/' + selectedCover.filename + '.jpg');
            selectedAuthor = selectedCover.author;
            selectedDescription = selectedCover.desc;
        }
    ]]>
</mx:Script>
<mx:states>
    <mx:State name="coverDetails">
        <mx:RemoveChild target="{coverThumbnails}" />
        <mx:AddChild position="lastChild">
            <mx:Canvas>
                <mx:Image id="coverState" y="10" />
                <mx:Text y="250" text="{selectedAuthor}" fontSize="18"➥
                  fontWeight="bold" />
                <mx:Text y="300" text="{selectedDescription}" ➥
                  fontSize="14" width="400" />
                <mx:Button label="Return to Book Covers"➥
                  click="currentState=''" y="400" />
            </mx:Canvas>
        </mx:AddChild>
    </mx:State>
</mx:states>
    <mx:HBox backgroundColor="#EE82EE" verticalAlign="middle"➥
        fontSize="12" >
        <mx:Label text="Select the Books:" />
        <mx:CheckBox label="All Books" />
        <mx:Label text="Select Book Category" />
        <mx:ComboBox>
            <mx:dataProvider>
```

10

```
            <mx:ArrayCollection>
                <mx:String>Dreamweaver</mx:String>
                <mx:String>Flash</mx:String>
                <mx:String>Graphics</mx:String>
                <mx:String>Web Design</mx:String>
                <mx:String>Other</mx:String>
            </mx:ArrayCollection>
        </mx:dataProvider>
    </mx:ComboBox>
</mx:HBox>

<mx:Tile width="500" id="coverThumbnails" >
    <mx:Repeater id="displayCovers" dataProvider="{coverData}">
        <comp:CoverDisplay➥
            coverImageData="{displayCovers.currentItem}"➥
            click="displayBookDetails➥
(event.currentTarget.getRepeaterItem())" />
    </mx:Repeater>
</mx:Tile>
</mx:VBox>
```

By this point, your wow factor is through the roof. However, you have a bit more to do yet. You will next get the shopping cart up and working.

Finishing the shopping cart

Of course, the publisher hopes users will buy the books they see on the site you are building, and in vast quantities. You built the shopping cart component, BookCart, in part 1. You now need to wire it up to accept orders.

1. For starters, open up BookCart.mxml and go to Source view. You should see the following code:

```
<?xml version="1.0" encoding="utf-8"?>
<mx:Canvas xmlns:mx="http://www.adobe.com/2006/mxml">
    <mx:states>
        <mx:State name="cartExpand">
            <mx:SetProperty target="{bookCart}" name="height"➥
                value="500"/>
            <mx:AddChild relativeTo="{bookCart}" position="lastChild">
                <mx:DataGrid width="214" height="336">
                    <mx:columns>
                        <mx:DataGridColumn headerText="Column 1"➥
                            dataField="col1"/>
                        <mx:DataGridColumn headerText="Column 2"➥
                            dataField="col2"/>
                        <mx:DataGridColumn headerText="Column 3"➥
                            dataField="col3"/>
                    </mx:columns>
                </mx:DataGrid>
```

```
        </mx:AddChild>
        <mx:AddChild relativeTo="{bookCart}" position="lastChild">
            <mx:Button label="Click to Checkout" id="checkOut"/>
        </mx:AddChild>
      </mx:State>
    </mx:states>
    <mx:Panel id="bookCart" width="250" layout="vertical">
        <mx:Label text="There are 0 items in your cart" />
        <mx:Button x="5" y="30" label="See the cart details"➥
            click="currentState='cartExpand'" />
    </mx:Panel>
</mx:Canvas>
```

2. At present, the DataGrid control has three columns. For the purposes of this exercise, you only need two columns. So, delete Column 3.

3. Change the headerText attribute of Column 1 to Book and make the width attribute 150.

4. Change the headerText attribute of Column 2 to Qty. and make the width attribute 30.

```
<mx:DataGrid width="214" height="336">
    <mx:columns>
        <mx:DataGridColumn headerText="Book" width="150"➥
            dataField="col1"/>
        <mx:DataGridColumn headerText="Qty." width="30"➥
            dataField="col2"/>
    </mx:columns>
</mx:DataGrid>
```

5. Switch to Design view and, in the States pane, click the cartExpand state. Your screen should look like Figure 10-18.

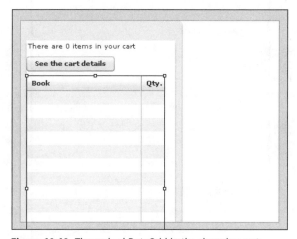

Figure 10-18. The revised DataGrid in the shopping cart

6. Save your work.

Creating a class for a custom event

Up to this point, you have been working with classes already created in ActionScript. As discussed in Chapter 3, classes are the basic unit of OOP. Many programmers would advocate putting nearly no code into the MXML file, instead putting it all into class files.

In this case study, you are going to control what goes into the shopping cart using the class file. However, more importantly, you are going to create a custom event.

If the term "custom event" sounds strange, let me explain. Up to this point, you have seen events such as click and creationComplete. The names of these events make sense to you. When either of these events happens, ActionScript knows what a click or creationComplete is due to internal code. But what you are going to do here is create your own event. In essence, it will take the selected book and place it in the shopping cart.

I am going to warn you here that some of this code will get a little involved. I will explain as best as I can. However, if you are new to OOP, you may have trouble with a few concepts at first. Just take your time and try to follow the flow.

You'll begin by putting your class file into its own directory. While this is not mandatory, it is a good idea to keep the various types of files for your projects organized into their own directories.

1. In the Navigator pane, select the root directory (onlinecomputerbooks), right-click, and select New ➤ Folder.

2. Call the new folder classes as shown in Figure 10-19.

Figure 10-19. Naming your folder in the New Folder dialog box

3. Click Finish. You should see the folder in the Navigator pane (see Figure 10-20).

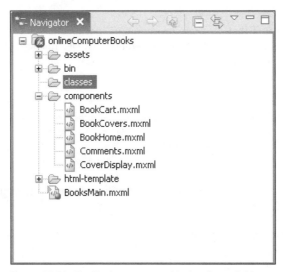

Figure 10-20. The Navigator pane with the classes folder

4. Right-click the new classes folder.

5. Select New ➤ ActionScript Class to bring up the dialog box shown in Figure 10-21.

Figure 10-21. The New ActionScript Class dialog box

Much of what you see here can be tied into the book's previous discussions of ActionScript.

Recall from Chapter 3 that, in OOP environments, *package* is a technical term for the directory structure the class file is located in. Notice that Flex Builder automatically enters the directory that you opened the New ActionScript class dialog box in as the package. You will leave this as is.

> *Unlike other OOP environments, ActionScript requires a package declaration in all class files. So, for this reason, the* Package *field must always contain information.*

Traditionally, class files begin with a capital letter. For the purposes of this exercise, you will call this class CartEvent.

6. Flex Builder makes inheritance easy to invoke with the Superclass field. Click the Browse button just to the right of the field; a list of available classes comes up (see Figure 10-22).

> *Chapter 3 discussed the concept of inheritance.*

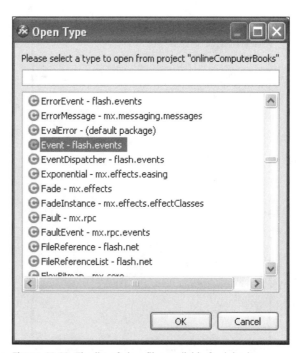

Figure 10-22. The list of class files available for inheritance

Since you are going to create a custom event with this class file, make the Event class the superclass. If you don't do so, you would have to define what an event is and all of the code associated with it. By using inheritance, all you have to do is add custom code for your particular needs.

7. After you select Event, which is part of the flash.events package, click OK.

You won't need to change any other setting. The dialog box should look like Figure 10-23.

Figure 10-23. The completed New ActionScript Class dialog box

8. Click Finish.

You should see that a file, CartEvent.as, was created with the following code:

```
package classes
{
    import flash.events.Event;

    public class CartEvent extends Event
    {
    }
}
```

Notice that all of the code is wrapped in the package declaration. This is sometimes referred to as the **package wrapper**. Following that are any required import statements. Finally, there is the class declaration. The name declared must be the same as the file name, minus the .as extension, or the class file will not work. The keyword extends means it is inherited from another class which, in this case, is Event.

The code necessary for the class file to run must be located between the curly braces of the class declaration.

Although this is not mandatory, most programmers traditionally declare the variables first. Here, you need to create a variable to hold the name of the book you selected. You could make it of type String, but for this example, you will keep things as generic as possible.

9. Since you will not be using any of the specialized functions of the String class, you will give the class a type of Object.

```
package classes
{
    import flash.events.Event;

    public class CartEvent extends Event
    {
        public var selectedBook:Object;
    }
}
```

After declaring your variables, you need to write a special function called a **constructor**. This function runs automatically as soon as the class is called. So you would place any code inside of it that must run automatically.

The name of the constructor must be the same as the class name, and there must be no return type, not even void.

10. You want to pass into the constructor the name of the book selected (selectedBook) and the type of event it was, which you will be creating shortly.

```
package classes
{
    import flash.events.Event;

    public class CartEvent extends Event
    {
        public var bookSelected:Object;

        public function CartEvent(selectedBook:Object, type:String)
        {

        }
    }
}
```

All the code necessary to handle the event, passed into the constructor with variable type, is located in the Event class. The Event class is called the superclass because the CartEvent class you created inherits from it.

11. You can send the event type back up to the constructor of the superclass, and thus take advantage of its functionality, by including a super() call as follows:

```
public function CartEvent(selectedBook:Object, type:String)
{
    super(type);
}
```

In all OOP environments, there are two levels of variables: A variable located inside of a function is called a **local property**. A variable located outside of a function is called an **object-level property**. Usually, an object-level property is referred to as simply a property.

12. The keyword this, when inside of a class file and referring to a property, means an object-level property. The name of the book comes into the constructor. You want to then set the object-level property, bookSelected, as follows:

```
public function CartEvent(selectedBook:Object, type:String)
{
    super(type);
    this.selectedBook = selectedBook;
}
```

> Many programmers frown upon the practice of making the object-level property name the same as the name of the function parameter. I don't share that view, because the this keyword can make the distinction.

10

Let's look at the flow of this so far:

Inside the MXML file, there will be a call to this class (you haven't created it yet). When the call is made, two parameters will be passed, the name of the book, of type Object; and the type of event it was, of type String. These parameters will pass to the constructor automatically. The constructor, in turn, will send the type back up to the parent class, Event, and let its already-created code handle it. Then the constructor will set the property selectedBook with the information passing into the parameter selectedBook.

So far, there does not seem to be anything going on that you probably couldn't have done right in the Event class. Here is where you start doing some customizing. Be careful here; things may get a little confusing.

Customizing your class

The Event class has a method called clone(). The clone() method makes a copy of the event type and allows you to create custom code for handling the event. However, you cannot do this directly in the Event class. Instead, you are going to use a powerful tool available in OOP environments. You are going to tell your class, CartEvent, to go up to the Event class, get the clone() method, and then add your customized code to it. In OOP environments, this is called **overriding** the method. An entire book could be devoted to just this subject. I think you will get the idea, however, shortly.

In order to do all this, you must use the keyword override.

1. Put the following code after the constructor:

```
public function CartEvent(selectedBook:Object, type:String)
{
        super(type);
        this.selectedBook = selectedBook;
}
override public function clone():Event
{

}
```

2. You are going to do something like you did earlier when you needed to access the details of the book you selected. You are going to tell ActionScript to create a new object from this class file and then return the information contained within that object to the caller. You saw that this is easier to do because all you need to do is make a call to the object to find the information you need.

```
override public function clone():Event
{
    return new CartEvent(selectedBook,type);
}
```

If you are a bit confused as to why you did this yet, don't worry . . . it is about to get very clear.

Your finished class code should look as follows:

```
package classes
{
    import flash.events.Event;

    public class CartEvent extends Event
    {
        public var selectedBook:Object;

        public function CartEvent(selectedBook:Object, type:String)
        {
            super(type);
            this.selectedBook = selectedBook;
        }
        override public function clone():Event
        {
            return new CartEvent(selectedBook,type);
```

```
        }
    }
}
```

Anytime this class is called, from anywhere, these events will run. What you need to do is assign this whole event a name.

3. Save your class file and reopen BookCovers.mxml, if necessary.

4. Right below the present import statement, import mx.collections.ArrayCollection, import your new class as follows:

```
import mx.collections.ArrayCollection;
import classes.CartEvent;
```

You can use a Metadata tag to predefine an event name. This way, every time you call an event of that name, the class file you just defined will run.

5. Under the opening VBox tag and above the script block, define the Metadata tag as follows:

```
<?xml version="1.0" encoding="utf-8"?>
<mx:VBox xmlns:mx="http://www.adobe.com/2006/mxml"➥
    width="500" xmlns:comp="components.*">
<mx:Metadata>

</mx:Metadata>
```

6. You can define the event as follows:

```
<mx:Metadata>
    [Event(name="bookSelected", type="classes.CartEvent")]
</mx:Metadata>
```

Notice that there is no semicolon at the end of the definition. If you put one in, an error would occur.

From here on in, you can now use bookSelected as an event to any file that imports the CartEvent class. You can treat bookSelected just as you would a click event or any other event. When the class CartEvent runs, the event is generated.

7. Scroll down to the coverDetails state and, below the existing button, add another Button control. Give it a label attribute of "Add to Cart", an x attribute of 200, a y attribute of 400, and a click event that will call a function (which you will need to create) called purchaseBook().

```
<mx:Canvas>
    <mx:Image id="coverState" y="10" />
    <mx:Text y="250" text="{selectedAuthor}" fontSize="18"➥
        fontWeight="bold" />
    <mx:Text y="300" text="{selectedDescription}" fontSize="14"➥
        width="400" />
```

10

```
        <mx:Button label="Return to Book Covers" click="currentState=''"➥
            y="400" />
        <mx:Button label="Add to Cart" x="200" y="400"➥
            click="purchaseBook()" />
    </mx:Canvas>
```

Figure 10-24 shows the new Add to Cart button.

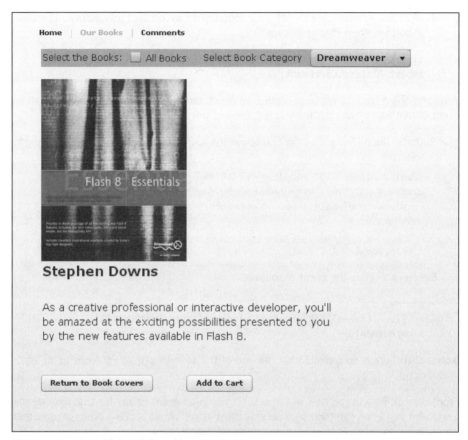

Figure 10-24. The addition of the Add to Cart button

If you want to test the positioning of the button, you will need to cut the click *event for now, or else an error will prevent the code from running.*

8. If you tested the position of this button, make sure you reinsert the click event after you have completed the test.

9. As you probably guessed, you need to create the purchaseBook() function at the end of the script block. The return type is void.

```
private function displayBookDetails(event:Object):void
{
    currentState = 'coverDetails';
    selectedCover = new Object();
    selectedCover = event;
    coverState.load('assets/' + selectedCover.filename + '.jpg');
    selectedAuthor = selectedCover.author;
    selectedDescription = selectedCover.desc;
}
private function purchaseBook():void
{

}
```

You already have a variable with all of the book information called selectedCover. This is the object created in the previous function and saved to the bindable variable defined at the start of BookCovers.mxml. You need to create a new object from the class CartEvent and then send over to the constructor the information in selectedCover and your new event, bookSelected.

10. Give the object a reference name of eventObj.

```
private function purchaseBook():void
{
    var eventObj:CartEvent = new CartEvent(selectedCover,➥
        "bookSelected");
}
```

11. Finally, to make it all happen, you have to use the trigger dispatchEvent, where you will dispatch the eventObj.

```
private function bookPurchase():void
{
    var eventObj:CartEvent = new CartEvent(coverData, "bookSelected");
    dispatchEvent(eventObj);
}
```

I hope you are taking the time to look up all of these structures in the ActionScript 3.0 Language Reference for even more details than I am presenting here. Also, I hope you are following the flow of the code.

If you save your code, there should be no errors generated. The code in BookCovers.mxml should now look as follows:

```
<?xml version="1.0" encoding="utf-8"?>
<mx:VBox xmlns:mx="http://www.adobe.com/2006/mxml"➥
    width="500" xmlns:comp="components.*">
```

10

```
<mx:Metadata>
   [Event(name="bookSelected", type="classes.CartEvent")]
</mx:Metadata>
<mx:Script>
   <![CDATA[
      import mx.collections.ArrayCollection;
      import classes.CartEvent;
      [Bindable]
      public var coverData:ArrayCollection;
      [Bindable]
      public var selectedCover:Object;
      [Bindable]
      public var selectedAuthor:Object;
      [Bindable]
      public var selectedDescription:Object
      private function displayBookDetails(event:Object):void
      {
         currentState = 'coverDetails';
         selectedCover = new Object();
         selectedCover = event;
         coverState.load('assets/' + selectedCover.filename + '.jpg');
         selectedAuthor = selectedCover.author;
         selectedDescription = selectedCover.desc;
      }
      private function bookPurchase():void
      {
         var eventObj:CartEvent = new CartEvent(selectedCover,➥
            "bookSelected");
         dispatchEvent(eventObj);
      }
   ]]>
</mx:Script>
<mx:states>
   <mx:State name="coverDetails">
      <mx:RemoveChild target="{coverThumbnails}" />
      <mx:AddChild position="lastChild">
         <mx:Canvas>
            <mx:Image id="coverState" y="10" />
            <mx:Text y="250" text="{selectedAuthor}" fontSize="18"➥
            fontWeight="bold" />
            <mx:Text y="300" text="{selectedDescription}"➥
               fontSize="14" width="400" />
            <mx:Button label="Return to Book Covers"➥
               click="currentState=''" y="400" /
            <mx:Button label="Add to Cart" x="200" y="400"➥
               click="bookPurchase()" />
         </mx:Canvas>
      </mx:AddChild>
```

```
            </mx:State>
        </mx:states>
            <mx:HBox backgroundColor="#EE82EE" verticalAlign="middle"➥
                fontSize="12" >
                <mx:Label text="Select the Books:" />
                <mx:CheckBox label="All Books" />
                <mx:Label text="Select Book Category" />
                <mx:ComboBox>
                    <mx:dataProvider>
                        <mx:ArrayCollection>
                            <mx:String>Dreamweaver</mx:String>
                            <mx:String>Flash</mx:String>
                            <mx:String>Graphics</mx:String>
                            <mx:String>Web Design</mx:String>
                            <mx:String>Other</mx:String>
                        </mx:ArrayCollection>
                    </mx:dataProvider>
                </mx:ComboBox>
            </mx:HBox>

            <mx:Tile width="500" id="coverThumbnails" >
                <mx:Repeater id="displayCovers" dataProvider="{coverData}">
                    <comp:CoverDisplay➥
                        coverImageData="{displayCovers.currentItem}"➥
                            click="displayBookDetails➥
                            (event.currentTarget.getRepeaterItem())" />
                </mx:Repeater>
            </mx:Tile>
        </mx:VBox>
```

Next is where everything you have been doing starts to come together.

Putting the pieces all together

All the information about the book is now in the CartEvent object. You now need to return to the BooksMain.mxml file.

1. Import the CartEvent class into this file.

```
<![CDATA[
    import mx.rpc.events.*;
    import mx.collections.*;
    import classes.CartEvent;
```

As soon as the BookCovers component is called, you want the event bookSelected to run, which will create the objects necessary for you to pass data to the shopping cart component.

2. Scroll down to where the call to the BookCovers component is located.

10

3. If you press the spacebar at the end of the tag, the Flex Builder help feature comes up (see Figure 10-25). If you scroll down, you will see that selectedBook, the custom event you created in BookCovers.mxml, is available because you imported the CartEvent class.

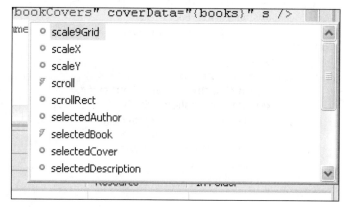

Figure 10-25. The selectedBook event availability

4. You are going to have it call an event, which you will write shortly, named bookSelectionHandler(). You will pass it the information using the event parameter.

```
<comp:BookCovers height="50%" width="50%" label="Our Books"➥
    id="bookCovers" coverData="{books}" ➥
selectedBook="bookSelectionHandler(event)" />
```

Notice once again that you can use bookSelected like any other event. The tough stuff is nearly done now, and things will start getting familiar again.

5. Go up to the script block and add the bookSelectionHandler() function as follows:

```
private function bookSelectionHandler(event:CartEvent):void
{

}
```

Notice the type is now CartEvent because the information is being passed from the CartEvent class.

Hopefully, users will purchase more than one book. For this reason, you may need to store more than one purchased book. Again, as you have done before, you will employ the class ArrayCollection.

6. Create another bindable variable called purchasedBooks and make it of type ArrayCollection. However, there is a twist here. The previous ArrayCollection uses were created for you by HTTPService. You need to create the object here.

```
import mx.rpc.events.*;
import mx.collections.*;
import classes.CartEvent;
[Bindable]
public var books:ArrayCollection;
[Bindable]
public var purchasedBooks:ArrayCollection=new ArrayCollection();
```

The ArrayCollection allows you to add to it with a method called addItem().

7. Come back down to the bookSelectionHandler() function and include the addItem() method as follows:

```
private function bookSelectionHandler(event:CartEvent):void
{
    purchasedBooks.addItem(event.selectedBook);
}
```

The CartEvent is passed to the function with the event parameter. The selectedBook property, in CartEvent, contains the book information. Notice that as soon as you type the period after event, you see selectedBook come up.

You have now gotten through the rough part. All you need to do is send the parameter over to the BookCart component.

8. Scroll down to where you called the BookCart component. Pass a variable called purchasedBooks and bind it to the purchasedBooks variable in this file as follows:

```
<comp:BookCart  x="750" y="291" purchasedBooks="{purchasedBooks}"/>
```

When you save now, you will see an error in the Problems pane. Don't worry about it; you will be fixing it in a few minutes.

9. Before you leave the code in BooksMain, please check it against the following code:

```
<?xml version="1.0" encoding="utf-8"?>
<mx:Application xmlns:mx="http://www.adobe.com/2006/mxml"➥
    height="100%" width="100%" layout="absolute" ➥
    backgroundColor="#FFFFFF" xmlns:comp="components.*"➥
    creationComplete="init()">
<mx:Script>
    <![CDATA[
        import mx.rpc.events.*;
        import mx.collections.*;
        import classes.CartEvent;
        [Bindable]
        public var books:ArrayCollection;
        [Bindable]
        public var purchasedBooks:ArrayCollection =➥
          new ArrayCollection();
    private function init():void
```

10

```
        {
            bookDataIn.send();
        }
        private function bookHandler(event:ResultEvent):void
        {
            books = event.result.books.stock;
        }
        private function bookSelectionHandler(event:CartEvent):void
        {
            purchasedBooks.addItem(event.selectedBook);
        }
    ]]>
</mx:Script>
<mx:HTTPService id="bookDataIn" url="assets/books.xml"➡
    result="bookHandler(event)" />
    <mx:Style>
        ComboBox
        {
            selectionColor:#32cd32
        }
        global
        {
            color:#00008b
        }
    </mx:Style>
    <mx:Image source="assets/logo1.gif"  x="357" y="10"/>
    <mx:LinkBar dataProvider="bookPages"  x="105" y="151"/>
    <mx:ViewStack id="bookPages" resizeToContent="true" x="118" y="185">
        <comp:BookHome height="50%" width="50%" label="Home" id="home" />
        <comp:BookCovers height="50%" width="50%" label="Our Books"➡
            id="bookCovers" coverData="{books}"➡
            bookSelected="bookSelectionHandler(event)" />
        <comp:Comments height="50%" width="50%" label="Comments"➡
            id="comments" />
    </mx:ViewStack>
    <comp:BookCart  x="750" y="291" purchasedBooks="{purchasedBooks}"/>
</mx:Application>
```

10. Save your work and go to the BookCart.mxml component.

11. Just below the opening Canvas tag, place a script block. Import the ArrayCollection class and make a bindable variable of purchasedBooks of type ArrayCollection.

```
<mx:Script>
    <![CDATA[
        import mx.collections.ArrayCollection;
        [Bindable]
        public var purchasedBooks:ArrayCollection;
    ]]>
</mx:Script>
```

12. Scroll down to the DataGrid and make the dataProvider attribute the purchasedBooks variable.

```
<mx:DataGrid width="214" height="336" dataProvider="{purchasedBooks}">
```

Since this contains the XML data, which was passed to CartEvent in BookCovers when you passed the selectedCover variable, which in turn was passed to purchaseBooks in the bookSelectionHandler in the BooksMain.mxml file, all you need to do is assign the node to the correct column of the DataGrid control.

The title of the book is listed in the XML file as title.

13. Change the dataField for Column 1 to title.

```
<mx:DataGridColumn headerText="Book" width="150" dataField="title"/>
```

Your finished BookCart code should look as follows:

```
<?xml version="1.0" encoding="utf-8"?>
<mx:Canvas xmlns:mx="http://www.adobe.com/2006/mxml">
<mx:Script>
  <![CDATA[
    import mx.collections.ArrayCollection;
    [Bindable]
    public var purchasedBooks:ArrayCollection;
  ]]>
</mx:Script>
  <mx:states>
    <mx:State name="cartExpand">
      <mx:SetProperty target="{bookCart}" name="height"➥
        value="500"/>
      <mx:AddChild relativeTo="{bookCart}" position="lastChild">
        <mx:DataGrid width="214" height="336"➥
          dataProvider="{purchasedBooks}">
          <mx:columns>
            <mx:DataGridColumn headerText="Book" width="150"➥
              dataField="title"/>
            <mx:DataGridColumn headerText="Qty." width="30"➥
              dataField="col 2"/>
          </mx:columns>
        </mx:DataGrid>
      </mx:AddChild>
      <mx:AddChild relativeTo="{bookCart}" position="lastChild">
        <mx:Button label="Click to Checkout" id="checkOut"/>
      </mx:AddChild>
    </mx:State>
  </mx:states>
  <mx:Panel id="bookCart" width="250" layout="vertical">
    <mx:Label text="There are 0 items in your cart" />
    <mx:Button x="5" y="30" label="See the cart details"➥
      click="currentState='cartExpand'" />
  </mx:Panel>
</mx:Canvas>
```

10

14. Save and run your application.

15. Go to the Our Books link.

16. Click a book cover and click the Add to Cart button.

17. If you expand your cart, you should see the book title in it (see Figure 10-26).

18. Try this for a few book titles by returning to the page displaying the book covers.

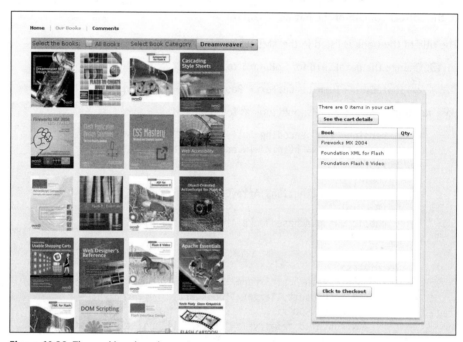

Figure 10-26. The working shopping cart

19. Close the browser and return to your code. While the tough part is over, you have a bit of cleanup work to do.

First of all, the ArrayCollection class has a property in it called length. This returns how many elements are in it.

20. Find the Label control in the BookCart.mxml file. Alter the text by replacing the number 0 with the code in bold.

```
<mx:Label text="There are {purchasedBooks.length} items in your cart"
/>
```

21. Go ahead and save your work and run the application again. Add a couple of items to your cart and you should see the counter incrementing, as shown in Figure 10-27.

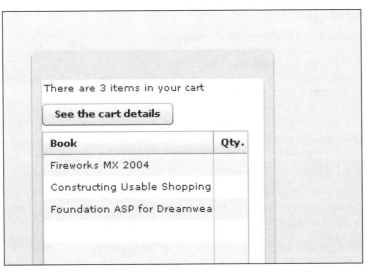

Figure 10-27. The incrementing counter

You have covered a lot of ground here and, for the most part, your shopping cart is now working. However, you have a few things still not fully operational:

- The quantity column of the DataGrid is still not functional. As a result, if you select a book twice, it will appear in the cart twice.

- You have no way to effectively remove items from the cart.

- The ComboBox control is still not being populated from the XML file, nor is it filtering the selection of books.

At the risk of irritating you, I am going to ask you to be patient. Toward the end of this book, we will be presenting a web site that will allow you to see and submit solutions using various dynamic technologies. However, there is a larger, less obvious, issue lurking that should be addressed right now: performance!

The TileList component

Right now, your application is only dealing with 20 or so books. A quantity of data this small does not create much of a demand on resources. However, what happens when your publisher's output grows to 200 books? How will that affect your performance?

As much as you may have fallen in love with the Repeater component, it is not the most efficient way of dealing with things as the data load grows. The reason is that it literally loads all of the images when the application loads.

The TileList component works a little differently. It does not load the images until they are actually needed. If you need to scroll through the images, they are not loaded until you scroll down to where they should appear. This can greatly reduce the time necessary to load the application.

1. Open the BookCovers component.

2. Scroll down to the Repeater component.

```
<mx:Tile width="500" id="coverThumbnails" >
  <mx:Repeater id="displayCovers" dataProvider="{coverData}">
    <comp:CoverDisplay➥
        coverImageData="{displayCovers.currentItem}"➥
        click="displayBookDetails➥
(event.currentTarget.getRepeaterItem())" />
  </mx:Repeater>
</mx:Tile>
```

There are two things you need to notice here. First of all, the id attribute of the Tile component is coverThumbnails, and the dataProvider of the Repeater component is coverData. You may want to make a note of these two items.

3. Delete the entire Tile structure, including the Repeater component.

4. In its place, start a TileList structure. Set the id attribute to coverThumbnails and the dataProvider to {coverData} as you have before.

```
<mx:TileList id="coverThumbnails" dataProvider="{coverData}" />
```

The event associated with a TileList component is not a click event, as you have used before, but a change event.

5. You need to set the change event to call the displayBookDetails() function, and you want to pass the event to the function.

```
<mx:TileList id="coverThumbnails" dataProvider="{coverData}" ➥
change="displayBookDetails(event)" />
```

You need to make a few minor adjustments to the function.

6. Change the function so it accepts an event of type Event.

```
private function displayBookDetails(event:Event):void
```

7. Change the selectedCover property so that it selects the event.currentTarget.selectedItem.

Recall that currentTarget is who generated the event, and the selectedItem is what was selected.

8. You have to do one additional chore. You will recall that the actual images come from the component CoverDisplay.mxml. The Tile component has an attribute called itemRenderer that will allow the Tile component to access the CoverDisplay component directly.

```
<mx:TileList id="coverThumbnails" dataProvider="{coverData}"➥
  change="displayBookDetails(event)"➥
  itemRenderer="components.CoverDisplay" />
```

9. Now open up the CoverDisplay component. You need to make a few minor changes.

10. For starters, delete the entire script block.

11. Change coverImageData in the source attribute of the Image tag to just data. This is how the TileList sends the data.

```
<mx:Image xmlns:mx="http://www.adobe.com/2006/mxml"➥
    source="assets/{data.filename}-small.jpg">

</mx:Image>
```

So, as you can see, you are using a bit less code than you needed to use with the Repeater component.

12. Save your work and run the application. You should see a much faster load time even with as few as 20 covers. However, you may have noticed a few new things (see Figure 10-28).

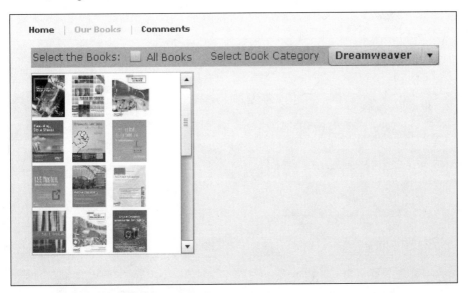

Figure 10-28. The added TileList component

13. If you click an image, the full image will appear as before. But when you return to the page displaying the book covers, the TileList component is full size. You can easily fix this bug by adding width and height attributes to the TileList component. You can also set the attributes for the column width and row height.

```
<mx:TileList id="coverThumbnails" dataProvider="{coverData}"➥
    change="displayBookDetails(event)"
    itemRenderer="components.CoverDisplay" width="500"➥
    height="400" columnWidth="120" rowHeight="110" />
```

14. When you run the application now, everything should be sized properly.

Summary

This chapter covered a lot of ActionScript code and, if you are a beginning programmer, you may have been confused by some of it. While the syntax is relatively easy, the concepts can sometimes take a while to fully grasp.

You will be returning to this case study for the next few chapters and do some tweaking and finishing up. We will also be talking about a web site that will present solutions based on various technologies.

You are now going to take a closer look at ArrayCollection to understand how to handle some of its many methods and properties.

11 **DRAG AND DROP**

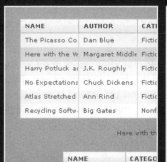 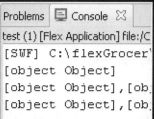 

How often do you drag and drop in desktop applications? You are probably answering that it is common. Now, here is a second question: How often do you drag and drop in a web application? The answer? Not often (although it is becoming more commonplace on the modern web).

Throughout this book, I have made frequent references to the distinction between desktop applications and web applications becoming blurred. Hopefully, you are seeing that for yourself. This chapter will blur that distinction even more.

You will be learning how to use one of the most unique features of Flex and the Flash Player: the Drag and Drop Manager.

As you will soon see, all the Flex components support the ability to drag and drop. In other words, by calling on a single property, you can grab one of the book covers, in the project you completed in the last chapter, and drag it into the shopping cart.

In this chapter, you will

- Implement dragging from DataGrid to DataGrid.
- Implement dragging from a DataGrid to List.
- Implement dragging a normally nondraggable component to a List.

You will have to learn some terminology first. So let's get started.

Understand the drag-and-drop concepts

Let's begin by thinking about the process of drag and drop.

A user initiates a drag-and-drop operation by selecting an item within a Flex component, such as a book cover. The user then holds down the mouse button as he or she moves the selected item around the screen. Finally, the user moves the item to another component and releases the mouse button to drop the item into that component.

Of course, like anything, you have to understand some terminology associated with this process.

The component from which the user is dragging the book cover from is called the **drag initiator**. The book cover itself would be the data that is being moved. This is called the **drag source**. While dragging the drag source around the screen, you will need to display the image while being dragged (or at least some image). This image is called the **drag proxy**. Finally, the component you drop the drag source into (usually the shopping cart) is called the **drop target**.

Just to see how easy it is to set up drag and drop, go to ActionScript Language Reference ➤ All Classes ➤ DataGrid control.

If you scroll down, you will see two properties: dragEnabled and dropEnabled (as shown in Figures 11-1 and 11-2).

---

dragEnabled property

dragEnabled:Boolean [read-write]

A flag that indicates whether you can drag items out of this control and drop them on other controls. If `true`, dragging is enabled for the control. If the `dropEnabled` property is also `true`, you can drag items and drop them within this control to reorder the items.

The default value is `false`.

Implementation
```
public function get dragEnabled():Boolean
public function set dragEnabled(value:Boolean):void
```

Figure 11-1. The dragEnabled property

---

dropEnabled property

dropEnabled:Boolean [read-write]

A flag that indicates whether dragged items can be dropped onto the control.

If you set this property to `true`, the control accepts all data formats, and assumes that the dragged data matches the format of the data in the data provider. If you want to explicitly check the data format of the data being dragged, you must handle one or more of the drag events, such as `dragOver`, and call the DragEvent's `preventDefault()` method to customize the way the list class accepts dropped data.

The default value is `false`.

Implementation
```
public function get dropEnabled():Boolean
public function set dropEnabled(value:Boolean):void
```

Figure 11-2. The dropEnabled property

> *You may need to click* Show Inherited Public Properties *to see these properties.*

Notice that both are properties that use a Boolean type that defaults to `false`.

The dragEnabled property makes the component a drag initiator and the dropEnabled property makes the component a drop target.

I am sure you are anxious to give this a little try. As I have done before, I will show you the concept in a simple setting. Later on, you will apply the concepts to the project you worked on in the last chapter.

Dragging to a DataGrid

By far the easiest way to handle drag and drop is to drag something to a DataGrid. This will become obvious as you progress. If you follow the steps I give you here, it should work each and every time.

1. Download the Chapter 11 files from the www.friendsofed.com site.

2. Start a new Flex basic project. You can call it whatever you choose and use a location of your own choosing also.

3. Set up an assets folder and using either the file import feature of Flex Builder (which you have used before) or Windows Explorer, put the books.xml file into it.

11

You have used this books.xml file before. But, if you want, take a moment and look at the structure.

4. In the default MXML file, enter the following code. There is nothing here you have not seen many times before.

```
<?xml version="1.0" encoding="utf-8"?>
<mx:Application xmlns:mx="http://www.adobe.com/2006/mxml"➥
    layout="absolute" creationComplete="bookStock.send()">
<mx:Script>
    <![CDATA[
        import mx.collections.ArrayCollection;
        import mx.rpc.events.ResultEvent;

        [Bindable]
        private var books:ArrayCollection;

        private function bookHandler(event:ResultEvent):void
        {
            books=event.result.books.stock;
        }
    ]]>
</mx:Script>
<mx:HTTPService url="assets/books.xml" id="bookStock"➥
    result="bookHandler(event)"/>
    <mx:DataGrid x="158" y="62" dataProvider="{books}">
        <mx:columns>
            <mx:DataGridColumn headerText="NAME" dataField="name"/>
            <mx:DataGridColumn headerText="AUTHOR" dataField="author"/>
            <mx:DataGridColumn headerText="CATEGORY" ➥
                dataField="category"/>
        </mx:columns>
    </mx:DataGrid>
</mx:Application>
```

5. Run the application; the result should look like Figure 11-3.

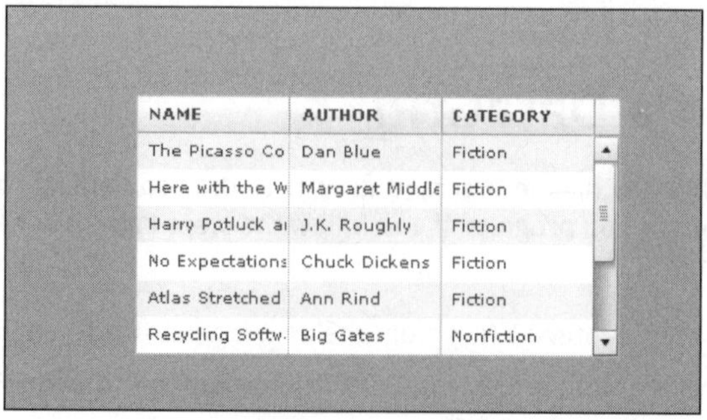

Figure 11-3. The results of the previous code

> You could have used the E4X standard for handling the XML data. But, for the time being, let's keep things as standardized as possible.

6. Give your DataGrid an id of dgInitiator.

```
<mx:DataGrid x="158" y="62" dataProvider="{books}" id="dgInitiator">
```

7. You now need to add a second DataGrid control that will receive the dragged data. It will only have two columns.

```
<mx:DataGrid x="158" y="62" dataProvider="{books}" id="dgInitiator">
    <mx:columns>
        <mx:DataGridColumn headerText="NAME" dataField="name"/>
        <mx:DataGridColumn headerText="AUTHOR" dataField="author"/>
        <mx:DataGridColumn headerText="CATEGORY" dataField="category"/>
    </mx:columns>
</mx:DataGrid>
<mx:DataGrid id="dgTarget" x="228" y="269">
    <mx:columns>
        <mx:DataGridColumn dataField="name" headerText="NAME"/>
        <mx:DataGridColumn dataField="category" headerText="CATEGORY"/>
    </mx:columns>
</mx:DataGrid>
```

8. Run the code; your results should now look like Figure 11-4.

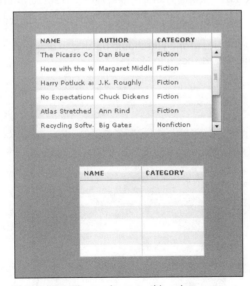

Figure 11-4. The results up to this point

You are now ready to set up the drag-and-drop process.

9. Go back to the dgInitiator DataGrid and set the dragEnabled property to true.

```
<mx:DataGrid x="158" y="62" dataProvider="{books}" id="dgInitiator"➡
  dragEnabled="true">
```

10. Again, run the code; you will be able to drag the information, but will have no place to drop it yet, as shown in Figure 11-5.

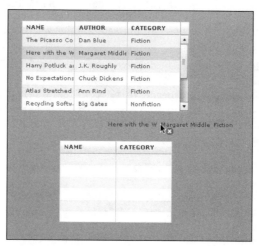

Figure 11-5. The dragEnabled property set to true

11. Set the dropEnabled property of the dgTarget DataGrid to true.

```
<mx:DataGrid id="dgTarget" x="228" y="269" dropEnabled="true">
```

12. Now test the application, and you should be able to drag and drop data items from one grid to another, as shown in Figure 11-6.

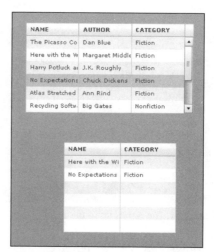

Figure 11-6. The data being dragged and dropped from one DataGrid to another

Notice that the Drag and Drop Manager handled all of the necessary connections and coding. Other than just setting up the initial DataGrid connections and enabling the drag-and-drop properties, you didn't need to do another thing in terms of coding.

Now that you have successfully transferred the data to a new DataGrid, what do you do with it? A little bit of logic will actually give you the answer to that.

As you have already seen, most data over the Internet is transferred via an XML file. Flex handles XML data as ArrayCollections. Thus, you need to save the data from the drop target into a new ArrayCollection.

13. Add the following bindable code to your script block:

```
<mx:Script>
  <![CDATA[
      import mx.collections.ArrayCollection;
      import mx.rpc.events.ResultEvent;

      [Bindable]
      private var books:ArrayCollection;

      [Bindable]
      private var purchasedBooks:ArrayCollection =
         new ArrayCollection();

      private function bookHandler(event:ResultEvent):void
      {
          books=event.result.books.stock;
      }
  ]]>
</mx:Script>
```

> As a reminder, you don't need to start a new ArrayCollection for the original data connection because HTTPService does that automatically in the background.

All you now need to do is bind the target DataGrid to the new ArrayCollection using the dataProvider property.

```
<mx:DataGrid id="dgTarget" x="228" y="269" dropEnabled="true"
    dataProvider="{purchasedBooks}">
```

Once the information is inside of the ArrayCollection, you can handle it any way you want, as you have already done. But, if you don't believe me, you can do a little test.

When a drag and drop is completed, an event called dragComplete is generated by the drag initiator.

1. In the dgInitiator DataGrid, add the following event:

```
<mx:DataGrid x="158" y="62" dataProvider="{books}" id="dgInitiator"➥
   dragEnabled="true" dragComplete="testDragDrop()">
```

2. In the script block, add the following function:

```
<mx:Script>
  <![CDATA[
      import mx.collections.ArrayCollection;
      import mx.rpc.events.ResultEvent;

      [Bindable]
      private var books:ArrayCollection;

      [Bindable]
      private var purchasedBooks:ArrayCollection =➥
         new ArrayCollection();

      private function bookHandler(event:ResultEvent):void
      {
          books=event.result.books.stock;
      }

      private function testDragDrop():void
      {
          trace(purchasedBooks);
      }
  ]]>
</mx:Script>
```

3. Now debug the application (remember, you cannot use Run with the trace() method) and drag and drop three items; you should see the results shown in Figure 11-7.

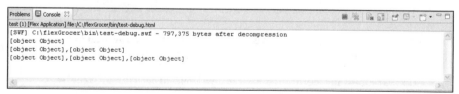

Figure 11-7. The results of the trace() method

Recall that you saw the [object Object] result when the ArrayCollection class was initially discussed. You will be taking a closer look at that in the next section. However, for the time being, rest assured that if you are seeing something similar to Figure 11-7, everything is working fine.

> *The* dgTarget *DataGrid has an event called* dragDrop, *which is broadcast when the user releases the mouse button over the target.*

4. Go ahead and remove the event, but leave the testDragDrop() function. You will be using it again.

As I stated at the outset, the easiest way to use drag and drop is to drag something to a DataGrid. But what happens if you want to drag to a List control where things aren't as clear-cut as before?

Dragging to a List control

In the last example, the Drag and Drop Manager had an easy job. It was able to match the column names of the dgInitiator DataGrid to the needed column names of the dgTarget DataGrid. But when you drag to a List control, there aren't any names to match.

Let's see how to handle this problem.

1. Remove the dgTarget DataGrid from the previous example.

2. In its place, put the following code:

```
<mx:List id="liTarget" width="225" dropEnabled="true" x="217" y="244"/>
```

3. Go ahead and run the application now and drag a few things into the List control; you will see a result similar to Figure 11-8.

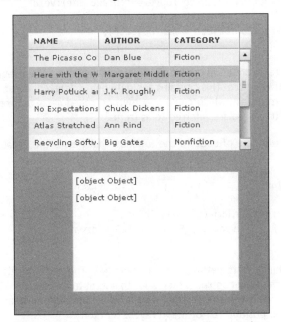

Figure 11-8. The result of dropping to the List control

You are getting [object Object] because Flex does not know how to match the data from the drag initiator to the drop target. You need to do a little programming to help it out.

Recall from the previous section that the event associated with the target is dragDrop.

4. Add the following parameter to the List control:

```
<mx:List id="liTarget" width="225" dropEnabled="true" x="217" ➡
    y="244" dragDrop="testDragDrop(event)"/>
```

5. In the script block, import the class mx.events.DragEvent (or you can use *).

```
<![CDATA[
    import mx.collections.ArrayCollection;
    import mx.rpc.events.ResultEvent;
    import mx.events.DragEvent;
```

6. Modify the signature of the testDragDrop() function as follows:

```
private function testDragDrop(event:DragEvent):void
{
    trace(purchasedBooks);
}
```

In order to populate the control properly, each item dragged into the List control must be saved to an object.

7. Replace the trace() statement with the creation of a new object.

```
private function testDragDrop(event:DragEvent):void
{
    var targetRow:Object = new Object();
}
```

As soon as you drag from an initiator, you create a DragEvent. The DragEvent class has a property called dragSource. This contains the data being dragged. It gets this information from the DragSource class, which contains a method called dataForFormat(). The pieces of data from the DataGrid are referred to as **items**.

8. Add a second line of code to the function that passes the DataGrid items to the Object.

```
private function testDragDrop(event:DragEvent):void
{
    var targetRow:Object = new Object();
    targetRow = event.dragSource.dataForFormat("items");
}
```

Here is where things start getting a bit convoluted. The code needs to look up the dataProvider of the List control. It then adds that item to the dataProvider by using the addItems function. But remember, since you are only adding one item at a time, it will always be added to position [0] of the ArrayCollection.

9. Add a dataProvider to the List control.

```
<mx:List id="liTarget" width="225" dropEnabled="true" x="217" y="244"→
    dragDrop="testDragDrop(event)" dataProvider="{purchasedBooks}"/>
```

10. Add the following third line to the testDragDrop() function.

```
private function testDragDrop(event:DragEvent):void
{
    var targetRow:Object = new Object();
    targetRow = event.dragSource.dataForFormat("items");
    liTarget.dataProvider.addItem(targetRow[0].name);
}
```

11. Save and run the application now; you should see the name property get transferred with some unwanted additional information, as shown in Figure 11-9. Don't worry, you will fix that in a bit.

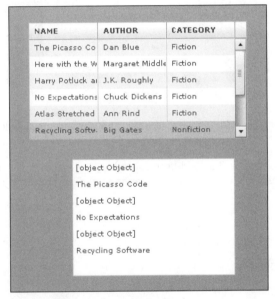

Figure 11-9. The List control populated

You are probably wondering why you are still getting the [object Object] code.

Flex, by default, still refers to the object for each item placed on the list. That default data can be stopped by adding a fourth line of code to the function as follows:

```
private function testDragDrop(event:DragEvent):void
{
    var targetRow:Object = new Object();
    targetRow = event.dragSource.dataForFormat("items");
    liTarget.dataProvider.addItem(targetRow[0].name);
    event.preventDefault();
}
```

12. Add the line to your code and run it; all should be well as shown in Figure 11-10.

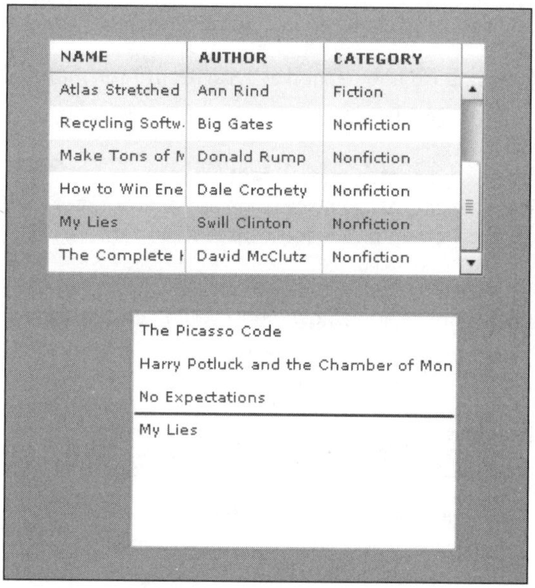

Figure 11-10. The corrected code results

Even if you didn't fully understand all the theoretical concepts behind the code, don't worry; you can use this code almost verbatim, and it should work each and every time.

All Flash components have drag-and-drop capability. However, not all capabilities are created equal. The following components have **enhanced drag-and-drop capability**.

- DataGrid
- List
- TileList
- HorizontalList
- Menu
- PrintDataGrid
- Tree

This means that ActionScript is doing most of the work for you. However, if you want to use any of the other components, such as Label, you need to do a bit of programming work on your own.

Let's have a look.

Nonenhanced drag and drop

Up to this point, most of the work has been done automatically. But when you get into nonenhanced drag-and-drop components, you need to do most of the work. Among the jobs are importing the necessary classes and checking that data types match.

1. Begin by starting a new MXML file using any name of your choice.

2. Add the following code to it:

```
<?xml version="1.0" encoding="utf-8"?>
<mx:Application xmlns:mx="http://www.adobe.com/2006/mxml"➥
   layout="vertical">
   <mx:Script>
     <![CDATA[
        import mx.collections.ArrayCollection;

        [Bindable]
        private var targetData:ArrayCollection=new ArrayCollection();
     ]]>
   </mx:Script>
   <mx:Label id="dragLabel" text="Drag this Label"/>
   <mx:List id="liTarget" width="225" dataProvider="{targetData}"/>
</mx:Application>
```

3. Run the application now; your results should look like Figure 11-11.

Figure 11-11. The example so far, with a label and empty list in place

There are four classes associated with drag-and-drop functionality:

- DragSource and IUIComponents: mx.core packages
- DragManager: mx.manager package
- DragEvent: mx.event package

4. Import the packages and classes just listed.

```
<![CDATA[
    import mx.collections.ArrayCollection;
    import mx.core.*;
    import mx.managers.DragManager;
    import mx.events.DragEvent;
```

In order to drag the Label component, you would need to create a mouseDown event that calls a function. However, in order for drag and drop to work, four parameters need to be passed.

The first parameter will be the ID of the Label component being dragged. The second parameter will be the data being passed. The third parameter will be the event being passed. Finally, the fourth parameter will be the format of the data.

5. Create the following mouseDown event for the Label component.

```
<mx:Label id="dragLabel" text="Drag this Label"➥
    mouseDown="dragTest(dragLabel,'This is the data', event,➥
    'stringFormat')"/>
```

In this case, you are just passing a simple string over as data.

6. Create the following function in the script block to handle the event:

```
private function dragTest(initiator:Label, myData:String,➥
    event:MouseEvent, format:String):void
{

}
```

Notice that the first argument is of the type component that you are associating with it. In this case, it is a Label control.

7. The first line of code needs to instantiate the DragSource class, which you imported previously in the mx.core package.

```
private function dragTest(initiator:Label, myData:String,➥
    event:MouseEvent, format:String):void
{
    var ds:DragSource = new DragSource();
}
```

8. You now want to add the data and format to the DragSource object using the addData() function.

```
private function dragTest(initiator:Label, myData:String,➥
    event:MouseEvent, format:String):void
{
    var ds:DragSource = new DragSource();
    ds.addData(myData,format);
}
```

9. You finally want to add the name of the component, the DragSource object, and the event to the DragManager class using the doDrag() function. Remember, the DragManager class is serving as a central managing point and, without the information, DragManager won't know what to do.

```
private function dragTest(initiator:Label, myData:String,➡
    event:MouseEvent, format:String):void
{
    var ds:DragSource = new DragSource();
    ds.addData(myData,format);
    DragManager.doDrag(initiator, ds, event);
}
```

If you save and give your application a try, you will see that you can drag the label. The only problem is that there is no place to drop it. It should look like Figure 11-12. Notice the red X. Its importance will be explained in a moment.

Figure 11-12. Dragging the Label control

In order to have a functional drop target, you need to do some programming on the List side now.

10. In the List tag, create a dragEnter event, passing the event and the format to a function you will soon create.

```
<mx:List id="liTarget" width="225" dataProvider="{targetData}"➡
    dragEnter="testDragEnter(event, 'stringFormat')"/>
```

Here things start getting a little tricky. You need to test to verify that the data is in the correct format. For instance, you couldn't pass a string if a number was expected. In the earlier examples, the Drag and Drop Manager handled all of that for you. But here, you have to test.

11. Set up the testDragEnter() function in the script block.

```
private function testDragEnter(event:DragEvent, format:String):void
{

}
```

11

> *There is a subtle, but important distinction here. At a very deep level, a* MouseEvent *and a* DragEvent *are two separate, but related, events, each with its own require-ments. Flex handles most of this in the background. Here, however, to test the data, you need to use a* DragEvent *so that the manager can do its job.*

12. The function is expecting the data to be a string. In order to test for this, you need to build an if statement using exactly the syntax shown here:

```
private function testDragEnter(event:DragEvent, format:String):void
{
   if(event.dragSource.hasFormat(format))
   {

   }
}
```

13. If the data is of the proper format, you need to tell the DragManager class to accept the data as follows:

```
private function testDragEnter(event:DragEvent, format:String):void
{
   if(event.dragSource.hasFormat(format))
   {
      DragManager.acceptDragDrop(IUIComponent(event.target));
   }
}
```

> *There are times, in OOP programming, where you sometimes have to accept syntax as is and working. This is one of those spots. When you are telling a com-ponent to accept a drag and drop manually, this syntax is used nearly verbatim. Anyone up for about 12 pages of convoluted code explanation?*

14. Go ahead and run the code now. You still won't be able to drop the Label control. But, if you notice, the red X will be missing (see Figure 11-13). This means that the List control is willing to accept the drop.

Figure 11-13. The List control, ready to accept the data

Before the List control will allow a drop, you need to do one last bit of programming.

15. You need to add a second event to the List control. A DragDrop event will call a function while passing the event and format parameters.

```
<mx:List id="liTarget" width="225" dataProvider="{targetData}"➥
    dragEnter="testDragEnter(event, 'stringFormat')"➥
    dragDrop="testDragDrop(event, 'stringFormat')"/>
```

16. Create the testDragDrop() function as follows:

```
private function testDragDrop(event:DragEvent, format:String):void
{

}
```

17. You will now get back to some familiar territory. You are going to create a new object to hold the data. You will then pass the event into that object and, finally, use the addItem() function to add the data to the List's dataProvider property.

```
private function testDragDrop(event:DragEvent, format:String):void
{
    var myData:Object = new Object();
    myData = event.dragSource.dataForFormat(format);
    liTarget.dataProvider.addItem(myData);
}
```

It may not hurt for you to have a look at what the finished code should look like:

```
<?xml version="1.0" encoding="utf-8"?>
<mx:Application xmlns:mx="http://www.adobe.com/2006/mxml"➥
    layout="vertical">
    <mx:Script>
        <![CDATA[
            import mx.collections.ArrayCollection;
            import mx.core.*;
            import mx.managers.DragManager;
            import mx.events.DragEvent;

            [Bindable]
            private var targetData:ArrayCollection=new ArrayCollection();
            private function dragTest(initiator:Label, myData:String,➥
                event:MouseEvent, format:String):void
            {
                var ds:DragSource = new DragSource();
                ds.addData(myData,format);
                DragManager.doDrag(initiator, ds, event);
            }
            private function testDragEnter(event:DragEvent,➥
                format:String):void
            {
                if(event.dragSource.hasFormat(format))
                {
```

11

```
                            DragManager.acceptDragDrop(IUIComponent(event.target));
                }
            }

            private function testDragDrop(event:DragEvent,➥
                format:String):void
            {
                var myData:Object = new Object();
                myData = event.dragSource.dataForFormat(format);
                liTarget.dataProvider.addItem(myData);
            }
        ]]>
    </mx:Script>
    <mx:Label id="dragLabel" text="Drag this Label"➥
        mouseDown="dragTest(dragLabel,'This is the data', event,➥
        'stringFormat')"/>
    <mx:List id="liTarget" width="225" dataProvider="{targetData}"➥
        dragEnter="testDragEnter(event, 'stringFormat')"➥
        dragDrop="testDragDrop(event, 'stringFormat')"/>
</mx:Application>
```

18. Go ahead and save and run your application. Notice the data when you drop it on the List control. It should look like Figure 11-14.

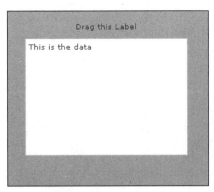

Figure 11-14. The finished drag and drop

Summary

You just covered three potential drag-and-drop scenarios that encompass many possibilities. Much of the code you used can be reproduced verbatim for your own projects. Later on in the book, you will revisit the project you completed in the last chapter and apply the concepts learned here.

You will now turn your attention to the server side of things.

12 FLEX AND COLDFUSION

"Welcome to ColdFusion, Powered by Flex."

These words were put on the Adobe site with the introduction of ColdFusion MX 7.02.

What Adobe is basically saying is that ColdFusion will continue to do its job serving as a powerful, yet easy-to-use application server. But the GUI duties will now be taken over by the Flex presentation server. As a matter of fact, ColdFusion MX 7.02 and Flex 2 have nearly seamless integration with each other.

In this chapter, you will

- Explore the ColdFusion/Flex Application Wizard, which works specifically with just ColdFusion.
- Build SQL queries in Flex while using data from ColdFusion.
- Create ColdFusion Components (CFCs) from within Flex Builder 2.
- Generate all of the necessary ColdFusion Meta Language (CFML) code to perform the necessary back-end operations.

Before you begin, if you have not done so already, please refer to the appendix, which discusses the installation of ColdFusion MX 7.02. It is important that you have this version or a later one installed, or you may not have access to some of the features discussed in this chapter.

I am assuming that you have never worked with ColdFusion before. Because of that, some of the early discussion in this chapter will be quite elementary.

> *You might be wondering, "But what about other server-side technologies such as PHP and ASP.NET?" I stuck to ColdFusion for the most part because it is the easiest server-side technology to integrate with Flex 2. However, in Chapter 15, I will discuss ways to learn how to use other dynamic technologies with Flex 2. Just as a little teaser, go to* www.charlesebrown.net.

Introducing ColdFusion

If you have never worked with ColdFusion before, you will be surprised to know that it was the philosophical basis for Flex's MXML language. The whole idea behind ColdFusion was to program using HTML-like tags rather than forcing the developer to learn the formalities of a development language like Java. For example, if you wanted to set a variable, it would go something like this:

```
<cfset myName = "Charles E. Brown">
```

Notice that there is no data typing and none of the formal requirements of XML structure.

The end result was that ASP-like applications could be developed quickly and easily. However, what many did not realize is that Java code was being generated in the background. As a matter of fact, I have a good friend that calls ColdFusion an easy-to-use Java development environment.

It's easy to see how this shares the same philosophy with Flex. Flex uses XML-like tags that ultimately generate ActionScript in the background.

While the ColdFusion language has not changed with Flex, many of the GUI functions are now better served by using Flex.

Assuming you have ColdFusion installed properly, the first thing you are going to need to do is install your data source. For the purposes of this example, you will use a small Access database. Since it's my goal to show you how to use Flex and ColdFusion together, and not to get into a discussion about database design or SQL, I kept this database very simple with just a few records.

You can download this database from www.friendsofed.com with the Chapter 12 downloads—do this now, as you'll need it in the upcoming text.

Installing a data source

ColdFusion makes installing a data source very simple.

1. Begin by going to Start ➤ Macromedia ➤ ColdFusion MX 7 ➤ Administrator. Your screen should look something like Figure 12-1.

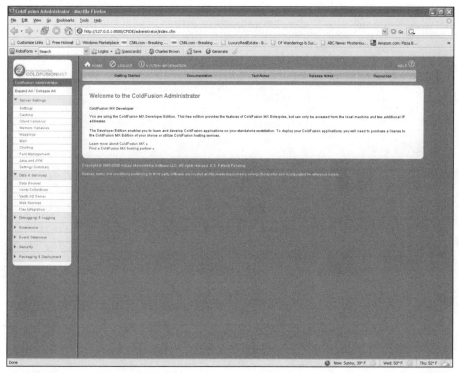

Figure 12-1. The ColdFusion Administrator

12

Notice that the ColdFusion Administrator opens up in your default web browser. Now look at the links along the left side.

2. Under the Data & Services category, click Data Sources. You'll now see the screen shown in Figure 12-2.

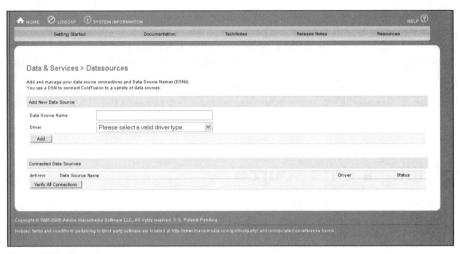

Figure 12-2. The Datasources screen

3. Now you will want to give your data source a name of your choosing. For the purposes of this exercise, I chose the name bookData as shown in Figure 12-3.

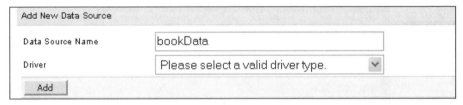

Figure 12-3. Naming the data source

As I stated at the beginning of this chapter, ColdFusion writes Java programming code in the background. Because of this, it can connect with any of the standard database environments by using the powerful Java Database Connector (JDBC) drivers. You're going to add one of these drivers next.

4. Click the Driver list as shown in Figure 12-4.

Data & Services > Datasources

Add and manage your data source connections and Data Source Names (DSNs).
You use a DSN to connect ColdFusion to a variety of data sources.

Add New Data Source

Data Source Name   bookData

Driver   Please select a valid driver type.

| Please select a valid driver type. |
| DB2 Universal Database |
| Informix |
| Microsoft Access |
| Microsoft Access with Unicode |
| Microsoft SQL Server |
| MySQL (3.x) |
| ODBC Socket |
| Oracle |
| other |
| Sybase |

Add

Connected Data Sources

Actions   Data Source Nam

Verify All Connections

Copyright © 1995-2006 Adobe Macromedia Software LLC. All rights reserved. U.S. Patents Pending.

Figure 12-4. The available JDBC drivers

> It is beyond the scope of this book to get into a detailed discussion of these drivers.

5. Select the Microsoft Access option, and click the Add button to reveal the screen shown in Figure 12-5.

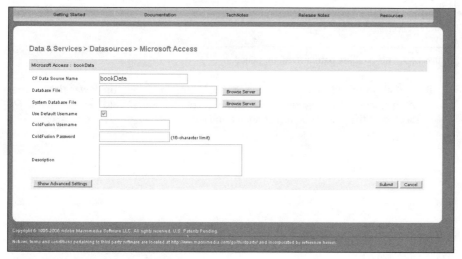

Figure 12-5. Microsoft Access driver screen

Your next step is to browse to the Access MDB file.

6. Click the Browse Server button for the Database File field. This will give you the screen shown in Figure 12-6.

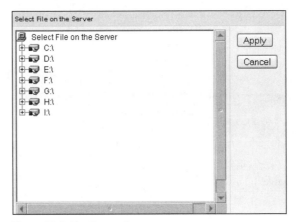

Figure 12-6. The Browse Server screen

7. Browse to the folder to which you downloaded the database for this chapter. Once you have located it, click the Apply button. You are brought back to the previous screen with all of the path information filled in, as shown in Figure 12-7.

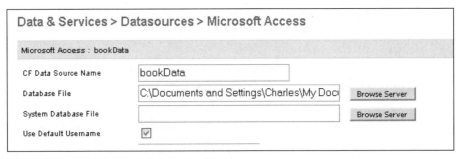

Figure 12-7. The database path information filled in

8. Next all you need to do is click the Submit button located in the lower-right corner of this screen. If everything was done correctly, you should see the word *OK* located in the status column as shown in Figure 12-8.

Figure 12-8. Here the Status column is showing that everything is ready to go!

As long as you have OK in the status column, ColdFusion is ready to go. That is how easy it is to use it.

9. Go ahead and close the ColdFusion Administrator. Believe it or not, you won't need to access it again.

Connecting Flex and ColdFusion

Next you need to connect Flex to ColdFusion.

1. Go ahead and open Flex Builder if necessary.

2. If you want, delete any projects you previously worked on. While this is not necessary, it might cause less confusion for now.

3. Select File ➤ New ➤ Other to bring up the screen shown in Figure 12-9.

Figure 12-9. Selecting the ColdFusion/Flex Application Wizard

4. Under the ColdFusion Wizards category, select ColdFusion/Flex Application Wizard.

5. Click Next. This brings up a screen, shown in Figure 12-10, that displays a description of the function of this wizard.

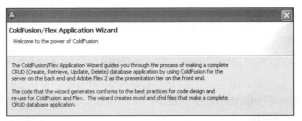

Figure 12-10. The ColdFusion/Flex Application Wizard Welcome

If you receive a prompt for a password to the RDS server, leave the password blank and continue on. I will be discussing configuration later on in this chapter.

6. After reading the description, click the Next button.

7. The next screen, as shown in Figure 12-11, allows you to load settings from previous ColdFusion/Flex applications. Since you don't have any, just click the Next button.

Figure 12-11. The Previous Wizard Settings screen

The next screen, shown in Figure 12-12, allows you to select the ColdFusion server address as well as any data sources located within the ColdFusion Administrator. Notice that it automatically found the data source you just set in the last section: bookData.

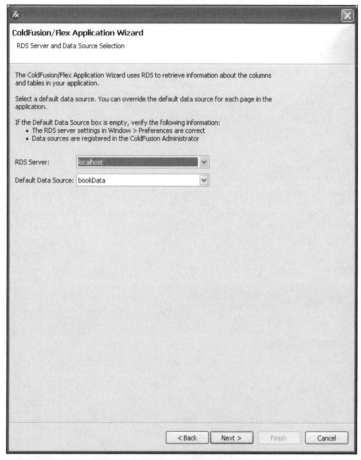

Figure 12-12. The RDS and Data Source Selection screen

8. ColdFusion, when run locally as you are doing here, runs as localhost:8500. It is sufficient to just select localhost here, so do so now.

> *RDS stands for **Remote Data Service** and it is how applications can access a ColdFusion data source.*

12

9. Click Next to get to the screen in Figure 12-13.

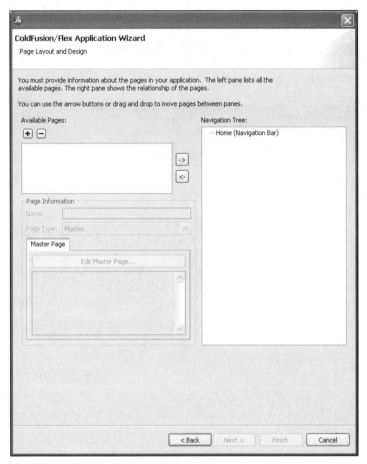

Figure 12-13. The Page Layout and Design screen

It is at this screen that the real work begins. This is where you will lay out your pages and decide what data you want to go into what page.

The first thing you want to do is design your main page. Again, for the purposes of this chapter, you are going to keep your designs very simple.

10. Under the Available Pages category, click the + button.

11. In the Name field, change the name to booksMain as shown in Figure 12-14.

Figure 12-14. The creation of the booksMain page

12. Click the Edit Master Page button. This page, shown in Figure 12-15, is where you assign the data to the page and build the SQL query.

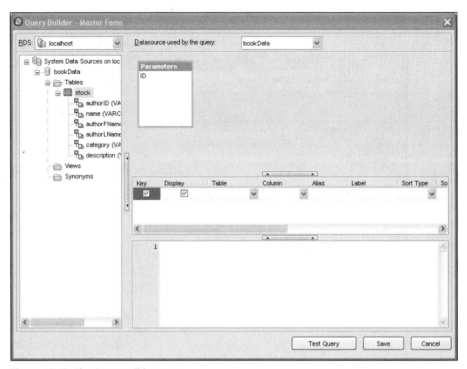

Figure 12-15. The Query Builder screen

As you can see, this screen shows you the structure of the database and allows you to build SQL queries using an Access-like interface. Your simple database has only one table. But that will serve the purpose for this simple example.

13. In the left window, double-click the stock table. Notice in Figure 12-16 that the SQL code has started to form in the bottom window.

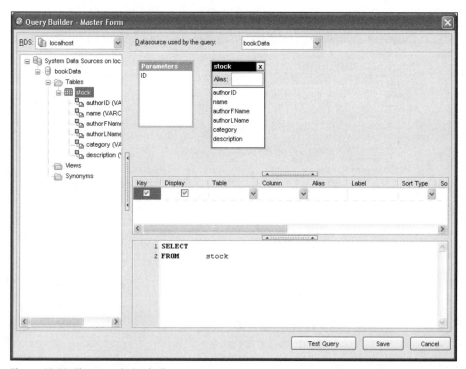

Figure 12-16. The query being built

Now, for your simple page, you just want the first and last name of the authors to appear. However, since you will link it to another page with the details, you will also need to include the authorID field.

14. Double-click the authorID, authorFName, and authorLName fields. Notice that the authorID field is listed as a key field and that its display status is turned off as shown in Figure 12-17.

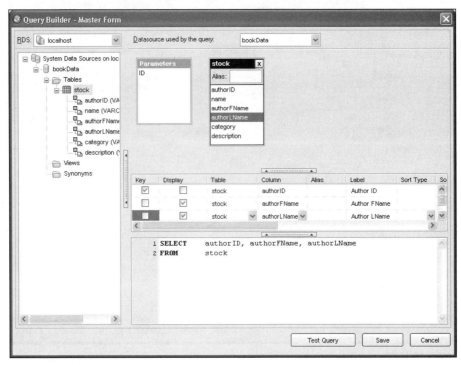

Figure 12-17. The fields added to the query

It is common to place fields on a page that may not display. This allows the query to use search criteria easily.

15. Give the query a quick test by clicking the Test Query button at the bottom of the screen. You should get the output shown in Figure 12-18.

autho...	authorF...	authorL...
1	Dan	Blue
2	Margaret	Middle
3	J.K.	Roughly
4	Chuck	Dickens
5	Ann	Rind
6	Big	Gates
7	Donald	Rump
8	Dale	Crochety
9	Swill	Clinton
10	David	McClutz

SELECT authorID, authorFName, authorLName FROM stock

Figure 12-18. Testing the query

Under Label you can also change how the labels will appear on the page. For instance, do you want authorFName to appear as a label?

16. Go ahead and change authorFName and authorLName to Author First Name and Author Last Name, as shown in Figure 12-19.

Figure 12-19. Changing the labels

17. Go ahead and close the test window and click the Save button. You are returned to the previous screen with all of the query information added in, as shown in Figure 12-20.

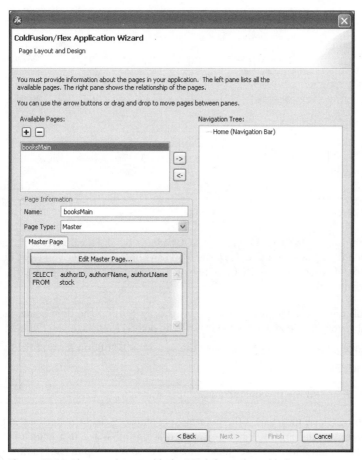

Figure 12-20. The page layout with the SQL information added

You now need to create a second page to show the details.

18. Click the + button and call the page bookDetails. This time, however, change the page type to Detail.

19. Click the Edit Detail Page button and, when in the query screen, double-click the stock table again—the details of this table will appear as shown in Figure 12-21.

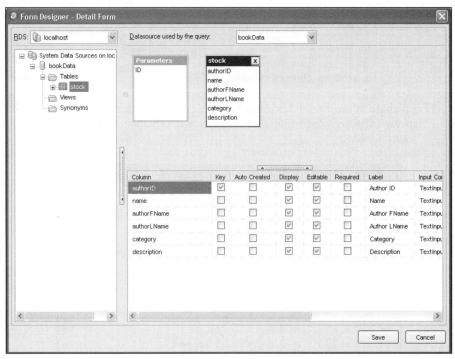

Figure 12-21. Editing the query of the Detail page

Notice in this case that you do not have SQL code to build. Flex Builder is doing a lot of work in the background for you. However, you can control whether you want fields to be required or whether you want them to be editable by the end user. Also, like the last form, you can control the labels.

20. You will be examining the other fields shortly. But, for the time being, make them all required, and change authorFName and authorLName like you did before.

21. Since authorID is a key field, select the Auto Created option for that field.

22. Click Save.

You are returned to the previous screen.

23. Home (Navigation Bar) is the outermost container. Select the booksMain page and, by either clicking the right arrow or dragging it, make it a child of the Home (Navigation Bar) container. Make sure you drop it on top of the Home (Navigation Bar) container.

24. Subsequently, make the bookDetails page a child of the booksMain page. Your finished setup should look like Figure 12-22.

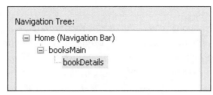

Figure 12-22. The navigation tree

25. Once you are finished, click the Next button to give you the screen shown in Figure 12-23.

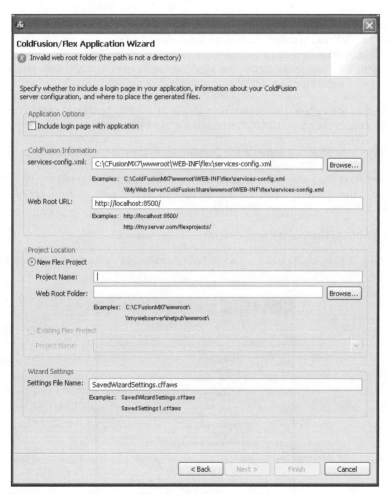

Figure 12-23. The server configuration page

We have a lot to talk about here. Let's take a few minutes and discuss this page line by line.

First of all, you may see the message "Invalid web root folder" at the very top. Don't worry about that for now. You will fix it shortly.

> If for some reason the config.xml file is not recognized, it might not have been installed correctly in the ColdFusion path. While there are a number of fixes, I have found the longest to be the most foolproof. Uninstall ColdFusion and Flex Builder. Reinstall ColdFusion 7.02 first and then Flex Builder 2 with the ColdFusion extensions. If the services-config.xml file is not recognized or can't be found, make sure the path to it is correct in the services-config.xml text field.

If you want to include a login page, you could select that option. For now, however, leave it off.

You should see the services-config.xml file with exactly the same information as shown in Figure 12-23. If you installed ColdFusion MX version 7.02 (not an earlier version), all you should need to do is browse to the directory shown in Figure 12-23. If the directory is not there exactly as shown in the figure, the application may not work correctly. Please take a moment and check this carefully.

As I stated at the outset, ColdFusion runs locally at http://localhost:8500. This is the localhost web server on port 8500. You can leave this setting as is for now.

26. Give your project a name. (I use BookProject in the following examples.)

All servers have their own root directory. This is the directory where they look for the information that needs to be found. All the files associated with your project have to be arranged in folders within that directory.

In the case of ColdFusion, the root directory is called wwwroot.

27. Click the Browse button to the right of the Web Root Folder field and drill down to the CFusionMX7\wwwroot directory as shown in Figure 12-24.

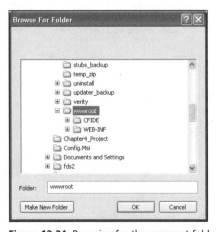

Figure 12-24. Browsing for the wwwroot folder

28. Click OK—you should now notice that the warning message about the invalid root folder has disappeared.

Your finished screen should look like Figure 12-25.

Figure 12-25. The finished project/server information screen

29. Leave the Wizard Settings file name as is for now and click Finish.

It may take a couple of minutes to compile, but Flex Builder is setting up all of the proper directories and writing the necessary code.

30. You should see an MXML document called Main.mxml. Go ahead and run it. It should begin with just the ControlBar opening and booksMain as a link, as shown in Figure 12-26. Don't worry, you will fix this name soon.

Figure 12-26. The opening screen of the application

31. Click the booksMain link and you will be taken to the first page populated with data, as shown in Figure 12-27.

Figure 12-27. The first page of the application

32. If you double-click a name, the bookDetails page opens, as shown in Figure 12-28.

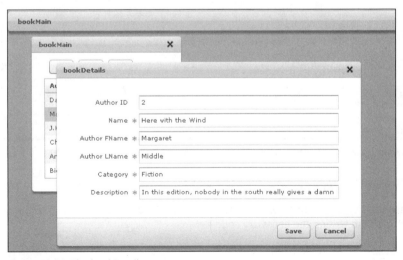

Figure 12-28. The bookDetails page

If you wanted, you could edit the data here, and it would be saved back to the database. Also, if you go back to the booksMain page and click the + above the data, a blank record opens that will allow you to add data.

Just think, you have a working application, linked to a database, in minutes. This is the power of ColdFusion/Flex applications.

Dissecting and modifying your application

If you return to Flex Builder and look at the code of the Main.mxml file, you won't see anything you haven't seen before.

```
<?xml version="1.0" encoding="utf-8"?>
<mx:Application xmlns:mx="http://www.adobe.com/2006/mxml"
    xmlns="*"
    xmlns:controllers="com.cfgenerated.controllers.*"
    layout="absolute"
    currentState="mainApplication">
    <mx:Style source="application.css" />

    <mx:states>
        <mx:State name="mainApplication">
            <mx:AddChild position="lastChild">
                <controllers:windowedApplication top="0" left="0"➥
                    right="0" bottom="0"/>
            </mx:AddChild>
        </mx:State>
    </mx:states>
</mx:Application>
```

When you click the booksMain link, it triggers a state, which calls the component booksMain.cfc.

Wait! Not booksMain.mxml?

OK, here is where things start getting interesting.

The file extension .cfc stands for ColdFusion Component. Flex has the capability of accessing and utilizing the full power of ColdFusion Components which, if you recall, are really running Java in the background.

The booksMain component is under the cfgenerated directory in the Project panel. Go ahead and open it.

```
<cfcomponent>
    <cffunction name="getMasterQuery" output="false"➥
        access="remote" returntype="query">
        <cfargument name="ID" required="false">
        <cfset var qRead="">
```

12

407

```
<cfquery name="qRead" datasource="bookData">
    SELECT    authorID, authorFName, authorLName
    FROM      stock
</cfquery>

<cfreturn qRead>
</cffunction>

<cffunction name="deleteItem" output="false"➥
    access="remote" returntype="void">
    <cfargument name="ID" required="true">

    <cfscript>
        stockGateway =➥
        createObject("component","BookProject.components.➥
        cfgenerated.bookDetails.stockGateway");
        stockGateway.deleteByID(arguments.ID);
    </cfscript>
</cffunction>
</cfcomponent>
```

Discussing in ins and outs of ColdFusion Components could be an entire book itself, with the programming language it uses another book yet again. As such, it is well beyond the scope of this book. However, you can see that the SQL query is built into the page. Also, notice that the two <cffunction> tags (all ColdFusion tags begin with *cf*) have an argument access = "remote". This argument allows the component to easily function as a web service.

> *ColdFusion Components can access many of the Java class files directly.*

Last of all, notice that because of the seamless integration between Flex and ColdFusion, no XML file is needed.

As you may have figured out already, every time you add a new "main" page to the application, the name of that page is entered in the ControlBar. booksMain is not exactly the most user friendly name in the world, so you need to make a few modifications to your application.

1. Select File ➤ New ➤ Other.
2. Once again, select the ColdFusion/Flex Application Wizard.

3. Click the Next button twice, and you will be greeted by the screen shown in Figure 12-29.

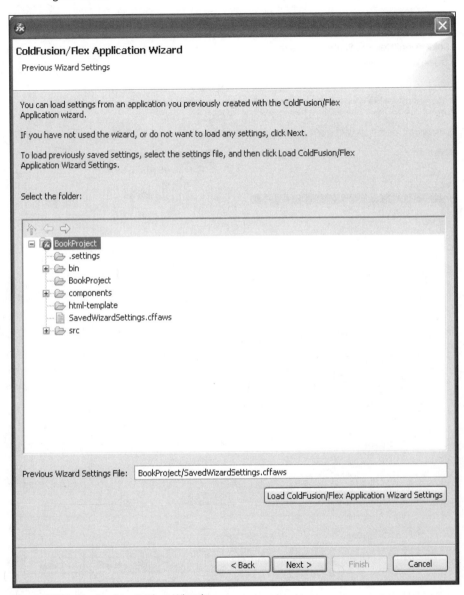

Figure 12-29. The Previous Settings Wizard

4. Select BookProject and click the Load ColdFusion/Flex Application Wizard Settings button.

5. Click Next twice; you should see the screen shown in Figure 12-30. This is the Page Layout and Design screen you saw earlier.

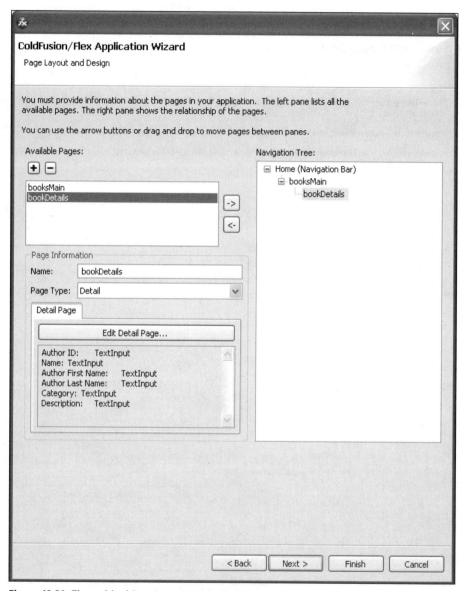

Figure 12-30. The revisited Page Layout and Design screen

6. Click the booksMain page and change the name to Find Books.

Since Flex is doing internal naming, you can use friendly names here, including spaces.

7. Make one more slight modification. Select the bookDetails page. You can change the name anytime you want (I changed it to Book Details), which will change the form's heading. Regardless of whether you change it here, next click the Edit Detail Page button.

8. For the Category field, scroll over to the Input Control category and change it from a TextInput to a ComboBox as shown in Figure 12-31.

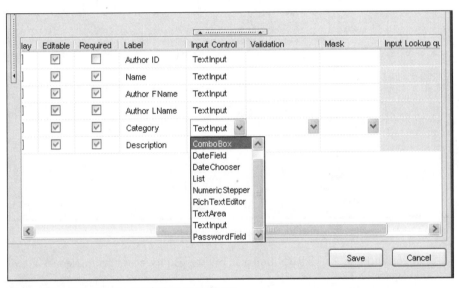

Figure 12-31. Selecting the ComboBox component

As you can see, all of the Flex components are available for your forms. However, when you select the ComboBox, you must select what the ComboBox must look up.

9. After selecting ComboBox, scroll over to the Input Lookup query (sub-select) field. You will see a small white button to the right of it. Click it.

12

This opens up a new query.

10. Double-click the Category field in the stock table. Your finished query should look like Figure 12-32.

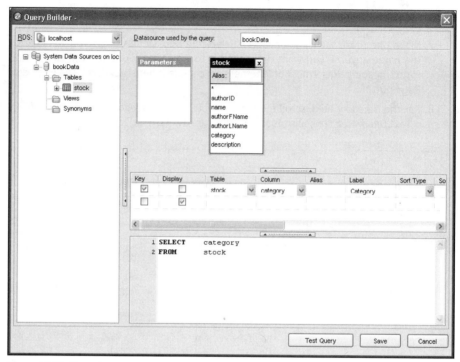

Figure 12-32. The subquery screen for the ComboBox component

11. If you click the Test Query button, you will see you have a small problem as shown in Figure 12-33.

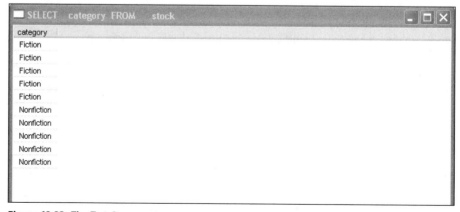

Figure 12-33. The Test Query screen

There is a listing of Fiction or Nonfiction for each record in the database. All you really want is just the two categories.

12. Fix this problem by scrolling over to the Condition column.

13. In the drop-down list (see Figure 12-34), select Group By.

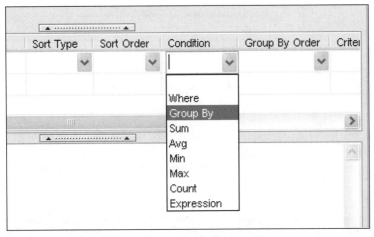

Figure 12-34. Setting the condition of the ComboBox component

14. If you test the query now, it should look like Figure 12-35.

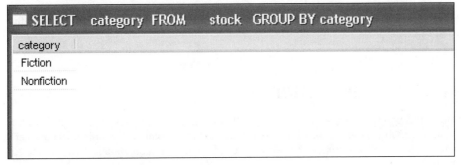

Figure 12-35. The corrected query

15. Close the Test Query screen, save the query, save the main query, and finally click Finish to recompile the code.

16. Once you are returned to the application, go ahead and run it—the first thing you should see is the corrected link label in the ControlBar (see Figure 12-36).

Figure 12-36. The corrected link label

12

17. Click this link as you did before and then select a record for details. Notice the functionality of the Category combo box as shown in Figure 12-37.

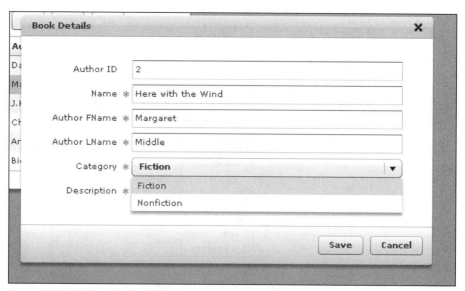

Figure 12-37. The functioning ComboBox component

Notice the changed heading.

I am sure that, by now, you are seeing the potential power of this easy-to-use tool. But that's not all!

Variations on a theme

Up to this point, you have been working with a single table database. As unrealistic as this would probably be in real life, it is serving you well in learning a few basic concepts. Let's use it for one last experiment before we look at a multiple table database with a one-to-many relationship.

1. As you did before, once again use the ColdFusion/Flex Application Wizard and go to the Page Layout and Design screen. Don't forget to use the Load ColdFusion/Flex Application Wizard Settings button, or your project will not load back in.

2. Once you get to the Page Layout and Design screen, use the – button to delete the two pages you already created.

3. Once they are deleted, click the + button to start a new page. You can call it whatever you want. I named it Books for this exercise.

4. For page type, select Master/Detail (as shown in Figure 12-38). This will keep the data all in one place rather than generating two different pages.

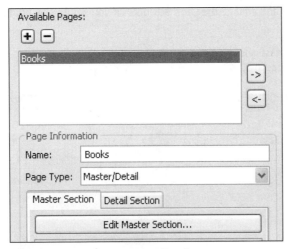

Figure 12-38. Setting up a Master/Detail page

Notice that there are two tabs available: one for the Master Section and one for the Detail Section. Past that, you set up your queries in much the same fashion as before.

5. Click the Master Section tab and then the Edit Master Section button and make changes to the fields as shown in Figure 12-39.

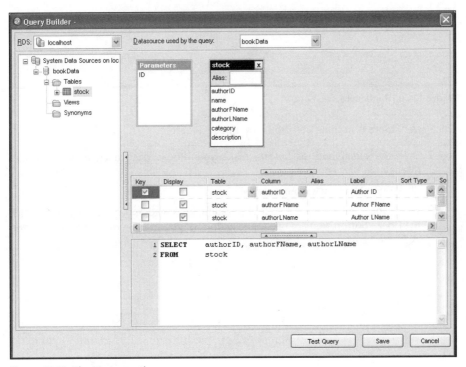

Figure 12-39. The Master section query

12

You can go ahead and change the Label attributes if you would like. I didn't in my example here.

6. After you test and save the query, go to the Detail Section and build the query shown in Figure 12-40.

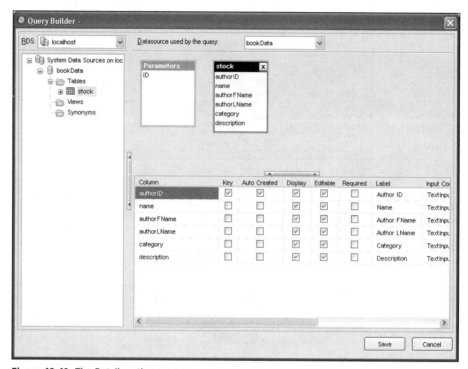

Figure 12-40. The Detail section query

Once again, there is nothing here you have not seen before.

7. Save the query and, as before, make your Books page a child of the Home (Navigation Bar) container.

8. Click Finish to compile your code.

9. When you are returned to your application, go ahead and run it. When you click the Books button, you are presented with all of your data in one location as shown in Figure 12-41.

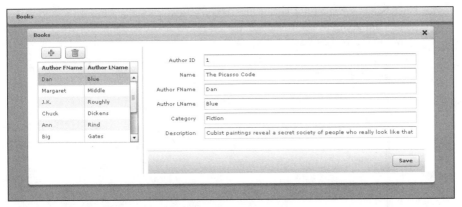

Figure 12-41. The finished Master/Detail page

> *Notice that the Master/Detail page information is in a* DataGrid *control. As a result, you can click a heading, for instance* Author LName, *and the data will sort on that column.*

You are probably asking yourself how often you would use a one-dimensional database. The answer is, most likely, not often.

When you downloaded the files for this chapter, there were two databases. The second one was multiBook.mdb, which you will use now.

10. Using the techniques discussed earlier, go ahead and register this database with the ColdFusion Administrator. I am giving it a data source name of multi as shown in Figure 12-42.

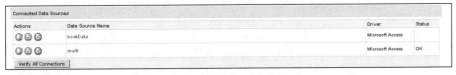

Figure 12-42. The multi data source in the ColdFusion Administrator

This database has a one-to-many relationship in two tables. The "one" table is named "authors" and the "many" table is named "books." You will add this as a second application to your bookProject application, like before:

11. Select File ➤ New ➤ Other.

You will use the ColdFusion/Flex Application Wizard once again; don't forget to load the previous settings.

12

12. Once you are in the Page Layout and Design screen, click the + button to add a new page. I am going to call this page Multiple Books and use the Master Page type, as shown in Figure 12-43.

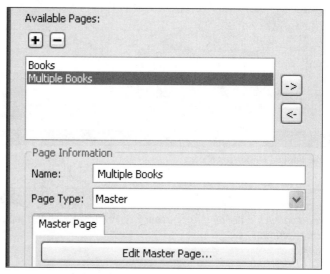

Figure 12-43. The Multiple Books Page added

13. Go ahead and click the Edit Master Page button. Notice that you can now see the two databases registered in the ColdFusion Administrator: bookData and multi (as shown in Figure 12-44).

Figure 12-44. Multiple data sources in the Query Builder

This is handy because you can now easily access multiple data sources with the click of a button.

14. Drag over the authors table from the multi database and select all of the fields, as shown in Figure 12-45.

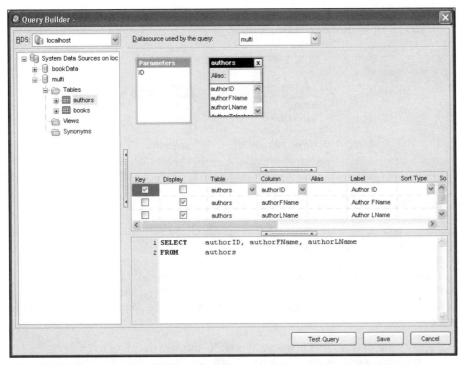

Figure 12-45. The query screen for the main page

Notice that, since the authorID is a key field, the Display check box option is unchecked. You can leave it so for now.

15. Test the query and save it.

16. Like you did before, create a Detail page called Books Written, as shown in Figure 12-46.

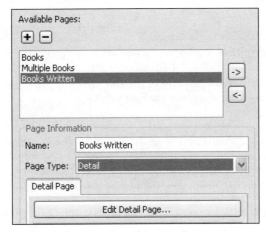

Figure 12-46. The Books Written Detail page

17. Now click the Edit Detail Page button. This time, bring over both the authors and books tables as shown in Figure 12-47.

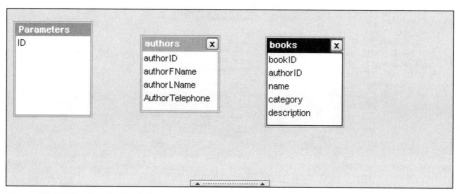

Figure 12-47. The two tables being set up

You need to create a logical connection between the two tables. As you can see, that logical connection would be authorID. However, there is nothing that says the connecting fields must contain the same name. As long as the data can be connected, the field names are irrelevant.

18. Click the authorID field in the authors table, and then drag it to the authorID field in the books table, as shown in Figure 12-48.

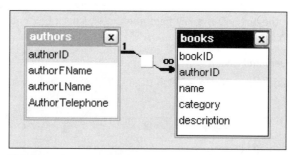

Figure 12-48. Connecting the two tables

Notice that there is a 1 on the left side of the line signifying the single-side table, and an infinity sign on the right signifying the multiple-side table.

> *As of this writing, there seems to be a slight quirk in Flex Builder 2. On some occasions, Flex Builder 2 will automatically detect the common field and make the connection. If this does not happen, just connect them as I am showing here.*

As you click each of the tables, you will see the fields in the Query Builder.

19. Click the books table and shut off the display option for bookID and authorID, as shown in Figure 12-49.

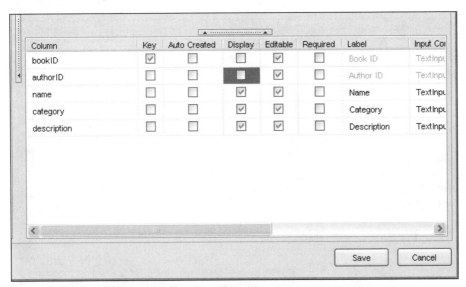

Column	Key	Auto Created	Display	Editable	Required	Label	Input Col
bookID	✓	☐	☐	✓	☐	Book ID	TextInpu
authorID	☐	☐	■	✓	☐	Author ID	TextInpu
name	☐	☐	✓	✓	☐	Name	TextInpu
category	☐	☐	✓	✓	☐	Category	TextInpu
description	☐	☐	✓	✓	☐	Description	TextInpu

Save   Cancel

Figure 12-49. Turning off the bookID and authorID fields

20. Save the query now.

21. You need to make the Multiple Books page a child of the Home (Navigation Bar) page and then make Books Written a child of that. Do this now, as shown in Figure 12-50.

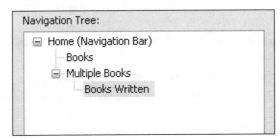

Navigation Tree:

- Home (Navigation Bar)
  - Books
  - Multiple Books
    - Books Written

Figure 12-50. The current navigation tree

Notice that there are now two "main" pages under Home (Navigation Bar): Books and Multiple Books.

22. Click Finish to compile the code.

23. After you are returned to Flex Builder, go ahead and run the application—the first thing you will notice is the name of the two "main" pages in the ControlBar.

12

24. Click Multiple Books and then double-click a record. Your results should look something like Figure 12-51.

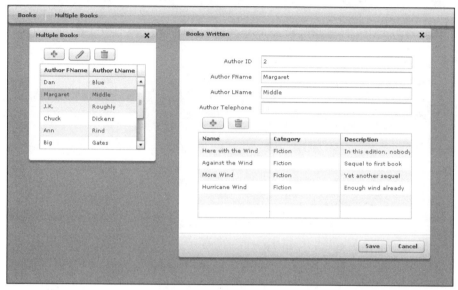

Figure 12-51. The complete application

Let's do one last refinement, assuming that you want the telephone number in a special format.

25. Once again, go into the ColdFusion/Flex Application Wizard and load the previous settings. You will need to edit the Books Written page by using the Edit Detail Page button.

26. Once you are in the query, click the authors table. You should see the field for Author Telephone.

27. Scroll over the field, and you should see a column for Mask.

28. Click the Mask field for the telephone number and select a format as shown in Figure 12-52.

29. Go ahead and recompile the code.

30. Run the application and select Multiple Books; you will see the Author Telephone field in the Detail page.

31. Enter a phone number. It should conform with the format selected, as shown in Figure 12-53.

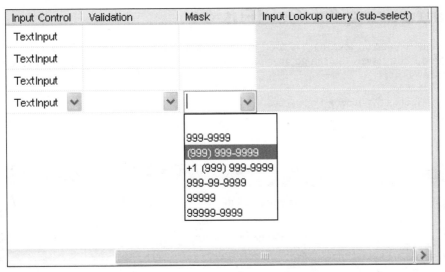

Input Control	Validation	Mask	Input Lookup query (sub-select)
TextInput			
TextInput			
TextInput			
TextInput			

999-9999
(999) 999-9999
+1 (999) 999-9999
999-99-9999
99999
99999-9999

Figure 12-52. The mask used for the telephone number

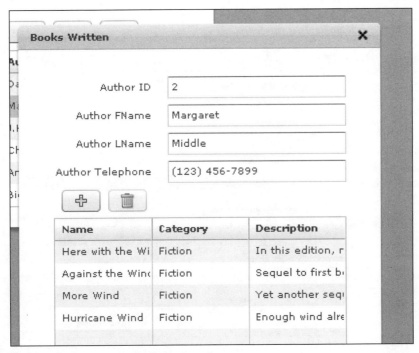

Figure 12-53. The formatted telephone number

As you can see, there are a lot of easy-to-implement possibilities here. But to complete your experience of ColdFusion and get used to using it in the context of a professional project, you need to take a look at how to configure Flex Builder to work with a nonlocal, full production server version of ColdFusion.

Configuring for ColdFusion

While running on localhost is good for testing, you would use an http:// address for a production server. You can go ahead and get that set up properly for ColdFusion/Flex as follows.

1. Select Window ➤ Preferences.

2. Once in Preferences, select RDS Configuration. The screen you get should be similar to the one shown in Figure 12-54.

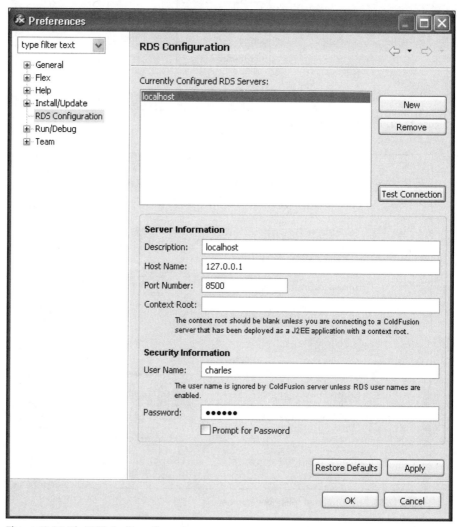

Figure 12-54. The RDS Configuration screen

Here you can set up your server's address, port number, and upload path as well as the user name and password. If you are working with multiple servers, you can add additional configurations by clicking New.

3. Once you have set up a configuration, test it by clicking the Test Connection button—this should give you the result shown in Figure 12-55.

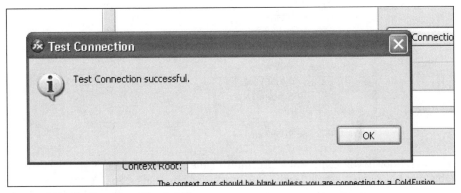

Figure 12-55. The Test Connection function

4. Once the configuration is set up, you can use views to help you manually do what you just did in the preceding sections. Select Windows ➤ Other Views to give you the screen shown in Figure 12-56.

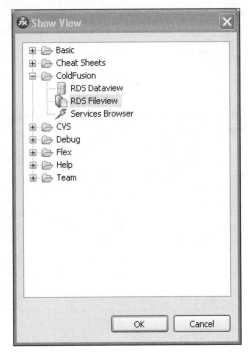

Figure 12-56. The Views screen

12

5. Select RDS Dataview and click OK. You can see the databases in the ColdFusion Administrator (see Figure 12-57).

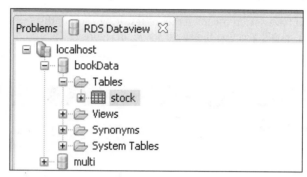

Figure 12-57. The RDS Dataview

If you drill down, you can see the structures of the tables. However, if you right-click a table name, you are presented with some interesting possibilities. For instance, you could right-click a table name and select Show Table Contents to get something like Figure 12-58.

authorID	name	authorFName	authorLName	category	description
1	The Picasso Code	Dan	Blue	Fiction	Cubist paintings...
2	Here with the ...	Margaret	Middle	Fiction	In this editio
3	Harry Potluck a...	J.K.	Roughly	Fiction	Young wizard fi...
4	No Expectations	Chuck	Dickens	Fiction	Dickens finally r...
5	Atlas Stretched	Ann	Rind	Fiction	Great inventors...
6	Recycling Softw...	Big	Gates	Nonfiction	How to just cha...
7	Make Tons of M...	Donald	Rump	Nonfiction	Rump explains ...
8	How to Win Ene...	Dale	Crochety	Nonfiction	The Ultimate ho...
9	My Lies	Swill	Clinton	Nonfiction	This former Am...
10	The Complete H...	David	McClutz	Nonfiction	McClutz gives y...

Figure 12-58. The contents of a table

That is not all. If you right-click a table name, you can build queries by selecting RDS Query Builder. You are presented with two buttons as shown in Figure 12-59.

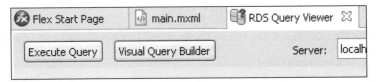

Figure 12-59. The Execute Query and Visual Query Builder buttons

If you click the Visual Query Builder button, you are presented with the Query Builder screen you saw earlier in the ColdFusion/Flex Application Wizard, as shown in Figure 12-60.

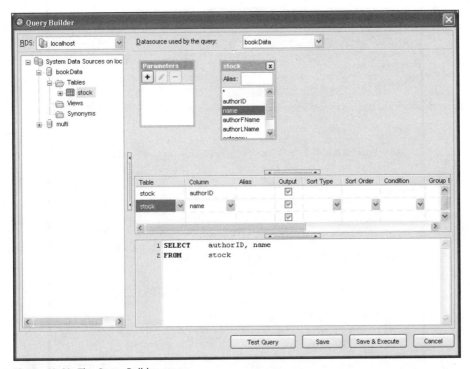

Figure 12-60. The Query Builder screen

12

But what do you do with the query once you have it built?

If you know the workings of ColdFusion Components, Flex Builder helps you out a bit.

6. Right-click a table name.

7. Select ColdFusion Wizards ➤ Create CFC, to give you the screen shown in Figure 12-61.

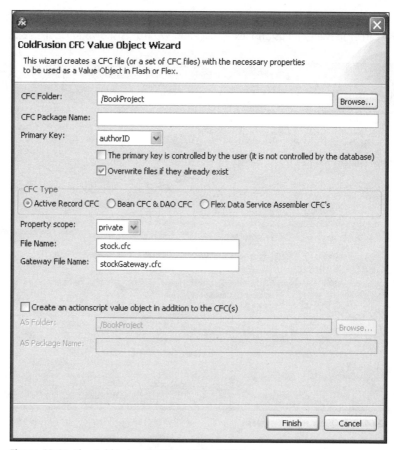

Figure 12-61. The ColdFusion CFC Value Object Wizard

It is beyond the scope of this book to get into all of the details about creating CFCs, but know that here you can select the type of CFC you want, as well as paths and names.

8. Click Finish, and all of the code necessary for the CFC to function is created as shown in Figure 12-62.

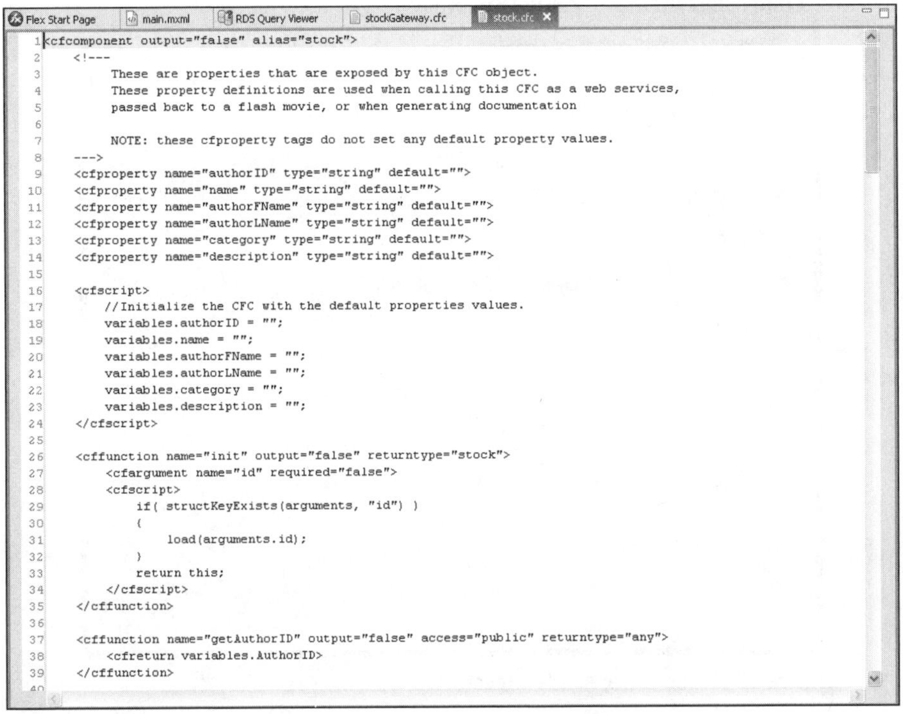

```
1  cfcomponent output="false" alias="stock">
2    <!---
3        These are properties that are exposed by this CFC object.
4        These property definitions are used when calling this CFC as a web services,
5        passed back to a flash movie, or when generating documentation
6
7        NOTE: these cfproperty tags do not set any default property values.
8    --->
9    <cfproperty name="authorID" type="string" default="">
10   <cfproperty name="name" type="string" default="">
11   <cfproperty name="authorFName" type="string" default="">
12   <cfproperty name="authorLName" type="string" default="">
13   <cfproperty name="category" type="string" default="">
14   <cfproperty name="description" type="string" default="">
15
16   <cfscript>
17       //Initialize the CFC with the default properties values.
18       variables.authorID = "";
19       variables.name = "";
20       variables.authorFName = "";
21       variables.authorLName = "";
22       variables.category = "";
23       variables.description = "";
24   </cfscript>
25
26   <cffunction name="init" output="false" returntype="stock">
27       <cfargument name="id" required="false">
28       <cfscript>
29           if( structKeyExists(arguments, "id") )
30           {
31               load(arguments.id);
32           }
33           return this;
34       </cfscript>
35   </cffunction>
36
37   <cffunction name="getAuthorID" output="false" access="public" returntype="any">
38       <cfreturn variables.AuthorID>
39   </cffunction>
40
```

Figure 12-62. The code created with the ColdFusion CFC Value Object Wizard

Notice it is well formed with appropriate comments.

As if that weren't powerful enough, you can also convert CFCs to AS files. Here's how:

9. Right-click a CFC in the Navigator pane and select ColdFusion Wizards.

12

10. From there, you can select Create AS Class (Based on CFC). The screen shown in Figure 12-63 should come up.

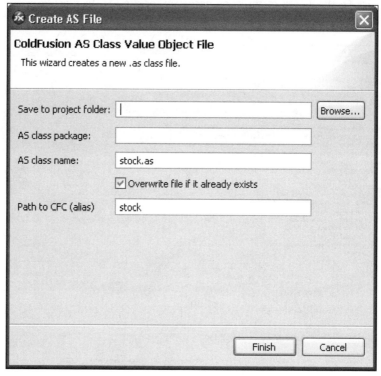

Figure 12-63. The Create AS File screen

This will allow you to convert a CFC into an AS class file. Likewise, you can convert an AS class file into a CFC. As a result, you can now mix and match entire libraries of components and AS class files as needed. The end result: seamless integration.

Summary

As you can easily see, I could devote a rather large book just to the subject of ColdFusion/Flex applications. More than ever, ColdFusion is going to hold an important role in the future development of RIAs.

I strongly recommend developing a good working knowledge of ColdFusion; and I can recommend no better source than the wonderful books written by Ben Forta. His *ColdFusion MX Web Application Construction Kit, 5th Edition* (Macromedia Press, 2002) is considered by many to be the Bible of ColdFusion. I hope you will spend time learning this powerful tool.

Next, let me turn your attention to the charting capabilities of Flex.

13 **CHARTING**

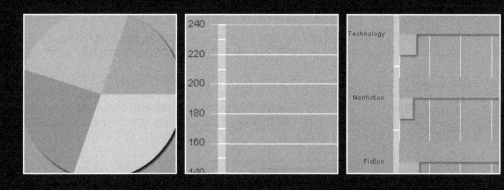

There is an old adage that a picture is worth a thousand words. You can show someone endless tables of data, but a picture will greatly simplify the interpretation of that data.

Flex comes with easy-to-use components that allow you to create many different types of charts with, as you will see, many variations within those types.

In this chapter, you will

- Create a chart.
- Link data to a chart.
- Examine the various parts of a chart.
- Create chart events.
- Animate a chart.
- Apply styles to a chart.

This chapter is assuming you have the Flex charting components installed and activated, as discussed in Chapter 1, with full access to all of their features.

Understand the Flex charting components

The charting capabilities of Flex are handled, like everything else, by components. However, these components are not free of charge. Once your initial trial period has expired, access to the components is blocked until you purchase a separate license code.

Assuming you have that activation code, or are in the trial period, the components allow you to build many different types of charts. To see a list of the chart types available, and a demonstration of the charting capability, go to http://examples.adobe.com/flex2/inproduct/sdk/explorer/explorer.html.

Figure 13-1 shows the screen that appears when you click the PieChart component located under Charts.

Here you will see that Adobe has provided an easy-to-follow model for creating charts. For a moment, let's focus in on the code model shown in Figure 13-2.

Notice that the outermost container, besides the container the chart is being built in, is the **chart type**, which determines what type of chart this will be (in this case, a PieChart). Here you can also set some options, which we will be getting into further, such as dataProvider, padding, DataTips (tooltips), and so forth.

Within that, you have the **series container**. This allows you to select the placement and style of the different fields of data.

Notice that the series container follows the programming pattern of state and transition you saw in Chapter 7. You have the outside container, with a lowercase name, with the specific instances created within by calling the proper class file.

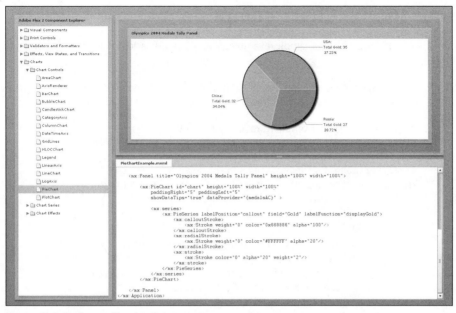

Figure 13-1. Understanding the chart components

```
PieChartExample.mxml

    <mx:Panel title="Olympics 2004 Medals Tally Panel" height="100%" width="100%">

        <mx:PieChart id="chart" height="100%" width="100%"
            paddingRight="5" paddingLeft="5"
            showDataTips="true" dataProvider="{medalsAC}" >

            <mx:series>
                <mx:PieSeries labelPosition="callout" field="Gold" labelFunction="displayGold">
                    <mx:calloutStroke>
                        <mx:Stroke weight="0" color="0x888888" alpha="100"/>
                    </mx:calloutStroke>
                    <mx:radialStroke>
                        <mx:Stroke weight="0" color="#FFFFFF" alpha="20"/>
                    </mx:radialStroke>
                    <mx:stroke>
                        <mx:Stroke color="0" alpha="20" weight="2"/>
                    </mx:stroke>
                </mx:PieSeries>
            </mx:series>
        </mx:PieChart>
```

Figure 13-2. The code model for creating a chart

13

Using the PieChart component

Let's start off by building a simple example. You will learn a lot of important concepts here.

If you need to, go ahead and start Flex Builder. If you want to, delete the Chapter 12 project and start a new project for this chapter using the name and location of your choice.

1. Begin by setting up a simple ArrayCollection that you can use to learn some simple chart concepts. Place the following code inside an MXML file:

```
<?xml version="1.0" encoding="utf-8"?>
<mx:Application xmlns:mx="http://www.adobe.com/2006/mxml"➥
    layout="absolute">
  <mx:Script>
    <![CDATA[
          import mx.collections.ArrayCollection;
          [Bindable]
        private var bookSales:ArrayCollection = new ArrayCollection( [
            {bookType: "Fiction", Sales: 143},
            {bookType: "Nonfiction", Sales: 189},
            {bookType: "Technology", Sales: 178},
            {bookType: "Self-help", Sales: 224} ]);
    ]]>
  </mx:Script>
</mx:Application>
```

You could have just as easily gotten your data from any data source, like the ones you've used in past chapters. However, though simple, this will serve the purpose of this example well.

The next step, under the script block, is to call the PieChart component. You will make the height and width 50%, and make the dataProvider the ArrayCollection you just created: bookSales.

2. Add the following underneath your <mx:script> tag:

```
<mx:PieChart width="50%" height="50%" dataProvider="{bookSales}">

</mx:PieChart>
```

If you were to run the application now, you wouldn't get any errors. You also wouldn't get any chart.

3. As stated just a few moments ago, Flex has no way of knowing what data to put where without the chart series. Using the model discussed earlier, you start off with the series container—add a container to your code, like so:

```
<mx:PieChart width="50%" height="50%" dataProvider="{bookSales}">
  <mx:series>

  </mx:series>
</mx:PieChart>
```

Within the series container, since you are creating a PieChart, you need to use the PieSeries element to indicate that we want to display our data as a pie chart. The series selected will coincide with the type of chart. Here you will specify what data to create the chart with by using the field attribute. Notice also that you do not enclose field inside curly braces.

4. Add the following to your code:

```
<mx:PieChart width="50%" height="50%" dataProvider="{bookSales}">
    <mx:series>
        <mx:PieSeries field="Sales" />
    </mx:series>
</mx:PieChart>
```

Here you told Flex to use the Sales field to create your pie chart.

5. Run the application now; your results should look something like Figure 13-3.

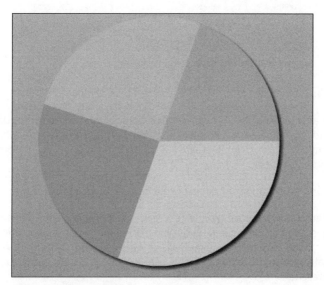

Figure 13-3. The basic PieChart component

It looks very nice. But without labels, the chart is meaningless. You want to label the pieces of the pie somehow.

6. Start by using the labelPosition attribute as follows:

```
<mx:PieChart width="50%" height="50%" dataProvider="{bookSales}">
    <mx:series>
        <mx:PieSeries field="Sales" labelPosition="inside" />
    </mx:series>
</mx:PieChart>
```

13

This adds the labels shown in Figure 13-4.

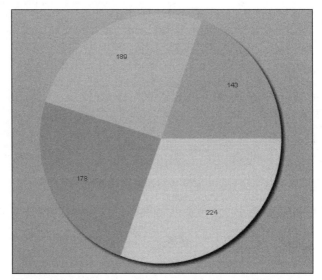

Figure 13-4. The PieChart component with the data added

This is a step in the right direction. However, the numbers, without labels, have little meaning.

You are probably looking for an attribute called label that will add the data from the bookType field now. That is not the way it is handled in Flex. Instead, when using the PieChart component, you need to create a function that will allow you to format the label exactly as it should appear.

The function you set up, using any name of your choice, will need to accept four parameters.

The first parameter will be of type Object and will represent the entire record being graphed. The second argument will be of type String and will represent the name of the field being graphed. The third parameter is of type int and is the item number being graphed. Finally, the fourth argument is of type Number and is the percentage of the pie this item represents.

The function must have a return type of String.

You may be thinking that you have a lot of programming ahead of you just to get a label. Don't worry, I have a few little surprises coming up.

7. Return to the script block and enter the following function. For the purposes of this exercise, I called it chartLabel.

```
private function chartLabel(dataItem:Object, field:String, index:int,➥
  dataPercent:Number):String
{
    return dataItem.bookType;
}
```

The names of the arguments are of your choice. However, the data types must be correct.

8. Now, here is the surprise—return to the PieSeries element and add the following labelFunction:

```
<mx:series>
    <mx:PieSeries field="Sales" labelPosition="inside"➥
        labelFunction="chartLabel" />
</mx:series>
```

The labelFunction attribute will call the function you just created and then return whatever you specify the return to be, as shown in Figure 13-5.

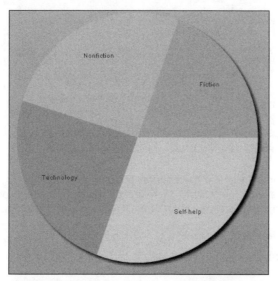

Figure 13-5. The labels added from the labelFunction attribute

Notice that the return of the labelFunction overrides just the data you saw before in Figure 13-4. This powerful feature now means your labels can look as you want them to and not be the products of some predefined format.

9. Make the following change to your function:

```
private function chartLabel(dataItem:Object, field:String, ➥
    index:int, dataPercent:Number):String
{
    return dataItem.bookType + " represents \n" + dataPercent +➥
        "% \n of our sales";
}
```

13

Recall from earlier chapters that \n is embedded into a string to create a new line. Here, you do a simple concatenation, with the result being as shown in Figure 13-6.

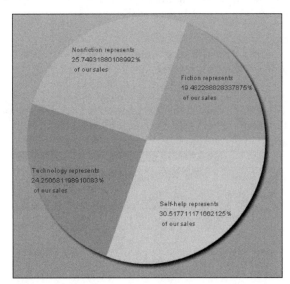

Figure 13-6. The fully concatenated label being returned

Unless you are working with the space shuttle program, that number may have a few more decimal places than you might want. There are a few ways you could approach this problem. However, using the round function of the Math class will return a rounded integer.

10. Make the following adjustments to the labelFunction:

```
private function chartLabel(dataItem:Object, field:String, ➡
    index:int, dataPercent:Number):String
{
    var rounded:Number = Math.round(dataPercent);
    return dataItem.bookType + " represents \n" + rounded +➡
        "% of our sales";
}
```

11. Run the application now, and you should see the results shown in Figure 13-7.

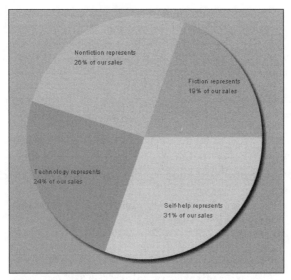

Figure 13-7. The adjusted label format in the chart

See how powerful this is. You can set up virtually any label format you might want.

It's beyond the scope of this book to discuss all of the options available in charts. However, let me point out a few key things.

12. For instance, change the labelPosition attribute of the PieSeries element as follows:

```
<mx:PieSeries field="Sales" labelPosition="callout"➥
    labelFunction="chartLabel" />
```

13. Run the application; your results should look like Figure 13-8.

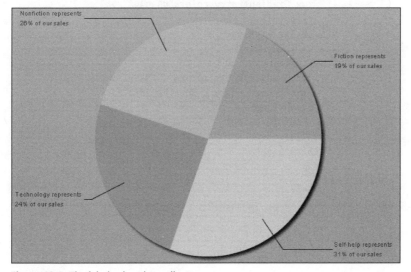

Figure 13-8. The labels placed as callouts

13

The chart could be made a lot more interesting visually by adding some gradient fills. This can be done easily by using the <mx:fill> container. Within that container, there would be an <mx:RadialGradient> for each slice of the pie. Within that, you would need to add an <mx:entries> with that tag containing two <mx:GradientEntry> tags: one for the opening color and one for the closing color.

Don't worry if you just got lost. The following example will clarify this concept for the four slices of your pie.

14. You need to place all of the following within the PieSeries element. For this reason, change the closing /> of the PieSeries tag to a > and add the following code:

```
<mx:PieChart width="50%" height="50%" dataProvider="{bookSales}">
   <mx:series>
      <mx:PieSeries field="Sales" labelPosition="callout"➥
         labelFunction="chartLabel">
         <mx:fills>
           <mx:RadialGradient>
             <mx:entries>
               <mx:GradientEntry color="#E9C836"/>
               <mx:GradientEntry color="#AA9127"/>
             </mx:entries>
           </mx:RadialGradient>
           <mx:RadialGradient>
             <mx:entries>
               <mx:GradientEntry color="#A1AECF"/>
               <mx:GradientEntry color="#47447A"/>
             </mx:entries>
           </mx:RadialGradient>
           <mx:RadialGradient>
             <mx:entries>
               <mx:GradientEntry color="#339933"/>
               <mx:GradientEntry color="#339998"/>
             </mx:entries>
           </mx:RadialGradient>
           <mx:RadialGradient>
             <mx:entries>
               <mx:GradientEntry color="#6FB35F"/>
               <mx:GradientEntry color="#497B54"/>
             </mx:entries>
           </mx:RadialGradient>
         </mx:fills>
      </mx:PieSeries>
   </mx:series>
</mx:PieChart>
```

15. Run your application; your results should resemble Figure 13-9.

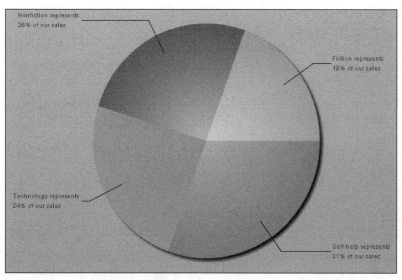

Figure 13-9. The chart with fills added

Now let me turn your attention to the ColumnChart component while still using the same data.

Using the ColumnChart component

A ColumnChart component uses a different set of class files than a PieChart component, as you'll see for yourself in the next example.

1. Create a new MXML file and just copy the ArrayCollection you created for the last exercise.

```
<?xml version="1.0" encoding="utf-8"?>
<mx:Application xmlns:mx="http://www.adobe.com/2006/mxml"➥
   layout="absolute">
   <mx:Script>
      <![CDATA[
         import mx.collections.ArrayCollection;
         [Bindable]
          private var bookSales:ArrayCollection = new➥
            ArrayCollection( [
            {bookType: "Fiction", Sales: 143},
            {bookType: "Nonfiction", Sales: 189},
            {bookType: "Technology", Sales: 178},
            {bookType: "Self-help", Sales: 224} ]);
      ]]>
   </mx:Script>
</mx:Application>
```

13

2. As you did with the `PieChart` component, call the `ColumnChart` component as follows below the script block:

```
<mx:ColumnChart dataProvider="{bookSales}" width="50%" height="50%">

</mx:ColumnChart>
```

3. Run the application; you will get a skeletal structure that won't be very informative as shown in Figure 13-10.

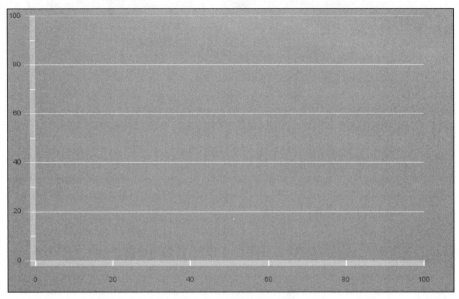

Figure 13-10. The basic structure for a ColumnChart component

The first thing you might want to do is set up categories along the x-axis. In order to do that, you need to set up a horizontalAxis container within the ColumnChart. Then, inside of the axis, you put the CategoryAxis component and assign it to a field; in this case bookType.

4. Make the following changes to your code:

```
<mx:ColumnChart dataProvider="{bookSales}" width="50%" height="50%">
    <mx:horizontalAxis>
        <mx:CategoryAxis categoryField="bookType"/>
    </mx:horizontalAxis>
</mx:ColumnChart>
```

5. Run the code; your results should be like Figure 13-11.

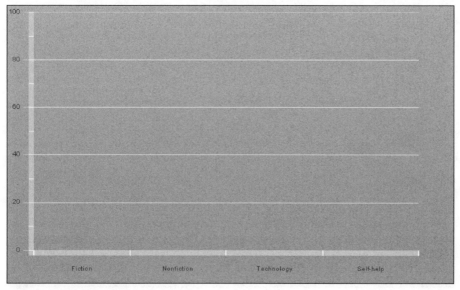

Figure 13-11. The categories added

The series container must be added now. In the case of a ColumnChart component, you will use the ColumnSeries element. However, slightly different from the PieSeries container, the xField and yField need to be specified.

6. Add the following bold lines:

```
<mx:ColumnChart dataProvider="{bookSales}" width="50%" height="50%">
    <mx:horizontalAxis>
        <mx:CategoryAxis categoryField="bookType"/>
    </mx:horizontalAxis>
    <mx:series>
        <mx:ColumnSeries xField="bookType" yField="Sales"/>
    </mx:series>
</mx:ColumnChart>
```

13

7. Run the application; your results should look similar to Figure 13-12.

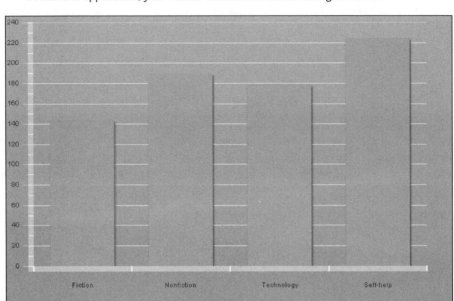

Figure 13-12. The completed ColumnChart component

One handy feature is the showDataTip attribute.

8. Return to line that calls the ColumnChart class and add the showDataTip attribute as follows:

```
<mx:ColumnChart dataProvider="{bookSales}" width="50%" height="50%"
    showDataTips="true">
```

9. Go ahead and run the application. Watch what happens when you roll your mouse over one of the columns (see Figure 13-13).

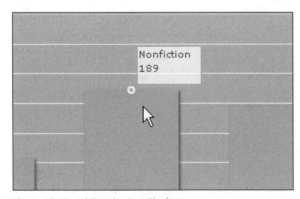

Figure 13-13. Adding the DataTip feature

What happens if you are working with multiple sets of data?

10. Begin by making a modification to your ArrayCollection as follows:

```
private var bookSales:ArrayCollection = new ArrayCollection( [
            {bookType: "Fiction", Sales: 143, returns: 13},
            {bookType: "Nonfiction", Sales: 189, returns: 9},
            {bookType: "Technology", Sales: 178, returns: 11},
            {bookType: "Self-help", Sales: 224, returns: 7} ]);
```

11. This new series would be added by adding a second ColumnSeries element to the series container, as shown here. Do so now.

```
<mx:series>
        <mx:ColumnSeries xField="bookType" yField="Sales" />
        <mx:ColumnSeries xField="bookType" yField="returns" />
</mx:series>
```

Notice that, in this case, the yField is returns.

12. Run the application, and you should get the results shown in Figure 13-14.

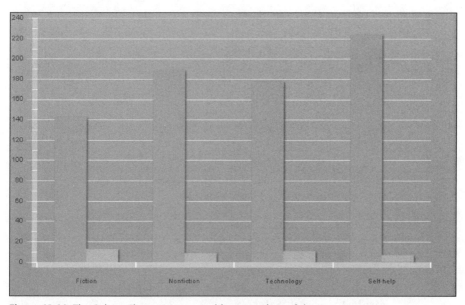

Figure 13-14. The ColumnChart component with a second set of data

You can easily see the second set of data charted, but, at this point, you have no idea what the columns mean. For that reason, you need to add a Legend component to the page. In order to do this, you need to make a few minor adjustments to the code.

13

13. Now give the chart an id attribute. For this example, I used myChart.

```
<mx:ColumnChart dataProvider="{bookSales}" width="50%" height="50%"➥
    showDataTips="true" id="myChart">
```

14. Next, underneath the closing ColumnChart tag, add the Legend component and bind it to myChart. Because the application is using absolute positioning, give the Legend component an x attribute of 630 and y attribute of 10.

```
<mx:Legend dataProvider="{myChart}" x="630" y="10"/>
```

15. Run the application now; you will see a problem in the upper-right side, as shown in Figure 13-15.

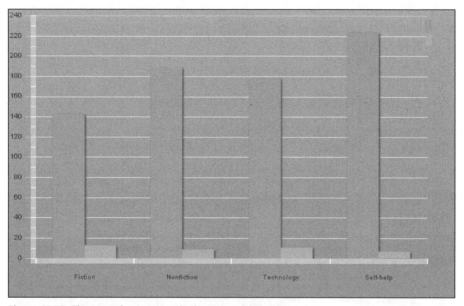

Figure 13-15. The Legend component in the upper-right corner

16. You see the colors associated with the columns, but no text to identify what they stand for. In order to get that, you need to add the displayName to the two ColumnSeries tags. Do this, as shown here:

```
<mx:series>
    <mx:ColumnSeries xField="bookType" yField="Sales"➥
        displayName="Book Sales"/>
    <mx:ColumnSeries xField="bookType" yField="returns"➥
        displayName="Book Returns"/>
</mx:series>
```

17. Run the application. The legend is now successfully completed, as shown in Figure 13-16.

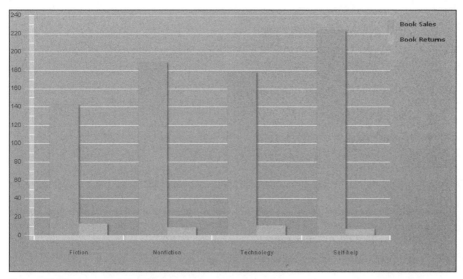

Figure 13-16. The complete Legend component

As you can see, you just created a nice-looking chart. You could also add the gradient effects that you used in the pie chart earlier. But, instead of doing that here, let's try something even more exciting: animating your charts.

Animating the chart

Let's say that you need to compare the data from Company A to Company B. With Flex, you can create great-looking transitions between the charts of the different companies. And, as you will soon see, the programming is not all that difficult.

You can use the ColumnChart component you created in the last exercise. However, you need to make a few adjustments to see the animation concept.

1. Rename your existing ArrayCollection bookSalesA. Then create a second ArrayCollection called bookSalesB. It should look as follows:

```
private var bookSalesA:ArrayCollection = new ArrayCollection( [
        {bookType: "Fiction", Sales: 143, returns: 13},
        {bookType: "Nonfiction", Sales: 189, returns: 9},
        {bookType: "Technology", Sales: 178, returns: 11},
        {bookType: "Self-help", Sales: 224, returns: 7} ]);

private var bookSalesB:ArrayCollection = new ArrayCollection( [
        {bookType: "Fiction", Sales: 91, returns: 20},
        {bookType: "Nonfiction", Sales: 142, returns: 18},
        {bookType: "Self-help", Sales: 182, returns: 23} ]);
```

13

2. You further need to adjust your chart series to accommodate the name change of bookSalesA. Make the following change:

```
<mx:ColumnChart dataProvider="{bookSalesA}" width="50%" height="50%"➥
    id="myChart">
```

You have three potential types of transitions:

- SeriesInterpolate
- SeriesSlide
- SeriesZoom

You will look at all three types by starting with SeriesInterpolate, which is the easiest to do.

3. Right below the script block, you will set up the `<SeriesInterpolate>` tag. To use this, it must be given id and duration attributes—add this now (recall from earlier chapters that duration is expressed in milliseconds).

```
<mx:SeriesInterpolate id="chartChange" duration="2000"/>
```

4. You now need to tie the ColumnSeries element to the effect which, in this case, is SeriesInterpolate. You will use the showDataEffect event as follows:

```
<mx:ColumnChart dataProvider="{bookSalesA}" width="50%" height="50%"➥
    id="myChart">
       <mx:horizontalAxis>
          <mx:CategoryAxis categoryField="bookType"/>
       </mx:horizontalAxis>
     <mx:series>
       <mx:ColumnSeries xField="bookType" yField="Sales"➥
          displayName="Book Sales"  showDataEffect="{chartChange}"/>
       <mx:ColumnSeries xField="bookType" yField="returns"➥
          displayName="Book Returns" showDataEffect="{chartChange}"/>
     </mx:series>
</mx:ColumnChart>
```

Notice that bookSalesA is still the default dataProvider. As you will see momentarily, this will be the initial data with the chart. Without stating this, the chart will not render.

The two ColumnSeries now use the attribute showDataEffect and references the id of the SeriesInterpolate class.

You now need to create a means of switching between the datasets, bookSalesA and bookSalesB. The best tool for doing this will probably be the RadioButton component. Since you have already learned to use this, I will not discuss it in great detail here. Of course, you could put them anywhere.

For this example, use the HBox container to contain the RadioButton component. Since the layout in this example is absolute, you give it an x and y attribute. In the example, x is 20 and y is 400.

5. Add this code wherever you feel is appropriate:

```
<mx:HBox x="20" y="400">
    <mx:RadioButton groupName="books" label="Book Sales A"
        selected="true" click="myChart.dataProvider=bookSalesA;"/>
    <mx:RadioButton groupName="books" label="Book Sales B"
        click="myChart.dataProvider=bookSalesB;"/>
</mx:HBox>
```

Notice that you made the Book Sales A button the default. When a RadioButton component is selected, a click event is created. This event will call the dataProvider attribute of the chart and call the desired dataset.

That is all there is to it.

6. Go ahead and run the application. Your results should resemble those in Figure 13-17.

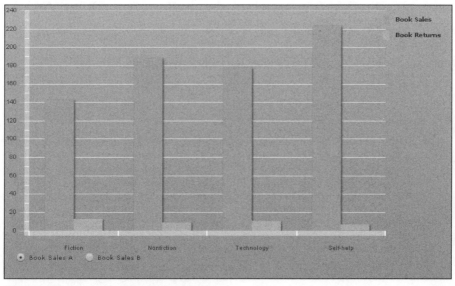

Figure 13-17. The chart with the radio buttons

When you click the RadioButton components, the background of the chart will rescale as the columns animate to their new sizes.

Now you'll make a few minor changes and look at the SeriesSlide effect.

To accomplish this, you need to create two effects . . . one to "slide" the columns in and one to "slide" the column out.

7. Replace the SeriesInterpolate tag with the two SeriesSlide tags shown here:

```
<mx:SeriesSlide id="chartSlideIn" duration="2000" direction="up"/>
<mx:SeriesSlide id="chartSlideOut" duration="2000" direction="down"/>
```

13

Notice that you need to specify a direction attribute. In this case, you will specify values that make the columns rise up to slide the new data in and collapse down to take the old data out. If you can't visualize this, you will in a moment.

In the ColumnSeries element, you will use the showDataEffect event as you did before. The showDataEffect event will this time reference the chartSlideIn SeriesSlide.

However, to take the chart out, you need to hide it. The hideDataEffect property will do this quite nicely by referencing the chartSlideOut id.

8. Make the following changes to your code:

```
<mx:series>
    <mx:ColumnSeries xField="bookType" yField="Sales"➥
        displayName="Book Sales" showDataEffect="{chartSlideIn}"➥
        hideDataEffect="{chartSlideOut}"/>
    <mx:ColumnSeries xField="bookType" yField="returns"➥
        displayName="Book Returns" showDataEffect="{chartSlideIn}"➥
        hideDataEffect="{chartSlideOut}"/>
</mx:series>
```

There is no need to make any changes to the RadioButton components.

9. Run the application. When you click a RadioButton component, you should find the effect quite stunning. The present columns are hidden and the new ones rise up.

10. To test out the SeriesZoom effect, substitute SeriesZoom for SeriesSlide and eliminate the direction attribute, as follows:

```
<mx:SeriesZoom id="chartSlideIn" duration="2000"/>
<mx:SeriesZoom id="chartSlideOut" duration="2000"/>
```

All other functionality is exactly the same as the SeriesSlide.

11. Go ahead and run the application. You will see the columns zoom in and out.

As you can see, you can create some really cool chart effects easily in Flex.

Using the BarChart component

As a final exercise, you can easily turn the column chart into a bar chart. As you may know already, a bar chart is a column chart turned on its side.

Use the ColumnChart component you created in the previous exercise and make a few modifications.

1. Begin by changing the opening and closing <mx:ColumnChart> tags to <mx:BarChart>.

```
<mx:BarChart dataProvider="{bookSalesA}" width="50%" height="50%"➥
    id="myChart">
</mx:BarChart>
```

All other attributes will remain the same.

2. In a ColumnChart component, the CategoryAxis is the horizontal axis. However, in a BarChart component, the CategoryAxis becomes the vertical axis. Your code needs to reflect that as follows:

```
<mx:verticalAxis>
    <mx:CategoryAxis categoryField="bookType"/>
</mx:verticalAxis>
```

3. Finally, you need to change the series from a ColumnSeries to a BarSeries. However, please remember that the xField and yField are also reversed within the series. Make the following changes:

```
<mx:series>
    <mx:BarSeries yField="bookType" xField="Sales"➥
        displayName="Book Sales" showDataEffect="{chartSlideIn}"➥
        hideDataEffect="{chartSlideOut}"/>
    <mx:BarSeries yField="bookType" xField="returns"➥
        displayName="Book Returns" showDataEffect="{chartSlideIn}"➥
        hideDataEffect="{chartSlideOut}"/>
</mx:series>
```

That is all there is to it—the complete chart code, excluding the animation code, should look as follows:

```
<mx:BarChart dataProvider="{bookSalesA}" width="50%" height="50%"➥
    id="myChart">
    <mx:verticalAxis>
        <mx:CategoryAxis categoryField="bookType"/>
    </mx:verticalAxis>
    <mx:series>
        <mx:BarSeries yField="bookType" xField="Sales"➥
            displayName="Book Sales" showDataEffect="{chartSlideIn}"➥
            hideDataEffect="{chartSlideOut}"/>
        <mx:BarSeries yField="bookType" xField="returns"➥
            displayName="Book Returns" showDataEffect="{chartSlideIn}"➥
            hideDataEffect="{chartSlideOut}"/>
    </mx:series>
</mx:BarChart>
```

13

451

4. Run the application now, and you should see something like Figure 13-18.

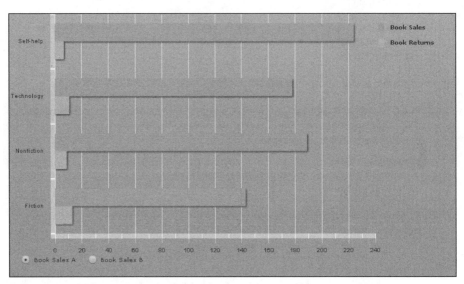

Figure 13-18. The BarChart component

Summary

As you can see, charting is an easy-to-use and effective way of presenting your data. Of course, you can use techniques you learned earlier in the book to import your data from XML files or ColdFusion sources.

You are near the homestretch; now let me turn your attention to how Flex can control printing of pages from applications next.

14 PRINTING

Book Name	Author Name
The Picasso Co	Dan Blue
Here With the V	Margaret Middle
Harry Potluck a	J.K. Roughly
No Expectations	Chuck Dickens
Atlas Stretched	Ann Rind
Recycling Softw.	Big Gates

Print

author
Dan Blue
Margaret Middle
J.K. Roughly
Chuck Dickens

Book Name
The Picasso Code
Here With the Wind
Harry Potluck and the
No Expectations

Sooner or later, you will probably want to print from a Flex application. In the past, printing from web applications has posed difficult challenges: users would need to print from a browser application, and web sites and applications are often not designed with the printed page in mind, so the look of the printout would be less than ideal.

Flex now addresses these problems with two new classes: `FlexPrintJob` and `PrintDataGrid`.

As you will see, the `FlexPrintJob` class manages the printing and serves as the interface with the printer. As a matter of fact, you will use the `start()` method to call the printer dialog box. What's more, you will add items to print by using the `addObject()` method of this class.

Along the way, you will need to make a few decisions, which we will discuss, about how you want the data to print. If you just want a page to print, the `FlexPrintJob` class handles that nicely. But if you want to format your data into a printable table, you will need to call the `PrintDataGrid` class.

An additional decision we will discuss is whether you want your printing handled by the main MXML file, or by a component. You will see the implications of that.

With Flex 2, printing is really an easy process once you get a few general concepts. Let's get to work.

The printing process

Sooner or later, you may want to print from Flex. For instance, if you are creating an e-commerce site, you may want to give the customer a printable receipt. There may be cases when you need a printout of data lists of some sort. As you are about to see, Flex makes the process a lot easier than traditional XHTML environments.

As I stated in the introduction to this chapter, the printing process revolves around two class files:

- `FlexPrintJob`: This class needs to be instantiated and serves as a container for the objects you want to print. What is great about this is you can use this class to split larger print jobs over multiple pages or scale the content to fit a specific page size.

- `PrintDataGrid`: You would use this class, which is a subclass of `DataGrid`, to print data that has to be in a grid or table format. It also allows you to print over multiple pages.

Let's begin by creating a new project using the name and location of your choice. You will start with a very simple exercise: printing out a label.

1. Set up the following simple code to create a label, located in a VBox container, which will serve as your first print test.

```
<?xml version="1.0" encoding="utf-8"?>
<mx:Application xmlns:mx="http://www.adobe.com/2006/mxml"➥
   layout="absolute">
```

```
        <mx:VBox id="printContent" backgroundColor="#FFFFFF">
            <mx:Label text="This is your first print test"/>
            <mx:Button label="Print" />
        </mx:VBox>
    </mx:Application>
```

2. Next, create a script block that will import the FlexPrintJob class. FlexPrintJob is located in the mx.printing package.

```
<mx:Script>
    <![CDATA[
        import mx.printing.FlexPrintJob;
        ]]>
</mx:Script>
```

If you don't import the FlexPrintJob class, Flex Builder 2 will do it automatically after you create the FlexPrintJob variable. You have seen this in earlier chapters; as I discussed then, I prefer to add my own import statements so I don't end up with a separate statement for each class imported.

From here on in, you will find the code very logical and easy to follow.

3. Create a function called testPrint(). The return type will be void.

```
<mx:Script>
    <![CDATA[
        import mx.printing.FlexPrintJob
        private function testPrint():void
        {

        }
    ]]>
</mx:Script>
```

4. The first line of code needs to create an instantiation of the FlexPrintJob class—add the following line to achieve this:

```
private function testPrint():void
{
    var myPrintJob:FlexPrintJob = new FlexPrintJob();
}
```

5. The next step is to open the Print dialog box. This can be done by using the start() method of the FlexPrintJob class, like so:

```
private function testPrint():void
{
    var myPrintJob:FlexPrintJob = new FlexPrintJob();
    myPrintJob.start();
}
```

14

Once the printer is selected, the object you want to print needs to be added to the FlexPrintJob container. In this case, you want to add the contents of the printContent VBox container, which consists of a label.

6. In order to add your object to the FlexPrintJob container, you need to use the addObject() method as follows:

```
private function testPrint():void
{
    var myPrintJob:FlexPrintJob = new FlexPrintJob();
    myPrintJob.start();
    myPrintJob.addObject(printContent);
}
```

7. Finally, the last step is to have the FlexPrintJob object send the object to be printed to the printer. This is accomplished with the send() method:

```
private function testPrint():void
{
    var myPrintJob:FlexPrintJob = new FlexPrintJob();
    myPrintJob.start();
    myPrintJob.addObject(printContent);
    myPrintJob.send();
}
```

That is all there is to the printing process (at least in its simplest form).

8. The one last thing you need to do is add this function as a click event to the button that will call testPrint():

```
<mx:VBox id="printContent" backgroundColor="#FFFFFF">
    <mx:Label text="This is our first print test"/>
    <mx:Button label="Print " click="testPrint()" />
</mx:VBox>
```

9. Go ahead and run the application, and you will see the Print button. Click it, and your Print dialog box should pop up, prompting you to print the label.

As you can see, it is all quite simple . . . *except* for one slight problem (and yes, it is slight).

10. Click the Print button again. When the Print dialog box appears, click Cancel.

You will see that the contents of the page suddenly disappear. The reason for this is a bit convoluted. If you cancel the print job, the function never gets to the send() method. The send() method has the functionality of returning back to the application after the print job is completed. So, in essence, it is never returning properly to the application.

The start() method returns a Boolean value. As a result, it can be easily placed as a test in an if statement block. In this case, you indicate that if start() isn't true (what happens if you cancel the print job), then return to the application.

11. Add the following to your application:

```
private function testPrint():void
{
    var myPrintJob:FlexPrintJob = new FlexPrintJob();
    if(myPrintJob.start() != true)
    {
        return;
    }
    myPrintJob.addObject(printContent);
    myPrintJob.send();
}
```

12. Run the application again, click the Print button, and then cancel the print job. The application should now function as expected.

Creating a separate Print container

In many cases, your data may not be in a form that is conducive for printing. If that is the case, you can create an invisible container to format your data and print the contents of that container using the techniques you have just learned.

Let's give it a try.

Use the books.xml file that you have used in earlier chapters and import it into your existing project using techniques discussed in earlier chapters. While you could put it into an assets folder if you want, the actual location can be one of your choice.

> You can download the books.xml file at www.friendsofed.com if necessary.

1. Start a new MXML file and modify it so it looks as shown here. This is a good place to refresh yourself in coding techniques learned earlier throughout this book.

```
<?xml version="1.0" encoding="utf-8"?>
<mx:Application xmlns:mx="http://www.adobe.com/2006/mxml"
    layout="vertical"
    creationComplete="bookDataRPC.send()">

    <mx:Script>
        <![CDATA[
            import mx.rpc.events.ResultEvent;
            import mx.collections.ArrayCollection;

            [Bindable]
            public var bookData:ArrayCollection;

            private function bookFunction(event:ResultEvent):void
            {
```

14

```
                        bookData = event.result.books.stock;
                }

        ]]>
    </mx:Script>

    <mx:HTTPService id="bookDataRPC" url="books.xml"➥
        result="bookFunction(event)"/>

    <mx:Form id="myForm">

        <mx:DataGrid id="bookInfo" dataProvider="{bookData}">
            <mx:columns>
                <mx:DataGridColumn dataField="name"➥
                    headerText="Book Name"/>
                <mx:DataGridColumn  dataField="author"➥
                    headerText="Author Name"/>
                <mx:DataGridColumn dataField="category"➥
                    headerText="Book Category"/>
            </mx:columns>
        </mx:DataGrid>
            <mx:Button id="myButton" label="Print"/>
    </mx:Form>

</mx:Application>
```

2. Go ahead and run the application; your screen should look like Figure 14-1 at this point. The button isn't functioning yet.

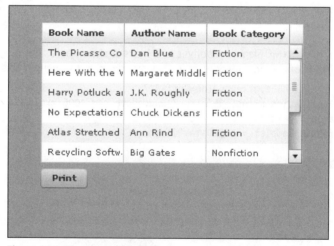

Figure 14-1. The DataGrid layout

As you can see, this is not ideal for printing. So you are going to create a flexible version for printing.

3. Create a new VBox container after the Form container. Give it an ID of printArea, a height of 300, a width of 500, a background color of white (a white background is usually preferable for most printing scenarios), and a visibility of false. Also, you will need an opening and closing tag.

```
<mx:VBox id="printArea" height="300" width="500"➟
    backgroundColor="#FFFFFF" visible="false" >

</mx:VBox>
```

The reason for setting the visibility to false will become apparent in a moment.

4. Within this VBox container, you will use the second of the two class files discussed previously: PrintDataGrid. Give it an ID of myPrintGrid and give it a width and height the same as the VBox container by specifying 100%.

```
<mx:VBox id="printArea" height="300" width="500"➟
    backgroundColor="#FFFFFF" visible="false" >
    <mx:PrintDataGrid id="myPrintDataGrid" height="100%"➟
        width="100%" />
</mx:VBox>
```

5. Now to return to the same syntax you used to create the function in the last exercise. Again, you are going to put the start() method, discussed in the previous section when using the FlexPrintJob class, as the test inside an if statement.

```
<mx:Script>
    <![CDATA[
        import mx.printing.FlexPrintJob;
        import mx.rpc.events.ResultEvent;
        import mx.collections.ArrayCollection;

        [Bindable]
        public var bookData:ArrayCollection;

        private function bookFunction(event:ResultEvent):void
        {
            bookData = event.result.books.stock;
        }

        private function printJob():void
        {
            var myPrintJob:FlexPrintJob = new FlexPrintJob();
            if(myPrintJob.start() != true)
            {
                return;
            }
        }

    ]]>
</mx:Script>
```

14

6. The next step, after the if block, is to make the dataProvider of PrintDataGrid, myPrintDataGrid, equal to the dataProvider of the actual DataGrid component, bookInfo.

```
private function printJob():void
{
    var myPrintJob:FlexPrintJob = new FlexPrintJob();
    if(myPrintJob.start() != true)
    {
        return;
    }

    myPrintDataGrid.dataProvider = bookInfo.dataProvider;
}
```

7. From here on in, this exercise works like the last one. Add the printArea VBox container to the FlexPrintJob object and then send it to the printer.

```
private function printJob():void
{
    var myPrintJob:FlexPrintJob = new FlexPrintJob();
    if(myPrintJob.start() != true)
    {
        return;
    }

    myPrintDataGrid.dataProvider = bookInfo.dataProvider;
    myPrintJob.addObject(printArea);
    myPrintJob.send();
}
```

8. The final thing you will need to do is add a click event to the Button control. Obviously, the function you will call here is printJob().

```
<mx:Button id="myButton" label="Print" click="printJob()"/>
```

9. Now run the application, print the page, and it should look something like Figure 14-2.

author	category	description	name
Dan Blue	Fiction	Cubist paintings reveal	The Picasso Code
Margaret Middle	Fiction	In this edition, nobody	Here With the Wind
J.K. Roughly	Fiction	Young wizard finds the	Harry Potluck and the (
Chuck Dickens	Fiction	Dickens finally reveals	No Expectations
Ann Rind	Fiction	Great inventors finally	Atlas Stretched
Big Gates	Nonfiction	How to just change the	Recycling Software
Donald Rump	Nonfiction	Rump explains how he	Make Tons of Money
Dale Crochety	Nonfiction	The Ultimate how-to bo	How to Win Enemies an
Swill Clinton	Nonfiction	This former American p	My Lies
David McClutz	Nonfiction	McClutz gives you the (	The Complete History (

Figure 14-2. The PrintDataGrid results

Notice that there seems to be a few things wrong—the application printed all the data, and it did not format the data like the DataGrid you wanted to print. This is not difficult to fix.

10. The syntax for PrintDataGrid is nearly identical to that of the DataGrid control. So you can adjust it in exactly the same way as you did the DataGrid control—change the code like so:

```
<mx:VBox id="printArea" height="300" width="500"➥
    backgroundColor="#FFFFFF" visible="false" >
    <mx:PrintDataGrid id="myPrintDataGrid" height="100%" width="100%">
    <mx:columns>
      <mx:DataGridColumn dataField="name" headerText="Book Name"/>
      <mx:DataGridColumn  dataField="author" headerText="Author Name"/>
      <mx:DataGridColumn dataField="category"➥
          headerText="Book Category"/>
    </mx:columns>
    </mx:PrintDataGrid>
</mx:VBox>
```

14

11. Now run the application and reprint the page, and you will see a very different result, as shown in Figure 14-3.

Book Name	Author Name	Book Category
The Picasso Code	Dan Blue	Fiction
Here With the Wind	Margaret Middle	Fiction
Harry Potluck and the Chamber	J.K. Roughly	Fiction
No Expectations	Chuck Dickens	Fiction
Atlas Stretched	Ann Rind	Fiction
Recycling Software	Big Gates	Nonfiction
Make Tons of Money	Donald Rump	Nonfiction
How to Win Enemies and Lose	Dale Crochety	Nonfiction
My Lies	Swill Clinton	Nonfiction
The Complete History of the W	David McClutz	Nonfiction

Figure 14-3. The reformatted PrintDataGrid output

As you can see, there is very little difference between using `PrintDataGrid` and `DataGrid`. In addition, it should now be obvious why you need to make this VBox container's visibility false: it is not needed for the web output, only for the printing.

> As mentioned before, column widths can be adjusted using the same syntax used by the `DataGrid` component. For instance, you may want to decrease the width of the Author Name and Book Category columns while increasing the width of the Book Name column to accommodate the longer names.

Printing and components

I am sure you can easily see why it might sometimes be better to relegate printing functions to a component. For instance, placing `PrintDataGrid`, and its subsequent invisible container, in a component could result in cleaner code. In addition, this could centralize many of your printing functions. Also, you may have multiple containers to handle a variety of potential printing situations.

Placing the printing functions in a component is not all that difficult. Let's take a look:

1. Open the file from the last exercise if necessary.

2. Create a new folder to hold your component using techniques discussed earlier in the book. For this example, I called it components.

3. Create a new component in the folder. For purposes of this exercise, I am calling it PrintComp. Base it on the VBox container. Make the background color white, the height 300, and the width 500. Finally, set the visibility to false.

```
<?xml version="1.0" encoding="utf-8"?>
<mx:VBox xmlns:mx="http://www.adobe.com/2006/mxml" width="500"➥
   height="300" backgroundColor="#FFFFFF" visible = "false">

</mx:VBox>
```

4. Cut and paste the PrintDataGrid tag from the MXML file in the previous exercise into this component.

The finished component should have the following code:

```
<?xml version="1.0" encoding="utf-8"?>
<mx:VBox xmlns:mx="http://www.adobe.com/2006/mxml" width="500"➥
   height="300" backgroundColor="#FFFFFF" visible="false">
   <mx:PrintDataGrid id="myPrintDataGrid" height="100%" width="100%">
      <mx:columns>
         <mx:DataGridColumn dataField="name" headerText="Book Name"/>
         <mx:DataGridColumn  dataField="author"➥
            headerText="Author Name"/>
         <mx:DataGridColumn dataField="category"➥
            headerText="Book Category"/>
      </mx:columns>
   </mx:PrintDataGrid>
</mx:VBox>
```

5. You are finished setting up the component now. Go back to the original MXML file and delete the rest of the VBox container.

6. At the top of the script block, import the component you just created.

```
<mx:Script>
   <![CDATA[
      import mx.printing.FlexPrintJob;
      import mx.rpc.events.ResultEvent;
      import mx.collections.ArrayCollection;
      import components.PrintComp;
```

7. Below the if block, in the printJob() function, instantiate the component. For the purpose of this exercise, I am calling it myPrintComp.

```
private function printJob():void
{
   var myPrintJob:FlexPrintJob = new FlexPrintJob();
   if(myPrintJob.start() != true)
   {
      return;
   }
   var myPrintComp:PrintComp = new PrintComp();
   myPrintDataGrid.dataProvider = bookInfo.dataProvider;
   myPrintJob.addObject(printArea);
   myPrintJob.send();
}
```

14

8. Under the instantiation, you are going to bring the component into this main file temporarily by using the addChild() method. It will not be seen because the VBox container in the component is set to a false visibility. Since you are going to add it to this MXML file, you will use "this" as the qualifier.

```
if(myPrintJob.start() != true)
{
    return;
}
var myPrintComp:PrintComp = new PrintComp();
this.addChild(myPrintComp);
```

9. You need to make a modification to the line that links the dataProvider properties. Remember that myPrintDataGrid is now located in the myPrintComp component. As such, you have to reference it there.

```
var myPrintComp:PrintComp = new PrintComp();
this.addChild(myPrintComp);
myPrintComp.myPrintDataGrid.dataProvider = bookInfo.dataProvider;
```

10. The object you are going to add to FlexPrintJob is going to be the myPrintComp object.

```
var myPrintComp:PrintComp = new PrintComp();
this.addChild(myPrintComp);
myPrintComp.myPrintDataGrid.dataProvider = bookInfo.dataProvider;
myPrintJob.addObject(myPrintComp);
myPrintJob.send();
```

11. Once the print job is finished, you will no longer need to use the component. You can remove it from the MXML file by simply using the removeChild() function after the myPrintJob.send() line.

```
var myPrintComp:PrintComp = new PrintComp();
this.addChild(myPrintComp);
myPrintComp.myPrintDataGrid.dataProvider = bookInfo.dataProvider;
myPrintJob.addObject(myPrintComp);
myPrintJob.send();
this.removeChild(myPrintComp);
```

The completed code should look as follows:

```
<?xml version="1.0" encoding="utf-8"?>
<mx:Application xmlns:mx="http://www.adobe.com/2006/mxml"
    layout="vertical"
    creationComplete="bookDataRPC.send()">

    <mx:Script>
        <![CDATA[
            import mx.printing.FlexPrintJob;
            import mx.rpc.events.ResultEvent;
            import mx.collections.ArrayCollection;
            import components.PrintComp;
```

```
    [Bindable]
    public var bookData:ArrayCollection;

    private function bookFunction(event:ResultEvent):void
    {
        bookData = event.result.books.stock;
    }

    private function printJob():void
    {
        var myPrintJob:FlexPrintJob = new FlexPrintJob();
        if(myPrintJob.start() != true)
        {
            return;
        }
        var myPrintComp:PrintComp = new PrintComp();
        this.addChild(myPrintComp);
        myPrintComp.myPrintDataGrid.dataProvider =➡
            bookInfo.dataProvider;
        myPrintJob.addObject(myPrintComp);
        myPrintJob.send();
        this.removeChild(myPrintComp);
    }

    ]]>
</mx:Script>

    <mx:HTTPService id="bookDataRPC" url="books.xml"➡
        result="bookFunction(event)"/>

    <mx:Form id="myForm">

        <mx:DataGrid id="bookInfo" dataProvider="{bookData}">
            <mx:columns>
                <mx:DataGridColumn dataField="name"➡
                    headerText="Book Name"/>
                <mx:DataGridColumn  dataField="author"➡
                    headerText="Author Name"/>
                <mx:DataGridColumn dataField="category"➡
                    headerText="Book Category"/>
            </mx:columns>
        </mx:DataGrid>
        <mx:Button id="myButton" label="Print" click="printJob()"/>
    </mx:Form>

</mx:Application>
```

14

If you run the application now, it runs exactly the same way as before, but this time, you have added flexibility due to centralizing your print code in a component.

Summary

As you can see, printing is a relatively simple process. The great part is that it uses consistent syntax in a wide variety of situations.

15 UNFINISHED SYMPHONY

As a person personally involved with computer books for many years, I have seen the following complaints about most computer books:

- Errors
- A feeling of incomplete discussion of topics
- Topics not covered

In addition to those three problems, there is one very nasty reality many computer books face (especially application-focused books such as this one): within 6 months, a sizable amount of information contained within it could be outdated due to software updates.

When I completed the chapter about ColdFusion (Chapter 12), my wonderful technical editor, Sas Jacobs, asked why I didn't cover PHP, Java, .NET, and so forth (apparently ColdFusion is not widely used in Australia). My chief editor, Chris Mills, asked, "Why don't you cover topic A and topic B?" All of these questions are valid. However, if I were to attempt to discuss all relevant topics, the book would never get out of the gate, and the beginning reader would end up with a 2,000-page tome, which presents its own set of complaints.

I am finishing this book by not finishing it. Instead, I would like you, dear reader, to look upon this book as a beginning and a challenge.

With the release of this book, a new website will be introduced, at www. charlesebrown.net.

This is not going to be just a typical author site, I hope, but also a continuation of this book. As issues come up, they will be posted there. As readers find better ways of accomplishing tasks, I will post them there with due credit. As software changes occur, they will be discussed there. And as topics come up, they will be presented there.

In addition, there will be discussions about how Flex fits in with other technologies. This will be especially important with the now-announced Apollo and revised Live Cycle technologies. When does one use the tools of Flash with Flex technology? Should video still be done in Flash and then added to Flex?

Each topic demands extensive discussion on its own, more than can be presented in a relatively short chapter.

I want the site to be looked upon as a means of making this book an organic being that will evolve as environment demands. Most importantly, I hope it serves as the generator of a new community of Flex developers.

Like this book, the site will be evolving as needs demand also. While I will begin with articles contributed by myself and various guest contributors, I hope to expand to live chat in a short time.

Finally, there is the challenge.

You may have noticed that I left a few small issues opened with the case study done earlier.

If you are an expert in PHP, ColdFusion, Java, or .NET, I challenge you to solve these open ends, and then contribute your solutions to the community at this site. Of course, full credit will be given with subsequent discussion.

Most importantly, as issues bubble to the surface, please contact me through the site, and I will see to it that they are addressed fully and as needed. Odds are if you have run into an issue, others have also.

Conclusion

I want to finish by thanking you for starting this journey with me. However, it is just that; a start. We have a long way to go with many possible roads we can take. Let's work together as a community as we navigate through this brave new world.

To paraphrase the closing tag of one popular television announcer: See you on the Net.

INSTALLING COLDFUSION MX 7

In Chapter 12 of this book, I use ColdFusion MX 7.02 to show dynamic connectivity with Flex Builder 2.

Happily, since the acquisition of Macromedia, Adobe has retained the policy of offering free Developer Editions of their server software. This software, which can be downloaded from www.adobe.com/cfusion/tdrc/index.cfm?product=coldfusion&loc=en_us, has no time limits and has the same functionality as the Enterprise Editions. However, it can be used only on one computer, and no more than one person can access the page at a time. So it cannot be used in a production environment.

The Developer Edition offers one additional benefit: it comes with its own web server that can be used on localhost:8500. For that reason, it is important to install ColdFusion exactly as I describe in this appendix.

One word of warning however: before you download the ColdFusion server, make sure you have a high-speed connection, as it is a whopping 281MB to download.

In this tutorial, I will be showing the installation on a Windows system. However, installation for other platforms is similar.

1. Download the server and start the installation; you should see the opening screen shown in Figure A-1.

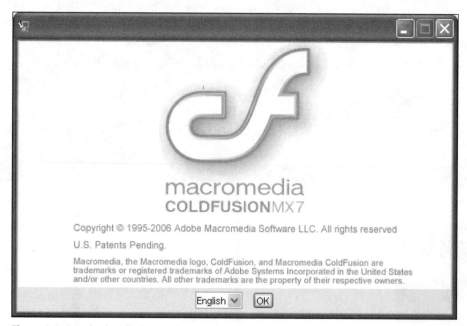

Figure A-1. Opening installation screen

2. Select the language you want to see ColdFusion in, and then click OK.

3. You next see the Welcome screen, shown in Figure A-2. Click Next.

4. The licensing screen comes up (see Figure A-3). Click the radio button to accept the terms and click Next.

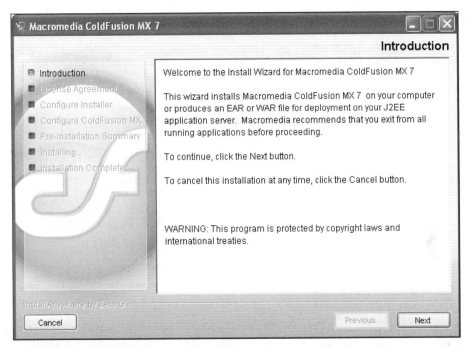

Figure A-2. Welcome screen

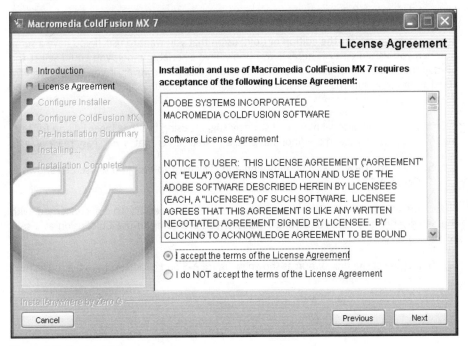

Figure A-3. License screen

The next screen that comes up is an important one (see Figure A-4).

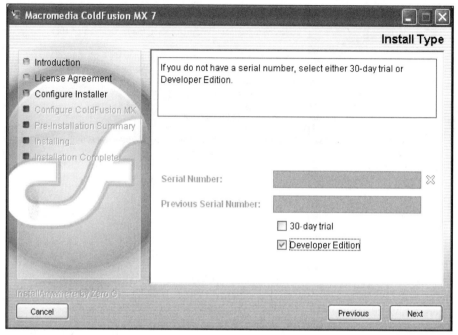

Figure A-4. Edition selection

This is where you select the edition of ColdFusion that you want to use. If you have a serial number, you would enter it here. If you don't have a serial number, you could select the 30-day trial edition and use it in production for 30 days. However, if you do not enter a serial number within that 30-day period, ColdFusion automatically reverts to the single licensed Developer Edition.

Even if you do have a serial number, I strongly suggest using the Developer Edition for testing. As you will soon see, this edition has a built-in web server that is very easy to work with.

5. Select the Developer Edition option and click Next to bring up the screen shown in Figure A-5.

Since you are using the Developer Edition, it is not necessary to be concerned with the Server configuration. For testing purposes, you are going to use ColdFusion as a self-contained server.

6. Just select the first option as shown in Figure A-5 and click Next to move to the next screen (see Figure A-6).

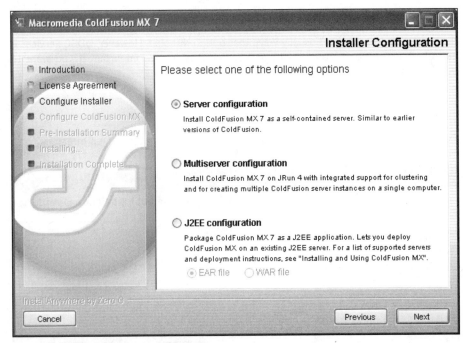

Figure A-5. Choosing the Server configuration

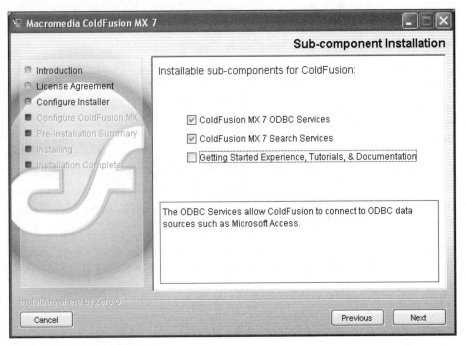

Figure A-6. Selecting components

A

Here you select the components you want. I have found the Getting Started Experience, Tutorials, & Documentation tend to pop up when you want to use some of the services of the server. To prevent this, I usually leave that option disabled. However, ODBC Services is important for database connectivity, and Search Services are important if you want to build a search engine.

7. Disable the Getting Started Experience, Tutorials, & Documentation option and click Next.

The next screen, shown in Figure A-7, will allow you to change the default directory.

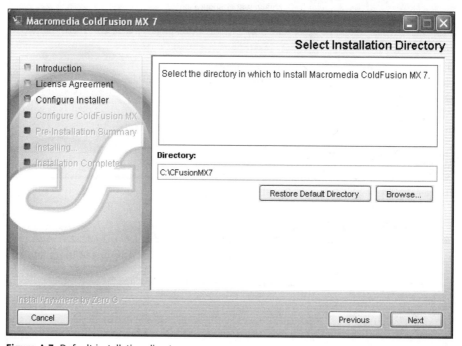

Figure A-7. Default installation directory

8. Unless you have a reason for changing the directory, accept the default and select Next to go to the next screen (see Figure A-8).

This screen will bring up a listing of any web servers you have active on the computer (for example, IIS or Internet Information Services).

ColdFusion will work over any web server. However, for testing purposes, it is far better to use the built-in web server that is available only if you selected the Developer Edition.

9. As shown in Figure A-8, select the option Built-in web server (Development use only) and click Next.

The next screen asks you to enter and confirm a password for the ColdFusion administrator (see Figure A-9).

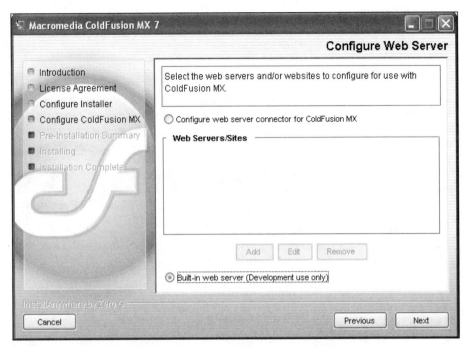

Figure A-8. Configuring ColdFusion

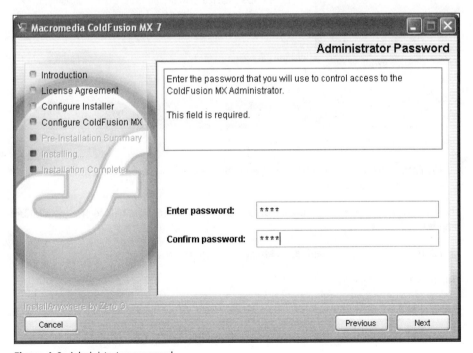

Figure A-9. Administrator password

A

You are required to enter a password here. However, since you will probably just be using this server locally for development and testing, you will delete the password after the installation is completed.

10. Enter a password of your choice and click Next.

Like the previous screen, you now have to enter a password for ColdFusion's Remote Data Services (RDS), as shown in Figure A-10. This is how outside development programs, like Dreamweaver and Flex, access databases in ColdFusion. Again, you are just entering a temporary password which you will delete later.

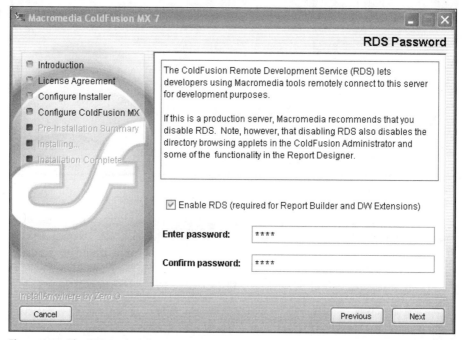

Figure A-10. The RDS password

11. Enter a password of your choice and click Next to move on to the final screen, as shown in Figure A-11.

This screen allows you to review all of the entered information before the installation begins.

12. If everything is as planned, go ahead and click the Install button.

This process may take several minutes.

If everything went all right, you will get the screen shown in Figure A-12.

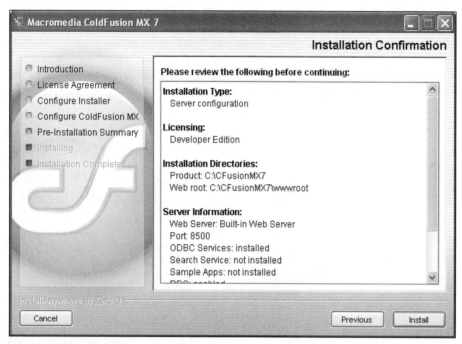

Figure A-11. Summary screen

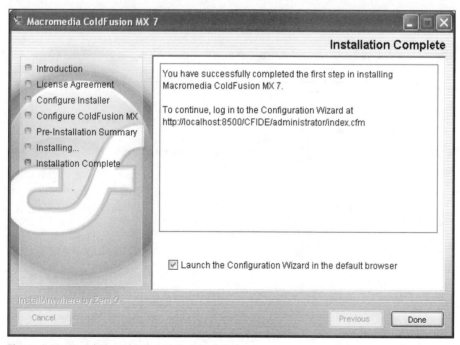

Figure A-12. Completion of Part 1 of the installation

A

Unfortunately, your job is not completed yet.

13. Make sure the Launch the Configuration Wizard in the default browser option is selected and click the Done button.

14. You now need to use the temporary password you set before and log in to the server, as shown in Figure A-13.

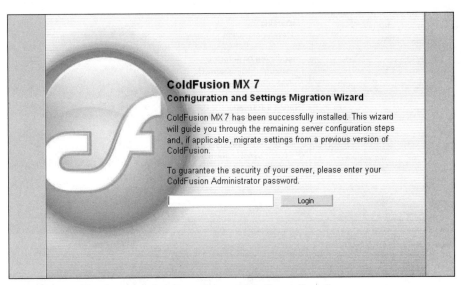

Figure A-13. Logging in as the administrator to complete the configuration

After you log in, you will get the message shown in Figure A-14.

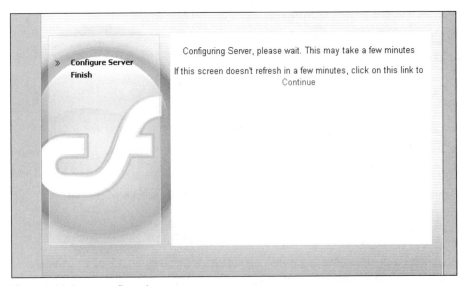

Figure A-14. Server configuration message

Upon successful completion, you should get the message shown in Figure A-15.

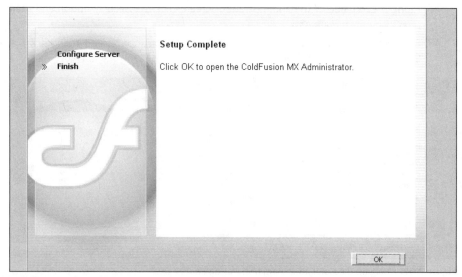

Figure A-15. Completion of server configuration

15. Click OK, and you are now brought into the ColdFusion Administrator (see Figure A-16).

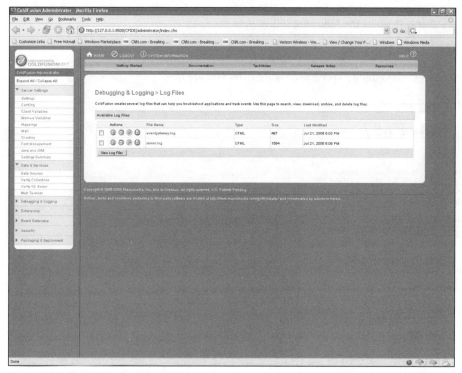

Figure A-16. The ColdFusion Administrator

You should go ahead and turn off the passwords you set earlier.

16. Along the left side of the administration screen, click the Security option and then select CF Admin Password.

17. Deselect the Use a ColdFusion Administration password option and then click the Submit Changes button. Your screen should match what you see in Figure A-17.

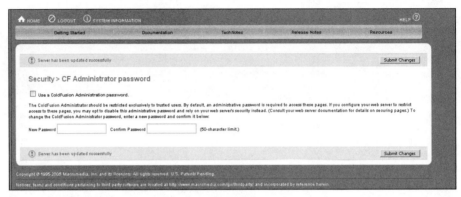

Figure A-17. Disabling the ColdFusion Administrator password

18. Click the Security link again and follow the preceding instructions to disable the RDS password. Don't forget to click the Submit Changes button again.

Theoretically, the installation is now finished. The fact that you are in the administrator is a pretty good indication that everything was successful. However, if you want to give it another test, go to the following URL in your browser:

```
http://localhost:8500
```

If you get something looking like Figure A-18, you are fine.

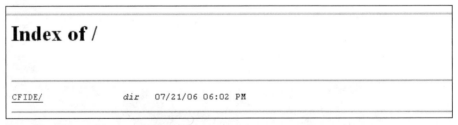

Figure A-18. The ColdFusion directory site

By default, ColdFusion starts automatically when the computer does. However, if for some reason it doesn't, you can manually start it using the following procedure in Windows:

1. Go to the Control Panel.

2. Go to Administrative Tools.

3. Go to Services.

4. Right-click each of the four ColdFusion services and select either Start or Restart.

INDEX

INDEX

friendsofed.com/forums

Join the friends of ED forums to find out more about our books, discover useful technology tips and tricks, or get a helping hand on a challenging project. *Designer to Designer*™ is what it's all about—our community sharing ideas and inspiring each other. In the friends of ED forums, you'll find a wide range of topics to discuss, so look around, find a forum, and dive right in!

■ Books and Information
Chat about friends of ED books, gossip about the community, or even tell us some bad jokes!

■ Flash
Discuss design issues, ActionScript, dynamic content, and video and sound.

■ Web Design
From front-end frustrations to back-end blight, share your problems and your knowledge here.

■ Site Check
Show off your work or get new ideas.

■ Digital Imagery
Create eye candy with Photoshop, Fireworks, Illustrator, and FreeHand.

■ ArchivED
Browse through an archive of old questions and answers.

HOW TO PARTICIPATE

Go to the friends of ED forums at **www.friendsofed.com/forums**.

Visit **www.friendsofed.com** to get the latest on our books, find out what's going on in the community, and discover some of the slickest sites online today!

friendsof ™

DESIGNER TO DESIGNER™

an Apress® company